Ensuring the Rights of Migrant Workers

Ensuring the Rights of Migrant Workers

Views from Origin Countries in Asia

Edited by Nguyen Thi Hong Yen, Nguyen Toan Thang, Nguyen Thi Kim Ngan, and Su Wai Mon

LEXINGTON BOOKS
Lanham • Boulder • New York • London

Published by Lexington Books
An imprint of The Rowman & Littlefield Publishing Group, Inc.
4501 Forbes Boulevard, Suite 200, Lanham, Maryland 20706
www.rowman.com

86-90 Paul Street, London EC2A 4NE

British Library Cataloguing in Publication Information Available

Library of Congress Cataloging-in-Publication Data

Names: Yen, Nguyen Thi Hong, editor. | Thang, Nguyen Toan, editor. | Ngan, Nguyen Thi Kim, editor. | Mon, Su Wai, editor. Title: Ensuring the rights of migrant workers : views from origin countries in Asia / edited by Nguyen Thi Hong Yen, Nguyen Toan Thang, Nguyen Thi Kim Ngan and Su Wai Mon. Description: Lanham, Maryland : Lexington Books, [2024] | Includes bibliographical references and index. | Summary: "This collection provides a picture of legal and practical issues of migrant workers, including documented and undocumented migrant workers in the Asian region. It concludes by summarizing the difficulties governments have in protecting the rights of migrant workers, setting out potential future solutions based on member states' practices"-- Provided by publisher. Identifiers: LCCN 2024008064 | ISBN 9781666940374 (cloth ; acid-free paper) | ISBN 9781666940398 (pbk ; acid-free paper) | ISBN 9781666940381 (ebook) Subjects: LCSH: Migrant labor--Asia. | Migrant labor--Law and legislation--Asia. | Foreign workers--Civil rights--Asia. | Noncitizens--Civil rights--Asia. Classification: LCC HD5856.A78 E57 2024 | DDC 331.5/44095--dc23/eng/20240322 LC record available at https://lccn.loc.gov/2024008064

Contents

Introduction

Labor migration is an international issue affecting most countries worldwide, including origin and destination countries. Economic hardship and geopolitical crises have led to a lack of sustainable jobs and the rise of increasingly diverse and growing migratory movements. In many economies, including emerging ones, aging populations and shrinking labor forces make contribution to increased worker mobility. Women are participating in migration flows in growing numbers as independent workers, with significant consequences for gender equality in both sending and receiving countries.[1]

There is no denying the positive contributions that migrant workers bring to countries' economic development and prosperity. For countries of origin, labor migration reduces tensions over unemployment or underemployment and contributes to development through remittances, skills transfer, and the creation of business and trade networks. For destination countries, labor migration can help address severe labor shortages, especially in the context of aging populations and changing demographics,[2] while also providing essential jobs in critical sectors such as health care, transportation, services, agriculture, and food processing.[3] However, many migrant workers are often held in temporary, informal, or unprotected jobs, exposing them to risks of insecurity, layoffs, and poor working conditions. It is especially likely to happen to undocumented/illegal labor migrants.

The increase in conflicts and civil wars, followed by severe consequences of climate change with extreme weather phenomena, poverty, disease, and unsustainable employment development in several countries, has made illegal labor migration flows more and more alarming. The COVID-19 epidemic at the end of 2019 has made this situation worse. The 2021 International Labor Organization (ILO) report shows that the estimated number of international migrants worldwide in 2019 was 272 million, including 245 million working-age people (15 years and older).[4] The number of international immigrant workers totaled 169 million in the same year. The 2019 estimate shows an increase of 5 million immigrant workers (3.0%) compared to the

2017 estimate of 164 million immigrant workers and an increase of 19 million (12.7%). Of the estimated 169 million international migrant workers, 113.9 million (67.4%) are in high-income countries, and 33 million (19.5%) are in upper-middle-income countries. The remainder is in lower-middle-income countries (9.5%) and low-income countries (3.6%). Women make up 41.5 percent, and men make up 58.5 percent of immigrant workers.[5]

This data shows the significant challenges of governments in managing international labor migration. Although significant efforts have been made in building a global legal framework to ensure fundamental human rights for migrant workers, specialized international legal instruments on this issue of the United Nations and the ILO have so far not attracted the attention of countries, as evidenced by the fact that the number of members participating in the International Convention on the Protection of the Rights of All Migrant Workers and Members of Their Families (ICMW Convention) or conventions within the ILO framework is still very modest. It causes these international treaties' roles to become hazy and less universal. Governments typically employ other fundamental international human rights conventions, including the Universal Declaration of Human Rights (UDHR), International Covenant on Civil and Political Rights (ICCPR), International Covenant on Economic, Social and Cultural Rights (ICESCR), or even their laws, to settle relevant concerns rather than ratifying these documents.

Asia is a vast continent with a sizable population and a plentiful labor force. It also provides a significant amount of migrant labor to industrialized nations. Migrant workers originating from Asia are mainly mid-level workers, skilled or unskilled. Although the pandemic has caused discrimination against individuals of Asian origin, the presence of migrant workers from Asia in developed countries is undeniable, despite the statistics showing that this rate tends to decrease during the COVID-19 epidemic period. Before the COVID-19 outbreak, migration from Asia to Organisation for Economic Co-operation and Development (OECD) countries had been steadily rising since 2012, according to Asian Development Bank (ADB). In 2019, an estimated 2.3 million people from Asian countries migrated to an OECD country; permanent migration in these countries fell by more than 30 percent in 2020, the most significant drop on record.[6] From 2022 until now, the situation has improved as the international labor market gradually recovered and waves of labor migration, including both documented and undocumented, have turned.

The book aims to clarify the current situation of international labor migration in Asian countries, legal and practical issues, as well as challenges for governments as the origin and destination countries in the governance of international labor migration. The book is divided into three parts. Part 1 concentrates on analyzing the global legal framework and mechanism for protecting the human rights of migrant workers. Part 2 of this book will analyze policies and laws of some Asian countries in protecting the human rights of migrant workers in sending countries; and in Part 3 of this research, the authors will concentrate on pointing out the assessments and recommendations for both governments and migrant workers to have a safety migration journey in the future. With much effort and openness, in this book, the authors wish to draw a general picture of both the legal and practical implications of migrant workers in Asian countries as the sending/original countries in the international labor market, from that contributing recommendations for promoting safety labor migration in this region in the coming time.

NOTES

1. ILO, Statistics on migrant workers, https://ilostat.ilo.org/topics/labor-migration/, accessed on 10 November 2023.
2. Source: https://roasiapacific.iom.int/labor-migration, accessed on 9 November 2023.
3. ILO, ILO Global Estimates on International Migrant Workers—Results and Methodology, Third edition, International Labor Office—Geneva, 2021, https://www.ilo.org/wcmsp5/groups /public/---dgreports/---dcomm/---publ/documents/publication/wcms_808935.pdf, accessed on 10 November 2023.
4. Ibid.
5. Ibid.
6. ADB, OECD, ILO, Labor migration in Asia: Covid-19 impacts, challenges, and policy responses, https://www.adb.org/sites/default/files/publication/797536/labor-migration-asia.pdf#page=12, accessed on 10 November 2023.

PART I

Are International Human Rights Standards Sufficient to Protect the Rights of Migrant Workers?

Although the movement of laborers across borders is not an abnormal phenomenon, the 20th and 21st centuries have experienced a surge in the numbers of migrant workers. The growing pace of economic globalization has created more migrant workers than ever before. The influx of migrant workers into advanced countries has emerged as a significant issue in the international community in recent centuries. Unemployment and increasing poverty have prompted many workers in developing countries to seek work elsewhere. According to the International Labor Organization (ILO), more than 70 percent of migrants are workers. In industrialized countries, the demand for labor, especially unskilled labor, has increased. As a result, millions of workers and their families travel to countries other than their own to find work. In the Asia-Pacific region, migrant workers contribute to the economies of both countries of origin and destination. However, migrant workers will likely enjoy inadequate social protection and are vulnerable to discrimination, exploitation, abuse, and human trafficking.

Since its establishment in 1945, the United Nations has built and expanded universal legal frameworks to ensure and promote fundamental human rights. The ILO is the international body with a mandate for international labor migration with the primary function of setting out international standards targeted at protecting the rights of migrant workers. With missions to foster dialogues and cooperation among countries to ensure human rights, the United Nations, in addition to related institutions such as the ILO, plays an essential and leading role in recognizing and safeguarding the rights of migrant workers on a global scale and impacting the requirement for safeguarding migrant workers on regional and national levels.

In 1990, the International Convention on the Protection of the Rights of All Migrant Workers and Members of Their Families (the ICMW) was ratified, marking a significant milestone in the United Nations' efforts in developing a universal legal framework to protect the rights of migrant workers. The Convention, formulated on the basis and development of the United Nations' existing principles of universal human rights framework, aims to end any forms of discrimination, abuse, or other discriminatory attitudes against migrant workers and ensure and improve the conditions for the current admission of migrants worldwide. The ICMW and other core human rights instruments offer some legal protection to migrant workers.

However, do these documents offer sufficient legal bases to protect the legitimate rights and interests of migrants? Are there any gaps or shortcomings arising from the implementation of these documents? To answer these questions, Part 1 analyzes and critiques current regulations of international law on migrant workers with a focus on those who are more vulnerable to discrimination, abuse, or other discriminatory forms such as women migrant workers, child laborers as migrants, and illegal migrant workers.

Chapter 1

International Legal Framework for the Protection of the Rights of Migrant Workers

Nguyen Thi Hong Yen and Tran Thi Thu Thuy

As the world's largest multilateral international organization, the restructuring of the United Nations (UN) in 1945 is evidence that the countries' aspiration to build a forum where "peace and security exist" is considered the highest principle and goal. Therefore, the Preamble of the United Nations Charter states that this organization "reaffirm[s] faith in fundamental human rights, in the dignity and worth of the human person, in the equal rights of men and women and of nations large and small" and identifies one of its operational purposes as "to achieve international co-operation in solving international problems of an economic, social, cultural, or humanitarian character, and in promoting and encouraging respect for human rights and fundamental freedoms for all without distinction as to race, sex, language, or religion."[1]

With those ideas and goals, the United Nations and its members have worked tirelessly for more than 70 years of establishment and advancement to perfect institutions and legal frameworks that safeguard fundamental human rights around the world, including migrant workers' rights. One may say that the UN has established a set of fundamental human rights norms through its focused and active efforts, which serve as broad guidelines for creating human rights legislation in various nations, areas, and the world at large. Regarding the rights of migrant workers, in addition to the general provisions in the Universal Declaration of Human Rights (UDHR), International Covenant on Civil and Political Rights (ICCPR), and International Covenant on Economic, Social and Cultural Rights (ICESCR), the United Nations has also made efforts to develop the International Convention on the Protection of the Rights of All Migrant Workers and Members of Their Families (ICMW) as a specialized document aimed at best protecting the rights of migrant workers and their family members. It has expanded the beneficiaries of protections not only to migrant workers themselves (including both documented and undocumented), but also to their family members.

While there isn't a single, widely agreed definition of irregular labor migration, this Convention has made notable strides in this regard by characterizing illegal migrant workers as those without proper documentation or, in an irregular situation, as anyone who isn't permitted to enter, remain, or work in the country of destination (ICMW, Article 5). The recognition of minimum rights for undocumented migrant workers further highlights the distinction between the ICMW and other international human rights treaties, even though there aren't many laws specifically pertaining to this category of people. Additionally, it creates interest in the subject among other nations. However, up to now, this Convention has yet to receive adequate attention from countries, as evidenced by the fact that the number of members joining the Convention is still very limited compared to the number of members of the United Nations. This comes from many different aspects.

To supplement the regulations within the framework of the United Nations, the International Labor Organization (ILO), as a specialized labor organization, also has to pay special attention to migrant worker groups. This organization has developed a series of documents to regulate issues related to the rights of migrant workers, such as: the Convention on Migration for Employment adopted in 1949 (No. 97); and the Convention relating to migration under abusive conditions and promoting equality of opportunity and treatment of migrant workers, adopted by the ILO General Assembly on June 24, 1975 at the sixtieth session (No. 143); the ILO also issued recommendations relating to Migration for Employment No. 86 and No. 151 in 1975.[2] The most significant of these are Conventions No. 97 and 143. These are considered two ILO initiatives to ensure the equal rights of migrant workers related to employment. However, like ICMW, these two Convention only have a few members.

The COVID-19 pandemic that broke out at the end of 2019 has brought many consequences for countries and the international community. It also contributes to exacerbating the vulnerability and insecurity of migrant workers in irregular situations.[3] As borders reopen and countries recover from the crisis, the movement of people will continue apace, including through irregular channels. Therefore, the issue of labor migration continues to become a topic that countries are more concerned about than ever, in addition to other critical international issues. In that context, completing the legal framework, including international, regional, and national laws, to better ensure the rights of migrant workers in general is extremely necessary. The delay and "consideration" of countries before international instruments such as ICMW, Conventions 97 and 143 also raise many questions about these documents' reasonableness, necessity, and effectiveness. From this perspective, this chapter will focus on analyzing and clarifying the current international legal framework on the rights of migrant workers as well as their monitoring mechanism, and provide related analysis and comments.

THE UNITED NATIONS' INTERNATIONAL HUMAN RIGHTS INSTRUMENTS AND MONITORING MECHANISM

The Bill of International Human Rights

Universal Declaration of Human Rights (UDHR) 1948

The idea of building the Bill of Human Rights arose and was implemented immediately after the adoption of the United Nations Charter in 1945. A United Nations Preparatory Commission on this issue was convened immediately after the conclusion of the San Francisco Conference and recommended that the Economic and Social Council (ECOSOC) quickly establish a committee on the promotion of human rights based on the content of Article 68 of the Charter. On the basis of this recommendation, ECOSOC established the Commission on Human Rights in early 1946. On December 10, 1948, by Resolution 217 A (III), the General Assembly adopted the UDHR three years after the United Nations was founded. The Declaration for the first time defined a set of specific fundamental human rights and freedoms in all aspects of politics, civil, economic, social, and cultural.

Although not an international treaty, the UDHR has enormous moral weight. Many provisions in the UDHR are considered international customary norms. Many of the Declaration's norms meet two conditions that constitute customary international law: general practice and *opinio juris*. Evidence can be found in the form of resolutions of the UN General Assembly as the Declaration is cited in important international treaties on human rights, and in bilateral agreements. The European Convention on Human Rights of 1950, the American Convention on Human Rights of 1969, and the African Charter on Human and Peoples' Rights also mention the fundamental role of the Declaration. Ian Brownlie points out that the Helsinki Document signed in 1975 and the Tehran Declaration in 1968 both contain the intention of states to adhere to the principles of the Declaration.[4] In 1993, the Vienna Declaration and Program of Action were adopted by 171 countries reaffirming their commitment to the principles enshrined in the UN Charter and Declaration.

From another perspective, the UDHR is the international community's first legal effort to limit states' traditional freedom of action in relations with their citizens. According to the rights–duty duality model, these efforts aim to impose obligations on states to respect and ensure the legitimate rights and freedoms of individual citizens.

UDHR is the basis for later building two important international treaties: the ICCPR and ICESCR. Although the group of migrant workers is not specifically mentioned in the UDHR, Article 2 of the UDHR recognizes equality and non-discrimination for any reason, therefore, migrant workers. Residents also enjoy and are protected by the state and all rights recognized in the UDHR.

International Covenant on Civil and Political Rights (ICCPR) 1966

The ICCPR was adopted under Resolution 2200A (XXI) of the United Nations General Assembly on December 16, 1966, and took effect from March 23, 1976, according to the provisions of Article 49. Currently, the Convention has 173 member states.[5] The ICCPR provisions recognize individuals' civil and political rights and impose obligations on member states to take necessary measures to ensure the enforcement of these rights. After more than 50 years of existence and being widely recognized, along with other international legal instruments on human rights of the UN, the ICCPR has contributed to creating global legal frameworks for ensuring and protecting human rights and to promote human rights values, especially civil and political rights for all individuals.[6]

Together with UHDR and ICESCR, ICCPR is the basis for creating the foundation for the creation of international treaties on human rights for specific subjects such as: children, women, people with disabilities, migrant workers, etc.

In the ICCPR, the group of migrant workers is not directly mentioned. However, for the rights recognized in the ICCPR, it is emphasized that all individuals enjoy those rights equally. Therefore, migrant workers, regardless of their status, will enjoy civil and political rights, especially some rights related to the right to life, the right to liberty and security of person, and the right to equality before the courts and tribunals, and so on.

International Covenant on Economic, Social and Cultural Rights (ICESCR) 1966

The ICESCR is one of the two pillar conventions on human rights (besides ICCPR) and is a component of the Bill of Human Rights (which includes these two conventions and the UDHR). More than nine years after being approved by the United Nations General Assembly and opened for countries to sign and ratify under Resolution No. 2200A dated December 16, 1966, ICESCR took effect on January 3, 1976, under Article 27 of the convention. To date, ICESCR has 170 member countries.[7] Similar to the ICCPR, ICESCR also establishes a system of basic human rights in the economic, social, and cultural fields and the obligations of states to ensure that all individuals enjoy these rights. All individuals, including groups of migrant workers, are treated equally in enjoying rights in the economic, social, and cultural fields, especially rights such as: the right to work, the right to join a trade union, the right to the enjoyment of just and favorable conditions of work, etc.

It can be seen that the UDHR, the ICCPR, and ICESCR do not directly regulate the rights of migrant workers. However, the number of members of the two Conventions is very large (accounting for the majority of UN member states); in addition, the provisions of the UDHR are customary norms. This leads to the obligation of member states to the Convention to comply with and ensure the human rights recognized in these two conventions. Although ICMW is a specialized convention for migrant workers (which will be analyzed later), the number of members is quite small (only 58 member countries). Therefore, in reality it must be recognized that, to ensure the rights of migrant workers, the Bill of International Human Rights still has great weight and is the basic obligation of countries without discrimination treatment between all individuals.

The United Nations' Monitoring Mechanism

The monitoring mechanism for ensuring and enforcing human rights within the United Nations framework is implemented through reports from countries. Implementing national reports is a mandatory obligation in most international human rights treaties. The reporting mechanism will include two mechanisms: (1) the universal periodic review mechanism of the United Nations Human Rights Council (UPR), and (2) the reporting mechanism under the Convention.

The UPR was established by the United Nations Human Rights Council (UNHRC) on March 15, 2006, on the basis of Resolution No. 60/251[8] and institution-building documents A/HRC/RES/5/1,[9] Resolution No. 16 /21,[10] and Decision No. 17/119 of the UNHRC.[11] With the UPR, countries must report on the implementation of all international human rights treaties to which they are members. The universal periodic review is based on three documents: (1) information prepared by the state concerned, which can take the form of a national report; (2) a compilation prepared by the Office of the High Commissioner for Human Rights of the information contained in the reports of treaty bodies, special procedures, including observations and comments by the state concerned, and other relevant official United Nations documents, which shall not exceed 10 pages; (3) additional credible and reliable information provided by other relevant stakeholders which should also be taken into consideration by the Council in the review. The Office of the High Commissioner for Human Rights will prepare a summary (which shall not exceed 10 pages) of such information based on the written submissions. This summary should contain, where appropriate, a separate section (included in the maximum 10 pages) for contributions by the national human rights institution of the state under review that is accredited in full compliance with the Paris Principles. Information provided by other accredited national human rights institutions will be reflected accordingly, as well as information provided by other stakeholders. Stakeholders, referred to in Human Rights Council Resolution 5/1, include inter alia, NGOs, national human rights institutions, human rights defenders, academic institutions and research institutes, regional organizations, and civil society representatives.[12]

During periodic reviews, countries report on how well they are respecting, promoting, and protecting human rights and improving the human rights situation in their country. States are reminded of their human rights obligations and responsibilities through the periodic review mechanism. The ultimate aim of the periodic review mechanism is to improve the human rights situation in all countries and address human rights violations wherever they occur. In addition, the UPR also promotes increased cooperation between countries and supports countries that are attempting to promote and protect human rights. It also encourages comprehensive collaboration and cohesion between states and international non-governmental organizations with UNHRC.

With the reporting mechanism under the Convention, normally, member states of an international treaty will have to submit an initial report one or two years after the Convention comes into force for that country. After that, countries will continue to have to submit periodic reports (possibly every 4 or 5 years, depending on the provisions of each convention). The initial report states that countries must submit one to two years after ratifying and joining the convention. This report usually includes information about the country's economic, political, and social issues affecting the implementation of the convention; the degree of compatibility of the country's current legal system with the provisions of the convention; as well as determining the measures the country intends to take to implement the convention. A periodic report is a report presented in accordance with the provisions of the conventions, after the initial report has been submitted. This report focuses on describing the progress made and difficulties in implementing the convention and suggests measures to overcome those difficulties.

The process of countries making national reports on ensuring and enforcing human rights is a process of dialogue between international institutions and countries on human rights issues of mutual concern, through which member states provide comprehensive information about the legal framework; announce legislative, executive, and judicial measures that the country has taken to improve the human rights situation in the country; and consider and evaluate positive developments and challenges that countries face in the process of implementing international treaties on human rights to which they are members. In addition, through the process of developing and protecting the report, countries can also share experiences and cooperate to support the promotion and protection of basic human rights.

THE INTERNATIONAL CONVENTION ON THE PROTECTION OF THE RIGHTS OF ALL MIGRANT WORKERS AND MEMBERS OF THEIR FAMILIES: THE CRYSTALLIZATION OF HUMAN RIGHTS VALUES

The International Convention on the Protection of the Rights of all Migrant Workers and Members of Their Families (ICMW) is one of the core human rights instruments of the United Nations. It was approved on December 18, 1990 and put into force on July 1, 2003.[13] The Convention is identified as a specialized legal instrument designed to provide specific legal protections for groups of migrant workers. The issue of ICMW marks an important step in the development of international human rights law as well as the international community's awareness of the importance of migrant workers to politics, economics, and societies in both origin and destination countries while also recognizing that migrant workers and their families are also an essential part of society.[14]

The purpose of the Convention is to establish minimal requirements that the member states have to impose on migratory laborers and family members residing under their jurisdiction, both during their employment and in odd circumstances.[15] The ICMW aims to fill legal gaps and is expected to become an effective legal instrument in "providing minimum universal standards to protect migrant workers and their family members."[16]

Scope and Object

Part I of the Convention contains a definition of migrant workers that will be found in any international instrument relating to the rights of migrants. Article 2(1) defines "migrant worker" as "a person who is to be engaged, is engaged or has been engaged in a remunerated activity in a State of which he or she is not a national." In addition, Article 4 explains that family members of migrant workers are "persons married to migrant workers or having with them a relationship that, according to applicable law, produces effects equivalent to marriage, as well as their dependent children and other dependent persons who are recognized as members of the family by applicable legislation or applicable bilateral or multilateral agreements between the States concerned."[17]

Compared to other international human rights instruments such as ICCPR or ICESCR, ICMW has expanded its scope of coverage to the rights of all migrant workers and their families, regardless of their status as documented or undocumented workers according to standards recognized in official human rights instruments.[18] The Convention's Preamble acknowledges that irregular migrants are frequently exploited and face serious human rights violations; that some employers seek such workers to benefit from unfair competition; that appropriate action to prevent and eliminate clandestine movements and trafficking of migrant workers while ensuring the protection of their human rights should be encouraged; and that recourse to the employment of migrant workers who are in an irregular situation will be discouraged if the fundamental human rights of all migrant workers are more widely recognized. This approach is critical to the Convention and is perhaps the least understood by countries reluctant to ratify the Convention.[19] However, due to certain limitations of undocumented migrant workers, the Convention only provides minimum legal protection for them to encourage all migrants and users to workers respect and comply with the laws and procedures established by the countries concerned.[20]

The Rights of Migrant Workers under the Convention

Article 7 of the Convention stipulates that, "States Parties undertake, in accordance with the international instruments concerning human rights, to respect and to ensure to all migrant workers and members of their families within their territory or subject to their jurisdiction the rights provided for in the present Convention without distinction of any kind such as to sex, race, colour, language, religion or conviction, political or other opinion, national, ethnic or social origin, nationality, age, economic position, property, marital status, birth or other status." It shows that the ICMW, similar to other international treaties on human rights, continues to recognize equality and non-discrimination as important fundamental principles to avoid creating discrimination between migrant workers and workers who are citizens of the receiving country.[21] Migrant women workers are protected from discrimination in the application of the Convention. According to Article 1, "All migrant workers and members of their families shall be covered by this Convention, unless otherwise provided herein, without distinction as to sex." However, a significant omission in the Convention is the lack of provisions addressing the specific issues that migrant women workers face. This also somewhat applies to youth.[22]

ICMW focuses on recognizing the rights of migrant workers in two main groups: (i) fundamental human rights to which all migrant workers, whether documented or undocumented, and their family members must be guaranteed; and (ii) rights regarding the documentation of migrant workers and their family members.[23] Namely, concerning the first group of rights, the ICMW essentially restates the main points of the UN human rights treaties, including the UDHR, ICCPR, and ICESCR, such as fundamental rights like the right to life and the prohibitions against torture or cruel, inhuman, or degrading treatment or punishment (Article 10); freedom of thought, conscience, and religion (Article 12); the right to liberty, security of person, and protection against arbitrary detention (Article 16); freedom from slavery, servitude, or forced or compulsory labor (Article 11); the right to freely leave any country, including their country of origin, and they have the right to return to or remain in their country of origin at all times (Article 8). Migrant workers or members of their families must not be subjected to forced or compulsory labor (Article 11), and they are entitled to equal treatment with nationals of the country of employment, relating to remuneration and other working conditions (Article 25); they also have the right to participate in meetings, trade union activities, and associations (Article 26) and the right to receive the same treatment as citizens of the state in which they are employed (Article 27); and their children have the fundamental right to access education on the basis of equal treatment (Article 30); as well as the right to procedural guarantees (Article 18). In addition, migrants have the right to urgently necessary medical care that keeps them alive or prevents irreversible harm to their health. This comprises a fundamental set of rights that affects migrant workers and their families, whether documented or undocumented migrant workers.[24]

The most differentiating point of ICMW is its focus on rights considered "special" for groups of migrant workers to ensure the best rights and safety for them during the migration process; for example, migrant workers and members of their families have the right to have recourse to the protection and assistance of the consular or diplomatic authorities of their state of origin or of a state representing the interests of that state whenever the rights recognized in the present Convention are impaired (Article 23); they have the right to recognition everywhere as a person before the law (Article 24); and the right to transfer their earnings and savings, in particular those funds necessary for the support of their families, from the state of employment to their state of origin or any other state. Although the Convention does not explicitly provide for the right to family reunification, states parties are encouraged to facilitate family reunification and protect family unity (Article 44). Article 50 stipulates that, "in the case of death of a migrant worker or dissolution of marriage, the State of employment shall favourably consider granting family members of that migrant worker residing in that State on the basis of family reunion an authorization to stay; the State of employment shall take into account the length of time they have already resided in that State."[25] And "members of the family to whom such authorization is not granted shall be allowed before departure a reasonable period of time in order to enable them to settle their affairs in the State of employment."[26]

To materialize these rights in practice, the Convention also defines the responsibilities of states, including both countries of origin and immigration, in ensuring the rights of migrant workers. One of the most interesting features of the Convention is that, in addition to establishing the obligations of states parties toward individual migrant workers, it also provides a framework, in Part VI, to promote sound, equitable, humane, and lawful conditions in connection with international migration of workers and members of their families.[27] States parties shall maintain appropriate services to deal with questions concerning international migration of workers and members of their families, as well as the formulation and implementation of policies regarding such migration; an exchange of information, consultation, and cooperation with the competent authorities of other states parties involved in such migration; the provision of appropriate information, particularly to employers, workers, and their organizations on policies, laws, and regulations relating to migration and employment, on agreements concluded with other states concerning migration and on other relevant matters (Article 65).[28] The freedom to conduct recruitment operations restricted to public services is outlined in Article 66. According to Article 67, states must take action to ensure that migrant workers and their families can safely and orderly return home. According to Article 68, member states must also work together to stop and eradicate the recruiting of migrant workers and their unauthorized or covert movements.[29] Article 69 of the Convention specifically states that member states are required to take appropriate action to ensure that migrant workers and their family members who are on their territory in violation of the law do not remain in that condition (Article 69).

Monitoring Mechanisms of the ICMW

In addition to recognizing the responsibility of states to ensure the rights of migrant workers, for the purpose of considering the application of this Convention, ICMW has established its own monitoring body in accordance with the provisions of Article 72 of the Convention called a Committee on the Protection of the Rights of All Migrant Workers and Members of Their Families.

The Committee has 14 independent experts who monitor the implementation of the Convention by member states. The members of the Committee are elected by secret ballot by the member states, taking into account an equitable geographical distribution, including the state of origin and the state of employment of migrant workers, as well as representing the world's leading legal systems. The Committee's members serve in their individual capacities for four-year terms.[30]

The Committee's primary duties include reviewing member states' reports and offering suggestions regarding migratory workers and their families residing in the state. Member states are obliged to submit regular reports to the Committee on how these rights are implemented in their territory. They must submit the first report one year after accession to the Convention and then every five years. The Committee shall examine each report and address its concerns and recommendations to the state party in the form of "concluding observations" (Articles 73–75). The Committee's other responsibilities include planning a day for general discussion and providing interpretations of the Convention's provisions as well as other matters pertinent to the Convention's mandate. When 10 member states have accepted these procedures under the terms of the Convention, the Committee may occasionally also take into consideration complaints or communications between states parties or individuals from states parties or individuals claiming that their rights under the Convention have been violated (Articles 76 and 77).[31]

In March 2004, the Committee held its first session and adopted interim rules of procedure. In October 2004, the Commission held informal meetings to develop guidelines for the preparation of the initial report for member states. The Committee formally adopted these guidelines at its second session in April 2005. At this session, the Committee also discussed working methods for examining the reports of member states.[32]

Until now, 58 countries have ratified the Convention, and 11 other countries have signed but have not ratified it. Thus, compared to other international treaties on human rights of the United Nations, ICMW has a relatively modest number of members. It dramatically reduced the "universality" of the Convention. Some recent studies believe that one of the reasons for this situation is because the Convention places too many responsibilities on receiving countries while "ignoring" the responsibilities of origin countries. It makes the Convention less "attractive" to countries.[33] According to some additional viewpoints, the Convention does not sufficiently distinguish between the rights of documented and undocumented migrant workers. They point out that for this reason, states would be required to offer excessive rights to migrant workers who do not have legal status in the state if they were to ratify the Convention.[34] Therefore, destination states are reluctant to ratify the Convention and assume new obligations. That is why the countries that have ratified the Convention are mainly the countries of origin of migrants.[35] However, it is undeniable that this Convention has contributed to perfecting the legal framework to protect the rights of migrant workers around the world and is still considered one of the core and specialized instruments of human rights protection reserved for migrant workers and their family members.[36]

ILO CONVENTIONS ON MIGRANT WORKERS

As a specialized international labor organization, many international labor standards adopted by the ILO's International Labor Conference over the years are important for protecting the dignity and rights of migrant workers. The most important ILO conventions pertaining to migrant workers are the Migration for Employment (Revised) Convention, 1949 (No. 97); the Migrant Workers (Additional Provisions) Convention, 1975 (No. 143); and the accompanying Recommendations. The instruments offer minimum standards of protection for all migrant workers, regardless of their migration status, and provide guidance on the fundamental components of an all-encompassing labor migration policy, as well as the protection of migrant workers, the development of their potential, and the measures to facilitate and control migratory movements.[37] However, the scope of these two conventions compared to ICMW is quite narrow, only applying to legal migrant workers.

The ILO adopted Convention 97 at its 30th plenary session on June 8, 1949, and put it into force on January 22, 1952.[38] According to Convention 97, the term "migrant worker" means "a person who migrates from one country to another with a view to being employed otherwise than on his own account and includes any person regularly admitted as a migrant for employment" (Article11[1]), and does not apply to frontier workers; short-term entry of members of the liberal professions and artists; and seamen (Article 11[2]). In addition to reiterating generally protected rights such as: the right to full, free (public) assistance, especially information (Article 2) and protection from misleading propaganda (Article 3); prohibiting deporting immigrant workers admitted for permanent residence in case of inability to work (Article 8); and allowing working migrants to transfer their income and savings (Article 9). The Convention also recognizes the principle of equality in treatment between migrant workers and nationals in terms of law and administrative practice regarding living and working conditions, social security, and access to justice, taxation, and procedure. Specifically, the Convention requires states to facilitate international migration for employment by establishing and maintaining free information and support services for migrant workers, and measures to combat false propaganda regarding migration and immigration.

States are required to treat citizens equally regarding some matters, such as social security, labor conditions, and association freedom.[39]

The ILO adopted Convention 143 at its 60th session on June 4, 1975, and put it into force on December 9, 1978. The Convention is the international community's first attempt to address the problems arising from illegal migration and the illegal employment of migrants, and sets out a general obligation to respect the fundamental human rights of all migrant workers (Article 1). It is also seen as a document designed to address some of the deficiencies of Convention 97, including (i) requiring members to ascertain whether any immigrant workers have been hired without authorization, and whether or not migrant laborers are being recruited unlawfully (Article 2); (ii) applying necessary and appropriate measures to prevent the clandestine movement of migrants in search of employment and the employment of illegal migrants (Article 3); (iii) prosecuting the authors of human trafficking (Article 5); (iv) taking necessary measures to facilitate the family reunification of all migrant workers who are legally residing in their country.[40] Additionally, under the 1949 Convention's provisions, the Convention broadens the definition of equality between legally resident migrant workers and foreign domestic workers. This guarantees equal opportunities and treatment in employment and occupation, social security, trade union and cultural rights, as well as individual and collective freedoms for migrant workers and their families who are lawfully residing in ratifying states. The Convention also calls on ratifying states to make it easier for migratory workers who are legally resident in their territory to reunite with their families.[41]

Convention No. 97 and 143 generally have no bearing on a member state's ability to reject admission, or choose the means of entry or stay. These conventions also state, however, that "Nothing in this Convention shall prevent Members from granting to persons unlawfully residing or working in the country the right to remain and work legally" and that "migrant workers shall be treated equally for employment security, provision of alternative employment, relief work, and retraining." After a maximum of two years, a member state may guarantee migrant workers' freedom to select their place of employment and their right to geographic mobility.[42]

Although there have been efforts to ensure rights for migrant workers, these two conventions have not received real attention from countries, as evidenced by the number of members of the two conventions, which is still quite limited. Until now, Convention No. 97 has only been ratified by 53 countries,[43] and 29 countries have ratified Convention 143.[44] Similar to the ICMW, several academic studies highlight why countries are still "indifferent" to these important international documents. Nonetheless, with the current increase in global migration, ensuring the rights of this group of people becomes even more urgent, and the presence of ICMW and other ILO instruments is undeniable. Optimistically, we can fully expect a more worthy position and attention for ICMW shortly.

REFERENCES

Anna Pawlak, *The rights of migrant workers in the United Nations system*, https://eurofur.eu/wp-content/uploads/2020/10/tr9.pdf, accessed on 8 November 2023;

C097 - Migration for Employment Convention (Revised), 1949 (No. 97), https://www.ilo.org/dyn/normlex/en/f?p=NORMLEXPUB:55:0::NO::P55_TYPE,P55_LANG,P55_DOCUMENT,P55_NODE:CON,en,C097,/Document, accessed on 8 November 2023.

General Assembly, United Nations, A/RES/60/251, 3 April 2006, https://www2.ohchr.org/english/bodies/hrcouncil/docs/a.res.60.251_en.pdf.

Human Rights Council, A/HRC/DEC/17/119, 19 July 2011, https://documents-dds-ny.un.org/doc/UNDOC/GEN/G11/150/36/PDF/G1115036.pdf?OpenElement.

Human Rights Council, A/HRC/RES/16/21, 12 April 2011, https://www.ohchr.org/sites/default/files/Documents/HRBodies/HRCouncil/RegularSession/Session23/TF/A-HRC-RES-16-21_en.doc.

ILO, Protecting the rights of migrant workers in irregular situations and addressing irregular labour migration: A compendium, https://www.ilo.org/wcmsp5/groups/public/---ed_protect/---protrav/---migrant/documents/publication/wcms_832915.pdf, accessed on 11 November 2023.

ILO, Ratification and implementation of ILO Conventions 97 and 143 on migrant workers to achieve fair labour migration governance, https://www.ilo.org/wcmsp5/groups/public/---africa/documents/publication/wcms_717848.pdf, accessed on 8 November 2023.

ILO, Rights, Labour Migration and Development: The ILO Approach, Background Note for the Global Forum on Migration and Development, 2007, https://www.gfmd.org/sites/g/files/tmzbdl1801/files/documents/gfmd_brussels07_contribution_ilo_rights_labour_mig_and_dev_en.pdf, accessed on 8 November 2023.

Institution-building of the United Nations Human Rights Council, A/RES/5/1, 18 June 2007, https://ap.ohchr.org/documents/dpage_e.aspx?si=a/hrc/res/5/1.

James A. R. Nafziger and Barry C. Bartel, "The Migrant Workers Convention: Its Place in Human Rights Law" (1991), 25. *International Migration Review*, tr. 771, 777.

Juhani Lonnröth, "The International Convention on the Protection of the Rights of All Migrant Workers and Members of Their Families in the Context of International Migration Policies: An Analysis of Ten Years of Negotiation," in *International Migration Review*, 25 (1991).

Mariette Grange, ICMC, "*Strengthening Protection of Migrant Workers and their Families with International Human Rights Treaties: A Do-it-yourself Kit*," International Catholic Migration Commission, Switzerland, 2006, 17–19.

Nguyen, Thi Hong Yen. "Challenges in Ensuring the Rights of Vietnamese Migrant Workers in the Globalization Context – The Two Sides of the Development

Process". In *Asian Yearbook of International Law*, (Leiden, The Netherlands: Brill | Nijhoff, 2021) doi: https://doi.org/10.1163/9789004501249_008.

Nguyen, Thi Hong Yen (Editor). *International Covenant on Civil and Political Rights 1966 and the implementation of recommendation of the Human Rights Committee for Vietnam.* National Political Publishing House, 2023.

OHCHR, The International Convention on Migrant Workers and its Committee, Fact Sheet No. 24 (Rev.1), New York and Geneva, 2005, https://www.ohchr.org /sites/default/files/Documents/Publications/FactSheet24rev.1en.pdf, accessed on 8 November 2023; Nguyen Thi Hong Yen, *Supra 3*, 130, 135.

OHCHR, Universal Periodic Review: Information and guidelines for relevant stakeholders' written submissions, https://www.ohchr.org/sites/default/files/Documents/HRBodies/UPR/TechnicalGuideEN.pdf.

Ratifications of C143—Migrant Workers (Supplementary Provisions) Convention, 1975 (No. 143), https://www.ilo.org/dyn/normlex/en/f?p=NORMLEXPUB:11300:::NO:11300:P11300_INSTRUMENT_ID:312288:NO, accessed on 8 November 2023.

Shirley Hune and Jan Niessen, "The First UN Convention on Migrant Workers' (1991), 9, *Netherlands Quarterly of Human Rights* 130, tr. 131–32.

Shirley Hune, "Migrant Women in the Context of the International Convention on the Protection of All Migrant Workers and Members of Their Families," in *International Migration Review*, 25 (1991), 800–817.

K. Touzenis and A. Sironi, *Current challenges in the implementation of the UN International Convention on the Protection of the Rights of All Migrant Workers and Members of Their Families*, European Union, 2013.

NOTES

1. United Nations Charter, https://www.un.org/en/about-us/un-charter/preamble, accessed on 11 November 2023.

2. Anna Pawlak, The rights of migrant workers in the United Nations system, https://eurofur.eu/wp-content/uploads/2020/10/tr9.pdf, accessed on 11 November 2023.

3. ILO, Protecting the rights of migrant workers in irregular situations and addressing irregular labour migration: A compendium, https://www.ilo.org/wcmsp5/groups/public/---ed_protect/---protrav/---migrant/documents/publication/wcms_832915.pdf, accessed on 11 November 2023.

4. Ian Brownlie, *Basic Documents on Human Rights* (Clarendon Press, 1981), 21.

5. https://tbinternet.ohchr.org/_layouts/15/TreatyBodyExternal/Treaty.aspx?Treaty=CCPR&Lang=en.

6. Nguyen, Thi Hong Yen (Editor). *International Covenant on Civil and Political Rights 1966 and the implementation of recommendation of the Human Rights Committee for Vietnam*. National Political Publishing House, 2023; Nguyen, Thi Hong Yen, *Đảm bảo quyền của người lao động di trú hợp pháp trong pháp luật quốc tế và pháp luật Việt Nam – thực trạng và giải pháp [Ensuring the rights of legal migrant workers*

in international law and Vietnamese law - current situation and solutions]. Tạp chí Khoa học pháp lý [Legal Sciences Journal], No.01(149)/2022, p.63-78; Nguyen, Thi Hong Yen, and Phuong Dung Nguyen. "Ensuring the Rights of Women Migrant Workers – Analysis and Practice from Viet Nam", *International Human Rights Law Review* 10, 2 (2021): 216-246. doi: https://doi.org/10.1163/22131035-10020001.

7. https://tbinternet.ohchr.org/_layouts/15/TreatyBodyExternal/treaty.aspx?treaty=cescr&lang=en

8. General Assembly, United Nations, A/RES/60/251, 3 April 2006, https://www2.ohchr.org/english/bodies/hrcouncil/docs/a.res.60.251_en.pdf.

9. Institution-building of the United Nations Human Rights Council, A/RES/5/1, 18 June 2007, https://ap.ohchr.org/documents/dpage_e.aspx?si=a/hrc/res/5/1.

10. Human Rights Council, A/HRC/RES/16/21, 12 April 2011, https://www.ohchr.org/sites/default/files/Documents/HRBodies/HRCouncil/RegularSession/Session23/TF/A-HRC-RES-16-21_en.doc.

11. Human Rights Council, A/HRC/DEC/17/119, 19 July 2911, https://documents-dds-ny.un.org/doc/UNDOC/GEN/G11/150/36/PDF/G1115036.pdf?OpenElement.

12. OHCHR, Universal Periodic Review: information and guidelines for relevant stakeholders' written submissions, https://www.ohchr.org/sites/default/files/Documents/HRBodies/UPR/TechnicalGuideEN.pdf.

13. Juhani Lonnröth, "The International Convention on the Protection of the Rights of All Migrant Workers and Memers of Their Families in the Context of International Migration Policies: An Analysis of Ten Years of Negotiation," in *International Migration Review*, 25 (1991).

14. Nguyen, Thi Hong Yen. "Challenges in Ensuring the Rights of Vietnamese Migrant Workers in the Globalization Context – The Two Sides of the Development Process". In *Asian Yearbook of International Law*, (Leiden, The Netherlands: Brill | Nijhoff, 2021) doi: https://doi.org/10.1163/9789004501249_008

15. Source: https://www.iom.int/sites/g/files/tmzbdl486/files/our_work/ICP/IDM/ICMC-Strengthening-Protection-of-Migrant-Workers-and-Their-Families.pdf, accessed on 6 November 2023.

16. Shirley Hune and Jan Niessen, "The First UN Convention on Migrant Workers" (1991), 9, *Netherlands Quarterly of Human Rights* 130, tr. 131–32.

17. OHCHR, The International Convention on Migrant Workers and its Committee, Fact Sheet No. 24 (Rev.1), New York and Geneva, 2005, https://www.ohchr.org/sites/default/files/Documents/Publications/FactSheet24rev.1en.pdf, accessed on 8 November 2023; Nguyen, Thi Hong Yen, *supra 14*.

18. Ibid.

19. Mariette Grange, ICMC, "Strengthening Protection of Migrant Workers and their Families with International Human Rights Treaties: A Do-it-yourself Kit," International Catholic Migration Commission, Switzerland, 2006, 17–19.

20. James A. R. Nafziger and Barry C. Bartel, "The Migrant Workers Convention: Its Place in Human Rights Law" (1991), 25, *International Migration Review*, tr. 771, 777.

21. Ibid.; Nguyen, Thi Hong Yen, *supra 14*.

22. Mariette Grange, ICMC, *supra 9*; Shirley Hune, "Migrant Women in the Context of the International Convention on the Protection of All Migrant Workers and Members of Their Families," in *International Migration Review*, 25, 1991, 800–817.

23. Ibid.

24. Mariette Grange, ICMC, *supra 9.*

25. OHCHR, *supra 7*, p. 8.

26. Ibid.

27. OHCHR, *supra 7*, p. 9.

28. Ibid.

29. Ibid.

30. OHCHR, *supra 7*, p. 10.

31. Source: https://www.ohchr.org/en/treaty-bodies/cmw/introduction, accessed on 8 November 2023.

32. OHCHR, *supra 7*, p. 10.

33. Nguyen, Thi Hong Yen, *supra 14.*

34. Anna Pawlak, *The rights of migrant workers in the United Nations system*, https://eurofur.eu/wp-content/uploads/2020/10/tr9.pdf, accessed on 8 November 2023; K. Touzenis and A. Sironi, *Current challenges in the implementation of the UN International Convention on the Protection of the Rights of All Migrant Workers and Members of Their Families*, European Union, 2013.

35. Anna Pawlak, *supra 23.*

36. Nguyen, Thi Hong Yen, *supra 14.*

37. ILO, Rights, Labour Migration and Development: The ILO Approach, Background Note for the Global Forum on Migration and Development, 2007, https://www.gfmd.org/sites/g/files/tmzbdl1801/files/documents/gfmd_brussels07_contribution_ilo_rights_labour_mig_and_dev_en.pdf, accessed on 8 November 2023.

38. C097 - Migration for Employment Convention (Revised), 1949 (No. 97), https://www.ilo.org/dyn/normlex/en/f?p=NORMLEXPUB:55:0::NO::P55_TYPE,P55_LANG,P55_DOCUMENT,P55_NODE:CON,en,C097,/Document.

39. ILO, *Supra 26*; C097 - Migration for Employment Convention (Revised), 1949 (No. 97), https://www.ilo.org/dyn/normlex/en/f?p=NORMLEXPUB:55:0::NO::P55_TYPE,P55_LANG,P55_DOCUMENT,P55_NODE:CON,en,C097,/Document, accessed on 8 November 2023.

40. Nguyen, Thi Hong Yen, *supra 14.*

41. ILO, *supra 26.*

42. ILO, Ratification and implementation of ILO Conventions 97 and 143 on migrant workers to achieve fair labour migration governance, https://www.ilo.org/wcmsp5/groups/public/---africa/documents/publication/wcms_717848.pdf, accessed on 8 November 2023.

43. Ratifications of C097 - Migration for Employment Convention (Revised), 1949 (No. 97), https://www.ilo.org/dyn/normlex/en/f?p=NORMLEXPUB:11300:0::NO::P11300_INSTRUMENT_ID:312242.

44. Ratifications of C143 - Migrant Workers (Supplementary Provisions) Convention, 1975 (No. 143), https://www.ilo.org/dyn/normlex/en/f?p=NORMLEXPUB:11300:::NO:11300:P11300_INSTRUMENT_ID:312288:NO, accessed on 8 November 2023.

Chapter 2

Agreements and Mechanisms for the Migrant Workers' Rights in Asia

Significant Challenges Confronted by a Highly Populated Continent

Nguyen Thi Kim Ngan

In globalization, migrant workers are becoming an indispensable element of the labor market. In many economies, including emerging economies, aging populations and a shrinking labor force contribute to the increasing mobility of workers. Currently, economic difficulties and geopolitical crises have led to a decent work shortage and increasingly diverse migration movements.

Based on figures for 2017 provided by the United Nations/Department of Economic and Social Affairs (UN/DESA), there are 258 million international migrants, 234 million migrants of working age (15 and older), and 164 million migrant workers worldwide. The previous International Labor Organization (ILO) global estimates on international migrant workers, which were also based on UN/DESA estimates and for which the reference year was 2013, reported that there were 232 million international migrants, 207 million migrants of working age, and 150 million migrant workers, suggesting increases from 2013 to 2017 of approximately 11 percent for international migrants, 13 percent for migrants of working age, and 9 percent for migrant workers. The substantially higher number of international migrants in 2017 could be attributed to migrant population growth.[1] In the following years, the number of international migrants, including migrant workers, also continued to increase. According to IOM (International Organization for Migration) statistics, compared to 2017, the number of international migrants in 2019 has increased from 258 million to 272 million; in 2020 it increased to 281 million. The number of migrant workers has increased from 164 million in 2017 to 169 million in 2019.[2]

Asia is the largest of the world's continents, covering approximately 30 percent of Earth's land area. It is also the world's most populous continent, with roughly 60 percent of the total population.[3] This continent includes the two most populous countries in the world, China (1.439 billion) and India (1.38 billion). Some other populous countries in Asia include Indonesia (273.5 million), Pakistan (220.8 million), Bangladesh (164.6 million), Japan (126.4 million), Philippines (109.5 million), Vietnam (97.3 million), and Turkey (84.3 million), according to 2020 statistics.[4] Asia is also one of the most dynamic regions in the world. Over the past two decades, labor migration has emerged as an important driver of economic growth and development in the region. Of the nearly 200 million migrant workers in the world, 5.2 percent are from countries in Central and Western Asia, 3.6 percent are from East Asia, 7.1 percent from Southeast Asia and the Pacific region, and 4.5 percent from South Asia.[5]

Recent trends suggest that there has been a shift in the flow of migrant workers in Asia. Previously, the flow of Asian migrant workers was mainly to destinations in the Middle East, Europe, or the United States. Nowadays, Asian workers from both traditional sending countries like India, Pakistan, Philippines, Indonesia, and Sri Lanka and emerging labor-sending countries like Bangladesh, Cambodia, Laos, and Vietnam are currently finding jobs in other Asian countries. The main receiving countries in Asia are Japan, South Korea, Malaysia, Singapore, Thailand, Brunei Darussalam, Hong Kong Special Administrative Region (China), and Taiwan. In fact, some Asian countries such as Thailand, Malaysia, and Singapore are both sending countries and receiving countries for migrant workers. Thai workers may migrate to Singapore, Malaysia, Japan, Taiwan, and Hong Kong in search of higher-paid jobs, while Cambodians, Laos, and Burmese migrate to Thailand to take the same kinds of jobs. Similarly, Singapore accepts foreign migrant workers; at the same time, many Singaporeans, mainly highly qualified workers, are finding jobs in the United States, Europe, and some other countries.

Asian countries have initially accessed international labor instruments as well as formed regional and bilateral agreements to protect the rights of migrant workers. International labor instruments lay out basic principles, articulate the rights and duties of employers and workers, establish policy objectives, outline areas of action, or provide guidance on means and procedures to be employed. International labor instruments are designed to promote decent work for workers of all nationalities. They take the legal form of either:

- Conventions or Protocols: Legally binding international treaties that may be ratified by member states, laying down the basic principles to be applied by ratifying countries. Conventions set out the minimum standards that were subject to extensive negotiations and resulting agreements between the governments, employers,' and workers' organizations from the member states; or
- Recommendations: Non-binding but authoritative guidelines that do not have to be ratified and become effective upon adoption by international organizations or at the international conference. Recommendations provide more specific guidance for national law and practice, as well as for international advocacy. Recommendations usually accompany and supplement a convention but can also be autonomous, not linked to any specific convention.

Based on international labor instruments, Asian countries concluded regional, sub-regional, and bilateral treaties that establish specific standards governing relations between member states.

AGREEMENTS ON MIGRANT WORKERS' RIGHTS IN ASIA

International Instruments on the Rights of Migrant Workers and Asian Countries' Ratification

States are entitled to develop their own labor and migration laws and policies. This requires coherent and comprehensive national policies to properly manage labor migration, including the protection of migrant workers' rights. In addition, national laws and policies on migrant workers' rights are compatible with relevant international labor standards. Special attention should be given to the numerous disadvantages and discrimination migrant workers frequently experience due to their sex, race or ethnicity, employment, and migratory status.

In the view of numerous problems affecting the rights of migrant workers in the Asian region, it would be helpful to review the range and scope of international instruments to assist in protecting these rights. There are two types of international instruments: (1) international instruments specifically deal with the rights of migrant workers, and (2) international human rights instruments apply to all persons, including migrant workers. Comparing to international human rights instruments, migrant specific instruments have the advantage that they draw attention to migrants as a separate target group for policy purposes. Both the ILO and the United Nations (UN) have developed international legal conventions which offer specific protection for migrant workers.

In the ILO's 1919 Constitution, member states agreed to protect the rights and interests of migrant workers. This commitment was reaffirmed in 1944 and 1998 when the ILO Declaration on Fundamental Principles and Rights at Work called for "special attention to the problems of persons with special social needs, particularly the unemployed and migrant workers." ILO's member states also adopted five up-to-date instruments (two conventions and three recommendations) specifically for international migrant workers:

- Migration for Employment Convention (Revised) 1949 (No. 97) and Recommendation (Revised) 1949 (No. 86)
- Protection of Migrant Workers (Underdeveloped Countries) Recommendation, 1955 (No. 100)
- Migrant Workers (Supplementary Provisions) Convention, 1975 (No. 143) and the Migrant Workers Recommendation, 1975 (No. 151)

In 1990, the United Nations adopted the International Convention on the Protection of the Rights of All Migrant Workers and Members of their Families (ICMW). Two UN Protocols supplementing the UN Convention Against Transnational Organized Crime adopted in 2000 have also served as essential instruments in the protection of the rights of migrant workers: the Protocol to Prevent, Suppress and Punish Trafficking in Person, Especially Women and Children and the Protocol Against the Smuggling of Migrant by Land, Sea and Air.

UN and ILO conventions and recommendations are applied to all workers regardless of nationality. In other words, migrant workers are subject to the same international labor standards as domestic workers. This means that, in principle, all international labor instruments are relevant to migrant workers as they set out the minimum standards that have been universally agreed upon at the international level.

Asian countries have gradually ratified ILO and UN conventions related to migrant workers toward protecting migrant workers' rights. Asian nations participated more in the ICMW than in ILO agreements. Ten Asian countries have ratified the ICMW, while two have signed but not ratified the convention. It is a remarkable number because the ICMW only has 58 state parties and 11 signatories. For the two ILO conventions, six Asian countries have ratified ILO Convention No. 97, and four countries joined ILO Convention No. 143. These conventions play an important role in protecting the rights of migrant workers in Asian countries. They inspire the development of national legislation, policies, and practices. Millions of workers have benefited from national laws adopted to comply with international labor standards, although only a small number of them may be aware of the connection between, for example, a poster on occupational safety and health standards in their factory, or rules on rest periods and maternity leave in the workplace, and the corresponding convention. In this way the UN and ILO standards have a real impact on the lives and working conditions of millions of workers, including migrant workers.

RATIFICATION STATUS OF MIGRANT WORKERS CONVENTIONS

As of May 1, 2023

ILO Migration for Employment Convention (Revised) 1949, (No. 97)

ILO Migrant Workers (Supplementary Provisions) Convention, 1975 (No. 143)

UN International Convention on the Protection of the Rights of All Migrant Workers and Members of their Families (ICMW), 1990

Status:

ILO Convention No. 97: 6 ratifications

ILO Convention No. 143: 4 ratifications

ICMW: State parties: 10

Non-ratified signatories: 2

Table 2.1.

States	***Ratification ILO C.97***[6]	***Ratification ILO C.143***[7]	***Ratification/Accession or Signature only ICMW***[8]
Afghanistan			
Armenia	Jan 27 2006	Jan 27 2006	Signature: 2013 No Ratification/Accession
Azerbaijan			Ratification/Accession:1999
Bahrain			
Bangladesh			Signature: 1998 Ratification/ Accession: 2011
Bhutan			
Brunei Darussalam			
Cambodia			Signature: 2004 No Ratification/Accession
China			
Cyprus	Sep 23 1960	Jun 28 1977	
Democratic People's Republic of Korea			

States	Ratification ILO C.97[6]	Ratification ILO C.143[7]	Ratification/Accession or Signature only UN MWC[8]
Georgia			
India			
Indonesia			Signature: 2004 Ratification/ Accession: 2012
Iran			
Iraq			
Israel	Mar 30 1953		
Japan			
Jordan			
Kazakhstan			
Kuwait			
Kyrgyzstan	Sep 10 2008		Ratification/Accession: 2003
Laos			
Lebanon			
Malaysia			
Maldives			
Mongolia			
Myanmar			
Nepal			
Oman			
Pakistan			
Philippines	Apr 21 2009	Sep 14 2006	Signature: 1993 Ratification/ Accession: 1995
Qatar			
Republic of Korea			
Saudi Arabia			
Singapore			
Sri Lanka			Ratification/Accession: 1996
State of Palestine			
Syria			Ratification/Accession: 2005
Tajikistan	Apr 10 2007	Apr 10 2007	Signature: 2000 Ratification/ Accession: 2002
Thailand			
Timor-Leste			Ratification/Accession: 2004
Turkey			Signature: 1999 Ratification/Accession: 2004
Turkmenistan			
United Arab Emirates			
Uzbekistan			
Vietnam			
Yemen			

[i] Ratifications of C097 - Migration for Employment Convention (Revised), 1949 (No. 97), https://www.ilo.org/dyn/normlex/en/f?p=NORMLEXPUB:11300:0::NO:11300:P11300_INSTRUMENT_ID:312242:NO

[ii] Ratifications of C143 - Migrant Workers (Supplementary Provisions) Convention, 1975 (No. 143), https://www.ilo.org/dyn/normlex/en/f?p=NORMLEXPUB:11300:0::NO:11300:P11300_INSTRUMENT_ID:312288:NO

[iii] STATUS OF RATIFICATION, International Convention on the Protection of the Rights of All Migrant Workers and Members of their Families, https://indicators.ohchr.org

Regional Agreements on the Rights of Migrant Workers

In the Asian region, there are some regional or sub-regional agreements on various aspects of labor migration. Regional or sub-regional agreements on the rights of migrant workers typically involve a series of meetings or agreements that allow participants to share experiences and develop relationships and a common understanding of mutual problems.

a. ASEAN agreements on the Protection and Promotion of the Rights of Migrant Workers

ASEAN member states share a common interest in and commitment to the promotion and protection of human rights and fundamental freedoms. The ASEAN Charter, which gave ASEAN a legal personality, was signed by ASEAN leaders in November 2007. The Charter calls for the establishment of an ASEAN human rights body for the "promotion and protection of human rights and fundamental freedoms of peoples in ASEAN." In accordance with the ASEAN Charter, respect for and promotion of human rights serve as the cornerstones for regional cooperation among ASEAN member states and its cooperation with relevant national, regional, and international institutions and organizations.

Human rights is the fundamental basis for peace, stability, and sustainable development. The adoption of the ASEAN Human Rights Declaration in 2012 attests to ASEAN's commitment to advance the promotion and protection of human rights in the region. The Declaration defines various internationally accepted rights, including civil, political, economic, social, and cultural rights. Furthermore, as recognized in the Declaration, the right to development entitles people of ASEAN to participate in and contribute to the process of narrowing the development gap within ASEAN and promoting equitable and sustainable development, fair trade practices, and effective international cooperation.

ASEAN has gradually expanded its regional human rights framework to encompass specific standards for women, children, persons with disabilities, migrant workers, and other vulnerable groups. ASEAN has adopted a number of human rights declarations:

- Jakarta Declaration on the Elimination of Violence Against Women in the ASEAN Region (2004)
- ASEAN Declaration Against Trafficking in Persons particularly Women and Children (2004)
- Vientiane Action Programme (2004)
- Declaration on the Establishment of the ASEAN Charter (2005)

- ASEAN Declaration on the Protection and Promotion of the Rights of Migrant Workers (2007)

The ASEAN Declaration on the Protection and Promotion of the Rights of Migrant Workers was adopted by the ASEAN heads of state in Cebu, Philippines, in 2007. The Declaration outlines the duties that countries of origin and destination must fulfil to protect migrant workers from exploitation, discrimination, and violence, as well as to manage labor movement and combat human trafficking. Following the signing of the Declaration, a Committee on the Implementation of the Declaration was set up to advance efforts in these areas. As one of the Committee's suggested activities, ASEAN holds an annual Forum on Migrant Labor (AFML), which provides a public forum for the review, discussion, and exchange of best practices and ideas between governments, workers' and employers' organizations, and civil society stakeholders on pressing issues affecting migrant workers in Southeast Asia. The Forum seeks to develop recommendations to advance the implementation of the principles of the ASEAN Declaration. The Forum provides opportunity to share stakeholder activities to implement the various recommendations from AFML meetings as well as the experience of developing the draft ASEAN Instrument on the Protection and Promotion of the Rights of Migrant Workers.

Ten years after the adoption of the Declaration on the Promotion and Protection of the Rights of Migrant Workers, the ASEAN heads of state have signed the ASEAN Consensus on the Promotion and Protection of the Rights of Migrant Workers following the 31st ASEAN Summit in Manila, Philippines. on November 14, 2017.

The Consensus has identified the general principles of ASEAN cooperation in protecting and promoting the rights of migrant workers; fundamental rights of migrant workers and the members of their families; specific rights of migrant workers; obligations of sending states; obligations of receiving states; and commitments of ASEAN member states in protecting and promoting the rights of migrant workers. The Consensus will serve as a guideline for the operation of ASEAN Committee on Migrant Workers, looking toward international standards applied in the ASEAN activities related to preserving and facilitating the rights of migrant workers, and further increasing the responsibility of states sending and receiving the laborers. The Consensus aims to establish a framework for closer cooperation among member states on addressing migrant workers' issues in the region. While it is non-legally binding (similar to the ASEAN Declaration on the Protection and Promotion of the Rights of Migrant Workers), the ASEAN Consensus is considered a living and evolving document.

SAARC Agreements on Human Rights

South Asian Association for Regional Cooperation (SAARC) comprises eight member states: Afghanistan, Bangladesh, Bhutan, India, Maldives, Nepal, Pakistan, and Sri Lanka. SAARC currently does not have an agreement on the rights of migrant workers. It has a cooperative approach of focusing on treaties linked with specific human rights issues. In 2002, SAARC adopted two treaties that impact the rights of migrant workers: the SAARC Convention on Preventing and Combating Trafficking in Women and Children for Prostitution and the SAARC Convention on Regional Arrangements for the Promotion of Child Welfare in South Asia.

The SAARC Convention on Preventing and Combating Trafficking in Women and Children for Prostitution, ratified in 2005, presented a significant step toward combating human trafficking at a regional level. It is "the first regional treaty of its kind and first treaty in Asia to address human trafficking."[9]

In 2004, SAARC adopted the SAARC Social Charter which impacts many economic, social, and cultural rights. The Charter defined the principles, goals, and objectives of SAARC cooperation on human rights, including the following:

- Promote participatory governance, human dignity, social justice, and solidarity at the national, regional, and international level;
- Ensure tolerance, non-violence, pluralism, and non-discrimination in respect of diversity within and among societies; and
- Promote universal respect for and observance and protection of human rights and fundamental freedoms of all, in particular the right to development.[10]

In the SAARC Social Charter, there are commitments to eradicate poverty, improve health services, foster educational access, and promote the status of women and children, population stabilization, and drug addiction rehabilitation. Members set up national coordination committees through an integrated program of action where core areas of cooperation are identified. Article 5 of the Charter recognized the obligations of member states related to the rights of the workers: create productive employment opportunities for all groups of people, including young people; provide enhanced job opportunities for young people through increased investment in education and vocational training; provide adequate employment opportunities and leisure time activities for youth to make them economically and socially productive.

The Arab League Agreements on Human Rights

The Arab League is bound by Arab culture and only 9 of its 22 member states are in Asia. In 1994 the Arab Charter on Human Rights was finalized by the Arab League. This was the first inter-governmental treaty for parts of West Asia laying down human rights standards and a monitoring mechanism in the form of an Arab Human Rights Committee. There is a monitoring role for the Arab Human Rights Committee that can make recommendations of a persuasive nature.

The Arab Charter on Human Rights (ACHR), adopted by the Council of the League of Arab States on May 22,2004, affirms the principles contained in the UN Charter, the Universal Declaration on Human Rights, the International Covenants on Human Rights, and the Cairo Declaration on Human Rights in Islam. ACHR provides for a number of traditional human rights, including the right to liberty and security of persons, equality of persons before the law, protection of persons from torture, the right to own private property, freedom to practice religious observance, and freedom of peaceful assembly and association. The Arab Charter on Human Rights requires states to ensure the prohibition of all forms of violence or abuse in relations among family members, particularly against women and children, and to take all necessary legislative, administrative, and judicial measures to guarantee the protection, survival, development, and well-being of the child in an atmosphere of freedom and dignity. It requires states to ensure special treatment to children at risk, which takes account of their age and protects their dignity, and to guarantee everyone's rights not to be subjected to physical or psychological torture or to cruel, degrading, humiliating or inhuman treatment and to equality and recognition as a person before the law.[11]

Despite not directly mentioning the rights of migrant workers, the Arab Charter on Human Rights identified a number of fundamental rights and freedoms. Therefore, the Arab Charter on Human Rights is also an essential regional legal instrument to protect the rights of migrant workers in Asian countries.

BILATERAL LABOR MIGRATION AGREEMENTS

In addition to participating in international and regional agreements, Asian countries also signed Bilateral Labor Migration Agreements (BLMAs) to enhance cooperation in labor migration, of which the important goal is to ensure the protection of labor migration. BLMAs include legally binding Bilateral Labor Agreements (BLAs) and Memoranda of Understanding

(MoUs). They can also include specific bilateral agreements between government ministries or agencies in countries of origin and destination, dealing with different aspects of labor migration. They can also cover framework or cooperation agreements that include labor migration along with other migration topics such as irregular migration, readmission, and migration and development. A BLMA describes in detail the specific responsibilities of each of the parties and the actions to be taken by them with a view to accomplishing their specific goals in terms of governance of labor migration.

For labor-receiving countries, BLMAs support better management, encourage cultural/political linkages and exchanges, and enable a flow of labor that satisfies the demands of employers and industrial sectors. For sending countries, these agreements ensure continued access to foreign labor markets and opportunities to advance the safety and welfare of their workforces.

Asian countries seem to prefer MoUs, probably because as non-binding agreements they are easier to negotiate, implement, and amend according to changing economic and labor market situations. Such agreements may be signed for political purposes, to display friendly relations or to strengthen collaboration in controlling irregular migration.

In the Asian region, the Philippines and the Republic of Korea have been the most successful among the labor-sending countries in their attempts to negotiate BLMAs. However, the number of BLMAs that the Philippines has successfully entered into over the last 40 years attests to the difficulty of such undertaking. The Philippines has been able to successfully sign with only 13 countries (12 labor-receiving countries: Norway, the United Kingdom, Papua New Guinea, Taiwan, Switzerland, Sweden, Libya, Jordan, Qatar, Iraq, Kuwait, and the Commonwealth of Northern Marianas Islands (CNMI); and 1 labor-sending country: Indonesia) since the overseas employment program began in 1974. While it has not been able to enter into such agreements with the largest labor-receiving countries of overseas Filipino workers such as Singapore, Japan, and Saudi Arabia.[12]

The Republic of Korea has MoUs with Bangladesh, Cambodia, China, Indonesia, Kyrgyzstan, Myanmar, Nepal, Pakistan, Philippines, Thailand, Timor-Leste, Uzbekistan, Vietnam, and Sri Lanka on the hiring of foreign workers under its Employment Permit System. Malaysia has signed MoUs with Bangladesh, China, Sri Lanka, Thailand, Pakistan, Vietnam, and Indonesia to regulate recruitment processes and procedures. Thailand has MoUs with Laos People's Democratic Republic, Cambodia, and Myanmar.[13]

People's Republic of China has been able to enter into four bilateral labor agreements with Bahrain, Mauritius, Russia, and Malaysia, and two social security agreements with Germany and Korea. Taiwan has forged bilateral labor agreements with Thailand and Vietnam through their respective

Economic and Cultural Offices for the employment of Thai and Vietnamese workers and MoUs with the Philippines, Mongolia, and Indonesia.[14]

Many countries of South and Southwest Asia have also signed bilateral labor agreements with countries outside the subregion. Bangladesh, India, Nepal, Pakistan, Sri Lanka, and Turkey have signed MoUs with receiving countries in East Asia, Europe, Southeast Asia, and Western Asia, with the majority of them made with Gulf Cooperation Council (GCC) countries, the area that has the largest concentration of migrant workers from South and Southwest Asia. India has signed MoUs with more than 17 countries, including numerous European countries. Nepal has so far signed bilateral agreements with three destination countries, Qatar, the Republic of Korea, and the United Arab Emirates, and is considering agreements with Bahrain, Israel, and Malaysia. Turkey has signed a number of bilateral labor arrangements with European countries: Federal Republic of Germany, Austria, Belgium, Netherlands, France, and Sweden.[15]

The nature, scope, content, and enforceability of the different bilateral agreements entered into by various Asian countries vary. For most of these agreements, however, monitoring and enforcement mechanisms tend to be weak, and typically they concentrate more on recruitment procedures and less on welfare and protection. There are some major issues to be covered in BLMAs:

- Exchange information
- Recruitment, testing, and certification of applicants
- Sectors, quotas, duration, and possibility of renewal
- Employment contracts and conditions of work
- Provisions to deal with migrant workers in irregular status
- Dispute settlement
- Social security arrangements
- Return provisions
- Jurisdiction and enforcement: Joint review committees

In formulating bilateral labor agreements, Asian countries can likewise be guided by international instruments such as the ILO Model Agreement on Temporary and Permanent Migration for Employment, including Migration of Refugees and Displaced Persons, annexed to Recommendation No. 86 on Migration for Employment (Revised), 1949[16]; the Guidance on Bilateral Labor Migration Agreements was prepared by the Thematic Working Group (TWG) 4 on BLMAs, under the auspices of the UN Network on Migration, co-chaired by ILO with IOM.[17]

OTHER INTERNATIONAL AGREEMENTS

In addition to international treaties on human rights, the rights of workers, including migrant workers, are also recognized in a number of bilateral or multilateral free trade agreements, economic partnership agreements, and general systems of preferences signed between Asian countries or between Asian countries and others, such as the Comprehensive and Progressive Agreement for Trans-Pacific Partnership (CPTPP) 2018, the Agreement establishing the ASEAN—Australia–New Zealand Free Trade Area 2010, the Free Trade Agreement between the European Union and its member states and the Republic of Korea 2011, the Free Trade Agreement between the European Union and its member states and the Socialist Republic of Vietnam 2020, and the Agreement between Japan and Mongolia for an Economic Partnership 2016.[18]

In the context of globalization, the issue of ensuring workers' rights is becoming increasingly critical. Based on considering workers as people who directly produce and supply goods and services in international trade, they must first be the beneficiaries and share the results of this process. In other words, they must be guaranteed fundamental rights, interests, and working conditions. This is the approach of the new generation of trade agreements and is becoming a trend worldwide in recent years. Labor standards are also considered a factor that makes the quality and difference of new generation trade agreements. The new generation trade agreements do not set labor standards but only reaffirm the labor standards in the eight Conventions of the International Labor Organization. These are Convention No. 87 and No. 98 on freedom of association and collective bargaining; Convention No. 29 and No. 105 on freedom from forced or compulsory labor; Convention No. 138 and No. 182 for the elimination of child labor; Convention No. 100 and No. 111 on the elimination of discrimination in employment and occupation. Labor clauses in trade agreements, economic partnership agreements, and general systems of preferences required the respect of labor standards and the protection of internationally recognized workers' rights.

MECHANISMS FOR PROTECTING MIGRANT WORKERS' RIGHTS IN ASIA

Mechanism of International Instruments on the Rights of Migrant Workers

ICMW established a mechanism to protect the rights of migrant workers. The Committee on the Protection of the Rights of All Migrant Workers and

Members of their Families (ICMW) is the body of independent experts that monitors implementation of the ICMW by its state parties. Its responsibilities include: examining reports from states parties and making recommendations on the topic of migrant workers and members of their families in that state; organizing days of general discussion; interpretations of the content of the substantive provisions in the Convention (general comments), and publishing statements and information or guidance notes on themes related to its mandate. The Committee will also, under certain circumstances, be able to consider inter-state or individual complaints or communications from states parties or from individuals who claim that their rights under the Convention have been violated.

For ILO conventions, ILO member states are required to submit periodic reports on the Conventions they have ratified and selected reports on the position of the state's law and practice with regard to matters dealt with in unratified conventions or recommendations. The Committee of Experts on the Application of Conventions and Recommendations and the Conference Committee on the Application of Standards examine the reports submitted by governments. When an individual state is not complying with the obligations under any ILO convention it has ratified, complaints may be submitted to the ILO under several procedures.

UN and ILO conventions' mechanisms are universal mechanisms to protect the rights of migrant workers. However, only Asian countries that ratified or accessed ICMW or ILO conventions are binding to those mechanisms (for more information, see Chapter 1).

Mechanism of Regional Agreements

Within the framework of ASEAN cooperation on human rights, the ASEAN Intergovernmental Commission on Human Rights (AICHR) was inaugurated in October 2009 as a consultative body of the ASEAN. This was further enhanced with the promulgation of the ASEAN Human Rights Declaration. AICHR exists to promote and protect human rights as well as regional co-operation on human rights in the member states of ASEAN. The establishment of the AICHR demonstrates ASEAN's commitment to pursue forward-looking strategies to strengthen regional cooperation on human rights. The AICHR is designed to be an integral part of ASEAN organizational structure, and is an overarching institution with overall responsibility for the promotion and protection of human rights in ASEAN. The AICHR members are called representatives, who are nominated by their respective governments. Decision-making of the AICHR is based on consultation and consensus. Since its establishment, the AICHR has adopted several key documents, including the Guidelines on the Operations of AICHR and the Guidelines on the AICHR's

Relations with Civil Society Organisations (CSOs). The AICHR's priority areas on human rights are found in the Five-Year Work Plan, which is based on the 14 mandates of the AICHR, mainly around the promotion and protection of human rights, capacity building, advice and technical assistance, and information gathering and engagement with national, regional, and international bodies. Each year, the AICHR specifies their high-priority programs and activities for the year based on the Work Plan and in response to emerging exigencies on human rights in the region. The AICHR holds two regular meetings annually and additional meetings when necessary, and reports to the ASEAN foreign ministers.

The ASEAN Committee to Implement the Declaration on the Protection and Promotion of the Rights of Migrant Workers (ACMW) was established in July 2007. The Committee is tasked with implementing the 2007 ASEAN Declaration on the Protection and Promotion of the Rights of Migrant Workers. ACMW's purpose is to ensure commitments made under the Declaration on Migrant Worker Rights are implemented, and to develop an ASEAN instrument on the protection and promotion of the rights of migrant workers. ACMW has divided its work into four areas: step up protection and promotion of the rights of migrant workers against exploitation and mistreatment; strengthen protection and promotion of the rights of migrant workers by enhancing labor migration governance in ASEAN countries; encourage regional cooperation to fight human trafficking in ASEAN; and develop an ASEAN Instrument on the Protection and Promotion of the Rights of Migrant Workers. ACMW's missions were reaffirmed in ASEAN Consensus on the Protection and Promotion of the Rights of Migrant Workers. The ACMW reports to the Senior Labor Officials Meeting (SLOM).

In the Arab League, the monitoring role institution of the Arab Charter on Human Rights is the Arab Human Rights Committee that can make recommendations of a persuasive nature. Member countries of ACHR have a reporting obligation. Although individual complaints cannot be currently made to the Committee, there is a possibility of protocols to add elements to the Arab Charter on Human Rights which could provide space for individuals to seek redress.

The state parties to the SAARC Convention on Preventing and Combating Trafficking in Women and Children for Prostitution established a Regional Task Force consisting of officials of the member states to facilitate implementation of the provisions of this Convention and to undertake periodic reviews. The state parties to the Convention may also, by mutual agreement, set up bilateral mechanisms to effectively implement the provisions of the Convention, including appropriate mechanisms for cooperation to interdict trafficking in women and children for prostitution. The state parties shall exchange, on a regular basis, information in respect of agencies, institutions, and individuals who are involved in trafficking in the region and also identify methods and routes used by the traffickers through land, water, or air. The information so furnished shall include information of the offenders, their fingerprints, photographs, methods of operation, police records, and records of conviction.[19]

MECHANISM OF BILATERAL LABOR MIGRATION AGREEMENTS

Bilateral Labor Migration Agreements (BLMA) identifies responsible institutions for the promotion, implementation, and enforcement of the agreed working and living conditions of migrant workers. The BLMA includes indications on the establishment of a governance structure, depending on the specific countries' needs. BLMA provisions are included for the supervision of working and living conditions of migrant workers, including the specific role of the labor inspection, other relevant institutions, and public health services in ensuring effective monitoring and enforcement of agreed commitments.

In some BLMAs, the parties establish a Ministerial Council, composed of ministers responsible for labor affairs of the parties, or their designees, to discuss matters of common interest, to oversee the implementation of the agreement, including cooperative activities, and to review progress under the agreement. The Council shall promote transparency and public participation in its work. The Council may consider any matter within the scope of the agreement and take such other action in the exercise of its functions as the parties may jointly decide, including working through the National Points of Contact to coordinate cooperative programs and activities, and establishing and assigning responsibilities to committees, working groups, or expert groups. The Council shall review the operation and effectiveness of the agreement, including the degree to which progress has been made in implementing the objectives of the agreement.

Under the MoU between Indonesia and the Philippines concerning migrant workers, a steering committee, composed of senior officials of both countries, was established to review the MoU's operation and coordinate the implementation of the program. The steering committee meets at least once a year. Joint working groups will also be established in receiving countries through the respective embassies or labor offices of the Philippines and Indonesia to promote and protect the welfare and rights of their migrant workers. These joint working groups are to meet regularly and pursue programs on-site in close coordination with the steering committee. The implementation of this agreement between the Philippines and Indonesia will be interesting to monitor since it can serve as a test case for the viability and effectiveness of collaborative efforts by receiving countries to gain leverage and to consolidate their strengths toward protecting the welfare and rights of their migrant workers.[20]

According to the Agreement on Bilateral Cooperation on Labor Migration between Italy and Philippines, the contracting parties establish a joint working group which holds regular consultations in order to monitor the implementation of the Agreement and submit proposals for ensuring a good functioning; regularly evaluate the Agreement; solve practical problems which could hamper the implementation of the Agreement; and recommend amendments to the Agreement, if necessary. The working group will be composed of at least three members from each part, led by a senior official, and will meet preferably annually or as necessary.[21]

CHALLENGES IN THE IMPLEMENTATION OF INTERNATIONAL AGREEMENTS AND MECHANISMS FOR MIGRANT WORKERS' RIGHTS IN ASIA

International cooperation to protect and promote human rights, whether on a global or regional scale, requires countries' efforts through many political and legal measures. Regarding the legal aspect, building and perfecting mechanisms and standard agreements on human rights plays a significant role in promoting and protecting human rights in a particular region. This has been proven through the success of human rights agreements and mechanisms in Europe, America, and recently in Africa.

Although a number of agreements and mechanisms have initially been formed to ensure and promote the rights of migrant workers in Asia, the implementation of these agreements and mechanisms has been facing many challenges:

- Countries in the Asian region have significant differences in political systems and levels of freedom and democracy. Some countries have lower levels of openness, slower economic and political integration, transparency, and rule of law than others. Integrating these countries into the region requires a lot of time and effort from other countries and the international community.
- Civil society in Asian countries has low levels of development. For example, ASEAN still needs to establish a dialogue between civil society and goverment. Recently, leaders of ASEAN countries have created some dialogue channels with people's organizations and civil society. However, this dialogue is generally more of a formality than sincere and responsible listening. Civil society's access to state agencies still faces

many difficulties, and people's proposals still need to have the opportunity to influence the standard policies of ASEAN and each member country's policies on human rights.

- Although a number of Asian countries have participated in international human rights treaties, including those on the rights of migrant workers, the level of commitment to implementation is generally low. In many countries, there is a strong tendency to support the "specificity" of human rights. These views were expressed in the Bangkok Declaration 1993 on human rights. During the lead-up to the World Conference on Human Rights, held in 1993, ministers from several Asian states adopted the Bangkok Declaration, which reaffirms their governments' commitment to the principles of the United Nations Charter and the Universal Declaration of Human Rights. The Bangkok Declaration recognized that "while human rights are universal in nature, they must be considered in the context of a dynamic and evolving process of international norm-setting, bearing in mind the significance of national and regional particularities and various historical, cultural and religious backgrounds."[22] The Bangkok Declaration is considered to be a landmark expression of Asian values concerning human rights, which offers an extended critique of human rights universalism.

Ministers from Asian states also believe that human rights are interdependent and indivisible, and stressed the need for universality, objectivity, and non-selectivity of human rights. However, at the same time, they emphasized the principles of sovereignty and non-interference. A rigid understanding of the principle of sovereignty and non-interference can prevent regional mechanisms from making recommendations that may not satisfy a particular state. Expanding the authority of regional human rights institutions also requires more time and effort.

In the Asian region, there are a number of key regional bodies including the ASEAN, SAARC, and and the Arab League. However, as migration is not an integral element of the mandates of any of these bodies, their dealings with migration issues are limited, particularly compared to regional bodies in other parts of the world. Asian countries still need to establish clear binding regulations and mechanisms for promoting appropriate working conditions and labor standards at the regional level.

The human rights protection mechanism of the Asian region is different from the human rights protection mechanism of large regions such as Europe, America, and Africa. To some extent, Asia countries in the ASEAN, SAARC, and the Arab League have adopted some regional instruments related to the rights of migrant workers and recognized the responsibility of the receiving and sending countries as well as of these organizations for the protection and promotion of the rights of migrant workers. However, many of the regional instruments are not binding. This makes the impact of these instruments very limited.

In recent years, ASEAN has conducted a number of studies and plans to reform and improve the operational efficiency of AICHR. ASEAN countries are amending and supplementing the regulations of AICHR in a more specific direction to the tasks of these institutions. Amending the AICHR regulations has been incorporated into the ASEAN Action Plan 2025. The development of a binding legal instrument on human rights in the region has also been realized. In addition, ASEAN plans to strengthen coordination activities between AICHR and other relevant organizations and institutions.

In the absence of regional mechanisms, many Asian countries, including labor-exporting countries, have not yet joined international treaties that protect migrant workers. Specifically, out of 69 countries and territories that have signed or ratified the UN convention on the rights of migrant workers, only 12 are in Asia, of which 10 have ratified it (including Azerbaijan, Bangladesh, Indonesia, Kyrgyzstan, Philippines, Sri Lanka, Syria, Tajikistan, Timor-Leste, and Turkey), and 2 countries (Armenia and Cambodia) have signed but not ratified the convention. As for the basic ILO conventions (including Convention Nos. 97 and 143), there are still many Asian countries that have not joined a number of important treaties.

BLMA agreements require particular administration to ensure their smooth operation—including the recruitment, testing, and certification of applicants for the program and timely data flow and information sharing between the two countries. For most of these agreements, monitoring and enforcement mechanisms tend to be weak, and typically they concentrate more on recruitment procedures and less on welfare and protection. The following are some areas that Asian parliamentarians and legislators can consider when reviewing agreements, particularly the implementation of rules and regulations, entered into by their respective countries or in drafting a possible legislative framework governing such agreements:

- Monitoring and enforcement mechanisms of the agreements: These are generally weak and not much is known about the extent of the implementation of these agreements.
- Provisions and mechanisms for worker welfare and protection: The economic interests and the interests of labor-receiving countries tend to dominate; consequently, the protective mechanisms are weak. Moreover, in some cases, worker's rights are denied, such as freedom of association, confiscation of travel documents by employers, and mandatory withholding of wages. To address the welfare and protective concerns, mechanisms for addressing violations of recruitment intermediaries can

be instituted. In addition, in cases where no separate social security agreement is entered into, social security provisions may be incorporated into bilateral labor agreements.

Regional cooperation on protecting migrant workers has recently brought certain benefits to countries and workers in the Asian region. However, in general, the results are still limited. There are many reasons, of which the lack of interest and determination of Asian countries is the main reason. Therefore, in the coming time, Asian countries need to make efforts on a national basis or coordinate with each other to overcome legal, economic, and social obstacles in this issue to better protect the rights of migrant workers in the region, thereby ensuring the stable development of labor cooperation in the region that benefits all countries.

REFERENCES

ILO. ILO Global Estimates on International Migrant Workers: Results and Methodology. 2017. https://www.ilo.org/wcmsp5/groups/public/---dgreports/-- -dcomm/---publ/documents/publication/wcms_652001.pdf. Accessed on September 15, 2023.

Monika Barthwal-Datta. *Understanding Security Practices in South Asia: Securitization Theory and the Role of Non-State Actor*. Routledge, 2012, New York.

Stella P. Go. *Asian Labor Migration: The Role of Bilateral Labor and Similar Agreements*, Regional Informal Workshop on Labor Migration in Southeast Asia: What Role for Parliaments, 21–23 September 2007, Manila, Philippines.

The Agreement on Bilateral Cooperation on Labor Migration between Italy and Philippines. https://www.dmw.gov.ph/archives/laborinfo/agreement/ITALY %20SIGNED %20AGREEMENT %20ON %20BILATERAL %20LABOR %20MIGRATION. . .pdf. Accessed on September 17, 2023.

The Bangkok Declaration 1993. https://unesdoc.unesco.org/ark:/48223/pf0000096128. Accessed on September 20, 2023.

The MOU between Indonesia and Philippines concerning migrant workers. https: //asean.org/wp-content/uploads/2016/05/IP1_Memo-of-Unds-bt-the-Dept-of-manpower-n-Trans-of-the-RI-n-Dept-of-Labor.pdf. Accessed on November 5, 2023.

The Situation Report on International Migration in South and South-West Asia. Bilateral cooperation, https://sitreport.unescapsdd.org/migration-policies/bilateral-cooperation. Accessed on July 5, 2023.

World Migration Report 2022. https://publications.iom.int/books/world-migration-report-2022. Accessed on July 5, 2023.

NOTES

1. https://www.ilo.org/wcmsp5/groups/public/---dgreports/---dcomm/---publ/documents/publication/wcms_652001.pdf, p. 5. Accessed on September 15, 2023.

2. World Migration Report 2022, https://publications.iom.int/books/world -migration-report-2022. Accessed on July 5, 2023.

3. https://education.nationalgeographic.org/resource/asia/. Accessed on January 5, 2023.

4. https://www.worldometers.info/population/countries-in-asia-by-population/. Accessed on January 5, 2023.

5. https://www.ilo.org/wcmsp5/groups/public/---dgreports/---dcomm/---publ/documents/publication/wcms_652001.pdf, pp. 14–15. Accessed on September 15, 2023.

6. Monika Barthwal-Datta. Understanding Security Practices in South Asia: Securitization Theory and the Role of Non-State Actor, Routledge, 2012, p.91. New York.

7 the SAARC Social Charter https://www.saarc-sec.org/index.php/resources/agreements-conventions/54-saarc-social-charter/file. Accessed on September 15, 2023.

8 The Arab Charter on Human Rights, https://digitallibrary.un.org/record/55136. Accessed on September 20, 2023.

9. Monika Barthwal-Datta. *Understanding Security Practices in South Asia: Securitization Theory and the Role of Non-State Actor*, Routledge, 2012, p.91.

10. The SAARC Social Charter, https://www.saarc-sec.org/index.php/resources/agreements-conventions/54-saarc-social-charter/file. Accessed on June 20, 2023.

11. The Arab Charter on Human Rights, https://digitallibrary.un.org/record/551368. Accessed on June 20, 2023.

12. https://www.ilo.org/asia/areas/labor-migration/WCMS_226300/lang--en/index.htm. Accessed on June 20, 2023.

13. https://www.ilo.org/asia/areas/labor-migration/WCMS_226300/lang--en/index.htm. Accessed on June 20, 2023.

14. Stella P. Go, *Asian Labor Migration: The Role of Bilateral Labor and Similar Agreements*, Regional Informal Workshop on Labor Migration in Southeast Asia: What Role for Parliaments, 21–23 September 2007, Manila, Philippines.

15. *The* Situation Report on International Migration in South and South-West Asia, Bilateral cooperation, https://sitreport.unescapsdd.org/migration-policies/bilateral -cooperation. Accessed on July 5, 2023.

16. https://www.ilo.org/dyn/normlex/en/f?p=NORMLEXPUB:12100:0::NO::P12100_INSTRUMENT_ID:312424.Accessed on June 20, 2023.

17. https://www.ilo.org/global/topics/labor-migration/publications/WCMS _837529/lang--en/index.htm. Accessed on June 20, 2023.

18. Labor Provisions in Trade Agreements, https://www.ilo.org/LPhub/. Accessed on June 20, 2023.

19. Article 8. The SAARC Convention on Preventing and Combating Trafficking in Women and Children for Prostitution, https://evaw-global-database.unwomen.org /-/media/files/un%20women/vaw/full%20text/asia/south%20asian%20association %20for%20regional%20cooperation/saarc%20convention%20on%20preventing

%20and%20combating%20trafficking%20in%20women%20and%20children %20for%20prostitution.pdf?vs=3229. Accessed on June 25, 2023.

20. The MOU between Indonesia and Philippines concerning migrant workers, https://asean.org/wp-content/uploads/2016/05/IP1_Memo-of-Unds-bt-the-Dept-of -manpower-n-Trans-of-the-RI-n-Dept-of-Labor.pdf. Accessed on July 6, 2023.

21. The Agreement on Bilateral Cooperation on Labor Migration between Italy and Philippines, https://www.dmw.gov.ph/archives/laborinfo/agreement/ ITALY%20 SIGNED%20AGREEMENT%20ON%20BILATERAL%20LABOR %20MIGRA-TION. . .pdf. Accessed on July 6, 2023.

22. The Bangkok Declaration 1993, https://unesdoc.unesco.org/ark:/48223/ pf0000096128, p. 44. Accessed on September 20, 2023.

Chapter 3

The Rights of Child Workers as Migrants

Chu Manh Hung

Children are vulnerable due to incomplete physical and mental development, so they are always in need of attention and protection from all legal systems, including both national and international law. Child labor is a violation of basic human rights and has been shown to hinder children's development, potentially leading to lifelong physical or psychological harm.[1]

In the context of the migrant labor crisis occurring globally, it is unfortunate that we still encounter instances of children being involved as workers. These children, whether with their parents or alone, undertake the risky journey in search of employment for themselves or to support their families. The sight of migrant children working on the streets has become all too familiar to the international community, serving as a painful reminder of the consequences of poverty, war, conflict, and natural disasters. It is disheartening that the term "migrant child labor" has become a phrase we are compelled to acknowledge and remember, as it signifies a problem that demands significant attention from countries and the international community as a whole.

The ILO's Global Estimates 2020 report on trends and the road forward has revealed a concerning rise in the number of child laborers aged 5–11. This age group now constitutes more than half of the total number of child laborers worldwide. Additionally, the report indicates that the number of children aged 5–17 engaged in hazardous work has increased by 6.5 million since 2016, reaching a staggering 79 million.[2]

Certainly, not all types of work performed by children can be considered child labor. In this context, we are referring to two specific aspects of child labor: (1) work that is hazardous and detrimental to children's mental, physical, social, moral, and ethical well-being, and (2) work that obstructs children's educational development by depriving them of learning opportunities, compelling them to prematurely leave school, or forcing them to balance demanding work hours with their studies.

The ILO report also shows that child labor today has some key characteristics as follows:[3]

- 70 percent of child laborers, totaling around 112 million children, are involved in the agricultural sector. Approximately 20 percent of child laborers, equivalent to 31.4 million children, work in the service sector. The remaining 10 percent are engaged in the industrial sector, encompassing around 16.5 million children.
- Nearly 28 percent of children aged 5–11 and 35 percent of children aged 12–14 are child laborers and do not go to school.
- Child labor is more common among boys than girls of all ages. If we take into account household chores that take at least 21 hours per week, the gender gap in child labor narrows.
- The rate of child labor in rural areas (14%) is nearly three times higher than in urban areas (5%).

Among the child labor population, the group of migrant child laborers stands out as particularly noteworthy. These young workers primarily find employment in the informal sector. Migrant children face a dual vulnerability as they are both minors and migrants. When these children cross borders without proper documentation and identification, they encounter limited access to essential social services such as education and health care.[4] Additionally, they face challenges in obtaining legal aid, further exacerbating their vulnerability and increasing the likelihood that they will be forced to continue working in various forms without adequate support.[5] Migrant child laborers are especially vulnerable to exploitation by unscrupulous employers and others. They often face various forms of abuse, including isolation; violence; substandard working conditions; unpaid wages; unfair practices concerning working hours, rest periods, and overtime; as well as harassment and threats if they attempt to report such abuses to authorities.[6] The absence of adult protection or lack of identification documents further exposes them to harassment by authorities and increases their vulnerability to human trafficking, sexual abuse, exploitation, and the risk of contracting diseases such as HIV/AIDS. Additionally, due to the lack of proper feedback mechanisms and information sharing, these children may be at risk of getting lost or "disappearing" during their journey.[7] Moreover, they are susceptible to drug abuse,[8] easily lured into social vices, and may become involved in criminal activities.

In migrant-receiving countries, unaccompanied migrant children who arrive without pre-arranged employment face significant challenges in finding work and securing housing. With limited resources, many of these migrant children end up living on the streets. Even if they manage to find employment at their destination, their lack of local connections, insufficient identification documents, and overall vulnerability make them easy targets for exploitation by unscrupulous employers. This exploitation can take various forms, including low wages, long working hours, unsafe working conditions, and other unfair practices. The absence of proper support networks and protections further exacerbates their vulnerability in the labor market.[9] However, it is important to note that not all migrant children are victims of trafficking or forced into child labor. Many children migrate voluntarily and without the involvement of intermediaries. However, it is still a concerning reality that some migrant children, particularly those working in domestic settings, agriculture, and the informal urban economy, are engaged in exploitative and hazardous labor conditions. These children are at a heightened risk of exploitation and abuse.[10]

The increasing occurrence of migrant child labor can be attributed to a range of factors, including economic shocks, prolonged school closures due to the COVID-19 pandemic, civil war, armed conflict, poverty, and natural disasters. These circumstances often force child laborers to work longer hours and endure harsher conditions. Additionally, many other children from vulnerable families are compelled to engage in exploitative forms of labor, particularly when their households experience job losses and reduced income.

This situation has raised significant concerns within the international community, highlighting the urgent need to strengthen efforts, including law enforcement, to eliminate child labor globally, including child labor within migration contexts. The objective is to safeguard and prioritize the rights of children, ensuring they receive appropriate care, protection, and support suited to their age and fundamental needs.

INTERNATIONAL STANDARDS ON THE RIGHTS OF MIGRANT CHILD WORKERS

Currently, there are three international instruments that directly regulate child labor and protect children's rights: the Convention on the Rights of the Child, the ILO Convention on Minimum Age for Employment (No. 138), and the ILO Worst Forms of Child Labor Convention (No. 182). These documents are considered to have established the legal boundaries of child labor and provided the basis for national and international action to effectively end the practice. In 2008, the 18th International Labor Statistics Conference adopted a resolution on child labor statistics, translating these legal standards into statistical terms for measurement purposes.[11]

The Basic Human Rights of Children in the Convention on the Rights of the Child (CRC) 1989

Among international treaties on human rights in general, the CRC is considered the only international treaty that specifically stipulates the rights reserved for children as a unique individual of the community. This is the first document that comprehensively addresses children's rights in a progressive direction, recognizing that every child has the right to live, develop, participate, and receive special care, protection, and help. The Convention applies to all children under 18 years of age and upholds the core principles of international human rights instruments of equality and non-discrimination.

> *1. States Parties shall respect and ensure the rights set forth in the present Convention to each child within their jurisdiction without discrimination of any kind, regardless of the child's or his or her parent's or legal guardian's race, color, sex, language, religion, political or other opinion, national, ethnic or social origin, property, disability, birth or other status.* (Article 2[1])[12]

Reiterating this principle, the Committee on the Rights of the Child has also declared that state obligations under the Convention apply to each child within the tsate's territory and to all children subject to its jurisdiction (Article 2 CRC). These state obligations cannot be arbitrarily and unilaterally curtailed either by excluding zones or areas from a state's territory or by defining particular zones or areas as not, or only partly, under the jurisdiction of the state. Moreover, state obligations under the Convention apply within the borders of a state, including with respect to those children who come under the state's jurisdiction while attempting to enter the country's territory.[13]

Up to now, the CRC is still the international document with the highest legal value on children's human rights. The Convention stipulates four groups of children's rights: right to survival, right to protection, right to development, and right to participation. In the field of labor, children's rights mentioned in the Convention include:

The right to be protected from economic exploitation and from doing heavy or harmful work: States parties recognize the right of the child to be protected from economic exploitation and from performing any work that is likely to be hazardous or to interfere with the child's education, or to be harmful to the child's health or physical, mental, spiritual, moral, or social development (Article 32).

Protecting children against sexual abuse and exploitation: States parties undertake to protect the child from all forms of sexual exploitation and sexual abuse. For these purposes, states parties shall in particular take all appropriate national, bilateral, and multilateral measures to prevent: (a) the inducement or coercion of a child to engage in any unlawful sexual activity; (b) the exploitative use of children in prostitution or other unlawful sexual practices; and (c) the exploitative use of children in pornographic performances and materials (Article 34). Child sexual abuse is understood as involving dependent, immature, and undeveloped children and minors in activities to which they do not fully understand and cannot give conscious intention, or violation of social taboos about family roles. Child abuse is often expressed by the following acts: child rape, incest, and lewdness with children.

Child sexual exploitation is the use of children to satisfy the desires of adults. The basis of this exploitation is the inequality of power and economic relationships between children and adults. Sexual exploitation of children often manifests itself in the following acts: child trafficking for commercial purposes, child prostitution, and child pornography. Child sexual exploitation is child sexual abuse, but it is associated with economic factors in order to profit.

Protection of children from trafficking and abduction: States parties shall take all appropriate national, bilateral, and multilateral measures to prevent the abduction of, the sale of, or traffic in children for any purpose or in any form (Article 35). According to the Additional Convention on the Abolition of Slavery, the Slave Trade and Institutions and Practices Similar to Slavery, adopted by the United Nations on April 30, 1956, and effective from April 30, 1957, child trafficking is understood as the transfer of children from one party (birth parents, guardians, and organizations and agencies assigned to take care of children) to another party for the purpose of taking care of children for any purpose or in any form in exchange for money or other things or compensation.

Protection of children against all forms of exploitation: States parties shall protect the child against all other forms of exploitation prejudicial to any aspects of the child's welfare (Article 36).

Protect children from inhumane treatment: States parties shall ensure that:

a. No child shall be subjected to torture or other cruel, inhuman, or degrading treatment or punishment. Neither capital punishment nor life imprisonment without possibility of release shall be imposed for offenses committed by persons below 18 years of age;
b. No child shall be deprived of his or her liberty unlawfully or arbitrarily. The arrest, detention, or imprisonment of a child shall be in conformity with the law and shall be used only as a measure of last resort and for the shortest appropriate period of time;
c. Every child deprived of liberty shall be treated with humanity and respect for the inherent dignity of the human person, and in a manner which takes into account the needs of persons of his or her age. In

particular, every child deprived of liberty shall be separated from adults unless it is considered in the child's best interest not to do so and shall have the right to maintain contact with his or her family through correspondence and visits, save in exceptional circumstances;

d. Every child deprived of his or her liberty shall have the right to prompt access to legal and other appropriate assistance, as well as the right to challenge the legality of the deprivation of his or her liberty before a court or other competent, independent, and impartial authority, and to a prompt decision on any such action (Article 37).

ILO Minimum Age Convention No. 138 (1973) And ILO Convention 182 on the Worst Forms of Child Labor

With a commitment "to pursue a national policy designed to ensure the effective abolition of child labour and to raise progressively the minimum age for admission to employment or work to a level consistent with the fullest physical and mental development of young persons,"[14] the convention has set specific regulations on the minimum working age, creating a legal corridor for limiting mechanisms and moving toward eliminating child labor in the future.

According to the International Convention on the Rights of the Child, a child is a person under the age of 18, unless national law recognizes the age of majority earlier (Article 1).[15] This provision is similar to the ILO Worst Forms of Child Labor Convention (No. 182).[16]

In the field of labor, to limit underage child labor, ILO Minimum Age Convention No. 138 (1973) sets the general minimum age for employment or work as 15 years old (13 years for light work) and the minimum age for hazardous work is 18 years (16 years under certain strict conditions). It provides for the possibility of initially setting a general minimum age of 14 (12 years for light work) when the economy and educational facilities are not yet fully developed.[17] Specifically:

1. *The minimum age for admission to any type of employment or work which by its nature or the circumstances in which it is carried out is likely to jeopardize the health, safety or morals of young persons shall not be less than 18 years.*
2. *The minimum age for admission to any type of employment or work which by its nature or the circumstances in which it is carried out is likely to jeopardize the health, safety or morals of young persons shall not be less than 18 years.* (Article 3)[18]

Or:

> *The minimum age (. . .) shall not be less than the age of completion of compulsory schooling and, in any case, shall not be less than 15 years.* (Article 2[3]).[19]

These regulations show that the ILO, with its objectives and operational functions, has made very specific records to avoid the situation of children participating in the informal labor market at an early age, not yet at the minimum age to perform certain jobs considered suitable. However, many countries in the South, especially in Africa, are facing migration of children below the minimum working age. As a rule, these children do not have valid (or fake) travel documents, making them easy targets for exploitation or blackmail. Due to their illegal status, these children may not dare contact the police to report crimes.[20]

In 2020, ILO Convention 182 on the worst forms of child labor, a historic document aimed at combating child labor, received ratification by most of the world's countries. To date, all 187 countries that are members of ILO have now ratified a convention aimed at protecting children from the worst forms of child labor, including slavery, prostitution, and human trafficking. This has partly shown the strong attention and commitment efforts of countries toward the issue of child labor and bad forms of labor for children. As ILO Director-General Guy Ryder once said, "Universal ratification of Convention 182 is an historic first that means that all children now have legal protection against the worst forms of child labour. (. . .) It reflects a global commitment that the worst forms of child labour, such as slavery, sexual exploitation, the use of children in armed conflict or other illicit or hazardous work that compromises children's health, morals or psychological wellbeing, have no place in our society."[21]

Child labor includes work that children are too young to perform and/or work that, by its nature or circumstances, is likely to be harmful to the child's health, safety, or morals.[22] In fact, whether specific forms of work can be called child labor depends on the age of the child, the type and hours of work performed, the conditions under which it is performed, and the objectives pursued by each country.[23] However, work that by its nature can cause harm or danger to children to a high degree will be called the worst forms of child labor. These are forms of child labor that are absolutely prohibited by international law and require countries to take immediate action to prevent and eliminate them. To clarify these forms of labor, ILO Convention No. 182, the worst forms of labor identified in Article 3, include:

a. *all forms of slavery or practices similar to slavery, such as the sale and trafficking of children, debt bondage and serfdom and forced or compulsory labour, including forced or compulsory recruitment of children for use in armed conflict;*

b. *the use, procuring or offering of a child for prostitution, for the production of pornography or for pornographic performances;*
c. *the use, procuring or offering of a child for illicit activities, in particular for the production and trafficking of drugs as defined in the relevant international treaties;*
d. *work which, by its nature or the circumstances in which it is carried out, is likely to harm the health, safety or morals of children.*[24]

In addition to the international documents mentioned above, there are also a number of other international conventions and documents that mention each area of protecting children's rights in labor such as: the convention on the suppression of human trafficking and commercial exploitation and prostitution (adopted by the United Nations on March 21, 1950, and effective from July 25, 1951); and the Convention against Transnational Organized Crime (adopted by the United Nations on November 15, 2000.

RESPONSIBILITIES OF STATES IN ENSURING THE RIGHTS OF MIGRANT CHILD WORKERS

Labor migration, including child labor, is a common phenomenon in the development process of countries, particularly in Southeast Asia. It has played a significant role in contributing to economic growth and regional development. Countries such as Malaysia, Singapore, and Thailand have long relied on migrant workers as essential contributors to their economies. In response to the flows of labor migration and the associated human rights challenges, countries have implemented various measures, including the signing of international treaties,[25] to enhance the protection of human rights, particularly for migrant child laborers. However, despite these efforts and expectations, ensuring the rights of migrant child workers in the 21st century continues to present numerous challenges.[26]

Develop a Regional Legal Framework to Protect the Rights of Migrant Child Workers

In Southeast Asia, ASEAN (Association of Southeast Asian Nations) has issued several important documents on human rights,[27] including the ASEAN Declaration on Human Rights,[28] the ASEAN Declaration on the Rights of Children in the Context of Migration,[29] and the ASEAN Convention against Trafficking in Persons, especially Women and Children.[30] ASEAN has also established permanent human rights institutions, namely, the

Intergovernmental Committee on Human Rights (AICHR), the Committee for the Promotion and Protection of the Rights of Women and Children (ACWC), and the Committee on Migrant Workers (ACMW). Additionally, ASEAN is one of the few regions, alongside Europe, to have a dedicated international treaty on combating human trafficking. However, the implementation of these conventions still faces certain limitations, particularly in terms of effective prevention and victim protection measures, especially for children.[31] ASEAN's mechanism for promoting and protecting human rights reflects the region's approach to balancing the protection of national sovereignty and the promotion of human rights. Southeast Asian countries prioritize respect for national sovereignty and the principle of non-interference in the internal affairs of other nations. Simultaneously, they seek to establish and promote a regional mechanism for human rights protection. ASEAN countries strive to reconcile these aspects, demonstrating their efforts in forming a regional human rights mechanism. However, it will take time for this mechanism to make significant progress and achieve its goals.[32]

AICHR (the ASEAN Intergovernmental Commission on Human Rights) was established under Article 14 of the ASEAN Charter.[33] The Committee held its inaugural session from March 28 to April 1, 2010, in Jakarta, Indonesia. Unlike human rights mechanisms in other regions, AICHR functions solely as an intergovernmental advisory body. Nevertheless, the regulations governing AICHR are subject to review five years after the Commission's establishment. This review is conducted by the ASEAN Foreign Ministers' Meeting with the objective of enhancing the effectiveness of promoting and protecting human rights in the region.[34] AICHR operates on the principles enshrined in the ASEAN Charter, with particular emphasis on respecting the independence, sovereignty, equality, territorial integrity, and national identity of all ASEAN member countries. It does not interfere in the internal affairs of ASEAN member countries and respects each member country's right to safeguard itself from external interference, subversion, or imposition. AICHR upholds the principles of the rule of law, good governance, democratic principles, and constitutional government. It promotes and protects fundamental freedoms, human rights, and social justice. AICHR also respects the United Nations Charter and international law, including international humanitarian law endorsed by ASEAN member states. Furthermore, it recognizes and respects the cultural, linguistic, and religious diversities among ASEAN countries while emphasizing common values in the spirit of unity in diversity.[35]

The AICHR holds two meetings annually, with each meeting lasting no more than five days. The annual meetings of the AICHR alternate between the ASEAN Secretariat and the member country holding the ASEAN chairmanship. The AICHR is required to submit its annual report and other reports to the ASEAN Foreign Ministers' Meeting. Additionally, the AICHR periodically disseminates information about its work and activities through appropriate public media channels.[36] In terms of its relationship with other human rights bodies within the ASEAN framework, the AICHR serves as the overarching human rights institution responsible for promoting and protecting human rights in ASEAN. Consequently, the AICHR collaborates with all other specialized human rights bodies within ASEAN to determine the best way to align their work with the AICHR. To achieve this, the AICHR engages in close consultation, coordination, and collaboration with these entities, aiming to enhance complementarity and cohesion in the promotion and protection of human rights.

The AICHR includes representatives from all ASEAN member countries. Each member state appoints a representative who is accountable to their respective government. The regulations governing the AICHR do not specify specific criteria for the selection of representatives but recommend that member countries consider factors such as gender equality, competence, and experience in the field of human rights when making appointments. Member states are also required to consult relevant entities in the process of appointing representatives to the AICHR. The term of each representative is three years and can be renewed for one additional term. The appointing government has the discretion to replace its representative if desired. Representatives are obligated to adhere to the ASEAN Charter, the AICHR statutes, and attend AICHR meetings. The chairperson of the AICHR is the representative from the member country holding the ASEAN chairmanship. The decision-making process of the AICHR is based on the principle of consultation and consensus, in accordance with Article 20 of the ASEAN Charter. As a result, the role of the AICHR is limited in certain cases, particularly when there is a human rights crisis in one of the member states. Serious human rights violations are still regarded as matters falling under the internal jurisdiction of each respective nation.[37]

At the 10th ASEAN Summit in October 2004, ASEAN leaders approved the Vientiane Action Program 2004–2010, which included the establishment of the ASEAN Committee on the Promotion and Protection of the Rights of Women and Children (ACWC).[38] The ACWC was created as part of the efforts to promote and safeguard the rights of women and children in the ASEAN region. Subsequently, at the 14th ASEAN Summit in February 2009, the Cha-am Hua Hin Declaration on the Roadmap for an ASEAN Socio-Cultural Community was approved. This Declaration emphasized the importance of promoting and protecting the rights of women and children as a means to ensure equitable development for these two vulnerable groups.[39] The operational regulations of the ACWC were adopted at the 15th Summit in

Bangkok, Thailand, held in October 2009. Following these developments, the ACWC was officially launched on April 7, 2010, in Hanoi, Vietnam.[40]

The ACWC includes two representatives from each member state, one for women's rights and one for children's rights. Thus, the Committee comprises a total of 20 members from the 10 ASEAN member countries. Each member serves a three-year term and can be re-elected for an additional term.[41] The main purpose of the ACWC is to promote and protect the human rights and fundamental freedoms of women and children in ASEAN. The ACWC is mandated to uphold the provisions of the Convention on the Elimination of All Forms of Discrimination Against Women (CEDAW) and the Convention on the Rights of the Child (CRC), both of which have been ratified by all ASEAN member states. The ACWC submits its annual report to the ASEAN Ministerial Meeting on Social Welfare and Development (AMMSWD) and shares it with the ASEAN Committee on Women (ACW) and other relevant ASEAN specialized agencies. Similar to the AICHR, the ACWC functions as a consultative body. Decisions within the ACWC are made through consultation and require the consensus of all member states. This consensus-based approach means that each member state has the power to veto issues it does not wish to discuss or act upon, which can limit the scope and effectiveness of the Committee. Additionally, the ACWC does not have a monitoring and evaluation mechanism in place.[42]

To protect the rights of migrant workers, the 12th ASEAN Summit, which took place on January 30, 2007, in Cebu, Philippines, adopted the ASEAN Declaration on the Protection and Promotion of the Rights of Migrant Workers (ACMW).[43] The objective of the Declaration was to ensure the effective implementation of commitments related to the rights of migrant workers within ASEAN member states. To operationalize this Declaration, ASEAN established the Committee to Implement the ASEAN Declaration on the Protection and Promotion of the Rights of Migrant Workers (ACMW) on July 30, 2007, in Manila, Philippines. The committee's primary purpose is to facilitate the implementation of the ASEAN Declaration on the Protection and Promotion of the Rights of Migrant Workers and to support the development of an ASEAN instrument specifically addressing the rights of migrant workers. The committee consists of representatives from each member state, as well as a representative from the ASEAN Secretariat. The chairmanship of the committee is held by the representative of the member state currently holding the rotating ASEAN chairmanship.

To address the protection of migrant child labor, ASEAN has implemented various measures. In 2017, ASEAN leaders adopted the ASEAN Consensus on the Protection and Promotion of the Rights of Migrant Workers, which emphasized the importance of safeguarding the rights of all migrant workers, including children.[44] Following that, in 2019, ASEAN Leaders adopted the ASEAN Declaration on the Rights of the Child in the Context of Migration.[45] Additionally, in 2021, ASEAN took note of the Regional Action Plan on Implementing the Declaration on the Rights of the Child in the Context of Migration (ASEAN RPA on CCM).[46] RPA ASEAN on CCM demonstrates ASEAN's dedication to respecting, protecting, and fully realizing the rights of migrant children. It complements the implementation of the ASEAN Regional Action Plan on the Elimination of Violence Against Children (ASEAN RPA on EVAC)[47] and aligns with ASEAN's efforts to achieve the Sustainable Development Goals. These initiatives are in accordance with the Global Compact for Safe, Orderly, and Regular Migration[48] and the Global Compact on Refugees.[49] Overall, ASEAN countries have adopted an approach that prioritizes the best interests of children in all relevant policies and practices concerning children in the context of migration.

Considering the emerging issues, concerns, and the heightened vulnerability of children in the context of migration, ASEAN has identified "child sensitivity" and "gender responsiveness" as core principles guiding its collective actions. These principles aim to strengthen national systems and address the specific needs of children in migration contexts, encompassing areas such as child protection, social sponsorship, education, health care, psychosocial support, safe environments, and access to justice. ASEAN is committed to enhancing the identification, protection, and support for all children in migration contexts. This includes children affected by trafficking, refugees, forced labor, and other circumstances requiring protection and support.

Addressing children's migration issues through the lens of children is imperative. Also, it is essential that the voices of children in migration situations and their stories of resilience are heard by leaders, policymakers, and key stakeholders. These voices should inform decision-making and prompt action. Empowering families, including those in migratory contexts, and enhancing their resilience to overcome challenges are also of particular importance. ASEAN is committed to adopting a pan-ASEAN strategy that takes a comprehensive family-centered approach. This approach aims to promote family well-being and development, strengthen family resilience, and foster family solidarity in adapting to the challenges faced by families. This commitment is reflected in the Bandar Seri Begawan Declaration on the Importance of Families for Community Development and Nation Building, which was adopted by ASEAN Leaders in 2021.[50] These initiatives are essential for fulfilling ASEAN's commitment to protecting and promoting the rights of children in the region.

It is true that ASEAN, as an intergovernmental organization dedicated to countries in the Southeast Asia sub-region, has a human rights protection mechanism that differs from the systems in major regions such as Europe, America, and Africa. Unlike these regions, ASEAN does not currently have a binding legal document specifically focused on human rights, and member countries themselves exhibit varying levels of commitment and international cooperation regarding human rights. In recent times, ASEAN has undertaken studies and initiatives aimed at reforming and enhancing the operational efficiency of the ASEAN Intergovernmental Commission on Human Rights and the ASEAN Commission on the Promotion and Protection of the Rights of Women and Children. This includes efforts to amend and clarify the regulations governing these institutions, making their tasks more specific. The research on amending the statute of the AICHR has been included in the ASEAN Plan of Action for the period up to 2025.[51] Furthermore, there have been endeavors to develop a binding legal instrument on human rights within the region. ASEAN also plans to strengthen coordination between AICHR, ACWC, and other relevant organizations, indicating a commitment to enhancing the practicality and effectiveness of these institutions in the future. These efforts provide a basis for hope that AICHR and ACWC will engage in more substantial and impactful activities going forward.

Cooperate to Protect Migrant Child Workers

Cooperation on the protection of child labor in the context of migration is an integral part of labor cooperation within the ASEAN region. Given the present circumstances, labor cooperation in ASEAN is essential to mitigate the negative impacts resulting from regional economic integration and globalization, particularly on vulnerable groups like migrant child workers. Regional labor cooperation should strive to establish the objective of promoting decent work and improving the lives of workers throughout ASEAN.[52] Currently, effective policies and collaborative initiatives addressing these issues are lacking in the ASEAN region. It is crucial to recognize that individual ASEAN countries cannot address the adverse effects of economic integration on their own or ensure decent work and livelihoods for both domestic and migrant workers without regional-level support and policies. Therefore, regional cooperation is necessary to develop comprehensive approaches and initiatives to protect the rights and well-being of migrant child laborers and other workers across ASEAN.

Labor cooperation among ASEAN countries needs to set the following priorities: prioritize labor policies that target social issues such as decent work, vocational training, social security, medical care, education, housing; prioritize building real social models for regional development to address unemployment, poverty, and social marginalization, with widespread participation of educational institutions and health care, as well as decent employment issues; and priority is given to ensuring basic social security standards, including medical care, sickness benefits, accident benefits, and family benefits.

In recent times, ASEAN countries have been actively involved in implementing various bilateral cooperation agreements to protect migrant child workers. Numerous agreements have been signed to combat trafficking in persons, particularly women and children, and to support the victims of such crimes. Examples of these agreements include those between Thailand and Cambodia,[53] Thailand and Myanmar,[54] and Thailand and Laos.[55] Bilateral agreements emphasize cooperation between countries in areas such as mutual legal assistance, information and data exchange, implementation of preventive and protective measures, and collaborative efforts to combat trafficking crimes. These agreements also address issues related to the repatriation and reintegration of trafficking victims, as well as outlining the responsibilities of relevant agencies and mechanisms to ensure effective implementation.[56] It has been observed that child protection activities and the implementation of procedures related to the repatriation and community reintegration of trafficking victims are carried out relatively effectively in some countries.[57] However, it is important to note that these agreements do not provide specific guidance on procedures to regulate child protection cases that fall outside the legal definition of child trafficking but still involve cross-border situations. Examples include unaccompanied vulnerable individuals who are not victims of trafficking or children who have been separated from their parents or caregivers due to immigration issues.[58]

ASEAN countries have made significant efforts to protect the rights of migrant workers, including child migrant workers. In recent years, they have achieved considerable progress in safeguarding and promoting the rights of migrant workers. The importance and benefits of bilateral and multilateral agreements in the field of migration have also been recognized. These agreements underline the shared and balanced responsibilities of ASEAN member states in protecting and promoting the rights of migrant workers and their families throughout the entire migration process. From a legal perspective, the development and establishment of common mechanisms and documents on human rights play a crucial role in promoting and protecting human rights in ASEAN. This has been demonstrated by the success of human rights mechanisms and documents in regions such as Europe, America, and more recently Africa. The ASEAN region is currently undergoing an institutionalization process, highlighted by the adoption of the ASEAN Charter, which includes provisions on fundamental principles for the protection of human rights. The establishment of the ASEAN Intergovernmental Commission on Human Rights has been a significant step in advancing the human rights protection mechanism in the region. However, for a comprehensive regional human rights mechanism, it is necessary to have adequate enforcement agencies and human rights documents that reflect the specific characteristics of the region. These documents will serve as the foundation for cooperation between countries in the field of human rights, as well as guide the activities of human rights agencies within the region.

REFERENCES

ACWC, Terms of Reference, https://acwc.asean.org/wp-content/uploads/2016/04/TOR-ACWC.pdf, accessed on 30 October 2023.AICHR Terms of Reference, Art. 3, 9.6, https://aichr.org/wp-content/uploads/2020/02/TOR-of-AICHR.pdf, accessed on 30 October 2023.

ASEAN 2025: Forging Ahead Together, https://www.asean.org/wp-content/uploads/2015/12/ASEAN-2025-Forging-Ahead-Together-final.pdf, accessed on 30 October 2023.

ASEAN Charter, https://aichr.org/wp-content/uploads/2019/01/ASEAN-Charter.pdf, accessed on 30 October 2023.

ASEAN Consensus on the Protection and Promotion of the Rights of Migrant Workers, https://asean.org/book/asean-consensus-on-the-protection-and-promotion-of-the-rights-of-migrant-workers-2/, accessed on 30 October 2023.

ASEAN Convention against Trafficking in Persons, Especially Women and Children, adopted in Kuala Lumpur, Malaysia, 21 November 2015, https://asean.org/asean-convention-against-trafficking-in-persons-especially-women-and-children/, accessed on 30 October 2023.

ASEAN Declaration on the Protection and Promotion on the Rights of Migrant Workers, https://hrasean.forum-asia.org/mechanism/asean-committee-on-migrant-workers/, accessed on 30 October 2023.

ASEAN Declaration on the Rights of Children in the Context of Migration, adopted at the 35th ASEAN Summit, Bangkok, Thailand, 2 November 2019, https://cil.nus.edu.sg/databasecil/2019-declaration-on-the-rights-of-children-in-the-context-of-migration/, accessed on 30 October 2023.

ASEAN Declaration on the Rights of Children in the Context of Migration, https://asean.org/asean-declaration-on-the-rights-of-children-in-the-context-of-migration/, accessed on 30 October 2023.

ASEAN Human Rights Declaration, 18 November 2012, https://asean.org/wp-content/uploads/2021/01/6_AHRD_Booklet.pdf, accessed on 30 October 2023.

ASEAN Regional Plan of Action on the Elimination of Violence against Children, https://violenceagainstchildren.un.org/sites/violenceagainstchildren.un.org/files/document_files/asean_regional_plan_of_action_on_elimination_of_violence_against_children_adopted.pdf, accessed on 30 October 2023.

American Bar Association Rule of Law Initiative. 2014. The ASEAN Human Rights Declaration: A Legal Analysis. Washington, DC: American Bar Association.

Anderson, Kirsten. Assessment of Child Protection Services for Migrant Children in Thailand, Coram International, UNICEF2019.

Bandar Seri Begawan Declaration on the Importance of the Family for Community Development and Nation-Building, https://asean.org/wp-content/uploads/2021/11/11.-BSB-Declaration-on-the-Importance-of-the-Family-for-Community-Development.pdf, accessed on 30 October 2023.

Binford, Warren, Michael Garcia Bochenek, Pablo Ceriani Cernadas, Emma Day, Sarah Field, Marci Hamilton, Ton Liefaard, Benyam Mezmur, Fasil Mulatu, Ann Skelton, and et al. 2023. "Report on Enforcing the Rights of Children in Migration," Laws 12, no. 5: 85. https://doi.org/10.3390/laws12050085.

Binford, Warren, Michael Garcia Bochenek, Pablo Ceriani Cernadas, Emma Day, Sarah Field, Marci Hamilton, Ton Liefaard, Benyam Mezmur, Fasil Mulatu, Ann Skelton, and et al. 2023. "Report on Enforcing the Rights of Children in Migration." *Op.cit.* note 27.

C138 - Minimum Age Convention, 1973 (No. 138), https://www.ilo.org/dyn/normlex/en/f?p=NORMLEXPUB:12100:0::NO::P12100_ilo_code:C138, accessed September 1, 2023.

C182 - Worst Forms of Child Labor Convention, 1999 (No. 182), https: // www .ilo .org /dyn /normlex /en /f ?p =NORMLEXPUB: 12100: 0: : NO: : P12100 ILO CODE: C182, accessed 30 October 2023.

Cha-am Hua Hin Declaration on the AICHR, https://aichr.org/wp-content/uploads/2020/02/Cha-am-Hua-Hin-Declaration-AICHR.pdf, accessed on 30 October 2023.

Consulting workshop on protecting the rights of workers abroad organized by the Vietnam Bar Association on March 3–4, 2008.

Convention on the Rights of the Child, https://www.ohchr.org/en/instruments-mechanisms/instruments/convention-rights-child , accessed September 1, 2023.

CRC Committee, General Comment No. 6, 2005, para. 12, https://www2.ohchr.org/english/bodies/crc/docs/gc6.pdf; IOM, HUMAN RIGHTS OF MIGRANT CHILDREN, *International Migration Law*, no.15, https://publications.iom.int/system/files/pdf/iml_15_en.pdf.

Global Compact for Refugees, https://www.unhcr.org/media/global-compact-refugees-booklet, accessed on 30 October 2023.

Global Compact for Safe, Orderly and Regular Migration, https://www.iom.int/resources/global-compact-safe-orderly-and-regular-migration/res/73/195, accessed on 30 October 2023.

Laos-Thailand MoU, articles 9–14, 17; Cambodia-Thailand MoU, articles 17, Part V; Myanmar-Thailand MoU, articles 13–16, Part VI.

Hans van de Glind and Anne Kou, Migrant children in child labor: A vulnerable group in need of attention, in "Children on the Move" IOM, 2013, https: // www .ilo.. org /ipec /Informationresources /WCMS 232634/ lang--en/index.htm, accessed on September 3, 2023.

ILO-IPEC, MIGRATION AND CHILD LABOUR—ESSENTIALS, https: // www .ilo .org /ipec /Informationresources /WCMS IPEC PUB 16975 /lang - -en /index .htm, accessed September 1 2023.

International Labour Office and United Nations Children's Fund, Child Labour: Global estimates 2020, trends and the road forward, ILO and UNICEF, New York,

2021. License: CC BY 4.0. https://data.unicef.org/resources/child-labour-2020-global-estimates-trends-and-the-road-forward/, accessed September 1, 2023.

Jovanovic, Marija. 2018. *Comparison of Anti-Trafficking Legal Regimes and Actions in the Council of Europe and ASEAN: Realities, Frameworks and Possibilities for Collaboration.* Strasbourg: Secretariat of the Council of Europe Convention on Action against Trafficking in Human Beings. Available online: https://rm.coe.int/coe-asean-study-thb/16808c1b91, accessed on 30 October 2023.

Memorandum of Understanding between the Government of the Kingdom of Cambodia and the Government of the Kingdom of Thailand on Bilateral Cooperation for the Elimination of Trafficking in Persons and Protection of Victims of Trafficking, 30 October 2014 (Cambodia-Thailand MoU).

Memorandum of Understanding between the Government of the Kingdom of Thailand and the Government of the Union of Myanmar on Cooperation to Combat Trafficking in Persons, Especially Women and Children, 24 April 2009 (Myanmar-Thailand MoU).

Memorandum of Understanding between the Government of the Kingdom of Thailand and the Government of the Lao People's Democratic Republic on Cooperation to Combat Trafficking in Persons, 12 July 2017 (Laos-Thailand MoU).

Regional Plan of Action on Implementing the ASEAN Declaration on the Rights of Children in the Context of Migration, https://asean.org/wp-content/uploads/2021/11/5.-ASEAN-RPA-on-CCM_Final.pdf, accessed on 30 October 2023.

Unicef, *Regional Situation Analysis on Children Affected by Migration in ASEAN Member States*, https://www.unicef.org/eap/reports/regional-situation-analysis-children-affected-migration-asean-member-states, accessed on 30 October 2023.

United Nations Children's Fund, A CHILD-RIGHTS APPROACH ON INTERNATIONAL MIGRATION AND CHILD TRAFFICKING: A UNICEF PERSPECTIVE, https://www.un.org/development/desa/pd/sites/www.un.org.development.desa.pd/files/unpd-cm3-2004_10_p06_unicef.pdf; ILO-IPEC, MIGRATION AND CHILD LABOUR—ESSENTIALS, https://www.ilo.org/ipec/Informationresources/WCMS_IPEC_PUB_16975/lang--en/index.htm.

Vientiane Action Programme (VAP) 2004–2010, Annex 1, 1.1.4.7, https://asean.org/wp-content/uploads/images/archive/VAP-10th%20ASEAN%20Summit.pdf, accessed on 30 October 2023.

NOTES

1. https://www.ilo.org/global/standards/subjects-covered-by-international-labour-standards/child-labour/lang--en/index.htm.

2. International Labour Office and United Nations Children's Fund, Child Labour: Global estimates 2020, trends and the road forward, ILO and UNICEF, New York, 2021. License: CC BY 4.0., https://data.unicef.org/resources/child-labour-2020-global-estimates-trends-and-the-road-forward/, accessed September 1, 2023.

3. Ibid.

4. Ibid.
5. Ibid.
6. Ibid.
7. United Nations Children's Fund, A CHILD-RIGHTS APPROACH ON INTERNATIONAL MIGRATION AND CHILD TRAFFICKING: A UNICEF PERSPECTIVE, https://www.un.org/development/desa/pd/sites/www.un.org.development.desa.pd/files/unpd-cm3-2004_10_p06_unicef.pdf; ILO-IPEC, MIGRATION AND CHILD LABOUR—ESSENTIALS, https://www.ilo.org/ipec/Informationresources/WCMS_IPEC_PUB_16975/lang--en/index.htm.
8. Ibid.
9. Hans van de Glind and Anne Kou, *Migrant children in child labour: A vulnerable group in need of attention*, in "Children on the Move," IOM, 2013, https://www.ilo.org/ipec/Informationresources/WCMS_232634/lang--en/index.htm, accessed on 3 September 2023, pp. 7–10.
10. ILO-IPEC, MIGRATION AND CHILD LABOUR—ESSENTIALS, https://www.ilo.org/ipec/Informationresources/WCMS_IPEC_PUB_16975/lang--en/index.htm.
11. International Labor Office and United Nations Children's Fund, *Supra note 1*.
12. Besides Article 2(1), this principle is also mentioned in Article 3(2), Article 4 of the Convention. See Convention on the Rights of the Child, https://www.ohchr.org/en/instruments-mechanisms/instruments/convention-rights-child.
13. CRC Committee, General Comment No. 6, 2005, para. 12. https://www2.ohchr.org/english/bodies/crc/docs/gc6.pdf; IOM, HUMAN RIGHTS OF MIGRANT CHILDREN, International Migration Law, No. 15, https://publications.iom.int/system/files/pdf/iml_15_en.pdf.
14. See Article 1 of the Convention, https://www.ilo.org/dyn/normlex/en/f?p=NORMLEXPUB:12100:0::NO::P12100_ilo_code:C13,8.
15. Convention on the Rights of the Child, https://www.ohchr.org/en/instruments-mechanisms/instruments/convention-rights-child, accessed September 1, 2023.
16. Article 2, C182 - Worst Forms of Child Labor Convention, 1999 (No. 182), https://www.ilo.org/dyn/normlex/en/f?p=NORMLEXPUB:12100:0::NO::P12100_ILO_CODE:C182.
17. Source: https://www.ilo.org/global/standards/subjects-covered-by-international-labour-standards/child-labour/lang--en/index.htm.
18. C138 - Minimum Age Convention, 1973 (No. 138), https://www.ilo.org/dyn/normlex/en/f?p=NORMLEXPUB:12100:0::NO::P12100_ilo_code:C13,8, accessed September 1, 2023.
19. Ibid.
20. van de Glind and Kou, *Migrant children in child labor*.
21. Source: https://news.un.org/en/story/2020/08/1069492.
22. International Labor Office and United Nations Children's Fund, Child Labor, p. 8.
23. Ibid.
24. C182 - (No. 182), https://www.ilo.org/dyn/normlex/en/f?p=NORMLEXPUB:12100:0::NO::P12100_ILO_CODE:C182.

25. Ex, Convention relating to the Status of Refugees, 28 July 1951 (189 U.N.T.S. 137) and its Protocols (1967); International Convention on the Protection of the Rights of All Migrant Workers and Members of their Families, 18 December 1990 (2220 U.N.T.S. 3); Convention on the Rights of the Child, 20 November 1989 (1577 U.N.T.S. 3) and its Protocols (2000, 2011).

26. Binford, Warren, Michael Garcia Bochenek, Pablo Ceriani Cernadas, Emma Day, Sarah Field, Marci Hamilton, Ton Liefaard, Benyam Mezmur, Fasil Mulatu, Ann Skelton, and et al. 2023. "Report on Enforcing the Rights of Children in Migration," Laws 12, no. 5: 85. https://doi.org/10.3390/laws12050085.

27. ASEAN Human Rights Declaration, 18 November 2012, https://asean.org/wp-content/uploads/2021/01/6_AHRD_Booklet.pdf, accessed on 30 October 2023.

28. ASEAN Declaration on the Rights of Children in the Context of Migration, adopted at the 35th ASEAN Summit, Bangkok, Thailand, 2 November 2019, https://cil.nus.edu.sg/databasecil/2019-declaration-on-the-rights-of-children-in-the-context-of-migration/, accessed on 30 October 2023.

29. Ibid.

30. ASEAN Convention against Trafficking in Persons, Especially Women and Children, adopted in Kuala Lumpur, Malaysia, 21 November 2015, https://asean.org/asean-convention-against-trafficking-in-persons-especially-women-and-children/, accessed on 30 October 2023.

31. Jovanovic, Marija. 2018. *Comparison of Anti-Trafficking Legal Regimes and Actions in the Council of Europe and ASEAN: Realities, Frameworks and Possibilities for Collaboration*. Strasbourg: Secretariat of the Council of Europe Convention on Action against Trafficking in Human Beings. Available online: https://rm.coe.int/coe-asean-study-thb/16808c1b91, accessed on 30 October 2023.

32. American Bar Association Rule of Law Initiative, 2014. The ASEAN Human Rights Declaration: A Legal Analysis. Washington, DC: American Bar Association.

33. ASEAN Charter, https://aichr.org/wp-content/uploads/2019/01/ASEAN-Charter.pdf, accessed on 30 October 2023.

34. AICHR Terms of Reference, Art. 3, 9.6, https://aichr.org/wp-content/uploads/2020/02/TOR-of-AICHR.pdf, accessed on 30 October 2023.

35. Ibid. Art. 2.1.

36. Source: https://aichr.org/aichr-meeting/, accessed on 30 October 2023.

37. Binford, Garcia Bochenek, Ceriani Cernadas, *Op.cit.* note 27.

38. Vientiane Action Programme (VAP) 2004–2010, Annex 1, 1.1.4.7, https://asean.org/wp-content/uploads/images/archive/VAP-10th%20ASEAN%20Summit.pdf, accessed on 30 October 2023.

39. Cha-am Hua Hin Declaration on the AICHR, https://aichr.org/wp-content/uploads/2020/02/Cha-am-Hua-Hin-Declaration-AICHR.pdf, accessed on 30 October 2023.

40. ACWC, Terms of Reference, https://acwc.asean.org/wp-content/uploads/2016/04/TOR-ACWC.pdf, accessed on 30 October 2023.

41. ACWC, Terms of Reference, Art. 6.

42. See more at: https://acwc.asean.org/, accessed on 30 October 2023.

43. ASEAN Declaration on the Protection and Promotion on the Rights of Migrant Workers, https://hrasean.forum-asia.org/mechanism/asean-committee-on-migrant-workers/, accessed on 30 October 2023.

44. ASEAN Consensus on the Protection and Promotion of the Rights of Migrant Workers, https://asean.org/book/asean-consensus-on-the-protection-and-promotion-of-the-rights-of-migrant-workers-2/, accessed on 30 October 2023.

45. ASEAN Declaration on the Rights of Children in the Context of Migration, https://asean.org/asean-declaration-on-the-rights-of-children-in-the-context-of-migration/, accessed on 30 October 2023.

46. Regional Plan of Action on Implementing the ASEAN Declaration on the Rights of Children in the Context of Migration, https://asean.org/wp-content/uploads/2021/11/5.-ASEAN-RPA-on-CCM_Final.pdf, accessed on 30 October 2023.

47. ASEAN Regional Plan of Action on the Elimination of Violence against Children, https://violenceagainstchildren.un.org/sites/violenceagainstchildren.un.org/files/document_files/asean_regional_plan_of_action_on_elimination_of_violence_against_children_adopted.pdf, accessed on 30 October 2023.

48. Global Compact for Safe, Orderly and Regular Migration, https://www.iom.int/resources/global-compact-safe-orderly-and-regular-migration/res/73/195, accessed on 30 October 2023.

49. Global Compact for Refugees, https://www.unhcr.org/media/global-compact-refugees-booklet, accessed on 30 October 2023.

50. Bandar Seri Begawan Declaration on the Importance of the Family for Community Development and Nation-Building, https://asean.org/wp-content/uploads/2021/11/11.-BSB-Declaration-on-the-Importance-of-the-Family-for-Community-Development.pdf, accessed on 30 October 2023.

51. ASEAN 2025: Forging Ahead Together, https://www.asean.org/wp-content/uploads/2015/12/ASEAN-2025-Forging-Ahead-Together-final.pdf, accessed on 30 October 2023.

52. Consulting workshop on protecting the rights of workers abroad organized by the Vietnam Bar Association on March 3–4, 2008.

53. Memorandum of Understanding between the Government of the Kingdom of Cambodia and the Government of the Kingdom of Thailand on Bilateral Cooperation for the Elimination of Trafficking in Persons and Protection of Victims of Trafficking, 30 October 2014 (Cambodia-Thailand MoU).

54. Memorandum of Understanding between the Government of the Kingdom of Thailand and the Government of the Union of Myanmar on Cooperation to Combat Trafficking in Persons, Especially Women and Children, 24 April 2009 (Myanmar-Thailand MoU).

55. Memorandum of Understanding between the Government of the Kingdom of Thailand and the Government of the Laos People's Democratic Republic on Cooperation to Combat Trafficking in Persons, 12 July 2017 (Laos-Thailand MoU).

56. Laos-Thailand MoU, articles 9–14, 17; Cambodia-Thailand MoU, articles 17, Part V; Myanmar-Thailand MoU, articles 13–16, Part VI.

57. Thailand is one of the countries that does a relatively good job of protecting children affected by migration. See: Anderson, Kirsten, Assessment of Child Protection Services for Migrant Children in Thailand, Coram International, UNICEF2019.

58. Unicef, *Regional Situation Analysis on Children Affected by Migration in ASEAN Member States*, https://www.unicef.org/eap/reports/regional-situation-analysis-children-affected-migration-asean-member-states, accessed on 30 October 2023.

Chapter 4

The Rights of Women Migrant Workers

From the Perspective and Experience of Origin Countries in Asia

Nguyen Thi Hong Yen and Nguyen Phuong Dung

> *"Times have changed, and today more and more women migrate not to join their partner, but in search of employment in places where they will be better paid than in their home country."*[1]

In recent decades, under the impact of globalization, more and more people have left their home countries and migrated to other countries and regions. One of the main reasons for migrants to leave their countries of origin is to seek decent work. The International Labor Organization (ILO) recorded that there were around 169 million international migrant workers, making up to 4.9 percent of the global labor force.[2] Of which, women migrant workers were estimated at 70 million, constituting 41.5 percent of the total international migrant workers. Men migrant workers still outnumbered women migrant workers with an estimated number of 99 million, accounting for 58.5 percent of the international migrant workers. Although women migrant workers were not the majority, during the 2013–2019 period, the number of women migrant workers was on the rise, significantly increasing from 66.6 million in 2013 to 68.1 million in 2017 and eventually to 70 million in 2019.[3]

As the most populous continent in the world with 4.6 billion people, by 2020, Asia contributed roughly 115 million people, accounting for over 40 percent of the global international migrants, indicating "intraregional migration increase," with big outflows of nationals from numerous countries such as

India, China, Bangladesh, Pakistan, the Philippines, Afghanistan, Indonesia, Myanmar, Vietnam and Nepal.[4] According to recent reports, a large number of international migrants of which almost half is contributed by women.[5] In Southeast Asia, emerging countries have continued to grow and industrialize, entailing the generation of more employment opportunities demanding a vast number of migrant workers. The statistics indicate a growth in the number of female migrant workers from ASEAN countries of origin such as Cambodia, Indonesia, Lao PDR, Myanmar, and Vietnam since 2012.[6] Female migrant workers comprise a large segment of the labor force in some ASEAN countries of destination including Brunei Darussalam, Singapore, Malaysia, and Thailand.[7] It was reported that the proportion of female migrant workers in the receiving countries was so high that in Singapore and Thailand, women migrant workers made up more than half, 58.24 percent and 50.24 percent, respectively, followed by Brunei (46.08%) and Malaysia (37.35%).[8] Data recorded in 2018 show that the contribution of international migrant workers in ASEAN net-receiving countries was considerable with a figure of 4.7 million, among which Malaysia and Singapore were documented as top destinations. The collated data describe the larger number of documented women migrant workers in Thailand, Brunei Darussalam, and Malaysia that female youth workers occupied the significant shares of the labor force and mostly engaged in the service and industry sectors, accounting for 45 percent and 22 percent, respectively.[9] Nevertheless, it is believed that the actual figure could be greater as the available data is just the tip of the iceberg describing the number of registered women migrant workers, while having yet to cover the attendance of the undocumented ones participating in the labor market.[10]

Labor mobility has played a crucial role in the economic development of some sub-regions such as Southern Asia and Southeast Asia, which are less affluent, despite the COVID-19 pandemic and its severe impacts. Labor migration has generated substantial international remittance influxes supporting several economies in these sub-regions. By 2020, some countries in these sub-regions listed in the top remittance recipients include India (USD 83 million), the Philippines (USD 35 million), Pakistan (USD 26 million), Bangladesh (USD 22 million), and Vietnam (USD 17 million).[11] Numerous countries, including the United States, Europe, the Gulf countries, Eastern Asian countries, Singapore, Malaysia, and Thailand showed significant reliance on foreign labor. These countries are the key labor market destinations for migrant workers and the origin of the majority of remittances. Although migrant workers generated remittances contributing to the development of many Southern Asian and Southeast Asian economies, they have experienced and suffered from manifold difficulties and different types of abuses including economic and social exploitation, and forced labor.[12]

It is undeniable that migration has opened the door to employment opportunities, facilitating a better life for migrant workers including women migrant workers and empowering women to improve their economic and social position. As a result, this trend has generated positive impacts on shifting traditional and obsolete beliefs in women's roles and responsibilities and made progress in the fight against gender inequality. In other words, migrating overseas to work is one of the effective ways of relieving women of the burden of social-cultural norms and subordinate gender roles and attaining women's liberation.[13] There are a variety of "pull" and "push" factors contributing to women's decision to move abroad to work. Women coming from poor communities in underdeveloped or developing countries are likely to migrate to work overseas. Similar to male migrants, insufficiency of employment opportunities with decent income earnings in their home countries in addition to the possibility of earning higher incomes in developed countries ascribe women's decision to migrate for employment abroad. Gender inequalities and discrimination against women and girls still exist in their communities of origin and labor markets, which makes it more difficult for women to sustain stable jobs at home. Women have been victimized by social and economic reform policies, particularly in former socialist countries when shifting to market economies and have been disregarded and made redundant on the grounds of health status, pregnancy, or maternity leave.[14] Family situations are also contributors to overseas migration for employment by women. Women are moving abroad to work in order to keep their families surviving. Female members are motivated to migrate overseas for employment to send remittances to finance other family members left behind, such as elderly members, young siblings, and children, to have adequate access to health care and education. In some cases, women are breadwinners and are encouraged by other male family members to work overseas to secure jobs for their male relatives. While at home there is no demand for their engagement in agricultural work and there are fewer alternative stable jobs offering good incomes in rural areas. In worst cases, families have chosen to sell their young daughters to traffickers in order to repay debts. Young women and girls sold to traffickers are likely to becomes victims of abuses.[15]

With the rise of feminization of international migration, the likelihood of risks and human rights violations that women migrant workers are confronted with is substantial. Due to their special status with dual features of being migrant workers and women, women migrant workers are vulnerable and exposed to difficulties and dangers from the beginning of the recruitment stage to the departure for destination countries and eventually in transit, living and working in foreign countries. Women migrant workers in irregular situations are likely to have more negative experience and face more vulnerabilities where they are outside the protective scope of regulations and only enjoy minimum human rights standards. Under the impact of harsher stances against migrants and gender bias attitudes and perspectives and in addition to the pressure of attempting to find jobs and settling into a new life abroad to take care of their families and children, they are likely to become irregular or undocumented migrant workers or victims of harassment, exploitation, abuse, gender-based and racial discrimination, trafficking into forced labor, debt bondage, servitude, and other forms of abuse and situations of captivity.[16]

Women migrant workers, especially those engaged in informal economies, are in a weaker position with higher exposure to exploitation and abuses, especially in "unregulated sectors" such as domestic work and the sex industry. Less preparation, deficiency in information on migration and employment, and migration and employment policies and regulations based on gender-biased sex selection in some receiving countries have placed women in more difficult situations, compared to men.[17] Thailand and Malaysia are the two destination countries in Southeast Asia recording the highest presence of undocumented female migrant workers. The "porous" borders between countries such as Thailand and Myanmar, Thailand and Lao PDR pose difficulties for administration and immigration management and control. This consequently has paved the way for organized crime beguiling women into emigration to other developed countries for jobs; however, smuggling them to fill jobs in the sex industry or domestic work sector, instead.[18] A huge emigration of women from Bangladesh, Pakistan, Nepal, and Sri Lanka to other countries such as Qatar, Bahrain, Oman, Libya, Kuwait, Saudi Arabia, and the United Arab Emirates for employment are engaged in domestic labor. Women migrant workers play a leading role in the domestic work sector, forming the enormous contribution to the sector with figures recorded in China (22 million), India (4.8 million), the Philippines (2 million), Bangladesh (1.5 million), and Indonesia (1.2 million). Migration for domestic work has also grown in other developing countries in the sub-regions including Vietnam, Lao PDR, Bangladesh, Sri Lanka, and Nepal with an increasing number of women migrant workers emigrating to the Middle East and East Asia, which have a higher demand for domestic and care work due to aging populations and reduction in popularity of the extended family care model.[19]

From the data on international migration, the significant proportion of women migrants contributing to the global migrant population constitutes "feminization of migration,"[20] "resulting from a number of worldwide forces in which gender roles and sex discrimination are intertwined with globalization."[21] Even though globalization has positive impacts on the development of the global economy, globalization engenders "trends contributing to this process including the growing demand for labor in fields dominated by women (particularly, the service sector); the lower cost of production when labor-intensive tasks are shifted to women migrant workers; and the sex-stereotyping of large business enterprises and government that may see women as cheap, temporary, or supplemental laborers whose 'docile' nature makes them easily exploited."[22] In the view of ILO, "feminization of migration," which is a term carrying a negative connotation, is described as "an over-representation of women migrants in extremely vulnerable positions, in so far as these positions are characterized by a strong bond of subordination between the employer and the employee and, above all, because those sectors are generally excluded from the scope of legal protection on employment, notably from the Labor Code."[23] Gender discrimination is attributable to the feminization of international labor migration, women's engagement in informal and unregulated sectors such as domestic work and the sex industry, and segmented and segregation of labor markets in origin and destination countries.[24]

Globalization has prompted the feminization of migration for employment with a variety of "pull" and "push" factors while concurrently leading to a reduction in the regulation of the labor market and a rise in the unregulated and irregular sector, the arrival of different kinds of gender-based exploitation. In response to these trends, there have been more stringent controls on migration for labor by several governments in developed countries. Although these trends benefit women from developing continents of the world with opportunities for empowerment and promotion of their labor skills when participating in labor markets in advanced countries, they also pose more vulnerability to exploitation and abuse to women migrant workers.[25]

INTERNATIONAL HUMAN RIGHTS STANDARDS ON ENSURING THE RIGHTS OF WOMEN MIGRANT WORKERS

International Human Rights Instruments of the United Nations

It is necessary to provide regulatory response to ensure the rights of women migrant workers since the discrimination they sustain is twofold, in particular: "first because they are foreigners and hence subject to the same discrimination as male migrant workers; and second because they are women and as such often victims of entrenched traditional attitudes in their country of origin or of employment concerning the place of women in society in general and in working life in particular."[26]

International legal instruments on human rights and fundamental freedom under the auspices of the United Nations offer fundamental and minimum legal protection for female migrant workers. The Universal Declaration of

Human Rights (UDHR) in 1948 represents a milestone in the history and development of human rights law.[27] Despite its nature of soft law, the UDHR acknowledges "basic rights and fundamental freedoms" that "are inherent to all human beings, inalienable and equally applicable to everyone, and that every one of us is born free and equal in dignity and rights" regardless of "our nationality, place of residence, gender, national or ethnic origin, colour, religion, language, or any other status."[28] The UDHR additionally laid the groundwork for the advent of the International Convention on the Elimination of All Forms of Racial Discrimination (ICERD), the International Covenant on Civil and Political Rights (ICCPR), the International Covenant on Economic, Social and Cultural Rights (ICESCR), and Convention on the Elimination of All Forms of Discrimination Against Women (CEDAW), which are of universal and far-reaching application.[29] Despite being deemed as the first critical human rights treaty broadly stipulating migrant workers' rights and their families, the International Convention on the Protection of the Rights of All Migrant Workers and Members of Their Families ("Migration Workers' Convention," or ICMW) has an insignificant effect on the protection of migrant workers' rights in practice due to its modest ratification.

International Convention on the Elimination of All Forms of Racial Discrimination (ICERD)

The ICERD is one of the core human rights treaties which was adopted by the UN General Assembly on 21 December 1965 and took effect on 4 January 1969. As of this chapter, ICERD has recorded a large number of around 185 participants including major migrant worker-receiving countries in East Asia, the Middle East, Europe, and America.[30] The ICERD is purposed to "speedily eliminate racial discrimination in all its forms and manifestations" and "prevent and combat racist doctrines and practices in order to promote understanding between races."[31] This Convention conceptualizes "racial discrimination" as "distinction, exclusion, restriction or preference based on race, colour, descent, or national or ethnic origin which has the purpose or effect of nullifying or impairing the recognition, enjoyment or exercise, on an equal footing, of human rights and fundamental freedoms in the political, economic, social, cultural or any other field of public life."[32]

Under the ICERD, state participants are under an obligation to ensure the right to equality before the law for everyone irrespective of race, color, or national or ethnic origin. This obligation of guaranteeing the right to equality before the law is extended to different spheres encompassing the rights "to work, to free choice of employment," "to just and favourable conditions of work," "to equal pay for equal work, to just and favourable remuneration," "to form and join trade unions," "to public health, medical care, social security and social services."[33] Upon their participation in this Convention, states parties should undertake various measures effectively including regulatory review, revision, and reform to attend to racial discrimination.

According to the UN Women's recent report in 2013, if states parties fail to acknowledge and include domestic work, which is majorly performed by migrant workers in labor laws, this can lead to non-compliance with the ICERD as they rule out the regulatory protection of migrant workers doing such work. Racial discrimination may take the form of abuse of women migrant domestic workers by private actors such as employers or recruiters.[34]

The International Covenant on Civil and Political Rights (ICCPR) and the International Covenant on Economic, Social and Cultural Rights (ICESCR)

The ICCPR and ICESCR are two of the highest participating treaties with the latest recorded numbers of 173 and 171 participants, respectively. Almost all United Nations member states, encompassing both migrant worker–sending and –receiving countries in the concerned regions, have ratified these covenants except Myanmar (in terms of the ICCPR), and of the major receiving countries, Singapore, Brunei, Malaysia, Saudi Arabia, and the United Arab Emirates have not become members of the ICCPR and the ICESCR.[35]

These two covenants endorse and validate the core principles of human rights and affirm the enjoyment of fundamental rights and freedoms "without distinction of any kind, such as race, colour, sex, language, religion, political or other opinion, national or social origin, property, birth or other status."[36] These two legal instruments additionally affirm the states' obligations to sustain the equal rights of men and women to the enjoyment of all civil and political rights, and economic, social, and cultural rights under the umbrella of the ICCPR and ICESCR.[37] The principle of non-discrimination reflected in the provisions of the ICCPR and ICESCR display no difference between the rights of nationals and non-nationals; the construal of "national origin" in these provisions is prohibition of discrimination on the basis of nationality.[38] Additionally, according to Article 2(3) of the ICESCR, only developing countries are allowed to limit the degree of guaranteeing the enjoyment by non-citizens of economic rights enshrined in the ICESCR "with due regard to human rights and their national economy." Thus, this means that migrants, including female migrant workers, are entitled to comprehensive social and cultural rights in all countries. With the accentuation of human rights and the national economy, this covenant explicitly does not excuse states from their duty of ensuring the economic rights for non-citizens. Moreover, any restrictions on economic rights that have gender-discriminatory impacts would not be allowable.[39]

The principle of non-discrimination is well reflected and incorporated in regulations of both the ICCPR and ICESCR. Under the ICCPR, the principle of non-discrimination is enshrined in several specific provisions on civil and political rights. In particular, Article 14 and Article 26 recognize the right to equality before the law and before judicial authorities, and to the entitlement to equal protection of the law for every person, which is applicable to women migrant workers regardless of their status as non-citizens.[40] This also offers equal treatment to women migrant workers when seeking recourse to the judicial systems for justice to claims against any contravention of rights or abuses targeted at them. These important articles are deemed as bases for all persons, including women migrant workers, who are under the state party's jurisdiction to defend and substantiate their legal rights.[41] Nevertheless, it was reported from the practice that it is impossible for women migrant workers to exercise this right as their legal residency is determined by their employment with employers. In case of disputes with their employers, women migrant workers, particularly those performing domestic work, would face cancellation of their residency permit and consequent expulsion. Further, in cases of unsettled dispute, due to fear of loss of income for the settlement period of the pending dispute and suspension of working, women migrant workers show reluctance to make any claim or take any legal action and rather are likely to accept the situation.[42] Slavery, slave trade, servitude, and forced labor are forbidden by the ICCPR.[43] This can apply to women migrant domestic workers who are suffering poor working conditions and are substantially underpaid. Despite not being considered to be forced labor or slavery, domestic work, with the involvement of debt bondage or trafficking, could potentially amount to forced labor or slavery.[44]

In addition, the ICESCR endorses the right to "just and favourable conditions of work" applicable to migrant workers, including women migrant workers. Following this, states parties are obligated to guarantee "fair wages and equal remuneration for work of equal value without distinction of any kind," the same conditions of work and payment for women to their counterparts when doing the same work, "safe and healthy working conditions," and "reasonable limitations on working hours and periodic holidays with pay."[45]

In general, the ICCPR and ICESCR are considered primary instruments forming the legislative framework of human rights standards. These instruments merely offer general and minimum protection as fundamental rights and freedoms contained therein apply to all citizens of the international community, including women migrant workers.

Convention on the Elimination of All Forms of Discrimination Against Women (CEDAW)

CEDAW plays an important role in the statutory frameworks for promoting and safeguarding the basic freedoms and rights of women, including women migrant workers. The advent of CEDAW in 1979[46] has made protecting rights for women migrant workers more possible. Currently, CEDAW has recorded a large number of participants with a total of 189 parties,[47] making the Convention's enforcement a significant influence. Thanks to the adoption of intersectional approach like other core human rights treaties such as the ICCPR and ICESCR, CEDAW concentrates more on different types of discrimination, exploitation, and abuse that women, including women migrant workers, may face in lieu of their characteristics or status. This helps to avoid the marginalization of obligations that states owe to female migrant workers, and to persist the implementation of human rights protections for female migrant workers in the countries that have yet to participate in the ICMW.[48]

On the basis of the primary human treaties, CEDAW places more emphasis on discrimination against women by providing a wide concept of discrimination against women and imposing obligations on states to eradicate this discrimination.[49] Despite no direct reference to women migrant workers in its text, by adopting the approach of intersectionality, CEDAW can be used to extend the protection for women migrant workers. In particular, while Article 1 of this Convention broadly defines discrimination, Article 2 provides the denouncement of "discrimination against women in all forms," and Article 3 provides that states parties should apply different measures "in all fields" to address multiple forms of discrimination.[50] According to Article 11 of CEDAW, states parties have the obligation to ensure women enjoy "equal rights in employment" on a basis of equality with men. This obligation encompasses guaranteeing various rights to employment opportunities, free choice of profession and employment, equal remuneration, social security, and protection of health and safety in working conditions.[51]

International Convention on the Protection of the Rights of All Migrant Workers and Members of Their Families ("Migration Workers' Convention" or ICMW)

The Migrant Workers' Convention is one of the important human rights treaties that exquisitely offers protection for migrant workers, including women migrant workers and their families. This Convention is further aimed to unify different standards pertaining to treatment of migrant workers applied by states and to strengthen the protection for migrant workers in addition to other instruments since this Convention is the first instrument acknowledging and describing all rights of migrant workers.[52] In addition, the ICMW extends its protection for undocumented migrant workers given that those in irregular situations sustain less favorable and unacceptable conditions. Although the ICMW is purposed for ensuring better living and working conditions for all migrant workers, including women migrant workers, regular or irregular situations notwithstanding, undocumented migrant workers are entitled to fewer rights compared to those who are documented. By covering those in an irregular situation, the ICMW attempts to reduce the number of undocumented migrant workers and end clandestine trafficking.[53]

The ICMW recognizes a number of rights in different fields encompassing civil, political, economic, social, and cultural rights in Parts III and IV.[54] The ICMW basically reaffirms fundamental rights recognized in core human rights instruments such as the UDHR, ICCPR, ICESCR, and ICERD.[55] The Convention reflects the same language as these instruments but singles migrant workers out for special mention. It reinforces several rights which have been already endorsed by the key human rights instruments, such as freedom from torture and inhuman or degrading treatment,[56] and freedom from slavery, servitude, or forced labor,[57] which are corresponding to those enshrined in the primary human rights instruments.[58] The Convention further describes other rights, such as the right to equality before the law and due process in a more detailed manner in comparison to other existing instruments. More importantly, the Convention introduces more obligations on states, for instance, dissemination of information to and for migrant workers regarding their rights,[59] provision of special protections to migrant workers regarding deportation from a country,[60] creation of procedures or institutions considering and addressing special needs of migrant workers,[61] and so forth.[62]

Nevertheless, the ICMW has failed to generate influence over the states. The number of states participating in this Convention is low and the majority of member states to the ICMW are sending countries. By the time of this chapter, there exists around 69 countries signing and/or ratifying the ICMW,[63] which are mainly sending countries located in Africa, Asia, and South America. Nevertheless, not all main countries of origin in the concerned sub-regions have become members of the ICMW. Among those, some main sending countries in the concerned sub-regions ratifying the ICMW include Bangladesh, Indonesia, the Philippines, Sri Lanka, and Timor-Leste. Cambodia has only signed but not yet ratified the Convention. Vietnam and Thailand have yet to participate in this Convention.[64] Principal destination countries additionally have yet to become members of the treaty, and the likelihood of ratifying the ICMW is minimal. Thus, the ICMW has a very humble impact on the protection of rights for women migrant workers.[65]

Additionally, according to some experts, the ICMW "underscores the age long conflict between the international norms of human rights and state sovereignty." The ICMW emphasizes the predominance of states in exercising their sovereign rights in managing and controlling their borders and setting requirements for migration toward non-nationals.[66] Several identified issues that migrant workers are confronted with pertain to visa status or work permits, which falls within the competence of state authorities.[67] Although through the addition of rights and benefits offered to documented migrant workers, the Convention motivates undocumented migrant workers to switch to be documented, they are under the influence of the jurisdiction of the host states and are unable to have their status legalized considering their states of employment. Further, for those whose status is legalized, national laws of the host states seem to prevail over the Convention in practice.[68]

From the scholars' perspectives, the ICMW has not received high ratification by governments in both sending and receiving countries due to numerous restraints. For sending countries, they may find the ratification and the implementation of the ICMW extravagant while they have already struggled on a shoestring budget and lack sufficient human resources for such tasks. In addition, there exists complicity between government circles and the labor export business. This has increased the need for establishing an effective governance with comprehensive and wide reforms. Further, upon the ratification of the ICMW, sending countries are under the obligations of supervising and monitoring unlawful export businesses and providing adequate embassy services to their citizens working overseas, while they have limited resources to conduct these tasks effectively. Another main impediment contributing to the non-ratification by sending countries is "the fear of being undercut by non-ratifying neighbors" and that "they will lose markets if they ratify."[69] In the case of receiving countries, political systems pose several hindrances, and transformation within the systems and national perspectives is needed. Despite the fact that migrant workers are offered protections, receiving countries show unwillingness to ensure all social, economic, and cultural rights to the extent expected in the ICMW in the midst of restructuring and reducing welfare provisions and redressing the balance to address the rights of other minority groups in multi-ethnic communities in accordance with international standards. Furthermore, receiving countries are reluctant to attend to irregular or undocumented migration and to extend protection to irregular or undocumented migrant workers. From the standpoint of receiving countries, extension of rights to irregular or undocumented migrant workers is considered "a form of encouragement," consequently placing more burdens on their national welfare systems.[70]

Treaties of the International Labor Organization (ILO) on Migration for Employment

The International Labor Organization is the UN agency specialized in constituting labor standards and developing policies and ensuring the rights for all workers at the international level. Within the ILO, there have been eight core conventions setting forth fundamental principles and rights at work, encompassing (i) freedom of association and the effective recognition of the right to collective bargaining; (ii) the elimination of all forms of forced or compulsory labor; (iii) the effective abolition of child labor; (iv) the elimination of discrimination in employment and occupation; and (v) a safe and healthy working environment. The 1998 ILO Declaration on Fundamental Principles and Rights at Work ("1998 ILO Declaration") also endorses these principles.[71]

In recent times, the ILO has strenuously formulated and adopted the Protocol of 2014 to the 1930 Forced Labor Convention as the ninth ILO "fundamental" instrument. The adoption of the resolution on the inclusion of a safe and healthy working environment in the ILO's framework of fundamental principles and rights at work by the International Labor Conference at the 110th Session in June 2022 has effectuated the amendment of the 1998 ILO Declaration on Fundamental Principles and Rights at Work, stimulating the 1981 Occupational Safety and Health Convention (No. 155) and the 2006 Promotional Framework for Occupational Safety and Healthy Convention (No. 187) to be fundamental conventions under the umbrella of the 1998 ILO Declaration.[72] In recognition of the cruciality of these principles, under the 1998 ILO Declaration, the ILO has the mandate to place an obligation on states which are members of the ILO but have yet to ratify the core conventions laying down such basic principles, "to respect, to promote and to realize, in good faith and in accordance with the Constitution, the principles concerning the fundamental rights which are the subject of those Conventions."[73] These fundamental principles are universally applicable to all workers, including women migrant workers. Moreover, throughout the 1998 ILO Declaration, the ILO has accentuated the issues of migrant workers, including female migrant workers, and stimulated states and other actors to attend to such issues.[74]

The 1949 Migration for Employment Convention (Revised) (C097) and Migration and Employment Recommendations (R086), and the 1975 Migrant Workers (Supplementary Provisions) Convention (C143) and the 1975 Migrant Workers Recommendation (R151) are the instruments directly targeted at migration and migration for employment. In light of the fundamental principle of non-discrimination, these instruments are aimed to ensure equality between citizens and regular migrant workers. By adopting the principle of non-discrimination, member states to the ILO C097 are obligated to ensure no discrimination to documented migrants, including women migrant workers, in terms of remuneration, working hours, overtime arrangements, paid leave, and social security. The ILO C143 requires states participants to acknowledge and respect fundamental human rights of all migrant workers, including women migrant workers, regardless of their status being legal or illegal and irregular or regular on the basis of loss of employment. States parties shall also undertake measures to ensure stable employment, and provide alternative employment, relief work, and training to workers. Unlike the ILO C097, the ILO C143 broadens its governing scope to deal with irregular migration and to promote the imposition of sanctions on traffickers.[75] Nevertheless, these ILO instruments have not received many ratifications. At present, the ILO C097 has recorded 53 ratifications and only Malaysia–Sabah and the Philippines ratified this instrument but with the exclusion of provisions in Annexes I–III.[76] The ILO C143 is no better, with only 28 ratifications, and the Philippines is the only nation to have ratified the ILO C143 in the concerned region.[77]

Furthermore, the ILO recently made an effort in safeguarding workers' rights through the adoption of the 2011 Convention on Domestic Workers (C189), underlining and facilitating the protection and promotion of rights of people performing domestic work, of which women migrants make up the majority. This Convention represents a milestone in the development of regulatory standards as it is targeted at protecting domestic workers' rights. Under this Convention, domestic workers are entitled to the same principal labor rights as those acknowledged for other workers in regard to reasonable working hours, resting, minimum wage, transparency in terms and conditions of employment, and reverence for the fundamental principles and rights at work.[78] This Convention is considered to "give these workers the dignity they are due and the same rights other workers have under the law" and is a crucial instrument laying the groundwork for approaching the issue of abuses and violence that vulnerable groups including women migrant workers experience and suffer.[79] The ILO C89 also recorded a lower number of ratification, with only 35 ratifications, and only received the ratification of the Philippines in the concerned region.[80]

LEGISLATIVE INSTRUMENTS FOR WOMEN MIGRANT WORKERS' RIGHTS IN ASIA

The Asia-Pacific is the most vibrant region in terms of migration. Several sending countries are located in this region, contributing a large number of migrant workers to the international workforce. Nevertheless, migratory channels and routes in this region are complicated, requiring the cooperation between the countries. This has led to the need for founding intergovernmental institutions or establishing regional governance aimed at addressing a wide range of affairs, including migration-related issues, beyond the national level.

A model of the best effort in forming regional governance is the Association of Southeast Asian Nations (ASEAN), which represents the primary effort of Southeast Asian countries in safeguarding the rights of female migrant workers at the regional level and promoting international cooperation.[81] The ASEAN consists of 10 states members, including Brunei, Cambodia, Indonesia, Lao PRD, Malaysia, Myanmar, Philippines, Singapore, Thailand, and Vietnam.[82] The majority of ASEAN countries are migrant-sending countries, apart from Singapore and Brunei, which are migrant-receiving countries, and of which the economies have been already developed and demand for labor is high. Thailand and Malaysia are hybrid sending and receiving countries.[83]

Recognizing that women and children are likely to become victims of human trafficking, the ASEAN made the Declaration Against Trafficking in Persons, Particularly Women and Children in 2004. This Declaration outlines some general principles in forming and facilitating collaborations between the ASEAN members in the prevention of and fight against human trafficking with a concentration on safeguarding women and children who are more vulnerable to abuses and exploitation.[84]

At a later time, ASEAN adopted the Declaration on the Protection and Promotion of the Rights of Migrant Workers on January 13, 2007, reflecting the commitments of the ASEAN members in resolving matters related to migrant workers, which can be read as encompassing female migrant workers. Under this Declaration, ASEAN countries set out the general principles for both receiving and sending states in the promotion of "the full potential and dignity of migrant workers in climate of freedom, equity, and stability in accordance with the laws, regulations and policies of respective ASEAN Member Countries." The Declaration highlights and encourages collaboration between the members to resolve the case of undocumented migrant workers.[85] The Declaration additionally sets forth obligations of receiving and sending states. Receiving states, according to this Declaration, are expected to ensure fundamental human rights for migrant workers which are enshrined in core human rights treaties such as (i) promotion of the welfare and human dignity of migrant workers; (ii) harmonization and tolerance between receiving states and migrant workers; (iii) facilitation of access to resources and remedies through information, training, and education, as well as access to justice and social welfare services; (iv) promotion of fair and appropriate employment protection, payment of wages, and adequate access to decent working and living conditions for migrant workers; (v) provision of support for migrant workers as victims of discrimination, abuse, exploitation, and violence with adequate access to the legal and judicial system of receiving states; and (vi) facilitation of the exercise of consular functions.[86] Sending states should ensure measures in support and protection of migrant workers' rights with a focus on (i) improvement of employment and livelihood opportunities for their citizens as sustainable alternatives to migration for employment; (ii) enactment of policies and procedures paving the way for different stages and processes related to migration for employment; and (iii) establishment and enhancement of statutory regulations and practices promoting formal migration routes and channels and eliminating malpractices and violations.[87]

In recent decades, the ASEAN has taken further steps to promote human rights standards. The advent of the ASEAN Human Rights Declaration (AHRD) in 2012 marks a critical step in the promotion and development of human rights standards in this sub-region. This instrument is deemed as a bare framework as it mainly reflects the same principles and fundamental rights and freedoms already prescribed in international human rights treaties by stating that the rights of women migrant workers are "an inalienable, integral and indivisible part of human rights and fundamental freedoms.[88] The adoption of the ASEAN Consensus on the Protection and Promotion of the Rights of Migrant Workers (the ASEAN Consensus) represents strenuous efforts of the ASEAN members in promoting and protecting the rights of migrant workers, including women migrant workers in the region. This ASEAN Consensus underlines the need to protect migrant workers' rights and their welfare and well-being. This instrument mirrors all basic principles and rights recognized in, and adopts the same language to, the core human rights conventions such as the principle of non-discrimination, the rights to fair and equal recruitment and employment, equality before the law with adequate access to justice, and adequate access to social security, education, and health care, family reunification, and others.[89] Since the inception of the ASEAN Consensus, the ASEAN members have inaugurated the ASEAN Commission on the Promotion and Protection of the Rights of Women and Children (ACWC) Work Plan for each five-year period (recently, the 2016–2020 period and the 2015–2021 period). The ACWC has a pivotal role in the region with the mission of "promoting and protecting the human rights and fundamental freedoms of women and children in ASEAN." In light of the CEDAW and other international human rights treaties, throughout the specific Work Plan, the ACWC is aimed to reinforce statutory frameworks on migrant workers in the member states to encourage the member states to abolish restrictions to migrant workers, including women migrant workers, ensure consistency with international human rights standards, and promote good practices. The specific Work Plan outlines indicators and strategies for actions and partnership and collaboration between the member states to achieve targets in guaranteeing and strengthening women migrant workers' rights in accordance with the relating instruments, including the Declaration on the Protection and Promotion of the Rights of Migrant Workers, the AHRD, and the ASEAN Consensus.[90]

CHALLENGES IN THE IMPLEMENTATION OF LEGISLATIVE INSTRUMENTS FOR ENSURING THE RIGHTS OF WOMEN MIGRANT WORKERS

There is no doubt that sub-regions in the Asia-Pacific such as South Asia and Southeast Asia have displayed considerable economic growth with the number of bilateral and multilateral treaties and regional cooperative mechanisms on investment and trading progressively increasing. The regional cooperation in pursuit of economic growth has engendered migration for employment associated with problematic issues. The rights of migrant workers, particularly women migrant workers, have received special attention from the states in the region. States' sovereignty and power are no longer absolute since the advent and development of human rights. However, in the region, mandates from member states would be required for regional institutions to implement or enforce any regulations or policies. From the practice, it was observed that the ASEAN member states "tend to shy away from tackling that issue in the ASEAN."[91] The comprehensive stimulation of rights for migrant workers including women migrant workers poses challenges in the region. This is attributable to different factors, including the deficiency of legally binding instruments, difficulties in the implementation of the rights-based framework due to economic policies, and hurdles arising from institutionalization in a region which is still under the process of developing regional integration.[92]

The Issue of State Sovereignty

From the governing scope of human rights treaties, women migrant workers in an irregular situation are entitled to very limited protection with some exceptions of minimum human rights standards endorsed by instruments which are universally applicable by essence. One of the main reasons that most human rights treaties avoid addressing undocumented female migrant workers is state sovereignty. Although the exercise of state sovereignty has been become faint upon the existence and development of human rights standards to redress the balance between states' supreme powers and their obligations in ensuring fundamental rights and freedoms for people, states are still the key actors under international law, and their powers over their territories are of paramount importance.[93]

The principle of state sovereignty is sturdily enshrined in the UN Charter.[94] States have the full entitlement to exercise their powers in managing migration by controlling borders and the entry of aliens. The majority of regional instruments have been articulated on the basis of this cardinal rule, especially those within the ASEAN. As such, states' powers are prevailing in regard to affairs within their territory borders. States are reluctant to grant more rights and protection to women migrant workers, including those who are undocumented as this would be considered encouragement of illegal migration, people smuggling and trafficking in persons for employment, which consequently gives rise to numerous problematic issues to their internal affairs. This presents hurdles in affording protection to women migrant workers, especially those in an irregular situation.[95]

Lack of Effective Governance and Absence of Legal Mechanisms

Although the Asia-Pacific in general and the concerned sub-regions such as Southeast Asia and South Asia mainly provide migrant workers to resolve labor shortages in other developed economies, and also host a large number of migrant workers, including females, there exists neither governance nor mechanisms effectively dealing with migration-related issues. Taking a more specific investigation of the sub-region: South Asia where there has been an attempt to establish and attain regional integration—the ASEAN. As analyzed above, the ASEAN has issued several commitments destined for protecting and promoting the rights for migrant workers including female migrant workers. Unlike the European Union, which is considered to be the most developed model of regional integration, despite strenuous endeavors in achieving regional integration and learning lessons from the EU experience, "ASEAN remains a strictly inter-governmental body and there is no indication of interest in sovereignty sharing."[96] The most recent achievement that the ASEAN has recently gained is the policy of visa exemption for citizens of the ASEAN members with the outlook to a "common visa."[97]

The Europe Union has developed common legal mechanisms to promote and protect human rights for the citizens with the support of the court systems. The European Court of Justice (ECJ) and the European Court of Human Rights (ECtHR) are the key actors in raising human rights–related issues and contributing to the implementation of human rights standards through case law.[98] Unfortunately, in comparison to the European Union, the ASEAN has yet to develop to the same degree. Not reaching the same level of integration as the European Union, from the observation of scholars, the ASEAN members has showed signs of constructing regional institutions resolving human rights issues, and the operation of such institutions would be mandated by the member states. The drafting process of the ASEAN Charter facilitated the possibility of instituting human rights–based mechanisms such as an ASEAN Court of Justice (ACJ) and an ASEAN Regional Human Rights Body (AHRB).[99] Nevertheless, upon the formation and signing of the ASEAN Charter in December 2007, the member states' sovereignty and authority are of supreme importance, enshrined in Article 2 thereof, which contributes to the nature of the ASEAN Charter as being a "soft" constitution.[100] As such, human rights have been left to wither within ASEAN principal instruments. The idea of establishing the ACJ was eventually removed as this would potentially face uncertainty over member states' decision by consensus. Only the idea of creating the AHRB was retained and reflected in Article 14 of the ASEAN Charter.[101]

In the following years, upon the adoption of the Cha-Am Hua Hin Declaration on the Intergovernmental Commission on Human Rights ("CAHN Declaration"),[102] the ASEAN Intergovernmental Commission on Human Rights (AICHR) was established as "a hopeful progress for the institutionalization of human rights not just in Southeast Asia but in the whole East Asian region."[103] In light of the CAHN Declaration, the formation of the AICHR is expected to strengthen the evolvement and development of the ASEAN cooperation on human rights and that "the AICRH will be the overarching institution responsible for the promotion and protection of human rights in the ASEAN."[104] The AICHR is mandated to play an "overarching role," striving to resolve human rights issues in ASEAN, including women migrant workers' rights at the regional level. As such, the AICHR promisingly generates positive impacts on the evolutionary process and promote good practices. Protection and promotion of human rights with an extension for migrant workers, including women migrant workers, by encouraging member states to accede to or ratify human rights treaties or collating related information from member states could be possibly conducted through this mechanism.[105] However, the primacy of state authority remains a challenge as "States have taken a realist-rationalist stance in regionalizing human rights cooperation" that no states could be brought to litigation and states would be the main actors screening and approving all processes on the basis of a consensual dialogue.[106] Thus, there is no doubt that AICHR falls short of authority to provide protection, which has been disparaged as ineffective mechanisms.[107]

The ASEAN member states have multiple differences and fragments in economic development, political and regulatory systems, cultures, and traditional values. The ASEAN was not founded to address the theme of human rights issues, but rather primarily set out to be a political organization. Under the earliest instrument of the ASEAN—the 1967 Bangkok Declaration—there was no mention of human rights. State governments within the ASEAN showed reluctance to address human rights issues.[108] The main concentration of the ASEAN is in the pursuit of economic development to ensure prosperity and freedom of the member states. Hence, it is more challenging for the member states to recognize human rights as common values and attain a common regulatory system of "hard" law on human rights and legally binding mechanisms.[109] In addition to the non-existence of parliamentary control, although the ASEAN members set up the ASEAN Intergovernmental Commission on Human Rights acknowledged by the High Level Panel, this Commission's key function is to promote the human rights standards in the sub-region, making its role of ensuring the rights of citizens, including women migrant workers, inadequate and limited. Thereby, the promotion and protection of women migrant workers' rights and human rights standards in ASEAN are slowly progressing. It will be a long process and difficult for the ASEAN to form and develop democratic rule-making as required for the protection of women migrant workers' rights and human rights standards in general.[110]

In general, even though the ASEAN countries have made efforts in human rights cooperation within the ASEAN recently, the institution of a regional human rights regime with proper enforcement shows little progress.[111] There is an absence of instruments laying groundwork for attending to a human rights regime that can comprehensively function to guarantee and support the rights of migrant workers, including female migrant workers. The establishment of the AICHR may indicate improvement of regional governance for human rights but still display shortcomings as a result of lacking institutionalized coercive measures. Additionally, there exists no "common language" in terms of human rights, particularly women migrant workers' rights, within the ASEAN due to differences in recognition and ratification. In the pursuit of a truly rights-based governance at the regional level, the ASEAN should achieve and maintain a "non-negotiable level of protection."[112]

In addition, the practices have indicated that the countries in the region prefer bilateral agreements to reform of national labor law. Countries of origin and destination have effectuated a cooperation mechanism in resolving issues of migrant workers in the form of bilateral agreements as formal agreements or memoranda of association setting forth principles and procedures as mutually agreed between them. A bilateral agreement recognizing undertakings of each party and quotas is more formal than a Memorandum of Understanding (MoU). Due to the non-binding essence, most countries are inclined to enter into MoUs as the negotiation, implementation, amendment, or revision of changes of economic and labor market conditions are simpler and more relaxed. In the spirit of establishing and strengthening economic, political, and amicable relationships, countries also sign agreements to jointly attend to migration issues. This cooperation mechanism benefits countries of destination and origins that provide policy bases for satisfying the need for labor, improving management, and promoting cultural ties and exchanges in destination countries, while providing opportunities for origin countries to access advanced labor markets and facilitating the protection and welfare for their workers.[113] In the region, there are numerous bilateral agreements and MoUs between countries, in particular:

- The Japanese government has sustained MoUs related to the Technical Intern Training Program (TITP) with numerous major sending countries of TITP participants including Bangladesh, Bhutan, Burma, Cambodia, India, Indonesia, Laos, Mongolia, Pakistan, the Philippines, Sri Lanka, Thailand, Uzbekistan, and Vietnam.[114]
- The South Korean government has operated its Employment Permit System on the basis of signing MoUs with other countries such as Bangladesh, Cambodia, China, Indonesia, Kyrgyzstan, Myanmar, Mongolia, Nepal, Pakistan, the Philippines, Thailand, Timor-Leste, Uzbekistan, Vietnam, and Sri Lanka.[115]
- Malaysia has entered into memoranda of cooperation with Bangladesh, China, Sri Lanka, Thailand, Pakistan, Vietnam, and Indonesia with the aim of regulating recruitment processes and governmental oversight procedures.[116]
- Thailand has signed MoUs with Lao PDR, Cambodia, and Myanmar.[117]

Nevertheless, this cooperation scheme has received criticism that states intend to use this collaboration mechanism as bilateral agreements or MoUs to circumvent the reform of national labor laws to be more in line with international standards. Rather, setting out and reinforcing the protection for migrant workers under legislation, states have chosen bilateral agreements or MoUs to restrict their commitments. As listed above, the majority of governments have employed bilateral agreements or MoUs as bare policy frameworks to attend to issues of migrant workers. However, the degree of protection under bilateral agreements and MoUs is different. Most MoUs are non-binding by nature and easily adjusted in case of changes in economic and labor market conditions, potentially instigating the implementation of undertakings and compliance of the signing countries, especially countries of destination which are normally in a stronger position, to be less effective. Such agreements coherently offer and secure less protection and few rights for migrant workers compared to national labor laws and international labor standards.[118] Several MoUs merely record general principles of cooperation between the states parties without addressing specific issues for migrant workers. For instance, the MoU signed by Indonesia and Malaysia in 2006 omitted to set out a weekly day off and penalties and enforcement mechanisms and allowed the withholding of domestic workers' documents.[119] Another example is the bilateral MoU between Malaysia and Bangladesh which failed to set forth responsibilities of recruitment agencies in Bangladesh, causing the addition of fees to workers that engendered debt bondage.[120] Recent practices additionally showed that governments of the UAE and Lebanon collaborated in the preparation of standard employment contracts. The government of Singapore and Saudi Arabia facilitated discussions with private recruitment agencies in articulating standard labor contracts. This approach of state administration and supervision mainly depending on contractual provisions was criticized for leaving the management of domestic migrant workers in the hands of private recruitment agencies. These standard labor contracts are no doubt deficient of guarantees for workers' rights.[121]

Absence of "Hard" Law on Human Rights

Limited legal frameworks remain a challenge to ASEAN governments in protecting migrant workers, including female migrant workers. The formulation of regulations within the ASEAN depends on the consensus of each member state and "is often done behind closed doors without public participation."[122] Although ASEAN has established agreements and frameworks covering the protection of women migrant workers, these documents are not legally binding and lack enforcement mechanisms. This means that member countries are not obligated to implement the policies, leaving women migrant workers vulnerable to exploitation and abuse. Human rights standards laying the groundwork for the protection of women migrant workers' rights are insufficient under the ASEAN Charter and other instruments. In addition to their voluntary status, these instruments contain general and fundamental rights similar to core human rights treaties without any further development and have yet to lay the groundwork for forming a human rights body and mechanisms.

All the relevant commitments that the ASEAN has developed and adopted are in the form of "soft" law, which is not legally binding. Thus, the arising problems in the implementation of regulations pertaining to migrant workers are ascribed to lack of enforcement.[123] The formulation of regional frameworks is based on one of the foremost principles recognized in the ASEAN Charter, which is "respect for the independence, sovereignty, equality, territorial integrity and national identity of all ASEAN Member States."[124] The principles of national sovereignty and non-interference are considered hindrances and accountable for the adoption of soft instruments with a more rights-based and people-centered approach within the ASEAN. Each of the ASEAN member states places more emphasis on that country's individual interest and benefit rather than collective benefits.[125] Although all the ASEAN members have recently expressed concern over human rights–related issues, especially the rights of women migrant workers, there exists a long process and a big gap among the ASEAN members. Despite the fact that all member states share the same perception of human rights standards as they participate in primary human rights treaties, the implementation and development of such human rights standards in the region contains some problematic issues. Each country interprets and applies human rights standards differently on the basis of "ASEAN way" or "ASEAN values," hindering the establishment and development of human rights mechanisms such as the European Union has. Some of the ASEAN members have showed interest and agreement in founding human rights mechanisms to ensure the rights of citizens in the sub-region. Nevertheless, the majority of the ASEAN states object to the idea of establishing a legally binding mechanism and insist on maintaining their "old way."[126]

According to the aforementioned Declaration on Migrant Workers, the principles and obligations imposed on the states members are restricted in terms of implementation and enforcement "in accordance with the laws, regulations, and policies of respective ASEAN Member Countries," or "without undermining the application by the receiving states of their laws, regulations and policies."[127] Similarly, according to the Declaration Against Human Trafficking, member states are obligated to take measures "to the extent permitted by their respective domestic laws" or undertake to achieve the objectives of the Declaration by adopting and implementing appropriate instruments "as may be necessary and consistent with their respective national laws and policies."[128] The absence of "hard" law undermines the efficacy of the implementation of the obligations of the states and makes the states less responsive to ensuring the rights of women migrant workers.[129]

INCONSISTENT AND DISPARATE IMPLEMENTATION AND CRITICAL FLAWS IN ENFORCEMENT UNDER THE LEGISLATIVE SYSTEMS AND PRACTICES OF MAJOR RECEIVING COUNTRIES

Despite the fact that there are frameworks and instruments on fundamental human rights and there have been efforts by governments in the region to improve the situation of women migrant workers, implementation varies widely between member countries. Radical changes in national laws are needed. Although women migrants are often engaged in doing domestic work when moving to other developed countries, labor laws and regulations in relevant countries have yet to acknowledge domestic workers' rights.

As aforementioned, the major receiving countries in the region, such as Singapore, Malaysia, and countries in the Gulf Cooperation Council (GCC), have not ratified several core human rights treaties. Legal protections even in the case of ratified instruments pale into insignificance in comparison to national laws. In countries where Islamic Shariah law is applicable, such as Bahrain, women's rights are not comprehensively recognized and a number of reservations were made to human rights treaties like CEDAW.[130] Migrant workers, especially domestic workers, have yet to be comprehensively guaranteed and recognized with multiple fundamental rights in national labor laws of several countries, such as Singapore,[131] Bahrain,[132] United Arab Emirates (UAE),[133] and Jordan,[134] offering little or even no legal protections for people, who are mostly foreign women, engaged in performing domestic work during different processes including recruitment, employment contract, or at work, and access to services. However, there has been progress that several GCC countries, such as the UAE, Kuwait, Bahrain, and Lebanon, have developed, for example, the idea of formulating specific law on domestic workers. But the progress has been stagnant, leaving little hope to offer more protection for female migrants doing domestic work in such countries.[135] In recent times, despite some efforts in reforming the *Kafala* system (which requires the visa and legal status of low-skilled workers to be secured by an in-country sponsor, making it difficult for migrant workers to change jobs or leave the host country without their employer's permission) made by governments of Bahrain, UAE, and Jordan, domestic migrant workers are still under the influence of the system. Consequently, this has posed risks of forced labor and debt bondage to a large number of women migrant workers. Further, female migrants doing domestic work subject to the *Kafala* system are unable to make complaints to authorities due to fear of deportation or employer retaliation.[136]

In Japanese jurisdiction, while having signed several international human rights treaties, the Japanese government has yet to enact a specific law directly guaranteeing the rights of migrant workers, including female migrant workers. Risks of discrimination, abuse, or exploitation that women migrant workers potentially face are disparately addressed in several laws such as Prostitution Prevention Law, the Act on Regulation and Punishment of Activities Relating to Child Prostitution and Pornography and the Protection of Children, or the Child Welfare Act. The Japanese government has also illegalized forced labor under the Employment Security Act and the Labor Standards Act. However, these acts were criticized for their definitions and governing scopes, which are more narrowed in comparison with international standards. In particular, exploitation has yet to be criminalized and there also exists an absence of laws imposing a ban on employers, recruiters, or labor agents withholding and retaining workers' personal documents.[137] The Technical Intern Training Program (TITP) aims to provide foreign workers with technical training and work experience in various industries. The

Japanese government recently continued to enact the Act on Proper Technical Intern Training and Protection of Technical Intern Trainees aimed to reform the TITP by requiring TITP participants and employers to collectively prepare work plans delineating working and living conditions, working hours, and other factors for the approval by the central labor authority. In 2018, the Special Skilled Worker visa program was launched by the Japanese government to deal with labor shortages in several sectors over a five-year period. However, these regulations and governmental policy programs have received censure for their exploitative nature, inducing more vulnerabilities to female migrants. Many women migrant workers were reported to be brought to Japan under such programs and forced to work long hours, often in unsafe conditions, for low pay, or even in informal industries. There has been no official reporting of traffickers exploiting TITP participants who were held criminally accountable.[138] The oversight measures are insufficient to protect foreign women from labor abuses. Children are not identified as victims of commercial sex exploitation unless there is third party facilitation. In addition to the authorities' misconception of sex and labor trafficking and child sex trafficking, the Japanese government has failed to conduct victim screening for trafficking indicators and sanctioned illegal traffickers, but instead, imposed drastic measures on victims such as arrestation, detention, or deportation.[139]

In the same vein, in South Korea, women migrant workers face a number of challenges in terms of their rights and protections. The Employment Permit System (EPS) was censured for engendering forced labor of migrant workers, particularly women migrant workers, by unscrupulous recruitment agencies. Migrant workers principally from Vietnam, the Philippines, Thailand, Cambodia, Indonesia, and Mongolia were excessively charged with huge amounts of dollars of debt. In addition, through the EPS, foreign women primarily from China, Thailand, the Philippines, Vietnam, Indonesia, and other countries in the region were trafficked to South Korea and forced to engage in commercial sex jobs at adult entertainment establishments.[140] Women migrant workers were recruited through unscrupulous recruitment agencies under misleading or deceptive promises of decent jobs, but instead, coerced to perform these acts. The South Korean government proscribed unscrupulous recruiters in its bilateral MoUs that can only be accessed by public sector entities and the government has yet to report investigating unscrupulous recruitment agencies. Women migrants were at risk of abuse and exploitation by their employers, as they were underpaid, enjoyed no holidays, experienced multiple abuses and violence, and had little leverage to negotiate better working conditions or to report abuse.[141]

Due to the fact that the Singaporean government has yet to abolish recruitment fees, coupled with the payment for fees for recruiters in Singapore and those in their home countries, migrant workers in Singapore are more at risk of debt bondage.[142] There also exists no provision of a minimum wage under Singaporean primary labor law. The Singaporean legal system is not structured to extend protection for domestic workers' rights, hence, foreign domestic workers subject to Singaporean jurisdiction are unable to enjoy and vindicate their legal rights under the law such as minimum wage, working hours, and paid holidays. Women migrant workers are required to pass a pregnancy test before entry and at a health check every six-month period. Women migrant workers are constrained to marry Singaporean citizens and such marriage is required to be approved by the central labor authority. This has even gone to the extreme in that domestic workers sustain "a lifetime ban" that they are never allowed to marry Singaporeans. Women migrant workers becoming pregnant or giving birth is impermissible. Domestic migrant workers could potentially be deported in case of pregnancy. Employers are in a stronger position with more power so it is easy for them to lodge a complaint to the central labor authority to "blacklist" a migrant worker, with the migrant worker consequently facing a migration ban of up to five years. Singaporean labor migration policies, especially on women migrant workers, have been condemned for harshness, discrimination against women migrant workers, and inconsistency with international standards. Under these domestic labor regulations, the rights to equal employment, to equality before the law, to privacy, to marriage, to establish family, and to protection of the reproductive health of female migrant workers are seriously contravened. These regulations are also contradictory to fundamental rights recognized in and ensured by core human rights treaties in the spirit of the UDHR. Several women's rights prescribed in Articles 11, 15, and 16 of CEDAW are solemnly breached.[143] The deficiency in legal protection is believed to contribute to the emergence of abuses and exploitation against domestic workers in Singapore.[144] Female migrants who have moved to Singapore to work bear large sums of debts from recruitment fees for recruiters in their countries of origin and those in Singapore. A large number of them engage in commercial sex acts and are confronted with more vulnerabilities to sex trafficking and physical and sexual abuse, and in addition to a prohibition of sex work, it is impossible for women to take any legal actions to defend themselves.[145]

Brunei and Malaysia consistently share the same situation as Singapore. These governments impose a prohibition on women migrant workers for becoming pregnant and a requirement for passing a pregnancy test before entry and on a periodic basis.[146] The key national labor laws of these countries do not embrace the protection for domestic workers. Hence, foreign female domestic workers literally have no proper legal protection under these jurisdictions. Employers in Brunei are not required to provide a written document recording terms and conditions to employees engaged in domestic work. In similar fashion, Malaysian employment law does not spare any protection for domestic workers in terms of minimum wage and maximum working hours.[147] These countries also forbid and illegalize commercial sex work. Nevertheless, it was documented that female migrants from other Southeast Asian countries migrating to Brunei and Malaysia were exploited to perform commercial sex acts, presenting more vulnerabilities to physical and sexual abuses and violence. In lieu of protecting foreign women as victims coerced to be engaged in commercial sex, the governmental authorities sanctioned them with detention and deportation.[148]

Thailand is one of the ASEAN countries showing the largest number of female migrant workers, of which the majority are engaged in the informal sector and there have been some movements in acknowledging the rights of women migrant workers. However, Thai labor law disregards and rules out domestic workers and sex workers. Protections for domestic workers are also restricted in ministerial regulations. Few existing labor regulations contain vagueness, paving the way for the exclusion of work in different fields of agriculture, fishery, domestic work, and others and the construal at the sole discretion of the Minister of Labor to ascertain the application of labor regulations. Despite reduction in several exclusions in the Labor Protection Act, the improvement is modest and the protection for domestic workers is narrowed regarding the entitlement to working hours, overtime compensation, minimum wage coverage, and social security. Health care, especially reproductive health care, is not critically guaranteed for domestic workers, who are likely to face dismissal in case of maternity leave or pregnancy.[149] In addition, workers in the adult entertainment industry enjoy no protections under relevant Thai regulations. Thai law has yet to acknowledge sex work and even considers this kind of work to be unlawful. The legal system also contains several flaws so obtaining operating licenses from local authorities is sufficient for establishments using workers to perform adult amusements. There are no regulations setting out requirements for those establishments to guarantee benefits or protections for workers, thus, leaving workers vulnerable to abuses and exploitation.[150] Moreover, despite no explicit exclusion of sex workers from mechanisms to access to justice, it is impossible for sex workers to file any claim or action against their employers in case of facing and suffering abuse or exploitation as they are afraid of being arrested, deported, and publicly shamed due to their irregular status and the kind of work that they are doing.[151]

CONCLUSION

In conclusion, migration in Asia has become an increasingly important phenomenon, driven by various economic, social, and political factors. The increasing number of women migrating for employment has transformed traditional gender roles and cultural and social norms, empowered them with more independence, and improved their position in societies. Women participating in labor markets of numerous countries in the region have contributed to the socio-economic development of sending and receiving countries and the whole region, in general. While women migrant workers may benefit from increased economic opportunities, by being female and migrants, they are more at risk of facing discrimination, exploitation, and abuse in host countries.

The international community and governments in the region have made strenuous efforts in constructing legislation and implementing policy programs aimed to safeguard and promote fundamental rights for women migrant workers. However, there exist shortcomings in the statutory instruments. There is no unifying instrument directly targeted at women migrant workers and it is necessary to refer to different instruments to determine the rights that they are entitled to. Under primary international human rights treaties, the rights that women migrant workers can enjoy are quite limited, and those who are in an irregular situation are afforded with only minimum human rights standards. In the midst of this, most major receiving countries in the region have shown their unwillingness to accede to treaties extending protection for migrant workers, including women migrant workers, or formulate a common robust legal system with full competent enforcement to effectively protect female migrants in the region. All regional instruments pertaining to migration issues are of voluntary and non-binding nature. State sovereignty and power remains prevailing with respect to migration control. There are no regional governance and mechanisms with competence of enforcement to effectively implement and ensure women migrant workers' rights. The majority of receiving countries have displayed flaws, inconsistence, or even violations of human rights standards in their legal systems and in practice. Most receiving countries have shown preference for entering into bilateral agreements or MoUs through which they can limit their commitments and manage the degree of compliance. Therefore, the insufficiency of legal protection afforded to women migrant workers has aggravated their vulnerability and poses risks to violence, harassment, and trafficking. And worse, little protection is provided to undocumented women migrant workers, leaving them in the hand of unscrupulous recruitment agencies and employers that mostly engage them in informal industries with more vulnerability to abuses, violence, forced labor, and trafficking.

To effectively protect the rights of women migrant workers, there is a need for a comprehensive and integrated approach that addresses the root causes of the issues, including formation of enforceable legal instruments and establishment of more robust and effective partnerships between countries in the region and intergovernmental mechanisms with complete competence to ensure the rights of women migrant workers. Protecting the rights of women migrant workers is not only a legal and moral imperative but also an economic necessity. Ensuring that women migrant workers are treated with dignity and respect will improve their lives and contribute to sustainable development and social cohesion in the region.

REFERENCES

ASEAN, "ASEN Member States," Association of Southeast Asian Nations—A Community of Opportunities for All, accessed February 28, 2023, https://asean.org/member-states/.

ASEAN, "Cha-Am Hua Hin Declaration on the Intergovernmental Commission on Human Rights," October 23, 2009, https://asean.org/wp-content/uploads/2021/09/Declaration-AICHR.pdf.

ASEAN, "ASEAN Declaration Against Trafficking in Persons Particularly Women and Children," in *Association of Southeast Asian Nations—A Community of Opportunities for All*, 2004, https://asean.org/asean-declaration-against-trafficking-in-persons-particularly-women-and-children/.

ASEAN, "ASEAN Declaration on the Protection and Promotion of the Rights of Migrant Workers," *Asia-Pacific Journal on Human Rights and the Law* 8, no. 2 (2007): 86–87.

ASEAN Secretariat, "ASEAN Human Rights Declaration," November 18, 2012, n. General Principles, para. 4, https://asean.org/wp-content/uploads/2021/01/6_AHRD_Booklet.pdf.

ASEAN Secretariat, "ASEAN Consensus on the Protection and Promotion of the Rights of Migrant Workers," November 14, 2017, https://asean.org/wp-content/uploads/2018/03/3.-March-2018-ASEAN-Consensus-on-the-Protection-and-Promotion-of-the-Rights-of-Migrant-Workers.pdf.

ASEAN Secretariat, "The ASEAN Commission on the Promotion and Protection of the Rights of Women and Children (ACWC) Work Plan 2016–2020," December 2018, https://asean.org/wp-content/uploads/2018/12/37.-December-2018-The-ASEAN-Commission-on-the-Promotion-and-Protection-of-the-Rights-of-Women-and-Children-ACWC-Work-Plan-2016-2020.pdf;

ASEAN Secretariat, "ASEAN Commission on the Promotion and Protection of the Rights of Women and Children (ACWC) Work Plan 2021–2025," August 2022, https://asean.org/wp-content/uploads/2022/10/09-2.-ASEAN-Commission-for-the-Protection-and-Promotion-of-the-Rights-of-Women-and-Children-ACWC-Work-Plan-2021-2025.pdf.

Benjamin Harkins, "Thailand Migration Report 2019" (United Nations Thematic Working Group on Migration in Thailand, 2019), 51, https://thailand.un.org/sites/default/files/2020-06/Thailand-Migration-Report-2019.pdf.

Bonny Ling, "The Role of ASEAN in Protecting the Rights of Migrant Workers in the Asia-Pacific," *Taiwan Journal of Democracy* 16, no. 1 (July 2020): 133–34.

Carolina G. Hernandez, "Institution Building Through an ASEAN Charter," in *Panorama: Insights into Southeast Asian and European Affairs*, 2007, 16–17, https://www.kas.de/c/document_library/get_file?uuid=c81cf9d9-b4d1-107b-6692-86b73e575ce8&groupId=252038;

Dina Deligiorgis, "Prevention of Gender-Based Violence and Harassment against Women Migrant Workers in South and Southeast Asia," Background Paper (UN Women, ILO, IOM and UNODC, 2022), 6, https://asiapacific.unwomen.org/sites/default/files/2022-11/PVAWMW-Background-paper-designed_FINAL.pdf.

Fraser Cameron, "The European Union as a Model for Regional Integration," Working Paper (International Institutions and Global Governance Program, September 2010), https://www.cfr.org/report/european-union-model-regional-integration.

ILO, "Domestic Workers Convention," C189 § (2011), https://www.ilo.org/dyn/normlex/en/f?p=NORMLEXPUB:12100:0::NO::P12100_ILO_CODE:C189; UN Women, "Review of Laws, Policies and Regulations Governing Labor Migration in Asian and Arab States: A Gender and Rights Based Perspective," 28.

ILO, "ILO Booklet 1," 2; ILO, "Preventing Discrimination, Exploitation and Abuse of Women Migrant Workers—Booklet 2" (International Labor Organization, June 1, 2003), 9, https://www.ilo.org/wcmsp5/groups/public/---ed_emp/documents/instructionalmaterial/wcms_116362.pdf.

ILO, "ILO Declaration on Fundamental Principles and Rights at Work and Its Follow-Up," June 18, 1998, 9, https://www.ilo.org/wcmsp5/groups/public/---ed_norm/---declaration/documents/normativeinstrument/wcms_716594.pdf; ILO, "Conventions and Recommendations," International Labor Organization, accessed February 28, 2023, https://www.ilo.org/global/standards/introduction-to-international-labor-standards/conventions-and-recommendations/lang--en/index.htm.

ILO, "MOUs, BLAs and Declarations Related to Migration," accessed February 28, 2023, https://www.ilo.org/asia/areas/labor-migration/WCMS_161105/lang--en/index.htm.

ILO, "Migration for Employment Convention (Revised)," C097 § (1949), https://www.ilo.org/dyn/normlex/en/f?p=NORMLEXPUB:12100:0::NO::p12100_instrument_id:312242; ILO, "Migrant Workers (Supplementary Provisions) Convention," C143 § (1975), https://www.ilo.org/dyn/normlex/en/f?p=1000:12100:0::NO::P12100_INSTRUMENT_ID,P12100_LANG_CODE:312288,fr:NO.

ILO, "Preventing Discrimination, Exploitation and Abuse of Women Migrant Workers: An Information Guide. Booklet 1 Introduction: Why the Focus on Women International Migrant Workers" (International Labor Organization [ILO], June 1, 2003), 9, https://www.ilo.org/wcmsp5/groups/public/---ed_emp/documents/instructionalmaterial/wcms_116360.pdf.

ILO, "Ratifications of C189 - Domestic Workers Convention, 2011 (No. 189)," accessed February 28, 2023, https://www.ilo.org/dyn/normlex/en/f?p=NORMLEXPUB:11300:0::NO:11300:P11300_INSTRUMENT_ID:2551460:NO.

International Labor Organization (ILO), "Making Women Migrant Workers Count: Sex Disaggregation of Labor Migration Statistics in ASEAN (2019 Data)" (International Labor Organization, 2020), 5, https://www.ilo.org/wcmsp5/groups/public/---asia/---ro-bangkok/documents/briefingnote/wcms_773226.pdf.

International Labor Office—Geneva: ILO, "Making Decent Work a Reality for Domestic Workers: Progress and Prospects Ten Years after the Adoption of the Domestic Workers Convention, 2011 (No. 189)" (International Labor Organization [ILO], June 15, 2021), 31–33, https://www.ilo.org/wcmsp5/groups/public/---ed_protect/---protrav/---travail/documents/publication/wcms_802551.pdf.

International Labor Office—Geneva: ILO, "ILO Global Estimates on International Migrant Workers: Results and Methodology, Third Edition" (International Labor Organization [ILO], June 30, 2021), 20, https://www.ilo.org/wcmsp5/groups/public/---dgreports/---dcomm/---publ/documents/publication/wcms_808935.pdf.

International Labor Organization (ILO), "ILMS Brief—ASEAN 2020," 45–46; Deligiorgis, "Prevention of Gender-Based Violence and Harassment against Women Migrant Workers in South and Southeast Asia," 6–7.

International Organization for Migration (IOM), "World Migration Report 2022" (International Organization for Migration [IOM], December 1, 2021), 73, https://publications.iom.int/books/world-migration-report-2022.

IOM, "IOM Asia-Pacific Regional Data Hub: Regional Secondary Data Review |March 2021" (International Organization for Migration [IOM], May 7, 2021), https://publications.iom.int/books/iom-asia-pacific-regional-data-hub-regional-secondary-data-review-march-2021.

Linda S. Bosniak, "Human Rights, State Sovereignty and the Protection of Undocumented Migrants Under the International Migrant Workers Convention," *International Migration Review* 25, no. 4 (December 1991): 742–43.

Jennifer S. Hainsfurther. A Right-Based Approach: Using CEDAW to Protect the Human Rights of Migrant Workers (2009) *American University International Law Review*, Vol. 24, No. 5, pp. 843–896, 880.

Margaret Satterthwaite, "Human Rights Protections Applicable to Women Migrant Workers: A UNIFEM Briefing Paper in UNIFEM Regional Programme on Empowering Women Migrant Workers in Asia—Roundtable on the Human Rights of Women Migrant Workers under CEDAW 11 July 2003" (United Nations Development Fund for Women [UNIFEM], 2003), 3–4.

Margaret L. Satterthwaite, "Crossing Borders, Claiming Rights: Using Human Rights Law to Empower Women Migrant Workers," *Yale Human Rights & Development Law Journal* 8 (2005): 7.

Margaret Satterthwaite, "Women Migrants' Rights under International Human Rights Law," *Feminist Review* 77 (2004): 168–69.

Narender Nagarwal, "Analysing the Legal Framework of Human Rights of Migrant Workers" (2014) 5 *Indian Journal of Law and Justice* 99, 103.

Nguyen, Thi Hong Yen and Nguyen, Phuong Dung. "Ensuring the Rights of Women Migrant Workers – Analysis and Practice from Viet Nam", *International Human Rights Law Review* 10, 2 (2021): 216-246, doi: https://doi.org/10.1163/22131035-10020001.

Nicola Piper and Robyn Iredale, "Identification of the Obstacles to the Signing and Ratification of the UN Convention on the Protection of the Rights of All Migrant Workers: The Asia Pacific Perspective," UNESCO Series of Country Reports on the Ratification of the UN Convention on Migrants (UNESCO, October 2003), 13.

Nisha Varia, "'Sweeping Changes': A Review of Recent Reforms on Protections for Migrant Domestic Workers in Asia and the Middle East," *Canadian Journal of Women and the Law* 23, no. 1 (2011): 275.

Patrick A. Taran and Eduardo Geronimi, "Globalization, Labor and Migration: Protection Is Paramount—ILO International Migration Programme: Perspectives on Labor Migration" (International Labor Office Geneva: International Labor Organization [ILO], December 11, 2013), 10, https://www.ilo.org/wcmsp5/groups/public/---ed_protect/---protrav/---migrant/documents/publication/wcms_232365.pdf;

Piper and Iredale, "Identification of the Obstacles to the Signing and Ratification of the UN Convention on the Protection of the Rights of All Migrant Workers: The Asia Pacific Perspective," 51–52.

Rachiminawati, "Lesson Learned for ASEAN from the Integration of Human Rights in the European Union (The EU)," *Indonesian Journal of International Law* 6, no. 3 (April 2010): 507.

Rebecca Napier-Moore, "Protected or Put in Harm's Way? Bans and Restrictions on Women's Labor Migration in ASEAN Countries" (International Labor Organization [ILO] and UN Women, 2017), 21, https://www.ilo.org/wcmsp5/groups/public/---asia/---ro-bangkok/---sro-bangkok/documents/publication/wcms_555974.pdf; US Department of State, "2022 Trafficking in Persons Report," 491.

Reena Arora, "Female Migration and Labor in Thailand: When Law and Society Continue to Exclude You," *UCLA Journal of International Law and Foreign Affairs* 21, no. 1 (2017): 74–76.

Robyn Iredale and Nicola Piper, "Identification of the Obstacles to the Signing and Ratification of the UN Convention on the Protection of the Rights of All Migrant Workers: The Asia-Pacific Perspective; Executive Summary," UNESCO Series of Country Reports on the Ratification of the UN Convention on Migrants (UNESCO, October 2003), 2–4, https://unesdoc.unesco.org/ark:/48223/pf0000139529.

Sriprapha Petcharamesree, "ASEAN and Its Approach to Force Migration Issues," *International Journal of Human Rights* 20, no. 2 (2016): 184.

James A. R. Nafziger and Barry C. Bartel, "The Migrant Workers Convention: Its Place in Human Rights Law," *International Migration Review* 25, no. 4 (December 1991): 774–75.

Jennifer S. Hainsfurther, "A Right-Based Approach: Using CEDAW to Protect the Human Rights of Migrant Workers," *American University International Law Review* 24, no. 5 (2009): 856.

Theoben Jerdan C. Orosa, "ASEAN Protection of the Rights of Migrant Workers: Evolving a Rights Regime for the Regional Protection of Labor," *Ateneo Law Journal* 59, no. 3 (December 2014): 726–27.

The ASEAN Secretariat Jakarta, "Women Migrant Workers in the ASEAN Economic Community" (UN Women Regional Office for Asia and the Pacific, 2017), 20, https://asiapacific.unwomen.org/sites/default/files/Field%20Office%20ESEAsia/Docs/Publications/2017/06/AEC-Women-migration-study.pdf.

United Nations, "The Foundation of International Human Rights Law," accessed February 28, 2023, https://www.un.org/en/about-us/udhr/foundation-of-international-human-rights-law.

United Nations, "Ratification Status for ICERD—International Convention on the Elimination of All Forms of Racial Discrimination," United Nations Treaty Collection, accessed February 28, 2023, https://treaties.un.org/Pages/ViewDetails.aspx?src=IND&mtdsg_no=IV-2&chapter=4&clang=_en#3.

United Nations, "International Convention on the Elimination of All Forms of Racial Discrimination," § Treaty Series (1965), https://treaties.un.org/Pages/ViewDetails.aspx?src=IND&mtdsg_no=IV-2&chapter=4&clang=_en.

UN Women, "Review of Laws, Policies and Regulations Governing Labor Migration in Asian and Arab States: A Gender and Rights Based Perspective" (United Nations Entity for Gender Equality and the Empowerment of Women [UN Women], 2013), 17, https://asiapacific.unwomen.org/sites/default/files/Field%20Office%20ESEAsia/Docs/Publications/2013/Review%20of%20Laws%20Policies%20and%20Regulations%20Governing%20Labor%20Migration%20in%20Asian%20and%20Arab%20States.pdf.

United Nations, "Ratification Status for ICCPR—International Covenant on Civil and Political Rights," United Nations Treaty Collection, accessed February 28, 2023, https://treaties.un.org/Pages/ViewDetails.aspx?src=TREATY&mtdsg_no=IV-4&chapter=4&clang=_en.

United Nations, "Ratification Status for ICESCR—International Covenant on Economic, Social and Cultural Rights," United Nations Treaty Collection, accessed February 28, 2023, https://treaties.un.org/Pages/ViewDetails.aspx?src=TREATY&mtdsg_no=IV-3&chapter=4&clang=_en.

United Nations, "International Convention on the Protection of the Rights of All Migrant Workers and Members of Their Families," A/RES/45/158 § Treaty Series, vol. 2220, p. 3 (1990), arts. 8–35, https://treaties.un.org/doc/Treaties/1990/12/19901218%2008-12%20AM/Ch_IV_13p.pdf.

US Department of State, "2022 Trafficking in Persons Report" (Office to Monitor and Combat Trafficking in Persons), 316, accessed February 28, 2023, https://www.state.gov/wp-content/uploads/2022/10/20221020-2022-TIP-Report.pdf.

UN Women, "Managing Labor Migration in ASEAN: Concerns for Women Migrant Workers" (United Nations Entity for Gender Equality and the Empowerment of Women [UN Women], 2013), 11, https://asiapacific.unwomen.org/sites/default/files/Field%20Office%20ESEAsia/Docs/Publications/2013/Managing%20Labor%20Migration%20in%20ASEAN%20Concerns%20for%20Women%20Migrant%20Workers.pdf.

Vitit MUNTARBHORN, "Development of the ASEAN Human Rights Mechanism," Briefing Paper, Directorate-General for External Policies (Policy Department: European Parliament, 2012), 6–7, https://www.europarl.europa.eu/RegData/etudes/note/join/2012/457120/EXPO-DROI_NT(2012)457120_EN.pdf.

NOTES

1. ILO. 2003. *Preventing Discrimination, Exploitation and Abuse of Women Migrant Workers—Booklet 2.* International Labor Organization. June 1. Accessed January 29, 2023. https://www.ilo.org/wcmsp5/groups/public/---ed_emp/documents/instructionalmaterial/wcms_116362.pdf.

2. ILO. 2021. *ILO Global Estimates on International Migrant Workers—Results and Methodology, Third Edition.* June 30. Accessed January 21, 2023. https://www.ilo.org/wcmsp5/groups/public/---dgreports/---dcomm/---publ/documents/publication/wcms_808935.pdf.

3. International Labor Office—Geneva: ILO, 21.

4. IOM. 2021. *World Migration Report 2022.* December 1. Accessed January 21, 2023. https://publications.iom.int/books/world-migration-report-2022; Deligiorgis, Dina. 2022. *Prevention of Gender-Based Violence and Harassment against Women Migrant Workers in South and Southeast Asia.* ILO, IOM and UNODC UN Women. https://asiapacific.unwomen.org/sites/default/files/2022-11/PVAWMW-Background-paper-designed_FINAL.pdf.

5. Deligiorgis, Dina. 2022. *Prevention of Gender-Based Violence and Harassment against Women Migrant Workers in South and Southeast Asia.* 6; IOM. 2021. *IOM Asia-Pacific Regional Data Hub: Regional Secondary Data Review.* March. Accessed January 21, 2023. https://publications.iom.int/books/iom-asia-pacific-regional-data-hub-regional-secondary-data-review-march-2021; The ASEAN Secretariat Jakarta. 2017. *Women Migrant Workers in the ASEAN Economic Community.* UN Women Regional Office for Asia and the Pacific. https://asiapacific.unwomen.org/sites/default/files/Field%20Office%20ESEAsia/Docs/Publications/2017/06/AEC-Women-migration-study.pdf.

6. ILO. 2020. *Making Women Migrant Workers Count: Sex Disaggregation of Labor Migration Statistics in ASEAN (2019 Data).* International Labor Organization. Accessed January 25, 2023. https://www.ilo.org/wcmsp5/groups/public/---asia/---ro-bangkok/documents/briefingnote/wcms_773226.pdf; The ASEAN Secretariat Jakarta. 2017. *Women Migrant Workers in the ASEAN Economic Community.* UN Women Regional Office for Asia and the Pacific. 40.

7. ILO. 2020. *ILMS Brief.* ASEAN. 6; The ASEAN Secretariat Jakarta. 2017. *Women Migrant Workers in the ASEAN Economic Community*; UN Women. 2013. *Managing Labor Migration in ASEAN: Concerns for Women Migrant Workers.* United Nations Entity for Gender Equality and the Empowerment of Women (UN Women). 11. Accessed January 29, 2023. https://asiapacific.unwomen.org/sites/default/files/Field%20Office%20ESEAsia/Docs/Publications/2013/Managing%20Labor%20Migration%20in%20ASEAN%20Concerns%20for%20Women%20Migrant%20Workers.pdf.

8. The ASEAN Secretariat Jakarta. 2017. *Women Migrant Workers in the ASEAN Economic Community.* 125.

9. ILO. 2020. *ILMS Brief.* ASEAN. 5–6.

10. The ASEAN Secretariat Jakarta. 2017. *Women Migrant Workers in the ASEAN Economic Community.* 44.

11. IOM. 2021. *World Migration Report 2022.* 85–86.

12. IOM. 2021. *World Migration Report 2022.* 85–86; The ASEAN Secretariat Jakarta. 2017. *Women Migrant Workers in the ASEAN Economic Community.* 40–41.

13. ILO. 2003. *ILO Booklet 1.* 2; ILO, "Preventing Discrimination, Exploitation and Abuse of Women Migrant Workers—Booklet 2" (International Labor Organization, June 1, 2003), 9, https://www.ilo.org/wcmsp5/groups/public/---ed_emp/documents/instructionalmaterial/wcms_116362.pdf.

14. ILO, "ILO Booklet 2," 11.

15. ILO, 11–14.

16. ILO, "ILO Booklet 1," 2; Margaret Satterthwaite, "Human Rights Protections Applicable to Women Migrant Workers—A UNIFEM Briefing Paper in UNIFEM Regional Programme on Empowering Women Migrant Workers in Asia—Roundtable on the Human Rights of Women Migrant Workers under CEDAW 11 July 2003" (United Nations Development Fund for Women [UNIFEM], 2003), 3–4.

17. Patrick A. Taran and Eduardo Geronimi, "Globalization, Labor and Migration: Protection Is Paramount: ILO International Migration Programme: Perspectives on Labor Migration" (International Labor Office Geneva: International Labor Organization [ILO], December 11, 2013), 10, https://www.ilo.org/wcmsp5/groups/public/---ed_protect/---protrav/---migrant/documents/publication/wcms_232365.pdf; Margaret L. Satterthwaite, "Crossing Borders, Claiming Rights: Using Human Rights Law to Empower Women Migrant Workers," *Yale Human Rights & Development Law Journal* 8 (2005): 7.

18. International Labor Organization (ILO), "ILMS Brief—ASEAN 2020," 45–46; Deligiorgis, "Prevention of Gender-Based Violence and Harassment against Women Migrant Workers in South and Southeast Asia," 6–7.

19. International Labor Office—Geneva: ILO, "Making Decent Work a Reality for Domestic Workers: Progress and Prospects Ten Years after the Adoption of the Domestic Workers Convention, 2011 (No. 189)" (International Labor Organization (ILO), June 15, 2021), 31–33, https://www.ilo.org/wcmsp5/groups/public/---ed_protect/---protrav/---travail/documents/publication/wcms_802551.pdf; Deligiorgis, "Prevention of Gender-Based Violence and Harassment against Women Migrant Workers in South and Southeast Asia," 6–7.

20. ILO, "ILO Booklet 1," 9.

21. Satterthwaite, "Crossing Borders, Claiming Rights: Using Human Rights Law to Empower Women Migrant Workers," 6.

22. Satterthwaite, "A UNIFEM Briefing Paper," 3.

23. ILO, "ILO Booklet 1," 9.

24. Taran and Geronimi, "Globalization, Labor and Migration: Protection Is Paramount: ILO International Migration Programme: Perspectives on Labor Migration," 10.

25. Satterthwaite, "Crossing Borders, Claiming Rights: Using Human Rights Law to Empower Women Migrant Workers," 8.

26. ILO, "ILO Booklet 1," 13.

27. Narender Nagarwal, "Analysing the Legal Framework of Human Rights of Migrant Workers" (2014) 5 *Indian Journal of Law and Justice* 99, 103.

28. United Nations, "The Foundation of International Human Rights Law," accessed February 28, 2023, https://www.un.org/en/about-us/udhr/foundation-of-international-human-rights-law. Nguyen, Thi Hong Yen and Nguyen, Phuong Dung. "Ensuring the Rights of Women Migrant Workers – Analysis and Practice from Viet Nam", International Human Rights Law Review 10, 2 (2021): 216-246, doi: https://doi.org/10.1163/22131035-10020001.

29. United Nations.

30. United Nations, "Ratification Status for ICERD—International Convention on the Elimination of All Forms of Racial Discrimination," United Nations Treaty Collection, accessed February 28, 2023, https://treaties.un.org/Pages/ViewDetails.aspx?src=IND&mtdsg_no=IV-2&chapter=4&clang=_en#3.

31. United Nations, "International Convention on the Elimination of All Forms of Racial Discrimination," § Treaty Series (1965), https://treaties.un.org/Pages/ViewDetails.aspx?src=IND&mtdsg_no=IV-2&chapter=4&clang=_en.

32. United Nations, art. 1(1).

33. United Nations, art. 5.

34. UN Women, "Review of Laws, Policies and Regulations Governing Labor Migration in Asian and Arab States: A Gender and Rights Based Perspective" (United Nations Entity for Gender Equality and the Empowerment of Women [UN Women], 2013), 17, https://asiapacific.unwomen.org/sites/default/files/Field%20Office%20ESEAsia/Docs/Publications/2013/Review%20of%20Laws%20Policies%20and%20Regulations%20Governing%20Labor%20Migration%20in%20Asian%20and%20Arab%20States.pdf.

35. United Nations, "Ratification Status for ICCPR—International Covenant on Civil and Political Rights," United Nations Treaty Collection, accessed February 28, 2023, https://treaties.un.org/Pages/ViewDetails.aspx?src=TREATY&mtdsg_no=IV-4&chapter=4&clang=_en; United Nations, "Ratification Status for ICESCR—International Covenant on Economic, Social and Cultural Rights," United Nations Treaty Collection, accessed February 28, 2023, https://treaties.un.org/Pages/ViewDetails.aspx?src=TREATY&mtdsg_no=IV-3&chapter=4&clang=_en.

36. "International Covenant on Civil and Political Rights," 999 UNTS 171 § (1966), art. 2(2), https://treaties.un.org/doc/Treaties/1976/03/19760323%2006-17%20AM/Ch_IV_04.pdf; "International Covenant on Economic, Social and Cultural Rights," 993 UNTS 3 § (1966), art. 2(2), https://treaties.un.org/doc/Treaties/1976/01/19760103%2009-57%20PM/Ch_IV_03.pdf.

37. International Covenant on Civil and Political Rights, art. 3; International Covenant on Economic, Social and Cultural Rights, art. 3.

38. Satterthwaite, "Crossing Borders, Claiming Rights: Using Human Rights Law to Empower Women Migrant Workers," 15.

39. Satterthwaite, 18.

40. International Covenant on Civil and Political Rights, arts. 14 and 26.

41. Satterthwaite, "Crossing Borders, Claiming Rights: Using Human Rights Law to Empower Women Migrant Workers," 16.

42. UN Women, "Review of Laws, Policies and Regulations Governing Labor Migration in Asian and Arab States: A Gender and Rights Based Perspective," 20.

43. International Covenant on Civil and Political Rights, art. 8.

44. UN Women, "Review of Laws, Policies and Regulations Governing Labor Migration in Asian and Arab States: A Gender and Rights Based Perspective," 21.

45. International Covenant on Economic, Social and Cultural Rights, art. 7.

46. "Convention on the Elimination of All Forms of Discrimination against Women," 1249 UNTS 13 § (1979), https://treaties.un.org/doc/Treaties/1981/09/19810903%2005-18%20AM/Ch_IV_8p.pdf.

47. Convention on the Elimination of All Forms of Discrimination against Women.

48. Margaret Satterthwaite, "Women Migrants' Rights under International Human Rights Law," *Feminist Review* 77 (2004): 168–69.

49. Jennifer S. Hainsfurther, "A Right-Based Approach: Using CEDAW to Protect the Human Rights of Migrant Workers," *American University International Law Review* 24, no. 5 (2009): 856.

50. Hainsfurther, 859.

51. Convention on the Elimination of All Forms of Discrimination against Women, art. 11; Satterthwaite, "A UNIFEM Briefing Paper," 9.

52. James A. R. Nafziger and Barry C. Bartel, "The Migrant Workers Convention: Its Place in Human Rights Law," *International Migration Review* 25, no. 4 (December 1991): 774–75.

53. Nafziger and Bartel, 777.

54. United Nations, "International Convention on the Protection of the Rights of All Migrant Workers and Members of Their Families," A/RES/45/158 § Treaty Series, vol. 2220, p. 3 (1990), arts. 8–35, https://treaties.un.org/doc/Treaties/1990/12/19901218%2008-12%20AM/Ch_IV_13p.pdf.

55. Nafziger and Bartel, "The Migrant Workers Convention: Its Place in Human Rights Law," 780.

56. United Nations, International Convention on the Protection of the Rights of All Migrant Workers and Members of Their Families, art. 10.

57. United Nations, art. 11.

58. Nafziger and Bartel, "The Migrant Workers Convention: Its Place in Human Rights Law," 782.

59. United Nations, International Convention on the Protection of the Rights of All Migrant Workers and Members of Their Families, art. 33.

60. United Nations, arts. 22 and 56.

61. United Nations, art. 25(3) and 42.

62. Nafziger and Bartel, "The Migrant Workers Convention: Its Place in Human Rights Law," 783.

63. United Nations, "Ratification Status for the International Convention on the Protection of the Rights of All Migrant Workers and Members of Their Families," accessed February 28, 2023, https://treaties.un.org/pages/ViewDetails.aspx?src=IND&mtdsg_no=IV-13&chapter=4&clang=_en.

64. United Nations.

65. Satterthwaite, "Women Migrants' Rights under International Human Rights Law," 167.

66. United Nations, International Convention on the Protection of the Rights of All Migrant Workers and Members of Their Families, art. 79. Article 79 of the ICMW provides that "Nothing in the present Convention shall affect the right of each Party to establish the criteria governing admission of migrant workers and members of their families."

67. Nicola Piper and Robyn Iredale, "Identification of the Obstacles to the Signing and Ratification of the UN Convention on the Protection of the Rights of All Migrant Workers—The Asia Pacific Perspective," UNESCO Series of Country Reports on the Ratification of the UN Convention on Migrants (UNESCO, October 2003), 13.

68. Nafziger and Bartel, "The Migrant Workers Convention: Its Place in Human Rights Law," 784.

69. Piper and Iredale, "Identification of the Obstacles to the Signing and Ratification of the UN Convention on the Protection of the Rights of All Migrant Workers—The Asia Pacific Perspective," 51–52; Robyn Iredale and Nicola Piper, "Identification of the Obstacles to the Signing and Ratification of the UN Convention on the Protection of the Rights of All Migrant Workers: The Asia-Pacific Perspective; Executive Summary," UNESCO Series of Country Reports on the Ratification of the UN Convention on Migrants (UNESCO, October 2003), 2–4, https://unesdoc.unesco.org/ark:/48223/pf0000139529.

70. Piper and Iredale, "Identification of the Obstacles to the Signing and Ratification of the UN Convention on the Protection of the Rights of All Migrant Workers—The Asia Pacific Perspective," 52–53; Iredale and Piper, "Identification of the Obstacles to the Signing and Ratification of the UN Convention on the Protection of the Rights of All Migrant Workers: The Asia-Pacific Perspective; Executive Summary," 3–4.

71. ILO, "ILO Declaration on Fundamental Principles and Rights at Work and Its Follow-Up," June 18, 1998, 9, https://www.ilo.org/wcmsp5/groups/public/---ed_norm/---declaration/documents/normativeinstrument/wcms_716594.pdf; ILO, "Conventions and Recommendations," International Labor Organization, accessed February 28, 2023, https://www.ilo.org/global/standards/introduction-to-international-labor-standards/conventions-and-recommendations/lang--en/index.htm.

72. ILO, "Conventions and Recommendations."

73. ILO, "1998 ILO Declaration," 9.

74. ILO, n. preamble.

75. ILO, "Migration for Employment Convention (Revised)," C097 § (1949), https://www.ilo.org/dyn/normlex/en/f?p=NORMLEXPUB:12100:0::NO::p12100_instrument_id:312242; ILO, "Migrant Workers (Supplementary Provisions) Convention," C143 § (1975), https://www.ilo.org/dyn/normlex/en/f?p=1000:12100:0::NO::P12100_INSTRUMENT_ID,P12100_LANG_CODE:312288,fr:NO; UN Women, "Review of Laws, Policies and Regulations Governing Labor Migration in Asian and Arab States: A Gender and Rights Based Perspective," 27.

76. ILO, "Ratifications of C097 - Migration for Employment Convention (Revised), 1949 (No. 97)," accessed February 28, 2023, https://www.ilo.org/dyn/normlex/en/f?p=NORMLEXPUB:11300:0::NO:11300:P11300_INSTRUMENT_ID:312242:NO.

77. ILO, "Ratifications of C143 - Migrant Workers (Supplementary Provisions) Convention, 1975 (No. 143)," accessed February 28, 2023, https://www.ilo.org/dyn/normlex/en/f?p=NORMLEXPUB:11300:0::NO:11300:P11300_INSTRUMENT_ID:312288:NO.

78. ILO, "Domestic Workers Convention," C189 § (2011), https://www.ilo.org/dyn/normlex/en/f?p=NORMLEXPUB:12100:0::NO::P12100_ILO_CODE:C189; UN Women, "Review of Laws, Policies and Regulations Governing Labor Migration in Asian and Arab States: A Gender and Rights Based Perspective," 28.

79. UN Women, "Review of Laws, Policies and Regulations Governing Labor Migration in Asian and Arab States: A Gender and Rights Based Perspective," 28.

80. ILO, "Ratifications of C189 - Domestic Workers Convention, 2011 (No. 189)," accessed February 28, 2023, https://www.ilo.org/dyn/normlex/en/f?p=NORMLEXPUB:11300:0::NO:11300:P11300_INSTRUMENT_ID:2551460:NO.

81. Bonny Ling, "The Role of ASEAN in Protecting the Rights of Migrant Workers in the Asia-Pacific," *Taiwan Journal of Democracy* 16, no. 1 (July 2020): 133–34.

82. ASEAN, "ASEN Member States," Association of Southeast Asian Nations—A Community of Opportunities for All, accessed February 28, 2023, https://asean.org/member-states/.

83. Ling, "The Role of ASEAN in Protecting the Rights of Migrant Workers in the Asia-Pacific," 134.

84. ASEAN, "ASEAN Declaration Against Trafficking in Persons Particularly Women and Children," in *Association of Southeast Asian Nations—A Community of Opportunities for All*, 2004, https://asean.org/asean-declaration-against-trafficking-in-persons-particularly-women-and-children/.

85. ASEAN, "ASEAN Declaration on the Protection and Promotion of the Rights of Migrant Workers," *Asia-Pacific Journal on Human Rights and the Law* 8, no. 2 (2007): 86–87.

86. ASEAN, 87.

87. ASEAN, 87–88.

88. ASEAN Secretariat, "ASEAN Human Rights Declaration," November 18, 2012, n. General Principles, para. 4, https://asean.org/wp-content/uploads/2021/01/6_AHRD_Booklet.pdf.

89. ASEAN Secretariat, "ASEAN Consensus on the Protection and Promotion of the Rights of Migrant Workers," November 14, 2017, https://asean.org/wp-content/uploads/2018/03/3.-March-2018-ASEAN-Consensus-on-the-Protection-and-Promotion-of-the-Rights-of-Migrant-Workers.pdf.

90. ASEAN Secretariat, "The ASEAN Commission on the Promotion and Protection of the Rights of Women and Children (ACWC) Work Plan 2016–2020," December 2018, https://asean.org/wp-content/uploads/2018/12/37.-December-2018-The-ASEAN-Commission-on-the-Promotion-and-Protection-of-the-Rights-of-Women-and-Children-ACWC-Work-Plan-2016-2020.pdf; ASEAN Secretariat, "ASEAN Commission on the Promotion and Protection of the Rights of Women and Children (ACWC) Work Plan 2021–2025," August 2022, https://asean.org/wp-content/uploads/2022/10/09-2.-ASEAN-Commission-for-the-Protection-and-Promotion-of-the-Rights-of-Women-and-Children-ACWC-Work-Plan-2021-2025.pdf.

91. Theoben Jerdan C. Orosa, "ASEAN Protection of the Rights of Migrant Workers: Evolving a Rights Regime for the Regional Protection of Labor," *Ateneo Law Journal* 59, no. 3 (December 2014): 726–27.

92. Orosa, 738.

93. Linda S. Bosniak, "Human Rights, State Sovereignty and the Protection of Undocumented Migrants Under the International Migrant Workers Convention," *International Migration Review* 25, no. 4 (December 1991): 742–43.

94. United Nations, "Charter of the United Nations," 1 UNTS XVI § (1945), art. 2, https://treaties.un.org/doc/publication/ctc/uncharter.pdf.

95. Bosniak, "Human Rights, State Sovereignty and the Protection of Undocumented Migrants Under the International Migrant Workers Convention," 742–43; Hainsfurther, "A Right-Based Approach: Using CEDAW to Protect the Human Rights of Migrant Workers," 880.

96. Fraser Cameron, "The European Union as a Model for Regional Integration," Working Paper (International Institutions and Global Governance Program, September 2010), https://www.cfr.org/report/european-union-model-regional-integration.

97. Orosa, "ASEAN Protection of the Rights of Migrant Workers: Evolving a Rights Regime for the Regional Protection of Labor," 725.

98. Rachiminawati, "Lesson Learned for ASEAN from the Integration of Human Rights in the European Union (The EU)," *Indonesian Journal of International Law* 6, no. 3 (April 2010): 507.

99. Carolina G. Hernandez, "Institution Building Through an ASEAN Charter," in *Panorama: Insights into Southeast Asian and European Affairs*, 2007, 16–17, https://www.kas.de/c/document_library/get_file?uuid=c81cf9d9-b4d1-107b-6692-86b73e575ce8&groupId=252038; Orosa, "ASEAN Protection of the Rights of Migrant Workers: Evolving a Rights Regime for the Regional Protection of Labor," 741.

100. Orosa, "ASEAN Protection of the Rights of Migrant Workers: Evolving a Rights Regime for the Regional Protection of Labor," 742.

101. Orosa, 742; Rachiminawati, "Lesson Learned for ASEAN from the Integration of Human Rights in the European Union (The EU)," 502.

102. ASEAN, "Cha-Am Hua Hin Declaration on the Intergovernmental Commission on Human Rights," October 23, 2009, https://asean.org/wp-content/uploads/2021/09/Declaration-AICHR.pdf.

103. Orosa, "ASEAN Protection of the Rights of Migrant Workers: Evolving a Rights Regime for the Regional Protection of Labor," 743.

104. ASEAN, "CAHN Declaration," para. 8.

105. Sriprapha Petcharamesree, "ASEAN and Its Approach to Force Migration Issues,"*International Journal of Human Rights* 20, no. 2 (2016): 184.

106. Orosa, "ASEAN Protection of the Rights of Migrant Workers: Evolving a Rights Regime for the Regional Protection of Labor," 743.

107. Petcharamesree, "ASEAN and Its Approach to Force Migration Issues," 184.

108. Vitit MUNTARBHORN, "Development of the ASEAN Human Rights Mechanism," Briefing Paper, Directorate-General for External Policies

(Policy Department: European Parliament, 2012), 6–7, https://www.europarl.europa.eu/RegData/etudes/note/join/2012/457120/EXPO-DROI_NT(2012)457120_EN.pdf.

109. Rachiminawati, "Lesson Learned for ASEAN from the Integration of Human Rights in the European Union (The EU)," 506.

110. Rachiminawati, 506.

111. Orosa, "ASEAN Protection of the Rights of Migrant Workers: Evolving a Rights Regime for the Regional Protection of Labor," 742; MUNTARBHORN, "Development of the ASEAN Human Rights Mechanism."

112. Orosa, "ASEAN Protection of the Rights of Migrant Workers: Evolving a Rights Regime for the Regional Protection of Labor," 745.

113. ILO, "MOUs, BLAs and Declarations Related to Migration," accessed February 28, 2023, https://www.ilo.org/asia/areas/labor-migration/WCMS_161105/lang--en/index.htm.

114. US Department of State, "2022 Trafficking in Persons Report" (Office to Monitor and Combat Trafficking in Persons), 316, accessed February 28, 2023, https://www.state.gov/wp-content/uploads/2022/10/20221020-2022-TIP-Report.pdf.

115. ILO, "MOUs, BLAs and Declarations Related to Migration."

116. ILO.

117. ILO.

118. Nisha Varia, "'Sweeping Changes' A Review of Recent Reforms on Protections for Migrant Domestic Workers in Asia and the Middle East," *Canadian Journal of Women and the Law* 23, no. 1 (2011): 275.

119. Varia, 275.

120. US Department of State, "2022 Trafficking in Persons Report," 367.

121. Varia, "'Sweeping Changes' A Review of Recent Reforms on Protections for Migrant Domestic Workers in Asia and the Middle East," 275–76.

122. Rachiminawati, "Lesson Learned for ASEAN from the Integration of Human Rights in the European Union (The EU)," 507.

123. Orosa, "ASEAN Protection of the Rights of Migrant Workers: Evolving a Rights Regime for the Regional Protection of Labor," 738.

124. ASEAN, "The ASEAN Charter," 2007, art. 2, https://asean.org/wp-content/uploads/2021/08/November-2020-The-ASEAN-Charter-28th-Reprint.pdf.

125. Rachiminawati, "Lesson Learned for ASEAN from the Integration of Human Rights in the European Union (The EU)," 501.

126. Rachiminawati, 505.

127. ASEAN, "ASEAN Declaration on the Protection and Promotion of the Rights of Migrant Workers," 86.

128. ASEAN, "ASEAN Declaration Against Trafficking in Persons Particularly Women and Children"; Petcharamesree, "ASEAN and Its Approach to Force Migration Issues," 182.

129. Orosa, "ASEAN Protection of the Rights of Migrant Workers: Evolving a Rights Regime for the Regional Protection of Labor," 725.

130. UN Women, "Review of Laws, Policies and Regulations Governing Labor Migration in Asian and Arab States: A Gender and Rights Based Perspective," 45.

131. UN Women, 120.

132. UN Women, 42–43; US Department of State, "2022 Trafficking in Persons Report," 107.

133. UN Women, "Review of Laws, Policies and Regulations Governing Labor Migration in Asian and Arab States: A Gender and Rights Based Perspective," 126; US Department of State, "2022 Trafficking in Persons Report," 568.

134. UN Women, "Review of Laws, Policies and Regulations Governing Labor Migration in Asian and Arab States: A Gender and Rights Based Perspective," 84.

135. Varia, "'Sweeping Changes': A Review of Recent Reforms on Protections for Migrant Domestic Workers in Asia and the Middle East," 274.

136. UN Women, "Review of Laws, Policies and Regulations Governing Labor Migration in Asian and Arab States: A Gender and Rights Based Perspective," 49, 56, 84, and 126.

137. US Department of State, "2022 Trafficking in Persons Report," 314.

138. US Department of State, 314.

139. US Department of State, 315.

140. US Department of State, 330–31.

141. US Department of State, 330–31.

142. US Department of State, 488.

143. UN Women, "Review of Laws, Policies and Regulations Governing Labor Migration in Asian and Arab States: A Gender and Rights Based Perspective," 110; Rebecca Napier-Moore, "Protected or Put in Harm's Way? Bans and Restrictions on Women's Labor Migration in ASEAN Countries" (International Labor Organization (ILO) and UN Women, 2017), 21, https://www.ilo.org/wcmsp5/groups/public/---asia/---ro-bangkok/---sro-bangkok/documents/publication/wcms_555974.pdf; US Department of State, "2022 Trafficking in Persons Report," 491.

144. US Department of State, "2022 Trafficking in Persons Report," 490; UN Women, "Review of Laws, Policies and Regulations Governing Labor Migration in Asian and Arab States: A Gender and Rights Based Perspective," 110.

145. US Department of State, "2022 Trafficking in Persons Report," 491.

146. Napier-Moore, "Protected or Put in Harm's Way? Bans and Restrictions on Women's Labor Migration in ASEAN Countries," 20.

147. US Department of State, "2022 Trafficking in Persons Report," 141 and 367.

148. US Department of State, 140 and 368.

149. Reena Arora, "Female Migration and Labor in Thailand: When Law and Society Continue to Exclude You," *UCLA Journal of International Law and Foreign Affairs* 21, no. 1 (2017): 74–76.

150. Arora, 76.

151. Benjamin Harkins, "Thailand Migration Report 2019" (United Nations Thematic Working Group on Migration in Thailand, 2019), 51, https://thailand.un.org/sites/default/files/2020-06/Thailand-Migration-Report-2019.pdf.

Chapter 5

The Rights of Illegal Migrant Workers

Tran Thi Thu Thuy and Nguyen Tien Duc

One of the globalization promises is better job opportunities with higher wages that has led to an increase in international labor migration. In return, migrant workers also contribute significantly to those economies and make up a significant portion of the workforce in their host countries.[1] They fill labor market gaps, stimulating the economies of the countries they live in, which in turn creates more jobs and generates more tax revenue.

The current situation of globalization is characterized by a significant impact from the COVID-19 pandemic, with cross-border flows plummeting in 2020. However, the latest data suggests that global business is not going away, but the landscape is shifting, with important implications for strategy and management.[2] Despite the challenges posed by the pandemic and geopolitical tensions, international flows show no signs of a sustained downturn.[3] The data shows a broad pattern of decoupling between the United States and China, but the flows of countries that are geopolitically aligned with the United States and China do not indicate a broader split between rival blocs.[4]

On the other hand, the trend of migrant workers has seen an increase. According to the International Labor Organization (ILO), the number of international migrant workers has increased from 164 to 169 million, indicating an increase of 5 million migrant workers since 2017.[5] Migrant workers made up one in 20 of the world's workforce in 2019, often carrying out key functions in critical sectors from health care to transportation and food processing.[6] The pandemic has caused a significant decrease in international labor migration due to travel restrictions and economic uncertainty.[7] This has had adverse effects on both countries of origin, which often rely on remittances sent home by migrant workers, and destination countries, which benefit from the labor provided by migrants.[8] Despite their value to the global economy, many migrant workers face uncertainty at work, a situation made worse by the COVID-19 pandemic. As the world recovers from the pandemic, it is expected that international labor migration will resume, perhaps even increase, as economies rebound, and countries lift travel restrictions. However, the experiences of the pandemic have underscored the need for better protections for migrant workers.[9]

Before moving forward, it is prerequisite to explain terminologies that will be used in this chapter. Although the rights of illegal, irregular, undocumented migrant workers have garnered increasing attention from various actors, national and international, the relevant concepts remain unclear and controversial. The definition of illegal migration for work or migrant worker is far from settled. An "illegal migrant" is often defined as a national from a country who works within the territory of another country without legal approval in the form of a work visa or residence permit. However, the usage of the term "illegal" is criticized for carrying a criminal connotation and is not preferred in many contexts.[10] As expounded by several international bodies, the usage of the term "illegal" may be inaccurate and harmful.[11] It is inaccurate in the sense that it gives a criminal image of migrant worker, while being undocumented constitutes administrative violation merely. It even violates due process principles codified in both international and national laws as it concludes the "illegal" status of a person, followed by punitive sanctions such as detention and deportation, without necessary procedural guarantees and safeguards. This way of thinking might even entitle states to ignore their international human rights obligations toward persons subject to their jurisdiction regardless of their immigration status. Moreover, the term is considered harmful in that because of the criminal label it has the dehumanizing effect on migrant workers as undignified, dishonest, and dangerous persons. The pervasive usage of the term would likely breed social discontent, intolerance, and xenophobia against migrant workers.

Attempts to rise above an endless array of derogatory terms, racial slurs, and demeaning labels against migrant workers have been made. In 1994, the International Conference on Population and Development proposed the adoption of the term "undocumented" to describe individuals who lack documentation of their legal status.[12] But, the term "undocumented" was considered deficient since it did not include those who obtained legal approval to enter the host country as a tourist but did not legally qualify for an occupation. Undocumented migrant workers might be different from the category of those with false documents, who were moved by traffickers across borders.

The term "irregular migrant" or "migrant workers in an irregular situation" is often used as an alternative to "illegal migrant." The descriptor was first proposed at the International Symposium on Migration held in

Bangkok in April 1999, and later endorsed at the International Labor Office's 2004 International Conference in Geneva.[13] The term indicates people who are employed in a foreign country without the necessary authorization. They are often referred to as "irregular" or "undocumented" migrants.[14] This definition includes individuals who may have entered the country without permission, are working in violation of their visa conditions, or have overstayed their visas. Irregularities in migration can occur at any stage of the migration process, from departure to return, and can be committed by either the migrant or the authorities.[15] The term "irregular" acknowledges that the person's migration status is not in line with established rules, but it avoids criminalizing the individual's existence, which can be implied by terms like "illegal." It's important to note that while their status may be irregular, these individuals still have rights that must be respected and protected.[16] This term helps to shift the discourse on migration away from a security paradigm that often seeks to combat or fight irregular migration, often through harsh border control measures and criminalizing irregular migrants.[17] Instead, it encourages a focus on the rights and well-being of these individuals. It bears noting that irregularity is a fluid concept, which means at a certain point in time or during a certain period a person might transfer "in and out" of the scope of "irregularity" as laws and policies change.

According to Article 5(b) of the International Convention on the Protection of the Rights of All Migrant Workers and Members of Their Families (ICMW), migrant workers:

a. Are considered as documented or in a regular situation if they are authorized to enter, to stay and to engage in a remunerated activity in the State of employment pursuant to the law of that State and to international agreements to which that State is a party;
b. Are considered as non-documented or in an irregular situation if they do not comply with the conditions provided for in subparagraph a. of the present article.

It is observed that international instruments have a clear tendency of adopting the descriptors "irregular" or "undocumented" when referring to migrant workers in an irregular situation, indicating that these individuals either entered a host country without official documentation or overstayed their permitted time. On the other hand, the term "illegal" is often used by governments and media, reflecting the emphasis placed by states on their domestic authority over immigration matters. The language used in international treaties underscores the importance of human rights for all individuals, regardless of their legal status under domestic law. For this reason, this chapter makes use of irregular migrant workers with a stress on inherent rights of this group.

According to a recent publication of ILO, labor market dynamics and asymmetries between countries of origin and destination are among the main drivers for irregular migration.[18] In the absence of safe and regular migration options, individuals may find themselves compelled to leave their place of residence due to health or survival reasons. On top of that, detrimental phenomena and factors such as climate change; sea level rise; environmental degradation; unequal access to economic and social rights including health care, decent work, food, land, or water; disparities in opportunities; as well as gender inequality and gender-based violence, can all serve as strong motivators for people to migrate through irregular channels. Other contributing factors or structural elements include gender-specific migration bans, recruitment costs, unscrupulous labor recruiters, misleading or incorrect information, or a lack of comprehension of intricate immigration regulations.

INTERNATIONAL HUMAN RIGHTS STANDARDS ON THE RIGHTS OF IRREGULAR MIGRANT WORKERS

On the one hand, it is generally accepted that states retain the sovereign right to regulate and manage their cross-border entry and labor influx.[19] Articles 34 and 79 of the ICMW confirms this reading.[20] On the other hand, the exercise of this power must observe states' international human rights and labor standards. Being an irregular migrant worker is not an indication of a lack of rights or that these rights should not be taken seriously. Since human rights are inherent, all migrants, irrespective of their migration status, are still holders of legitimate rights. Ensuring these rights, including labor rights, is crucial for addressing irregular labor migration and should form the groundwork for effective management and cooperation at all levels. To this end, international human rights and labor standards and instruments have mushroomed over time. For protecting irregular migrant workers' rights there are mainly two international mechanisms at stake: one developed by human rights treaty-based bodies, the other by ILO, a UN labor-specialized body.

The 1990 International Convention on the Protection of the Rights of All Migrant Workers and Members of Their Families universally safeguards the fundamental rights of migrant workers and their families, regardless of their immigration status. Many of these rights, outlined in Part III, are also enshrined in other international human rights treaties, such as the International Covenant on Civil and Political Rights (ICCPR) and the International Covenant on Economic, Social and Cultural Rights (ICESCR). Part III of the ICMW specifically addresses civil and political rights tailored to the unique circumstances of migrant workers, such as the right to personal liberty and security (Article 16) and the right to humane treatment for those deprived of their liberty (Article 17). The ICMW also extends protection to migrant workers' rights not explicitly covered in other human rights treaties, including protection against unauthorized seizure or destruction of personal documents (Article 21), procedural safeguards during individual expulsion proceedings (Article 22), and the right to seek consular or diplomatic protection and assistance (Article 23). In addition to civil and political rights, the ICMW also recognizes the economic, social, and cultural rights of all migrant workers. Two unique rights enshrined in the ICMW are the right to respect for cultural identity (Article 31) and the right to transfer earnings and savings upon the end of their stay in the employment state (Article 32). Furthermore, Part III emphasizes the obligation of all migrant workers and their families to abide by the laws of the state of employment or transit (Article 34).

The ILO's International Labor Conference has established international labor standards that apply to migrant workers, including those in an irregular situation, unless specified otherwise. The eight fundamental ILO Conventions outline the basic principles and rights at work that pertain to all migrant workers, regardless of their nationality or migration status.[21] The 1998 ILO Declaration on fundamental principles and rights at work and its follow-up obliges all ILO member states to promote and realize the principles concerning the fundamental rights contained in these Conventions. Several other ILO standards, both of general application and those with specific provisions for migrant workers in areas such as employment, labor inspection, social security, wage protection, occupational safety and health, and sectors like agriculture, construction, hotels and restaurants, and domestic work, are particularly relevant to migrant workers in an irregular situation. In addition, when formulating national laws and policies on labor migration and the protection of migrant workers in an irregular situation, states are guided by ILO Convention No. 97 (1949) concerning Migration for Employment (Revised), Convention No. 143 (1975) concerning Migrations in Abusive Conditions and the Promotion of Equality of Opportunity and Treatment of Migrant Workers (Supplementary Provisions), and the accompanying Recommendation Nos. 86 and 151.

Equality and Non-Discrimination

Non-discrimination is a fundamental principle underpinning all international human rights instruments, including the United Nations Charter, the Universal Declaration on Human Rights, ICCPR, and ICESCR. For example, Articles 1 and 2(1) of the Universal Declaration of Human Rights recognize the concept of human dignity that is inherent to everyone, irrespective of their migration status. Additionally, while the International Convention on the Elimination of All Forms of Racial Discrimination permits differentiation between citizens and non-citizens, it also ensures that both groups are protected against discrimination. The ICMW explicitly prohibits discrimination based on nationality in Article 7. Human rights treaty bodies have broadened the scope of non-discrimination to encompass non-nationals, including migrant workers, regardless of their legal status or documentation.[22] The rights enshrined in Part III of the ICMW extend to all migrant workers, even those in an irregular situation. Consequently, any differential treatment based on nationality or migration status constitutes discrimination unless it is grounded in law, pursues a legitimate aim under the ICMW, is necessary in the specific circumstances, and is proportionate to the legitimate aim pursued.[23]

The ICMW mandates that states parties respect and ensure the rights provided therein for all migrant workers and their families without discrimination. However, Article 7 does not create a standalone right. Its application is limited to the rights of irregular migrant workers that are protected in the ICMW, particularly in Part III. Article 7 encompasses both legal and actual discrimination. States parties must ensure that their laws, regulations, and administrative practices do not discriminate against migrant workers. According to the ICMW Committee, merely addressing de jure discrimination will not guarantee de facto equality.[24] Therefore, states parties are obligated to implement proactive measures to prevent, mitigate, and eliminate the conditions and attitudes that give rise to or perpetuate de facto discrimination against migrant workers. Article 7 extends its prohibition to both direct and indirect discrimination against migrant workers. Indirect discrimination manifests when a seemingly neutral law, policy, or practice has a disproportionate adverse impact on the rights of migrant workers. For example, a requirement for birth certificates for school enrollment may disproportionately affect irregular migrant workers, who often lack such certificates or have been denied them due to their immigration status.

In addition, the fundamental principles of equality and non-discrimination are deeply embedded in international human rights agreements, various labor standards, and the established ILO standards on rights at work. These principles are explicitly guaranteed in the Equal Remuneration Convention, 1951 (No. 100) and the Discrimination (Employment and Occupation) Convention, 1958 (No. 111). The ILO Convention No. 143 on migrant workers states in Article 9(1) that even migrants who have entered a country irregularly and cannot obtain legal status are entitled to equal treatment. This includes rights related to previous employment, such as remuneration, social security, and other benefits.

Personal Liberty and Security

Irregular migrants face increased risks of abuse and exploitation due to their vulnerable status. Their undocumented condition makes them more susceptible to coercion and abuse, with the fear of being reported or deported, further exacerbating their vulnerability. It bears noting that women migrants are more vulnerable to ill-treatment and other forms of violence from both state and non-state actors such as employers and state officials.

According to Article 16 of the ICMW, states parties are obligated to safeguard all migrant workers from violence, physical harm, threats, and intimidation, whether perpetrated by public officials or private individuals, groups, or institutions. This obligation necessitates that states parties: (i) Enact and enforce laws that prohibit such actions; (ii) Thoroughly investigate instances of abuse and violence; (iii) Bring to justice and appropriately penalize the perpetrators; (iv) Provide sufficient compensation to victims and their families; (v) Offer human rights training to public officials; and (vi) Effectively oversee the behavior of state agents and regulate that of private individuals and entities to prevent such actions. Moreover, states parties are under an obligation to effectively combat all forms of prejudice, discrimination, and hatred directed toward migrant workers and their families, particularly those in irregular situations. This includes hate crimes, incitement to hatred, and hate speech, regardless of the source, whether it be politicians or the media. Furthermore, states must intensify effort to raise public awareness about the illegality of such acts and promote respect for the fundamental human rights of all migrant workers.

Article 16 of the ICMW also complements Article 9 of the ICCPR in terms of personal liberty and security in the sense that migrant workers, regardless of their immigration status, shall not be arbitrarily detained or arrested, whether individually or collectively. To avoid arbitrariness, the arrest or detention of migrant workers must have a legal basis, pursue a valid objective under the Convention, be necessary in specific circumstances, and be proportionate to the legitimate goal being pursued. While Article 16(4) of the ICMW does not explicitly outline the acceptable reasons for detention, it clearly states that migrant workers shall not be deprived of their liberty unless it is in accordance with established lawful grounds and procedures. Furthermore, detention must be authorized by law, serve a legitimate Convention objective, be necessary in specific circumstances, and be proportionate to the legitimate aim being pursued. According to the ICMW Committee, any liberty-restricting measure, custodial or non-custodial, must be exceptional and always based on a thorough and individualized assessment.[25] This assessment should consider the necessity and appropriateness of any liberty restriction, including whether it is proportionate to the objective to be achieved.

The principle of proportionality mandates that states parties detain migrant workers only as a last resort, prioritizing less coercive measures, particularly non-custodial measures, whenever such measures are sufficient to achieve the intended objective. In all such instances, the least intrusive and restrictive measure possible should be applied in each individual case.

In addition, Article 16, paragraphs 6–9, and Article 17 of the ICMW provides for fair trial rights for irregular migrant workers when they are in custody and pretrial detention. It includes the right to contact consular or diplomatic authorities of their state of origin, the right to legal assistance and the assistance of an interpreter, if necessary, without cost, and the right to compensation for migrant workers who have been victims of unlawful arrest or detention. Importantly, states must guarantee that migrant workers and their families are not expelled during the processing of their claims. In addition, during detention, irregular migrant workers enjoy the right to be treated with humanity, and with respect for their inherent dignity and cultural identity. States have a duty to ensure that migrant workers and their families are provided with living conditions that comply with recognized international standards. This encompasses access to proper sanitation, bathing and shower facilities, sufficient food that respects religious dietary rules, clean drinking water, means of communication with family, competent medical care, and opportunities for religious practice. Furthermore, countries must protect migrant workers and their families from any form of cruel treatment, including sexual violence and abuse, committed by guards or other detainees or inmates.

International human rights law mandates specific protections for refugees and migrant workers in relation to expulsion. First, irregular migrant workers should not bear the costs of their expulsion, including legal proceedings or administrative detention costs.[26] Furthermore, if their irregular situation is not their fault, such as due to redundancy or contract expiration, or if the employer failed to complete necessary formalities, migrant workers should not be responsible for any expulsion-related costs, including travel costs.[27]

In addition, irregular migrant workers who are detained and facing expulsion should be informed of the reasons and given the opportunity to contest them. They should have equal and effective access to justice to appeal against the deportation or expulsion order, and the appeal should suspend the expulsion order. This also means access to legal assistance and interpretation assistance, if needed, and the right to stay in the country while their claims are being evaluated.[28] An expulsion decision should be communicated in a language they understand, in writing, and with reasons. These rights are crucial to ensure due process.[29] A person affected by an expulsion decision should also have a reasonable opportunity before or after departure to settle any wage claims and other entitlements due to them and any pending liabilities.

This is particularly important in situations where migrant workers fall into irregular situations for reasons beyond their control, such as redundancy before the expected end of their contract, or failure of the employer to fulfill the necessary immigration formalities, in which the worker may have claims arising from the past or promised employment.[30]

Freedom from Forced Labor, Equal Renumeration, Labor, and Health-Related Rights

Irregular migration can place migrants in perilous situations and make them susceptible to various forms of exploitation, forced labor, and human trafficking. The lack of documentation is often a significant factor in coercion and potential forced labor and trafficking, with the threat of exposure and deportation. The ILO Protocol of 2014 to the Forced Labor Convention, 1930, acknowledges in its Preamble the heightened risk of forced labor among migrants. Consequently, preventive measures against forced labor should encompass protecting individuals, particularly migrant workers, from potential abusive and fraudulent practices during the recruitment and placement process.

Article 11 of the ICMW compels states parties to take decisive action to eliminate all forms of forced or compulsory labor among migrant workers. This includes eradicating harmful practices such as debt bondage, passport confiscation, and unlawful confinement. States parties are required to prevent employers and recruiters from seizing or destroying migrant workers' travel or identity documents.[31] States parties should provide training to law enforcement personnel and guarantee that occupations predominantly filled by migrant workers, particularly female migrant workers, such as domestic work and certain forms of entertainment, are safeguarded by labor laws and are subject to regular inspections.[32]

Measures for vulnerable groups such as children and women should be taken to mitigate the adverse impacts on those. According to Article 25(1)(b) of the ICMW, laws and regulations governing the minimum employment age apply equally to migrant children. The minimum age should not be below 15 years, consistent with Article 2 of ILO Convention No. 138 (1973) concerning Minimum Age for Admission to Employment. Furthermore, in compliance with Article 11 of the Convention, states parties are mandated to shield child migrant workers from any form of slavery, prostitution, or work that could endanger their education, safety, morals, and health, such as prolonged working hours. States parties must safeguard child migrant workers from violence and guarantee their rights to education, leisure, and occupational health.[33]

The obligation to respect and ensure the rights of migrants who are victims of forced labor and are in an irregular situation involves several measures. These include: 1) taking steps to ensure that victims of forced labor are not penalized for their irregular migration status; 2) raising awareness and prevention through training, organizing workers, and providing them with the necessary assistance to assert their rights and report abuses; and 3) implementing protective measures, such as a period for reflection and recovery, short- or long-term residence permits, and facilitating repatriation if desired.[34] In practice, states most commonly provide repatriation assistance, followed by short- or long-term residence permits as seen in Bosnia-Herzegovina, Canada, and Italy; work authorization for freed migrants; and periods for recovery and reflection (to decide on repatriation).[35]

The ICMW stipulates that migrant workers, regardless of their status, are entitled to the same treatment as nationals in terms of remuneration and other work conditions and employment terms.[36] While states parties may deny access to their labor markets to migrant workers who lack work permits, once an employment relationship has been established, all migrant workers, including those in an irregular situation, have the right to equal work conditions and employment terms.[37] Noted that the work conditions and employment terms outlined under Article 25 are not exhaustive. The principle of equal treatment also applies to any other aspect that is considered a work condition or employment term according to national law and practice, such as maternity protection.

The ICMW upholds the principle of equal treatment in terms of compensation and other working conditions between nationals and migrants, regardless of their immigration status. This right also applies to private employment contracts. It emphasizes that employers cannot be excused from any legal or contractual obligations, nor can their obligations be limited in any way due to any irregularity in the migrant workers' stay or employment.[38] States are obligated to impose proportionate penalties on employers who violate the principle of equal treatment in private employment contracts with irregular migrant workers and ensure that these migrant workers have access to labor courts or other legal remedies when their rights are violated, without fear of deportation.[39] According to the ICMW Committee, to effectively implement this provision, a national monitoring system for workplaces should be established, particularly in industries known to employ irregular migrant workers.[40]

Empowering migrant workers in an irregular situation is one of the most effective strategies for safeguarding their rights. The rights to freedom of association and collective bargaining are essential tools for enhancing working conditions and pay, and all migrant workers ought to be able to exercise their trade union rights without fearing harassment. However, migrant workers in an irregular situation are often legally or practically prohibited from joining or forming trade unions, barred from holding leadership positions in trade unions, or lack protection against discrimination based on their trade union activities.[41] Women migrant workers are the least represented and frequently face additional obstacles to organizing due to the industries in which they work.[42]

In line with the Freedom of Association and Protection of the Right to Organize Convention, 1948 (No. 87) and the Right to Organize and Collective Bargaining Convention, 1949 (No. 98), states must guarantee, both legally and practically, that migrant workers in irregular situations have the right to organize and bargain collectively without facing any form of discrimination. It is crucial to eliminate barriers to unionization, such as the fear of retaliation that some workers on temporary contracts, including migrant workers, may have about joining a union. Trade unions may be an avenue to advocate for the labor rights of irregular migrant workers, such as providing information and services to migrant workers, irrespective of their status, including information on undocumented workers' rights in the union's education programs and incorporating undocumented workers' rights into the union's collective bargaining agenda to ensure equal treatment and prevent exploitative practices.[43]

In terms of social security, Article 27 of the ICMW emphasizes that migrant workers' access to social security benefits is subject to existing bilateral and multilateral treaties. The relevant authorities of the migrant worker's home country and the country of employment can collaborate at any time to establish the necessary arrangements for determining the application procedures for these benefits. As recommended in the ILO Multilateral Framework on Labor Migration, nations should consider entering into bilateral, regional, or multilateral agreements to ensure that irregular migrant workers have access to social security coverage, benefits, and portable social security entitlements. However, this provision should not be interpreted as denying migrant workers access to benefits they would otherwise be entitled to under the applicable legislation of the country of employment, solely based on the absence of a reciprocity agreement between that country and their home country.[44]

Article 9(1) of ILO Convention No. 143 ensures that irregular migrant workers are treated equally in terms of rights stemming from previous employment, particularly regarding social security and other benefits. However, irregular migrants are only entitled to a specific right if the legislation of the destination country grants such a right to legally employed migrants. As a result, social security rights should typically arise equally from all past employment, whether authorized or unauthorized. Nonetheless, this poses significant practical challenges, especially when it comes to accessing benefits, which often require the person to legally reside in the national territory.[45] If the migrant worker leaves the national territory, mechanisms should be in place to allow for acquired rights and rights in the process of acquisition to follow them upon their return to their country of origin. This highlights the importance and value of establishing bilateral or multilateral social security agreements that can address such situations. In the absence of such an agreement, the Migrant Workers Recommendation, 1975 (No. 151) advocates for the reimbursement of any social security contributions that have not and will not result in rights under national laws or regulations or international arrangements. However, where social security contributions do not permit entitlement to benefits, every effort should be made to conclude bilateral or multilateral agreements to protect the rights of migrants.

Article 28 of the ICMW stipulates that migrant workers and their family members have the right to receive any medical care urgently needed to preserve their life or prevent irreversible damage to their health, on an equal footing with nationals. However, when read in conjunction with other international human rights instruments, Article 28 may impose broader obligations on states parties. Article 12 of the ICESCR guarantees the right to the highest attainable standard of health for all individuals. Therefore, states parties are obligated to ensure that all individuals, regardless of their migration status, have effective access to at least a minimum level of health care on a non-discriminatory basis. The Committee on Economic, Social and Cultural Rights interprets this to include primary health care, as well as preventive, curative, and palliative health services. The Committee on the Rights of the Child asserts that every migrant child is entitled to the same health care as nationals under Article 24 of the Convention on the Rights of the Child. Consequently, states parties must ensure, among other things, that all migrant workers and their families have access to essential medicines and that migrant children are immunized against major infectious diseases. They must also ensure that migrant women have access to appropriate prenatal and postnatal health care, safe reproductive health services, and emergency obstetric care.

AGREEMENTS AND MECHANISMS FOR IRREGULAR MIGRANT WORKERS' RIGHTS IN ASIA

The escalating intricacy of cross-border labor migration underscores the necessity for global collaboration in managing migration procedures and safeguarding migrant workers' rights. This collaboration can manifest in various forms, from multilateral and regional frameworks to national arrangements. Generally, those agreements are favored over bilateral ones due to the potential power imbalance between the states involved in the latter.[46] However, achieving multilateral agreements can be challenging, making bilateral labor agreements (BLA) and memoranda of understanding (MoU) often the only viable options for source countries. Since 2000, Asia has seen a surge in BLAs and MoUs concerning labor migration. Those agreements aim to improve the governance of labor migration, ensure access to foreign labor markets, and protect migrant workers, although their effectiveness remain questionable.[47]

BLAs and MoUs are common mechanisms for regulating interstate labor migration in Asia.[48] The ILO has long recognized the importance of BLAs in managing labor migration and protecting migrant workers. The ILO Migration for Employment Convention No. 97 (1949) encourages countries to establish BLAs when necessary to regulate migration for employment, especially when the number of migrants is large. The accompanying ILO Recommendation (No. 86) includes a model agreement that has served as a guide for developing BLAs worldwide. The 1990 ICMW also recognizes the value of BLAs in protecting the rights of irregular migrant workers. In a similar vein, the ILO Tripartite Technical Meeting of November 2013 called on the ILO to provide guidance to governments and social partners on developing, negotiating, and implementing BLAs.[49] However, it is crucial to understand that these agreements necessitate specific administrative measures to ensure their seamless execution. This includes the recruitment, examination, and certification of program applicants, as well as the prompt exchange and sharing of information between the two countries. Despite their widespread use, the efficacy of these agreements can be hindered by inadequate monitoring and enforcement mechanisms. They often prioritize recruitment procedures over the welfare and protection of workers.

BLAs and MoUs, which can be formal and binding or less formal and more flexible, are designed to address common concerns related to labor migration.[50] Several Asian countries have contracted BLAs. For instance, the Republic of Korea has MoUs with several countries including Bangladesh, Cambodia, China, Indonesia, Kyrgyzstan, Myanmar, Mongolia, Nepal, Pakistan, Philippines, Thailand, Timor-Leste, Uzbekistan, Vietnam, and Sri Lanka for the hiring of foreign workers under its Employment Permit System.[51] Malaysia and Thailand also have MoUs with various countries to regulate recruitment processes and procedures. The country of origin with the most bilateral agreements is the Philippines with 13–12 labor-receiving countries and one labor-sending country, Indonesia.

Contents of BLAs and MoUs vary dependending on the needs and capacity of the contracting states. Normally, these agreements lay out requirements for visas and work permits that migrant workers need to obtain in order to work in the host country; employment conditions such as wages, working hours, and working conditions for migrant workers; social security; occupational safety and health; and return and re-admission. Coordination mechanisms are also established for information sharing and urgent response. For instance, the 1997 BLA between the Philippines and Qatar regulates the employment of Filippo migrant workers in Qatar. The Philippines is responsible for vetting workers and providing them with information about life in Qatar before they travel. Qatari employers must first request for Philippine workers through the Qatari government. Unless the workers breach their contract, the cost of travel is borne by the employers. Employers are required to provide written contracts, with copies to be given to the governments. Any disputes between workers and employers will be resolved by the Qatari government. A joint committee is established to oversee the implementation of the agreement. The MoU between South Korea and Nepal in 2007 places substantial responsibilities on both governments' agencies. The Nepalese government is tasked with screening and assisting workers, while the Korean government is responsible for monitoring them upon arrival. Workers are required to pass a Korean language test, as well as medical and criminal record checks. The governments have agreed to engage in various forms of cooperation, including sharing information through computerized systems. Korea retains the right to decrease the number of permits if the number of Nepalese workers who stay in Korea illegally surpasses a specified percentage.

Southeast Asian countries have been a major sending source of migrant workers. The Association of Southeast Asian Nations (ASEAN) has adopted several agreements and mechanisms to address the issue of irregular migration. These agreements and mechanisms aim to protect the rights of irregular migrant workers, promote labor mobility, and combat human trafficking. The ASEAN Declaration on the Protection and Promotion of the Rights of Migrant Workers (1999) commits ASEAN member states to protect the rights of all migrant workers, including irregular migrants. It outlines various principles that should guide the treatment of migrant workers, including the right to non-discrimination, the right to freedom of movement, the right to work, and the right to protection from exploitation and abuse. The Bangkok Declaration on Irregular Migration (1999) complements the ASEAN Declaration. It focuses on the specific challenges of irregular migration and outlines a regional framework for managing irregular migration, promotes humane and orderly migration, and calls for cooperation between countries of origin and of destination to address the root causes of irregular migration. In 2017, ASEAN issued the Consensus on the Protection and Promotion of the Rights of Migrant Workers, which builds on the 1999 ASEAN Declaration with greater detailed guidance on how to protect the rights of migrant workers, including irregular migrants. The Consensus also includes a commitment to develop a regional instrument on the protection and promotion of the rights of migrant workers. In 2023, in the aftermath of the COVID-19 pandemic, ASEAN adopted Guidelines on Protection of Migrant Workers and Family

Members in Crisis Situations to call for the protection of migrant workers in conflict or crisis situations within and outside ASEAN.

In addition, ASEAN has established a variety of mechanisms for the promotion of migrant workers' rights. For example, the ASEAN Senior Officials Meeting on Labor, a forum for ASEAN member states to discuss labor migration issues, meets twice a year and is responsible for developing and implementing ASEAN labor migration policies. The ASEAN Forum on Migrant Labor (AFML) is an annual event that brings together governments, workers' and employers' organizations, and civil society stakeholders to discuss key issues affecting migrant workers in Southeast Asia. The forum serves as a platform for sharing best practices, exchanging ideas, and developing recommendations to improve the protection of migrant workers' rights. It also provides an opportunity for stakeholders to share their experiences in implementing AFML recommendations and in developing the draft ASEAN Instrument on the Protection and Promotion of the Rights of Migrant Workers.

CHALLENGES IN THE IMPLEMENTATION OF AGREEMENTS AND MECHANISMS FOR IRREGULAR MIGRANT WORKERS' RIGHTS

Safeguarding the rights of migrant workers is a multifaceted issue that involves 'numerous parties, including governments, employers, and labor unions, and presents a range of legal and ethical dilemmas. There is an increasing acknowledgment of the need to protect the rights of migrant workers, as evidenced by various international instruments. However, a substantial disparity exists between legislation and actual practice. A multitude of migrant workers are still deprived of their fundamental rights due to factors such as ineffective enforcement mechanisms, the vulnerability of migrant workers, and some governments' hesitance to safeguard their rights. Despite these obstacles, there is a burgeoning movement advocating for the promotion and protection of migrant workers' rights, spearheaded by diverse stakeholders, including the migrant workers themselves, labor unions, human rights organizations, and governments. Economic migration has surged both within and across regions, typically from less affluent states and regions toward more prosperous ones. However, not all migrants are received warmly. Immigration policies and laws restrict the admission of migrants, which are considered undesirable. These individuals have been labeled as economic migrants and, over time, have come to be known as illegal migrants or immigrants.

Weak Commitments and Enforcement of International Labor Standards

The 1990 ICMW is a comprehensive international treaty that aims to protect the rights of all migrant workers, regardless of their status or nationality. However, despite its importance, the ICMW has faced a number of obstacles to its implementation. One of which is the low number of ratifications. As of 2023, only 57 states have ratified the Convention, which means that it is not binding on a majority of countries in the world.[52] Notably, few major host states are signatories to the ICMW.

Frail political will and the populist concern in relation to the domestic electorates are the main drivers for the restrictive approach to the ICMW.[53] Traditionally, the attainment of rights has been tightly linked to citizenship or, at the very least, to a robust membership in the political community. The ICMW, by extending rights to all foreigners, including those in an undocumented situation, questions the privileges associated with citizenship and blurs the distinction between members and non-members of the community. For example, Mauritius's diverse ethnic composition and constitutional structure make it challenging to ratify the ICMW. The country's constitution divides the population into distinct communities, and ratifying the ICMW could alter this demographic balance, potentially requiring a constitutional review. As a result, Mauritian politicians have been cautious in their approach to maintaining ethnic harmony.

In addition, the economic consequences of labor migration necessitate a careful cost-benefit analysis before ratifying the ICMW. The ICMW's potential impact on labor costs, stemming from increased protections for migrant workers, may deter states from adopting the treaty. There may be financial and administrative burdens associated with ratifying and implementing the ICMW, including expenditures related to law enforcement, due process, official training, and public education.[54]

Legal barriers are also a factor in considering ratification of the ICMW, whose provisions often clash with existing domestic laws in some nations. Even in Western constitutionalist jurisdictions, the ICMW may necessitate substantial legislative changes. In Canada, ratifying the ICMW would require a reevaluation of the government's legal and institutional framework for employing low-skilled foreign workers.[55] Similarly, Japanese authorities have cited conflicts between the ICMW and domestic laws and the constitution as reasons for their reluctance to ratify the Convention.[56] In the United States, ratifying the ICMW would also have significant legal repercussions. While national laws and the US Constitution already provide some protections for migrant workers and their families, discrepancies exist regarding undocumented migrants and the rights of migrant workers to hold public jobs, receive social security benefits, and enjoy immigration and civil rights.[57]

Lack of Comprehensive Data on Irregular Migration

Irregular migration presents an intricate challenge, and data on irregular migration and irregular migrants often prove insufficient. The majority of official data systems fail to adequately capture either the number or the circumstances of migrants, and many international migration datasets do not accurately account for irregular migrants. Some data are available on those irregular migrants who encounter state intervention, such as arrests at border control points, numbers in immigration detention, and return figures. However, this information rarely provides an accurate representation of the total irregular migrant population. Irregular migrants are seldom included in population censuses, which remain the primary statistical source of information about migrant populations.

The Committee on the Rights of the Child has highlighted the critical need for comprehensive data on migrant children to effectively formulate, implement, and monitor public policies that safeguard their economic and social rights. The lack of reliable data, particularly on children in irregular migration situations, poses significant challenges. The Committee urges all responsible authorities to prioritize addressing the scarcity of national statistics and estimates on irregular migrants, with a particular focus on irregular migrant children. This entails: (1) enhancing the collection of disaggregated data while implementing safeguards to prevent data misuse; (2) ensuring that migration-affected households are included in local statistical and data systems, as well as in nationally representative surveys of living standards, expenditure, and labor force; and (3) establishing a shared responsibility for monitoring the situation of migrant children among all involved countries, including countries of origin, transit, and destination. Furthermore, the Committee on the ICMW has expressed its worry about the lack of data concerning the situations of irregular migrants, including aspects such as school enrollment. This data deficiency could prevent states from effectively assessing and addressing the circumstances of migrant children.[58] Hence, states parties are strongly encouraged to collect data for in-depth research and effective enforcement purposes.

REFERENCES

Adam S Chilton and Eric A Posner, "Why Countries Sign Bilateral Labor Agreements" (2018) 47 *Journal of Legal Studies* S45.

Antonio Martín Artiles, “Towards a Fair Deal for Migrant Workers in the Global Economy” (2008), 14, *Transfer: European Review of Labour and Research* 706.

Arthur C Helton, “The New Convention from the Perspective of a Country of Employment: The U.S. Case” (1991) 25 *International Migration Review* 848.

“Bilateral Agreements and Regional Cooperation” (18 October 2013) <http://www.ilo.org/asia/areas/labour-migration/WCMS_226300/lang--en/index.htm>.

Bureau international du travail (ed.), *ILO Global Estimates on International Migrant Workers: Results and Methodology* (3rd ed., International labour organization, 2021).

Committee on Economic, Social and Cultural Rights, “General Comment No. 20 on Non-Discrimination in Economic, Social and Cultural Rights” (2009).

“Conclusions of Tripartite Technical Meeting on Labour Migration” <https://www.ilo.org/wcmsp5/groups/public/---ed_protect/---protrav/---migrant/documents/meetingdocument/wcms_232352.pdf>.

“Irregular Migrant” <https://home-affairs.ec.europa.eu/networks/european-migration-network-emn/emn-asylum-and-migration-glossary/glossary/irregular-migrant_en>.

European Parliament. Directorate General for External Policies of the Union, *Current Challenges in the Implementation of the UN International Convention on the Protection of the Rights of All Migrant Workers and Members of Their Families* (Publications Office, 2013) <https://data.europa.eu/doi/10.2861/31224>.

European Trade Union Confederation and others, “Trade Unions. Organising and Promoting Undocumented Migrant Workers Rights” (2017) <http://picum.org/wp-content/ uploads/2017/12/Trade_Union_Participation_EN_2017.pdf>.

François Crépeau and Maja Vezmar, “Words Matter: ‘Illegal,’ ‘Irregular,’ ‘Unauthorized,’ ‘Undocumented’” <https://www.knomad.org/sites/default/files/2021-07/Policy%20Brief%2015%20%20-%20Words%20matter%20illegal%20irregular%20unauthorized%20undocumented%20-%20June%202021.pdf>.

“How COVID-19 Has Affected International Labour Migration” (*World Economic Forum*, 31 May 2021) <https://www.weforum.org/agenda/2021/05/how-covid-19-has-affected-international-labour-migration-and-the-path-to-enduring-reintegration/>.

International Labor Organization, “Ending Forced Labour by 2030: A Review of Policies and Programmes” (2018) <https://www.ilo.org/wcmsp5/groups/public/---ed_norm/---ipec/documents/publication/wcms_653986.pdf>.

International Labor Organization, “Protecting the Rights of Migrant Workers in Irregular Situations and Addressing Irregular Labour Migration: A Compendium” (International Labor Organization, 2022) <https://www.ilo.org/wcmsp5/groups/public/---ed_protect/---protrav/---migrant/documents/publication/wcms_832915.pdf>.

International Labor Organization, “Temporary Labour Migration: Two Studies on Workers’ Perspectives and Actions” (2021) <https://www.ilo.org/wcmsp5/groups/public/---ed_protect/---protrav/--migrant/documents/publication/wcms_816182.pdf>.

"International Labour Office, Towards a Fair Deal for Migrant Workers in the Global Economy" <https://www.ilo.org/public/libdoc/ilo/2004/104B09_110_engl.pdf>.

Irena Omelaniuk (ed.), "Irregular Migration: Causes, Patterns, and Strategies," Global Perspectives on Migration and Development (Springer, Dordrecht, 2012) <https: // doi .org /10 .1007 /978 -94 -007 -4110 -2>.

Laurie Berg, "At the Border and Between the Cracks: The Precarious Position of Irregular Migrant Workers Under International Human Rights Law" (2007) 8 *Melbourne Journal of International Law*, 16–18.

"Migrant Worker Numbers Rise by Five Million: ILO | UN News" (30 June 2021) <https://news.un.org/en/story/2021/06/1095082>.

"Migrant Workers Still at Great Risk despite Key Role in Global Economy | UN News" (16 December 2021) <https://news.un.org/en/story/2021/12/1108082>.

"Migration in an Interconnected World: New Directions for Action" <https://www .iom.int/sites/g/files/tmzbdl486/files/jahia/webdav/site/myjahiasite/shared/shared/ mainsite/policy_and_research/gcim/GCIM_Report_Complete.pdf>.

MWC Committee, "General Comment No. 2 on the Rights of Migrant Workers in an Irregular Situation and Members of Their Families" (2013), 6.

Nicola Piper, "Obstacles to, and Opportunities for, Ratification of the ICRMW in Asia," in Antoine Pecoud, Paul de Guchteneire, and Ryszard Cholewinski (eds.),

Migration and Human Rights: The United Nations Convention on Migrant Workers' Rights (Cambridge University Press 2009) <https://www.cambridge.org/core/ books/migration-and-human-rights/obstacles-to-and-opportunities-for-ratification -of-the-icrmw-in-asia/8F0F22E7CE7318C73BD1896B98323163>.

"OECD International Migration Outlook 2020: What Is the Impact of the COVID-19 Pandemic on Migrants and Their Children? | European Website on Integration" <https://ec.europa.eu/migrant-integration/library-document/oecd-international -migration-outlook-2020-what-impact-covid-19-pandemic-migrants_en>.

P. Douglas, M. Cetron, and P. Spiegel, "Definitions Matter: Migrants, Immigrants, Asylum Seekers and Refugees" (2019), 26, *Journal of Travel Medicine* taz005.

Piyasiri Wickramasekara, "Assessment Guide for Bilateral Agreements and Memoranda of Understanding on Labour Migration, with a Special Focus on Bangladesh" (ILO Country Office for Bangladesh, 2018) 1 <https://www.ilo.org /wcmsp5/groups/public/---asia/---ro-bangkok/---ilo-dhaka/documents/publication/ wcms_683744.pdf>.

Piyasiri Wickramasekara, "Labour Migration in South Asia: A Review of Issues, Policies and Practices, International Migration Paper No. 108" (International Labour Office, 2015) <http://www.ilo.org/public/english/protection/migrant/ download/imp/imp108.pdf>.

Steven A. Altman and Caroline R. Bastian, "The State of Globalization in 2021" [2021] *Harvard Business Review* <https://hbr.org/2021/03/the-state-of -globalization-in-2021>.

"The Bangkok Declaration on Irregular Migration" <https://www.iom.int/sites/g/files /tmzbdl486/files/jahia/webdav/site/myjahiasite/shared/shared/mainsite/policy_and _research/rcp/APC/BANGKOK_DECLARATION.pdf>.

"The Need for a Rights-Based Approach to Migration in the Age of Globalization," in Cholewinski R., Pécoud A., and de Guchteneire P. (eds.), *Migration and Human Rights: The United Nations Convention on Migrant Workers' Rights* (Cambridge University Press, New York, 2009).

"The State of Globalization in 2023" <https://hbr.org/2023/07/the-state-of-globalization-in-2023>.

Victor Piché, Eugénie Depatie-Pelletier and Dina Epale, "Obstacles to Ratification of the ICRMW in Canada," in Antoine Pecoud, Paul de Guchteneire, and Ryszard Cholewinski (eds.), Migration and Human Rights: The United Nations Convention on Migrant Workers' Rights (Cambridge University Press, New York, 2009) <https://www..cambridge.org/core/books/migration-and-human-rights/obstacles-to-ratification-of-the-icrmw-in-canada/D37DF890E6F7BE1963746ACBEB34E775>.

"Why 'Undocumented' Or 'Irregular'?" <https://www.unhcr.org/cy/wp-content/uploads/sites/41/2018/09/TerminologyLeaflet_EN_PICUM.pdf>.

NOTES

1. "Migrant Workers Still at Great Risk despite Key Role in Global Economy | UN News" (16 December 2021) <https://news.un.org/en/story/2021/12/1108082> accessed 7 November 2023.

2. Steven A. Altman and Caroline R. Bastian, "The State of Globalization in 2021" [2021] *Harvard Business Review* <https://hbr.org/2021/03/the-state-of-globalization-in-2021> accessed 7 November 2023.

3. "The State of Globalization in 2023" <https://hbr.org/2023/07/the-state-of-globalization-in-2023> accessed 7 November 2023.

4. Altman and Bastian (n 2).

5. Bureau international du travail (ed.), *ILO Global Estimates on International Migrant Workers: Results and Methodology* (3rd ed., International Labour Organization, 2021); "Migrant Worker Numbers Rise by Five Million: ILO | UN News" (30 June 2021) <https://news.un.org/en/story/2021/06/1095082> accessed 7 November 2023.

6. Bureau international du travail (n 5).

7. "OECD International Migration Outlook 2020: What Is the Impact of the COVID-19 Pandemic on Migrants and Their Children? | European Website on Integration" <https://ec.europa.eu/migrant-integration/library-document/oecd-international-migration-outlook-2020-what-impact-covid-19-pandemic-migrants_en> accessed 7 November 2023.

8. "How COVID-19 Has Affected International Labour Migration" (*World Economic Forum*, 31 May 2021) <https://www.weforum.org/agenda/2021/05/how-covid-19-has-affected-international-labour-migration-and-the-path-to-enduring-reintegration/> accessed 7 November 2023.

9. "Migrant Workers Still at Great Risk despite Key Role in Global Economy | UN News" (n 1).

10. "Irregular Migrant" <https://home-affairs.ec.europa.eu/networks/european-migration-network-emn/emn-asylum-and-migration-glossary/glossary/irregular-migrant_en> accessed 7 November 2023; François Crépeau and Maja Vezmar, "Words Matter: 'Illegal,' 'Irregular,' 'Unauthorized,' 'Undocumented'" <https://www.knomad.org/sites/default/files/2021-07/Policy%20Brief%2015%20%20-%20Words%20matter%20illegal%20irregular%20unauthorized%20undocumented%20-%20June%202021.pdf> accessed 7 November 2023.

11. "Why 'Undocumented' Or 'Irregular'?" <https://www.unhcr.org/cy/wp-content/uploads/sites/41/2018/09/TerminologyLeaflet_EN_PICUM.pdf> accessed 7 November 2023.

12. "International Labour Office, Towards a Fair Deal for Migrant Workers in the Global Economy" <https://www.ilo.org/public/libdoc/ilo/2004/104B09_110_engl.pdf> accessed 8 November 2023.

13. "The Bangkok Declaration on Irregular Migration" <https://www.iom.int/sites/g/files/tmzbdl486/files/jahia/webdav/site/myjahiasite/shared/shared/mainsite/policy_and_research/rcp/APC/BANGKOK_DECLARATION.pdf> accessed 7 November 2023.

14. "Migration in an Interconnected World: New Directions for Action" <https://www.iom.int/sites/g/files/tmzbdl486/files/jahia/webdav/site/myjahiasite/shared/shared/mainsite/policy_and_research/gcim/GCIM_Report_Complete.pdf> accessed 7 November 2023.

15. Antonio Martín Artiles, "Towards a Fair Deal for Migrant Workers in the Global Economy" (2008) 14 *Transfer: European Review of Labour and Research* 706.

16. P. Douglas, M. Cetron, and P. Spiegel, "Definitions Matter: Migrants, Immigrants, Asylum Seekers and Refugees" (2019) 26 *Journal of Travel Medicine* taz005.

17. Irena Omelaniuk (ed.), "Irregular Migration: Causes, Patterns, and Strategies," *Global Perspectives on Migration and Development* (Springer Dordrecht, 2012) <https://doi.org/10.1007/978-94-007-4110-2> accessed 8 November 2023; United Nations (ed.), *The Economic, Social and Cultural Rights of Migrants in an Irregular Situation* (United Nations, 2014).

18. International Labor Organization, "Protecting the Rights of Migrant Workers in Irregular Situations and Addressing Irregular Labour Migration: A Compendium" (International Labor Organization, 2022) <https://www.ilo.org/wcmsp5/groups/public/---ed_protect/---protrav/---migrant/documents/publication/wcms_832915.pdf> accessed 8 November 2023.

19. MWC Committee, "General Comment No. 2 on the Rights of Migrant Workers in an Irregular Situation and Members of Their Families" (2013), 6.

20. Laurie Berg, "At the Border and Between the Cracks: The Precarious Position of Irregular Migrant Workers Under International Human Rights Law" (2007) 8 *Melbourne Journal of International Law* 16–18.

21. It includes Conventions No. 29 (1930) concerning Forced Labour; No. 105 (1957) concerning the Abolition of Forced Labour; No. 138 (1973) concerning Minimum Age for Admission to Employment; No. 182 (1999) concerning the Prohibition and Immediate Action for the Elimination of the Worst Forms of Child Labour; No. 87 (1948) concerning the Freedom of Association and Protection of the Right to

Organize; No. 98 (1949) concerning the Right to Organize and Collective Bargaining; No. 100 (1951) concerning Equal Remuneration; and No. 111 (1958) concerning Discrimination (Employment and Occupation).

22. Committee on Economic, Social and Cultural Rights, "General Comment No. 20 on Non-Discrimination in Economic, Social and Cultural Rights" (2009).

23. Human Rights Committee, "General Comment No. 18 on Non-Discrimination" (1989).

24. MWC Committee, "General Comment No. 1 on Migrant Domestic Workers" (n 19) 7–8.

25. Ibid., 9.

26. Article 22(8) MWC; Article 9(3) ILO Convention No. 143.

27. MWC Committee, "General Comment No. 1 on Migrant Domestic Workers" (n 19) 16–17.

28. Article 22(4) MWC; ILO Recommendation No. 151.

29. Article 22(3) MWC.

30. Article 9(1) ILO Convention No. 143.

31. Article 21 MWC.

32. MWC Committee, "General Comment No. 1 on Migrant Domestic Workers" (n 19).

33. Ibid.

34. International Labor Organization, "Protecting the Rights of Migrant Workers in Irregular Situations and Addressing Irregular Labour Migration: A Compendium" (n 18) 17.

35. International Labor Organization, "Ending Forced Labour by 2030: A Review of Policies and Programmes" (2018) <https://www.ilo.org/wcmsp5/groups/public/---ed_norm/---ipec/documents/publication/wcms_653986.pdf>.

36. Article 25(1) MWC.

37. ILO Convention No. 111 (1958) concerning Discrimination (Employment and Occupation).

38. Article 25(3) MWC.

39. Article 83 MWC.

40. MWC Committee, "General Comment No. 2 on the Rights of Migrant Workers in an Irregular Situation and Members of Their Families" (2013) 17.

41. International Labor Organization, "Protecting the Rights of Migrant Workers in Irregular Situations and Addressing Irregular Labour Migration: A Compendium" (n 18) 19.

42. International Labor Organization, "Temporary Labour Migration: Two Studies on Workers" Perspectives and Actions" (2021) <https://www.ilo.org/wcmsp5/groups/public/---ed_protect/---protrav/--migrant/documents/publication/wcms_816182.pdf>.

43. European Trade Union Confederation and others, "Trade Unions. Organising and Promoting Undocumented Migrant Workers Rights" (2017) <http://picum.org/wp-content/ uploads/2017/12/Trade_Union_Participation_EN_2017.pdf>.

44. See, e.g., *Koua Poirrez v. France*, Application No. 40892/98 (30 December 2003).

45. International Labor Organization, "Protecting the Rights of Migrant Workers in Irregular Situations and Addressing Irregular Labour Migration: A Compendium" (n 18) 25.

46. Piyasiri Wickramasekara, "Assessment Guide for Bilateral Agreements and Memoranda of Understanding on Labour Migration, with a Special Focus on Bangladesh" (ILO Country Office for Bangladesh, 2018) 1 <https://www.ilo.org /wcmsp5/groups/public/---asia/---ro-bangkok/---ilo-dhaka/documents/publication/ wcms_683744.pdf>.

47. Piyasiri Wickramasekara, "Labour Migration in South Asia: A Review of Issues, Policies and Practices, International Migration Paper No. 108" (International Labour Office, 2015) <http://www.ilo.org/public/english/protection/migrant/ download/imp/imp108.pdf>.

48. "Bilateral Agreements and Regional Cooperation" (18 October 2013) <http: //www.ilo.org/asia/areas/labour-migration/WCMS_226300/lang--en/index.htm> accessed 9 November 2023.

49. "Conclusions of Tripartite Technical Meeting on Labour Migration" <https: //www.ilo.org/wcmsp5/groups/public/---ed_protect/---protrav/---migrant/documents/ meetingdocument/wcms_232352.pdf> accessed 9 November 2023.

50. Adam S Chilton and Eric A Posner, "Why Countries Sign Bilateral Labor Agreements" (2018) 47 *Journal of Legal Studies* S45.

51. "Bilateral Agreements and Regional Cooperation" (n 48).

52. "- OHCHR Dashboard" <https://indicators.ohchr.org/> accessed 9 November 2023.

53. "The Need for a Rights-Based Approach to Migration in the Age of Globalization," in Cholewinski R., Pécoud A., and de Guchteneire P., *Migration and Human Rights: The United Nations Convention on Migrant Workers' Rights* (Cambridge University Press, New York, 2009)

54. European Parliament. Directorate General for External Policies of the Union., *Current Challenges in the Implementation of the UN International Convention on the Protection of the Rights of All Migrant Workers and Members of Their Families* (Publications Office, 2013) <https://data.europa.eu/doi/10.2861/31224> accessed 9 November 2023.

55. Victor Piché, Eugénie Depatie-Pelletier, and Dina Epale, "Obstacles to Ratification of the ICRMW in Canada," in Antoine Pecoud, Paul de Guchteneire, and Ryszard Cholewinski (eds), *Migration and Human Rights: The United Nations Convention on Migrant Workers' Rights* (Cambridge University Press, New York, 2009) <https://www.cambridge.org/core/books/migration-and-human-rights/obstacles-to -ratification-of-the-icrmw-in-canada/D37DF890E6F7BE1963746ACBEB34E775> accessed 9 November 2023.

56. Nicola Piper, "Obstacles to, and Opportunities for, Ratification of the ICRMW in Asia" in Antoine Pecoud, Paul de Guchteneire, and Ryszard Cholewinski (eds.), Migration and Human Rights: The United Nations Convention on Migrant Workers" Rights (Cambridge University Press, New York, 2009) <https://www.cambridge.org/core/ books/migration-and-human-rights/obstacles-to-and-opportunities-for-ratifica-

tion-of-the-icrmw-in-asia/8F0F22E7CE7318C73BD1896B98323163> accessed 9 November 2023.

57. Arthur C. Helton, "The New Convention from the Perspective of a Country of Employment: The U.S. Case" (1991) 25 *International Migration Review* 848.

58. ICMW Committee, "MWC/C/DZA/CO/1."

PART II

Laws of Some Asian Origin Countries on the Rights of Migrant Workers

Globalization, together with the promotion of the free flow of capital, finance, technology, also boosts the liberalization of the flow of labor on a global scale. The rising rates of unemployment and poverty have induced workers in developing countries to look elsewhere for work. The flow of international migrant workers is indicative of three main trends as follows: (i) from developing countries to other developing countries; (ii) from developing countries to developed countries; (iii) from developed countries to other developed countries.

Thus, for the developing countries themselves, there are always two flows of migrant and immigrant workers. However, with developing countries in Asia under this study, the percentage of migrant workers is higher than that of immigrant workers. Therefore, the laws and policies of these countries also pay more attention to the rights of migrant workers.

As discussed in the previous part, the primary migrant workers studied in this book include legal migrant workers, illegal migrant workers, and vulnerable groups. Therefore, this part of the book will also look at the laws and policies of several developing countries in Asia related to these three groups of subjects.

The question here is, for each country, whether the policies and laws of that country have met to guarantee the rights of migrant workers. For the group of legal migrants, issues that need to be considered are: state management to ensure the workers' path for work abroad; prevention of fraud, human trafficking, illegally sending people abroad for work; protecting the interests of workers; organizing financial resources for them to borrow before leaving; providing loans to create jobs; helping to reintegrate migrants into the community upon return; maintaining a good relationship between workers and overseas employment recruitment and consulting agencies, and others. Additionally, the existing legal policies to protect the rights of illegal migrant workers are meager and inadequate. Therefore, it is necessary to learn from good practices to build an institutional framework to protect the interests of this group of workers.

In addition to analyzing policies and laws, this section will also give a general overview of implementing these regulations, thereby highlighting the challenges and difficulties encountered by countries to ensure the rights of migrant workers.

Chapter 6

Protecting the Rights of Migrant Workers in Vietnam

Assessing the Effectiveness of Laws and Associated Instruments

Nguyen Thi Thanh Hai

Migration for work or economic migration is a dominent and, arguably, growing trend in the international intergration process. For example, this is the case at a regional level in Association of Southeast Asian Nations (ASEAN) where the Master Plan on ASEAN Connectivity (MPAC) 2025 includes opportunity for migration within ASEAN that will promote competitiveness for the region, inclusiveness and a greater sense of community.[1] Migration has long been an important characteristic of labor markets in many countries but has taken on added significance with the globalization of the economy.[2] Migration is significant economically and socially for countries in terms of in-migration (immigration), out-migration (emigration), and internal migration (within country) with benefits and challenges to the domestic economy resulting from each of these flows of human mobility.

Vietnam is a country whose population ranks 15th in the world, 8th in Asia, and 3rd in ASEAN. Vietnam has a large workforce for whom there are significant opportunities for migration.[3] Vietnam is one of the largest suppliers of out-migrants with over 540,000 workers employed in more than 43 countries.[4] According to the Vietnam Migration Profile 2016, migrant workers account for about 3.1 percent of the population.[5] Each year, Vietnam deploys about 80,000 wokers to work overseas through formal, government-sponsored programs.[6] In addition, a very significant number of Vietnamese workers migrate to other countries without work permits or related documentation to seek work as illegal or undocumented migrants. Their number is not known.

The remittances of migrant workers are a key contributor to the Gross Domestic Product (GDP) and to the income of many families in Vietnam. Overseas migrant workers can have a positive impact on the economy. Vietnam is among the top 10 recipients of international remittances in the world.[7] Vietnam ranks 6th in Asia and 11th in the world as a recipient country of international remittances.[8] The annual remittances from migrant workers to Vietnam has reached about US$2 billion in recent years.[9] Because 90 percent of Vietnamese workers abroad are low-skilled with limited expertise, coming from rural areas with poor language capabilities,[10] they are at risk of human rights abuses or other forms of exploitation at all stages of their migration process. Vietnamese migrant workers, in particular undocumented workers, face many challenges, including social stigma and discrimination and are frequently exploited, physically abused, and otherwise mistreated,[11] or even become victims of debt bondage, forced labor, human smuggling, and trafficking. During their time working abroad, workers who are being exploited or abused often opt to keep silent rather than reporting or making formal complaints because of the fear of visa cancellation or of revoking permission to stay in the country.[12]

Despite these concerns, the current legal framework in Vietnam is not strong enough to protect migrant workers so as to ensure their effective access to legal protection during the recruitment process, while working abroad and after returning home. Vietnam has not ratified the International Convention on the Protection of the Rights of All Migrant Workers and Members of Their Families, which was agreed upon by the United Nations in 1990, and this limits the protection afforded to Vietnamese workers overseas, whether legally documented or illegal migrants. This chapter argues that, although there are certain legal protections in Vietnam, the legal framework and its implementation on protection of rights of migrant workers remain quite weak and there is a lack of protection for all migrant groups, in particular, undocumented workers.

THE LEGAL FRAMEWORK FOR ENSURING THE RIGHTS OF MIGRANT WORKERS

This section provides information about the core legal and institutional instruments and attendant arrangements that are in place which impact migrant workers from Vietnam.

The Development of Vietnam's Legal Framework on Migrant Workers

Commencing in the early 1980s, a policy was implemented to send workers and officials to work in countries in the former socialist bloc, namely the Soviet Union and Eastern European countries, the German Democratic Republic, Bulgaria, and Czechoslovakia (see, for example, Schwenkel, 2014; 2016;[13] and Iglicka, 2005[14]). The first legal document referencing this issue was the Government's Decision No. 46/CP, dated November 2,1980, regarding the sending of workers and officers for training to strenthen their capacity and to work for a period of time in other socialist countries. The main purpose of the policy of sending Vietnamese people to study and work abroad in this period was "to foster and improve skills, improve technical, professional and management skills, and work."[15] At the same time, the purpose of this policy was also to give workers a fixed period of time in the economic establishments of selected socialist countries in order to enhance and contribute to meeting the skills needs of Vietnam and help the host countries overcome, in part, their labor shortages. Furthermore, although not yet included in the provisions of the law, Vietnam also issued a number of guiding principles and documents in the form of decisions, directives, and decrees to regulate this mobility, including

- Decision of the Council of Ministers No. 263/HDBT dated July 24, 1984;
- Directive of the Council of Ministers No. 08/HDBT dated June 30, 1988;
- Decree of the Council of Ministers No. 370/HDBT dated September 20, 1991.

In addition to regulations on the state's management of Vietnamese workers relocating abroad for employment, these documents also initially set out regulations on workers' rights when working abroad, such as Decree No. 370/HDBT, the Decision of the Council of Ministers, dated September 20, 1991, which affirms that the employment of workers must ensure the rights of the workers, including "the right to request to be provided with complete and accurate information about employment, workplace, contract term, working conditions, meals, accommodation and rest, salary regime, bonus, social insurance and other necessary conditions."[16] Directive 41/CT-TW of the Politburo on the Export of Labour and Professionals, passed on September 22, 1998, continues this affirmation that labor export is an important long-term strategy, contributing to the country's economic growth and national reconstruction in the period of industrialization and modernization.[17]

On the basis of these political directives, the rights of Vietnamese workers to work abroad are officially protected in the Labour Code 1994 and continue to be recognized in later revised labor regulations, specifically the Codes of 1994, 2012, and 2019. The first provision prohibits sending people abroad to work illegally and requires that the sending of Vietnamese citizens abroad to work requires a permit from the Ministry of Labour, War Invalids and Social Affairs and relevant competent authorities. These requirements are recognized in Article 184 of the Labour Code 1994. Following that, the legal provisions on the protection of Vietnamese citizens working abroad continues to be recognized in many legal documents related to Vietnamese abroad in general, with specific consideration for the rights and needs of Vietnamese citizens opting to work overseas.

Based on the provisions of the 2013 Constitution on the state's obligation to protect the legitimate rights and interests of employees (Article 57 [2]) and fundamental human rights in Chapter 2, Vietnam has developed a policy and legal framework on the rights of migrant workers to be protected through the following groups of legal and policy documents:

- The Protection of Vietnamese people going to work abroad through the provisions of the existing labor law: The 2013 Constitution affirms the right to work, the right to fair and safe working conditions, enjoyment of fair wages, access to suitable rest periods and the right not to be discriminated against, forced, or exploited, as affirmed in Article 35 (1). This right is applicable to Vietnamese workers in all contexts including when working abroad. The rights of Vietnamese workers to work abroad are affirmed in the current Labour Code 2019, within which Vietnam affirms the imperative that labor migration abroad under contract complies with Vietnamese laws, the laws of the host countries, and international, bilataral treaties between Vietnam and contracting states.[18]
- To further codify regulations on the export of labor in general, and to protect Vietnamese workers while working abroad in particular, the National Assembly passed the Law on Vietnamese Guest Workers on November 29, 2006. This is the first act on protecting the rights of Vietnamese workers abroad. This law was recently revised by the National Assembly in 2020 and changes took effect from January 1, 2022. Compared with the 2006 law, the Law on Vietnamese Labourers Working Abroad under Contract shows some amendments that include the expansion of the guarantee of workers' rights to work abroad based on international labor standards. To implement this law, the government has issued a number of decrees guiding the implementation of the law on Vietnamese working abroad including:
- Decree No. 112/2021/ND-CP regulating expenses and detailing a number of articles and guiding the implementation of the Law on Vietnamese workers working abroad under contracts, effective from January 1, 2022;

- Decision No. 40/2021/QD-TTg on Overseas Employment Support Fund, effective from February 21, 2022;
- Circular No. 21/2021/TT-BLDTBXH detailing a number of articles of the law on Vietnamese workers working abroad under contracts, effective from February 1, 2022;
- Circular No. 20/2021/TT-BLDTBXH stipulating the database system on Vietnamese workers working abroad under contract, effective from February 1, 2022;
- Decree No. 12/2022/ND-CP dated January 17, 2022, of the government stipulating penalties for administrative violations in the fields of labor, social security, and Vietnamese workers working abroad according to the provisions of the Decree; and
- Decision No. 40/2021/QD-TTg dated December 31, 2021, of the prime minister on the Overseas Employment Support Fund.

The protection of workers is, therefore, enshrined in the legal provisions on the migration activities of Vietnamese people abroad. In this context, the rights of Vietnamese migrant workers are also protected through the provisions on citizen protection in Vietnam and foreign countries, especially rights related to nationality, freedom of movement, and other civil rights in Article 23 of the 2013 Constitution; Law on Overseas Representative Offices of the Socialist Republic of Vietnam 2009; the Nationality Law 2008, amended and supplemented in 2015; and civil law 2015 (amended in 2017). In addition, the protection of the rights of migrant workers is also established in legal regulations to prevent serious human rights violations such as forced labor as in the Criminal Law 2015 (Article 279), and human traffficking in the Human Trafficking Prevention and Control law 2011.

In recent years, the protection of migrant workers has been addressed by the Communist Party of Vietnam. On December 12, 2022, the Central Committee of the Communist Party adopted its new Party Directive 20-CT/TW on labor migration. This policy document indicates strong support from the highest policy-making levels in Vietnam.

In addtion to the policy and legal framwork, there has been some voluntary standards promulgated such as the Code of Conduct to ensure responsible and ethical recruitment developed by the Vietnam Labour Export Association in 2010 (updated in 2018).[19]

Over the years, the government of Vietnam has developed law, policy, and guidance to "Protect legal rights and benefits of Vietnamese workers, enterprises, organizations and individuals in bringing Vietnamese workers abroad to work."[20] These legal documents also recognized the rights, obligations, and prohibited acts of enterprises or organizations sending workers to work abroad. However, Vietnam's policies and laws on migration still need to be improved.[21] The gaps in this existing legal framework, among others, include the following:

First, although the existing laws aim to protect the legitimate rights and interests of guest workers, there is a lack of a strong human rights–based approach on the protection of the rights of migrant workers. Throughout recent history, this policy and legal framework reflects the aim of giving workers the opportunity to work abroad in order to earn a better income and recognizes employment opportunities for the workers, reducing poverty, stabilizing society, and building a highly skilled and professional workforce. Acccordingly, the main focus of the law is state management and rights and obligation of enterprises and non-business organizations sending workers abroad under contract.[22]

Second, the existing policy and legal framework only provides protection for *Guest workers under contract*, which means "Vietnamese citizens residing in Vietnam who meet all the conditions prescribed by laws of Vietnam and the host country, and work abroad in accordance with this Law."[23] Compared to the definition of migrant workers in international treaties and regional intruments such as the *International Convention on the Protection of the Rights of All Migrant Workers and Members of Their Families* and ASEAN Consensus on the protection and promotion of the rights of migrant workers, the concept of "guest workers" or "worker working abroad" is narrower than the concept of migrant workers.[24]

This means that the law only applies to contracted workers rather than to any person who is to be engaged, is engaged, or has been engaged in a remunerated activity in a state of which he or she is not a national.[25] Accordingly, the scope of these laws fails to protect other groups of migrant workers such as illegal and undocumented workers, seasonal migrant workers, as well as members of the migant workers's family. This practice leads to poor enforcement and needs to be considered in time to ensure the full enjoyment of the rights of Vietnamese workers abroad.

RIGHTS OF VIETNAMESE MIGRANT WORKERS WORKING ABROAD WITH CONTRACT

This section looks at the regulations on the rights of migrant workers in comparision with the international framework on the human rights of migrant workers. Guest workers, as any other workers, are under the protection of labor laws incuding the Labour Code 2020. As noted earlier, the key legal document that guarantees the rights of Vietnamese migrant workers is the 2020 Law on Vietnamese Guest Workers. Compared to the 2006 Law on Việtmanse guest workers, this revised law provides better guarantees to human rights for migrant workers from pre-departure, upon arrival, during employment in receiving countries, and when returning. Vietnam migrant workers under contract are protected, by law, the following human rights:

- In line with the International Labour Organization (ILO) Convention and related human right treaties that Vietnam has ratified recenttly,[26] including the most recent ILO Convention Number 105 on Elimination of Forced Labour, the Law on Vietnamese Guest Workers provides 17 prohibited acts pertinent to Vietnamese guest workers. Accordingly, Vietnamese guest workers are protected from being provided false information, or other tricks to deceive workers; from abuse, trafficking, exploiting workers or practicing forced labor; or from committing illegal acts.[27] The law also protects migrant workers from being abused or becoming victims of debt bond, brokerage commissions, and other forms of service fees, and forced labor from recruitment agencies or foreign employers.[28]
- The key human rights principle of non-discrimination and gender equality is incorporated into in the 2020 law on Vietnamese guest workers.[29] For the first time the revised Law on Vietnamese Guest Workers provides a definition of "discrimination" and "forced labor" in line with ILO Convention Nos. 111 and 29.

In addition, with the existing recognition of labor rights under the 2020 Labour Code and relevant labor laws, as migrant workers, the laws on the protection of Vietnamese guest workers also guarantees other fundamental human rights throughout the process of migration. Article 6 of the 2022 Law on Guest Workers regulates the rights and obligations of Vietnamese guest workers. Certain human rights are recognized under this law such as:

- The right to receive training in occupational skills and foreign languages and orientation education for Vietnamese guest workers;
- The right to be provided with information on policies and laws, customs and practices of Vietnam and the host countries and the rights and obligations of parties when going abroad to work as guest workers;
- The right to to be provided with counseling and support for exercising their rights and obligations;
- The right to be entitled to salaries, wages, medical examination and treatment, social security, and occupational accident insurance policies and to transfer their salaries, wages, incomes, and other lawful assets back home;

- The right to be protected while working abroad in accordance with the laws of Vietnam and the host country as well as international law and practices;
- The right to unilaterally terminate their labor contracts when employers maltreat them or force them to work against their will, or when they face risks directly threatening their life or health or experience sexual harassment while working abroad;
- The entitlement to labor and employment support policies and benefits from the Fund for Overseas Employment Support in accordance with the law;
- The right to be not required to pay double social security or personal income tax;
- The right to file complaints, denunciations, and lawsuits about violations in the field of Vietnamese guest workers;
- The right to be provided with counseling and support in job creation and start-up activities upon their return home and to access voluntary psychosocial counseling services.[30]

Although the law on migrant workers in Vietnam has improved in terms of recognition of migrant workers' rights and legitimate interests, from the human rights perspective, some human rights are still missing and there is a failure to recognize this in the existing policies and laws of Vietnam including the following:

- The existing national laws fail to address the rights of members of migrant workers' families and some vulnerable migrant groups such as seasonal workers, project-tied workers, specified-employment workers, self-employed workers, the growing number of gig economy workers, as well as other undocumented migrant workers including children. This legal gap leads to the increasing of vulnerablity and human rights abuses for these groups in practice.
- Certain international human rights and labor standards have not yet been addressed and recognized in the current policy and legal documents on migrant workers. These rights include the right to freedom from being subjected to torture or to cruel, inhuman, or degrading treatment or punishment; freedom from slavery or servitude; the right to freedom of thought, conscience, and religion; the right to hold opinions without interference; the right to liberty and security of person; and the right to cultural identity and cultural links with their state of origin.

In the main, Vietnam is well-provided with a range of policies, laws, and other statutes in national and international law that are designed to protect the human and wider rights of Vietnamese migrant workers. This is recognition in law of the status of Vietnamese citizens and the consequent rights they have when working overseas, whether in a legal or undocumented manner. There are shortcomings to the laws and related instruments designed to protect the rights of Vietnamese workers abroad, notably for workers migrating outside of the protection of contracted and state-sponsored work abroad. On top of this, enforcement is generally poor as a result of inadequate resources to address issues and a lack of understanding on the part of key stakeholders in the process.

IMPLEMENTATION OF INTERNATIONAL INSTRUMENTS AND VIETNAMESE LAWS ON ENSURING THE RIGHTS OF MIGRANT WORKERS

Although Vietnam has not yet ratified the Convention on Migrant Workers and Members of their Families, the country has taken appropriate measures to fulfill its obligation on the protection of migrant workers under international core human rights treaties and ILO conventions that it has ratified. Under the 3rd Universal Periodic Review (UPR), Vietnam received recommendations from UN member states that sought to improve the legal framework on the protection of migrant workers and ratification of International Convention on the Protection of the Rights of All Migrant Workers and Members of Their Families (ICMW) and to address the risk of labor abuses.[31] In the concluding observations on the combined seventh and eighth periodic reports of Vietnam, the Committee noted that cross-border migration has rapidly increased in recent years and that women and girls migrating abroad are often victimized by fraudulent recruitment agencies and brokers for international marriage; and that migrant women who are victims of exploitation and violence face barriers in filing complaints and gaining access to justice.[32]

The UN Committee on Economic, Social and Cultural Rights (CESCR) has indicated in its note that the regulatory framework governing the recruitment of Vietnamese migrant workers for employment abroad retains issues that make migrant workers vulnerable to abuse and exploitation.[33] The Committee on the Rights of the Child recently recommend that Vietnam establish a mechanism for the early identification of migrant children who may have been recruited or used in hostilities abroad.[34] The prime minister of Vietnam has adopted plans to implement, such as Decision No. 1975/QD-TTg, dated December 31, 2019, of the prime minister approving the Master Plan for Implementation of the Recommendations that Vietnam accepts under the Universal Periodic Review Mechanism, and Decision No. 668/QD-TTg of the prime minister, approving the plan to implement the recommendations of the Committee on Elimination of All Forms of Discrimination against Women, May 16, 2017. Vietnam has made commitments to implement the UN's Sustainable Development Goals (SDGs); it is recognized that the goverment needs to focus efforts in areas that impact migrant workers in terms of the SDG Targets under 8.8, 10.7, and 10.

At a regional level, Vietnam hasbeen active in supporting ASEAN intiatives to address legal issues regarding migrant workers by implementing the ASEAN Declaration on the Protection and Promotion of the Rights of Migrant Workers (2007), and he ASEAN Consensus on the Protection and Promotion of the Rights. However, since these instruments are not legally binding, their implementation is limited.[35] The goverment of Vietnam has also signed bilaral agreements with other countries on the return of Vietnamese citizens who are not legally permitted to reside abroad.[36]

At the national level, according to the 2020 Law on Vietnamese Guest Workers, the Ministry of Labour, Invalids and Social Affairs (MOLISA) is the designated state management body accountable to the government for performance of the state's management of Vietnamese guest workers. MOLISA is responsible for posting on its portal information on opportunities for Vietnamese workers to relocate overseas as guest workers: building, managing, operating, updating, and sharing the database on Vietnamese guest workers; and coordinating with the Ministry of Foreign Affairs in assigning civil servants to, and guiding worker management skills for, overseas Vietnamese representative missions.[37] The Department of Overseas Labour (DoLAB) and the Department of Employment in MOLISA have the primary responsibility for the management and coordination of activities of international labor migration from Vietnam to other countries. In addition, Vietnamese migrant workers are entitled to protection in relation to their lawful rights and interests from Vietnamese embassies and missions overseas.[38] For activities to support migrant workers' reintegration, People's Committees at all levels and, locally, Department of Labour, War Invalids and Social Affairs (DOLISA) are obligated to perform the state's role in the management of Vietnamese guest workers when overseas.[39] They are also obligated to assist workers in accessing, making contributions to, carrying out procedures for receiving support from, and receiving support from, the Fund for Overseas Employment Support while they work abroad.[40]

Dispite such efforts in law-making and strengthening the institutional framework in relation to approved legislation, there are still big gaps at the point of implmentation:

- Although there are no comprehensive statistics or data, it does appears that there are large numbers of Vietnamese undocumented migrant workers who are smuggled into other countries.[4142] It is estimated that there are in the region of 600,000 undocumented workers from Vietnam working in Asia, Europe, and the United States although this may well be a significant underestimate.[43] These workers are located in specialist areas of work in their destination countries, for example, tobacco smuggling in Germany and both cannabis cultivation (men) and nail bars/beauty salons (women) in the UK.[44]

- Undocumented workers from Vietnam are subject to appalling travel and working conditions. They are frequently trafficked via established smuggling routes into their destination country, sometimes with tragic consequences for the smuggled workers.[45] It is estimated that at least 18,000 workers are smuggled from Vietnam into Europe alone each year.[46]
- Once they have arrived in their destination country, undocumented workers are subject to dreadful workplace abuse and very poor living conditions, with much of their already low pay held back for accommodation, food, insurance, and other "fees."[47]
- What is clear is a total failure of the current legal and institutional framework to address the abuse of vulnerable migrant workers from Vietnam, especially those who are undocumented and, therefore, deemed "illegal" in their host countries. Workers themselves are unwilling or unable to bring attention their situation with the competent authorities or with Vietnamese diplomatic missions for fear of deportation or reprisals against them and their families by criminal smuggling gangs.
- The complaints mechanisms and legal assistance for workers and their families seeking to make a complaint about their working conditions (whether documented or undocumented) are totally ineffective, and the authorities responsible for managing complaints are powerless to intervene in an effective manner.[48]

CHALLENGES TO THE RIGHTS OF MIGRANT WORKERS FROM VIETNAM TO OTHER COUNTRIES

Effecting meaningful change to the working lives of Vietnamese workers overseas, whether documented or undocumented, represents a number of challenges that will require multi-stakeholder engagement to redress in any effective manner. These include:

- The incomplete legal framework: Vietnam remains a non-state member of the migrant convention. During the third UPR review, Vietnam received eight recommendations from UN member states and recommendations for the Committee on the Rights of the Child (CRC

Committee) in its concluding observations on the combined fifth and sixth periodic reports of Vietnam in 2022.[49]

- Existing domestic law only provides protection for one particular group of migrants, which are migrants under contract. The large number of undocumented migrant workers is beyond the protection of national law. The case of 39 victims of smuggling to the UK is an alarm or wake-up call for Vietnam to take further action, beginning with strengthening its legal system.[50]
- The challenge to address the human rights risks of migrant workers includes issues related to forced labor, debt bondage, smuggling, and trafficking. Athought there has been progress in setting up the legal framework necessary to eradicate forced labor[51] and other forms of abuse, Vietnamese migrant workers remain at risk. In particular, COVID-19 has further increased this risk. These risks are complicated and cannot be eradicated without tackling their root causes. This requires collaboration within and between governments, international agencies, Non-governmental organizations (NGOs), and many other stakeholders.
- The lack of an effective and confidential complaints mechanism through which workers and their representatives can seek redress from abuse and exploitation. Currently even where mechanisms do exist, it is unlikely that undocumented workers would have the confidence in them to actually use them.
- The lack of legal protection for the families of migrant workers, notably children, especially the families of those who are undocumented.
- The absence of reliable data on migration from Vietnam hinders both law makers and those seeking to protect their rights, an issue highlighted by ILO in 2022 and pointing to the wide range of agencies that hold partial but unlinked data on this matter.[52]
- Finally, the current global turbulence, caused by a combination of climate change and the increased severity of natural disasters,[53] the legacy of COVID-19,[54] and war/conflict has increased migrant and refugee mobility from affected areas and also creates increasing vulnerabilities for migrant workers across the globe. The wider uncertainties created by the impact of these changes has also increased hospitality to outsiders in many countries and resulted in the tightening of laws designed to discourage illegal migration.[55] There is increasing recognition of the vulnerability of migrant workers in a globalized world, but it is also clear that protecting their rights in a turbulent world remains hugely challenging.[56]

CONCLUSION

Labor migration is a vitally important economic concern for many countries in the Global South, perhaps none more so than for Vietnam. It is the source of significant remittance income and, at one level, aspects of the processes involved with out-migration for contracted workers are formally organized by the state and supported by law and statute. At the other end of the spectrum, Vietnam also experiences high levels of undocumented or "illegal" migration within the region, to Europe and to North America, and these workers are unprotected by law and vulnerable to exploitation, abuse, and deprivation of the meager weages that they do earn. Neither the law in Vietnam, bilateral agreements with outher countries or international laws, nor conventions appear to have the "teeth" to tackle this social and economic exploitation of the most vulnerable and poorest members of the migrant community.

Vietnam is not alone in facing the challenges than emanate from growing levels of economic migration. Globally, the world is witnessing unprecedented levels of mobility in response to economic and social turbulence caused by a combination of climate change and the increased severity of natural disasters, the legacy of COVID-19, and war/conflict alongside increasing insularity and anti-migrant political rhetoric in countries that have traditionally welcomed migrants from other countries.

On paper at least, Vietnam has a relatively robust legal framework for the protection of its workforce, both in-country and when working abroad. In addition, Vietnam is signatory to most (but not all) international conventions promulgated by the ILO and by the United Nations and its agencies. However, the narrow definitions applied to the state's understanding of its obligations to Vietnamese workers located abroad (focusing on contract workers) means that the vast majority of Vietnamese migrant workers (particularly those who travel without formal documentation) are largely unprotected by the extant legal framework. Furthermore, enforcement of existing laws and recognition of the obligations of competent agencies (such as embassies and other diplomatic missions) is weak so that those protections that are afforded to migrant workers are ineffective.

Looking to the future, it is likely that global mobility of a vulnerable workforce, fleeing drought, famine, war, and wider economic hardship will only increase. Vietnam must act to ensure that its migrant workers are better protected at all stages of the recruitment, out-migration, and return processes so that the economic and social benefits of migration are fully realized at the individual, community, and national levels.

REFERENCES

Castles, S. (2000) International Migration at the Beginning of the Twenty-First Century: Global Trends and Issues, *International Social Science Journal*, 52(165), 269–81.

Complaint mechanisms for Vietnamese migrant workers: An overview of law and practice / Tripartite Action to Protect the Rights of Migrant Workers within and from the Greater Mekong Subregion (GMSTRIANGLE project), ILO Regional Office for Asia and the Pacific. - Hanoi: ILO, 2015 at https://abcnews.go.com/International/6000-mile-journey-scores-vietnamese-migrants-smuggled-trafficked/story?id=67318722.

Council of Ministers, Decree No. 370/HDBT of the Council of Ministers: Decree promulgating the Regulation on sending Vietnamese workers to work abroad for a fix term (Nghị định số 370/HĐBT của Hội đồng Bộ trưởng: Nghị định ban hành Quy chế về đưa người lao động Việt Nam đi làm việc có thời hạn ở nước ngoài), dated September 20, 1991, Article 6(1), https://vanban.chinhphu.vn/default.aspx?pageid=27160&docid=1422.

European Union, Consular Department, Ministry of Foreign Affairs of Vietnam, and International Organization for Migration, *"Overview Report on the Migration of Vietnamese Citizens Abroad in 2011" (Hanoi, May 2012)*, https://vietnam.iom.int/sites/vietnam/files/IOM_Files/Projects/MigrationPolicyManagement/Review_Vietnamese_Migration_Abroad_2012_VN.pdf.

Government Council, Decision of the Government Council No. 46-CP, dated February 11, 1980, on sending workers and officials to improve their qualifications and work for a fix period in the socialist countries (Quyết định của Hội đồng Chính phủ số 46-CP ngày 11 tháng 2 năm 1980 về việc đưa công nhân và cán bộ đi bồi dưỡng nâng cao trình độ và làm việc có thời hạn tại các nước xã hội chủ nghĩa), https://thuvienphapluat.vn/van-ban/Lao-dong-Tien-luong/Quyet-dinh-46-CP-dua-cong-nhan-can-bo-di-boi-duong-nang-cao-trinh-do-va-lam-viec-co-thoi-han-tai-cac-nuoc-XHCN-44226.aspx.

Iglicka, K. (2005) "Labour migration into Poland: The case of the Vietnamese community," in (eds.) Spaan, E., Hillmann, F., and van Naerssen, T., *Asian Migrants and European Labour Markets*. London: Taylor and Francis, 101–13.

ILO Global Business Network on Forced Labour, and ILO, Vietnam Policy Brief 1: Addressing forced labour at its root in Vietnam, 23 August 2020, https://respect.international/wp-content/uploads/2021/01/ILO-GBNFL_Viet-Nam_Forced-labour_Brief1.pdf.

ILO, World Migration Report 2022, p. 42, https://publications.iom.int/books/world-migration-report-2022.

National Essembly, Labour Code 2020, Law No. 45/2019/QH14 45/2019/QH14.

Nguyen, C. H. (2014) Development and brain drain: A review of Vietnamese labour export and skilled migration, *Migration and Development*, 3(2): 181–202.

Nguyen, T. (2019) Government-sponsored crime: The case of Vietnamese undocumented immigrants in Germany and the UK, accessed at http://dspace.univd.edu.ua/xmlui/handle/123456789/5839.

Nguyen, Thi Hong Yen. "Challenges in Ensuring the Rights of Vietnamese Migrant Workers in the Globalization Context – The Two Sides of the Development Process". In *Asian Yearbook of International Law,* (Leiden, The Netherlands: Brill | Nijhoff, 2021) doi: https://doi.org/10.1163/9789004501249_008

Nguyen, Thi Hong Yen, and Tran Thi Thu Thuy. "Ensuring the Rights of Vietnamese Migrant Workers in the Context of the Covid-19 Pandemic: Challenges and Solutions" (2022) 2:1 *Contemporary Sociological Issues 40–58.*

Politburo, Degree on export of labor and experts, (Chỉ thị về xuất khẩu lao động và chuyên gia), September 22, 1998, https://thuvienphapluat.vn/van-ban/Xuat-nhap-khau/Chi-thi-41-CT-TW-nam-1998-xuat-khau-lao-dong-chuyen-gia-170756.aspx.

Pratheepwatanawong, M. (2021). "Opportunities for New Trend of Labour Mobility from Vietnam as a Result of *Doi Moi*, ASEAN Connectivity and Belt and Road Initiative," in Jaiswal, P., and Bhatt, D. P. (eds.), *Rebalancing Asia.* Singapore: Springer. https://doi.org/10.1007/978-981-16-3757-5_7.

Schwenkel, C. (2014) Rethinking Asian mobilities: Socialist migration and post-socialist repatriation of Vietnamese contract workers in East Germany, *Critical Asian Studies*, 46(2), 235–58.

Schwenkel, C. (2016) Socialist Mobilities: Crossing New Terrains in Vietnamese Migration Histories, *Central and Eastern European Migration Review*, 4(1), 13–25.

Tappe, O., and Nguyen, M. T. N. (2019) TRaNS: Trans-Regional and -National Studies of Southeast Asia, 7(1), 1–18, DOI: https://doi.org/10.1017/trn.2019.4.

The 6,000-mile journey: How scores of Vietnamese migrants are smuggled or trafficked into the UK each year, https://abcnews.go.com/International/6000-mile-journey-scores-vietnamese-migrants-smuggled-trafficked/story?id=67318722.

The National Assembly, Law on Vietnamese guest workers, 2020. Law No. 69/2020/QH14.

Truong, N., and Tuong, V. (2022) The Dragon's Underbelly. Dynamics and Dilemmas in Vietnam's Economy and Politics. Singapore: ISEAS Publishing.

UN Committee on Economic, Social and Cultural Rights (CESCR), Concluding observations on the second to fourth periodic reports of Vietnam, No. E/C.12/VNM/CO/2–4. Dated 15 December 2014. Available at: https://tbinternet.ohchr.org/_layouts/15/treatybodyexternal/Download.aspx?symbolno=E/C.12/VNM/CO/2-4&Lang=En. Accessed on 20 September 2019.

Vietnam News, Viet Nam among world's 10 biggest recipients of remittances, accessed 20 May 2023, http://bizhub.vn/markets/viet-nam-among-worlds-10-biggest-recipients-of-remittances_341190.html.

Vietnam News, VN population tops 96.2 million, ranking 15th in the world, July 12, 2019, https://vietnamnews.vn/society/522544/vn-population-tops-96-2-million-ranking-15th-in-the-world.html.

VN Express, Vietnamese illegal workers abroad risk all to make a living, 6 September 2022. Accessed 1 May 2023, https://e.vnexpress.net/news/trend/vietnamese-illegal-workers-abroad-risk-all-to-make-a-living-4507926.html.

VN Express International, 90% of Vietnamese migrant workers are low-skilled: Expert, accessed 20 April 2023, https://e.vnexpress.net/news/news/90-of-vietnamese-migrant-workers-are-low-skilled-expert-4500735.html.

NOTES

1. Pratheepwatanawong, M. (2021). Opportunities for New Trend of Labour Mobility from Vietnam as a Result of *Doi Moi*, ASEAN Connectivity and Belt and Road Initiative. In: Jaiswal, P., and Bhatt, D. P. (eds.), *Rebalancing Asia.* Singapore: Springer, https://doi.org/10.1007/978-981-16-3757-5_7.

2. Castles, S. (2000) International Migration at the Beginning of the Twenty-First Century: Global Trends and Issues, *International Social Science Journal*, 52(165), 269–81.

3. Tappe, O., and Nguyen, M. T. N. (2019) TRaNS: Trans-Regional and -National Studies of Southeast Asia, 7(1), 1–18, DOI: https://doi.org/10.1017/trn.2019.4.

4. Vietnam News, VN population tops 96.2 million, ranking 15th in the world, July 12, 2019, https://vietnamnews.vn/society/522544/vn-population-tops-96-2-million-ranking-15th-in-the-world.html.

5. ILO, World Migration Report 2022, https://publications.iom.int/books/world-migration-report-2022P, p. 202.

6. ILO, Labour migration in Viet Nam, accessed 26 April 2023, https://www.ilo.org/hanoi/Areasofwork/labour-migration/lang--en/index.htm.

7. Vietnam News, Viet Nam among world's 10 biggest recipients of remittances, accessed 20 May 2023, http://bizhub.vn/markets/viet-nam-among-worlds-10-biggest-recipients-of-remittances_341190.html.

8. ILO, World Migration Report 2022, p. 42, https://publications.iom.int/books/world-migration-report-2022.

9. ILO, Labour migration in Viet Nam, accessed 26 April 2023, https://www.ilo.org/hanoi/Areasofwork/labour-migration/lang--en/index.htm.

10. VN Express International, 90% of Vietnamese migrant workers are low-skilled: Expert, accessed 20 April 2023, https://e.vnexpress.net/news/news/90-of-vietnamese-migrant-workers-are-low-skilled-expert-4500735.html.

11. Nguyen, Thi Hong Yen. "Challenges in Ensuring the Rights of Vietnamese Migrant Workers in the Globalization Context – The Two Sides of the Development Process". In *Asian Yearbook of International Law*, (Leiden, The Netherlands: Brill | Nijhoff, 2021) doi: https://doi.org/10.1163/9789004501249_008

12. See Nguyen, T. (2019) Government-sponsored crime: The case of Vietnamese undocumented immigrants in Germany and the UK, KhNUIA, URI: http://dspace.univd.edu.ua/xmlui/handle/123456789/5839 https://doi.org/10.32631/ccc19.03.

13. Schwenkel, C. (2014) Rethinking Asian mobilities: Socialist migration and post-socialist repatriation of Vietnamese contract workers in East Germany, *Critical Asian Studies*, 46(2), 235–58;

14. Iglicka, K. (2005) "Labour migration into Poland: The case of the Vietnamese community," in (eds.) Spaan, E., Hillmann, F., and van Naerssen, T., *Asian Migrants and European Labour Markets*, London: Taylor and Francis, 101–13.

15. Government Council, Decision of the Government Council No. 46-CP, dated February 11, 1980, on sending workers and officials to improve their qualifications and work for a fix period in the socialist countries (Quyết định của Hội đồng Chính

phủ số 46-CP ngày 11 tháng 2 năm 1980 về việc đưa công nhân và cán bộ đi bồi dưỡng nâng cao trình độ và làm việc có thời hạn tại các nước xã hội chủ nghĩa), https://thuvienphapluat.vn/van-ban/Lao-dong-Tien-luong/Quyet-dinh-46-CP-dua-cong-nhan-can-bo-di-boi-duong-nang-cao-trinh-do-va-lam-viec-co-thoi-han-tai-cac-nuoc-XHCN-44226.aspx.

16. Council of Ministers, Decree No. 370/HDBT of the Council of Ministers: Decree promulgating the Regulation on sending Vietnamese workers to work abroad for a fix term (Nghị định số 370/HĐBT của Hội đồng Bộ trưởng: Nghị định ban hành Quy chế về đưa người lao động Việt Nam đi làm việc có thời hạn ở nước ngoài), dated September 20, 1991, Article 6(1), https://vanban.chinhphu.vn/default.aspx?pageid=27160&docid=1422.

17. Politburo, Degree on export of labor and experts (Chỉ thị về xuất khẩu lao động và chuyên gia), September 22, 1998, https://thuvienphapluat.vn/van-ban/Xuat-nhap-khau/Chi-thi-41-CT-TW-nam-1998-xuat-khau-lao-dong-chuyen-gia-170756.aspx.

18. National Essembly, Labour Code 2020, Law No. 45/2019/QH14 45/2019/QH14.

19. Nguyen, Thi Hong Yen. "Challenges in Ensuring the Rights of Vietnamese Migrant Workers in the Globalization Context – The Two Sides of the Development Process". In *Asian Yearbook of International Law*, (Leiden, The Netherlands: Brill | Nijhoff, 2021) doi: https://doi.org/10.1163/9789004501249_008.

20. The National Assembly, Law on Vietnamese guest workers, 2020. Law No. 69/2020/QH14, Article 4 (2).

21. Nguyen, Thi Hong Yen. "Challenges in Ensuring the Rights of Vietnamese Migrant Workers in the Globalization Context – The Two Sides of the Development Process". In *Asian Yearbook of International Law,* (Leiden, The Netherlands: Brill | Nijhoff, 2021) doi: https://doi.org/10.1163/9789004501249_008.

22. The National Assembly, Law on Vietnamese guest workers, 2020. Law No. 69/2020/QH14.

23. The National Assembly, Law on Vietnamese guest workers, 2020. Law No. 69/2020/QH14, The National Assembly, Law on Vietnamese guest workers, 2020. Law No. 69/2020/QH14. Article 3(2).

24. Nguyen, Thi Hong Yen. "Challenges in Ensuring the Rights of Vietnamese Migrant Workers in the Globalization Context – The Two Sides of the Development Process". In *Asian Yearbook of International Law*, (Leiden, The Netherlands: Brill | Nijhoff, 2021) doi: https://doi.org/10.1163/9789004501249_008

25. International Convention on the Protection of the Rights of All Migrant Workers and Members of Their Families.

26. Vietnam has ratified 7/9 core human rights convention and 25 ILO Convention.

27. The National Assembly, Law on Vietnamese guest workers, 2020. Law No. 69/2020/QH14, Article 7 (1).

28. The National Assembly, Law on Vietnamese guest workers, 2020. Law No. 69/2020/QH14, Article 7.

29. The National Assembly, Law on Vietnamese guest workers, 2020. Law No. 69/2020/QH14, Article 4(4).

30. The National Assembly, Law on Vietnamese guest workers, 2020. Law No. 69/2020/QH14, Article 6.

31. 3rd UPR.

32. Committee on the Elimination of Discrimination against Women, observations on the combined seventh and eighth periodic reports of Vietnam, 29 July 2015.

33. UN Committee on Economic, Social and Cultural Rights (CESCR) , c oncluding observations on the second to fourth periodic reports of Vietnam, No. E/C.12/VNM/CO /2 – 4, d ated 15 December 2014. Available at: https://tbinternet .ohchr.org/_layouts/15/treatybodyexternal/Download.aspx?symbolno=E/C.12/VNM/ CO/2-4&Lang=En . Accessed on 20 September 2019.

34. Committee on the Rights of the Child, concluding observations on the combined fifth and sixth periodic reports of Vietnam, 21 October 2022.

35. Nguyen, Thi Hong Yen, and Tran Thi Thu Thuy, "Ensuring the Rights of Vietnamese Migrant Workers in the Context of the Covid-19 Pandemic: Challenges and Solutions" (2022) 2:1 *Contemporary* Sociological Issues, 40–58.

36. European Union, Consular Department, Ministry of Foreign Affairs of Vietnam, and International Organization for Migration, *"Overview Report on the Migration of Vietnamese Citizens Abroad in 2011"*

(Hanoi, May 2012),

https://vietnam.iom.int/sites/vietnam/files/IOM_Files/Projects/ MigrationPolicyManagement/Review_Vietnamese_Migration_Abroad_2012_VN .pdf.

37. The National Assembly, Law on Vietnamese guest workers, 2020. Law No. 69/2020/QH14, Article 70.

38. The National Assembly, Law on Vietnamese guest workers, 2020. Law No. 69/2020/QH14, Article 71.

39. The National Assembly, Law on Vietnamese guest workers, 2020. Law No. 69/2020/QH14, Article 70(4).

40. The National Assembly, Law on Vietnamese guest workers, 2020. Law No. 69/2020/QH14, Article 71(6).

41. Truong, N., and Tuong, V. (2022) *The Dragon's Underbelly: Dynamics and Dilemmas in Vietnam's Economy and Politics*, Singapore: ISEAS Publishing.

42. Nguyen, T. (2019) Government-sponsored crime: The case of Vietnamese undocumented immigrants in Germany and the UK, accessed at http://dspace.univd .edu.ua/xmlui/handle/123456789/5839; and

https://doi.org/10.32631/ccc19.03, 5 May 2023.

43. VN Express, Vietnamese illegal workers abroad risk all to make a living, 6 September 2022. Accessed 1 May 2023, https://e.vnexpress.net/news/trend/vietnamese -illegal-workers-abroad-risk-all-to-make-a-living-4507926.html.

44. Nguyen, T. (2019) Government-sponsored crime: The case of Vietnamese undocumented immigrants in Germany and the UK, accessed at http://dspace .univd.edu.ua/xmlui/handle/123456789/5839; and https://doi.org/10.32631/ccc19.03, 5 May 2023.

45. The 6,000-mile journey: How scores of Vietnamese migrants are smuggled or trafficked into the UK each year, https://abcnews.go.com/International/6000-mile -journey-scores-vietnamese-migrants-smuggled-trafficked/story?id=67318722.

46. Ibid.

47. VN Express, Vietnamese illegal workers abroad risk all to make a living, 6 September 2022. Accessed 1 May 2023. https://e.vnexpress.net/news/trend/vietnamese-illegal-workers-abroad-risk-all-to-make-a-living-4507926.html.

48. *Complaint mechanisms for Vietnamese migrant workers: An overview of law and practice / Tripartite Action to Protect the Rights of Migrant Workers within and from the Greater Mekong Subregion (GMSTRIANGLE project)*, ILO Regional Office for Asia and the Pacific. - Hanoi: ILO, 2015.

49. UPR and CRC.

50. https://abcnews.go.com/International/6000-mile-journey-scores-vietnamese-migrants-smuggled-trafficked/story?id=67318722.

51. ILO Global Business Network on Forced Labour, and ILO, Vietnam Policy Brief 1: Addressing forced labour at its root in Vietnam, 23 of August 2020, https://respect.international/wp-content/uploads/2021/01/ILO-GBNFL_Viet-Nam_Forced-labour_Brief1.pdf.

52. https://www.gso.gov.vn/wp-content/uploads/2023/01/Data-gaps-report-eng-14h-30.12-web.pdf.

53. ILO, World Migration Report 2022, p. 42, https://publications.iom.int/books/world-migration-report-2022.

54. Nguyen, T. H. Y., and Trn, T. T. T. (2022) Ensuring the Rights of Vietnamese Migrant Workers in the Context of the Covid-19 Pandemic: Challenges and Solutions, *Journal of Contemporary Sociological Issues*, 2(1), 40–58.

55. See, for example, https://www.theguardian.com/uk-news/2023/mar/07/suella-braverman-asylum-migration-bill-law-change-small-boats.

56. Nguyen, Thi Hong Yen. "Challenges in Ensuring the Rights of Vietnamese Migrant Workers in the Globalization Context – The Two Sides of the Development Process". In *Asian Yearbook of International Law,* (Leiden, The Netherlands: Brill | Nijhoff, 2021) doi: https://doi.org/10.1163/9789004501249_008

Chapter 7

International Labor Migration Governance in Myanmar

Challenges and the Way Forward

Su Wai Mon

Migration across international borders is not a new phenomenon and this practice has been significantly increasing in today's globalized world as millions of people are leaving their home countries to look for better economic and social opportunities. According to a report by the United Nations, it is estimated that the number of persons living outside of their country of origin reached 281 million in 2020, which equates to 3.6 percent of the global population. Within two decades, between 2000 and 2020, the number of international migrants increased by 108 million globally.[1] The reasons for migration vary where some people move in search of work or economic opportunities, to join family or to study, while others move to escape conflict, persecution, terrorism, or human rights violations. In addition, migration occurs in response to the adverse effects of climate change, natural disasters, or other environmental factors.[2] Although there is no universally accepted definition of who is a "migrant," the International Organisation for Migration (IMO) defines:

> "Migrant" is defined as "any person who is moving or has moved across an international border or within a State away from his/her habitual place of residence, regardless of (1) the person's legal status; (2) whether the movement is voluntary or involuntary; (3) what the causes for the movement are; or (4) what the length of the stay is.[3]

The term "migrant" covers a number of well-defined legal categories of people, such as migrant workers; persons whose particular types of movements are legally defined, such as smuggled migrants; as well as those whose status or means of movement are not specifically defined under international law, such as international students.[4]

MIGRANT WORKERS

Among all the categories of migrants, there are 164 million migrant workers globally based on the 2020 World Migration Report.[5] A migrant worker means "a person who migrates from one country to another with a view to being employed otherwise than on his own account and includes any person regularly admitted as a migrant for employment."[6] In addition, a migrant worker is also defined as a person who "is to be engaged or has been engaged in a remunerated activity in a state of which he or she is not a national."[7]

Although international migration can be a positive experience for workers, there have been growing concerns relating to the treatment of migrant workers including the violation of human rights such as exploitation, unsafe work environments, lack of access to social security, denial of freedom of association, and worker's rights, discrimination, and xenophobia.[8] Migrant workers face several challenges in receiving countries such as language barriers, unfamiliar surroundings, lack of information or social support, and conflict with immigration law leavening them vulnerable to exploitation, including forced labor. The lack of legal framework coupled with insufficient enforcement of labor protection legislation leaves migrants vulnerable to abuse by employers. People in search of work and better livelihood opportunities face a greater risk of being deceived or trafficked, by falling victim to unscrupulous job brokers and employers.

MYANMAR LABOR MIGRATION OUTLOOK

Myanmar, despite being an advantaged country in terms of natural resources and beautiful landscapes, has been in political turmoil for many years, affecting the economic and social conditions of its nationals. Therefore, migration has been the most favorable option for the people of Myanmar as a survival strategy for safe refuge and for livelihood. Myanmar is home to about 55.2 million and its labor force is about 23.4 million. Labor migration has long been an important livelihood strategy for the people in Myanmar to survive periods of severe economic and political hardships. The military coup in 2021 increased the momentum of internal and external migration even more primarily for security concerns while some left their homes for better economic opportunities.

According to the latest Myanmar Population Census of 2014, more than two million Myanmar citizens migrated abroad where more than 70 percent of all migrants were in Thailand, and a smaller number were working in Malaysia, China, and Singapore. Other countries of destination for Myanmar migrant workers include the Republic of Korea, Japan, and the Gulf Cooperation Council (GCC) countries.[9] It is estimated that about 10 percent of its labor force (approximately 1.5 million Myanmar migrant workers) is working abroad mainly in Thailand and Malaysia. In terms of remittance, an estimated US$ 2.25 million was remitted by migrants in 2020, approximately 2.9 percent of the GDP, excluding the millions which are remitted informally through brokers or hand-carried back home to family members.[10] There is is yet to establish a comprehensive labor migration governance framework to manage such immense labor migration flow in Myanmar.

Therefore, migration remains largely unregulated and inequitable, divided between regular migrants, who typically work in more developed economies within Asia and the Middle East through formal recruitment, and irregular or undocumented migrants, who travel via illegal channels to work in neighboring middle-income countries. Since formal recruitment through licensed agencies is a complex, costly, as well as time-consuming procedure, most migrants continue to seek the assistance of unlicensed brokers or go abroad independently. Therefore, it is easier for Myanmar migrant workers, particularly undocumented workers, to fall prey to smugglers, traffickers, and unscrupulous actors, which eventually leads to abuse and exploitation. On the other hand, it is unfortunate that this is the only avenue available to them to access livelihoods and safety, especially in the current economic and political climate.

This chapter aims to assess the existing legal and collaborative actions in ensuring and providing Myanmar migrant workers their rights abroad based on the legal and policy initiatives of relevant international and regional organizations.

INTERNATIONAL MIGRATION GOVERNANCE: LEGAL AND POLICY FRAMEWORK

International Standards and Policies

The fundamental international instruments relating to migration governance include the eight ILO Core Conventions concerning forced labor, child labor, discrimination, and freedom of association. In addition, the most significant instruments that address the rights of migrant workers are the International Labor Organisation's (ILO) Convention on Migration for Employment (No. 97), and Migrant Workers (Supplementary Provisions) Convention (No. 143), and the UN Convention on the Protection of All Migrant Workers and Members of Their Families (1990). Along with the more general human rights treaties, these instruments provide a very comprehensive set of civil, political, economic, social, and other rights for migrants, including the rights to equal protection under labor laws, anti-discrimination laws, and family laws.

Despite its very limited number of ratifications by states, the International Convention on the Protection of the Rights of All Migrant Workers and Members of Their Families (ICMW) can be considered as the cornerstone of the rights-based approach to migration, which is also recommended by many international organizations and Non-governmental organizations (NGOs) relating to the protection of migrant workers.[11] Moreover, the ILO Multilateral Framework on Labor Migration (non-binding instrument) provides a comprehensive set of principles, guidelines, and best practices to assist governments in developing effective labor migration policies and management using a rights-based approach. It addresses the important themes of migration governance such as decent work for all, promoting migration and development linkages, and expanding international cooperation. Moreover, it also advocates gender-sensitive migration policies that address the special problems faced by women migrant workers.[12]

ASEAN Initiatives to Improve Migration Policies and Governance

As of 2020, Association of Southeast Asian Nations (ASEAN) is home to a total of 10 million migrant workers, with more than seven million being from the region. It is no doubt that labor migration has a far-reaching impact on the socio-economic development of both countries of origin and destination[13] where labor market pressures are lessened as migrant workers fill up labor market demands in countries of employment while reducing unemployment rates in home countries. At the household level, remittances of migrants elevate their families' quality of life. Over the years, ASEAN has taken regional actions in various areas ranging from education/information, protection, enforcement, legal recourse, and reintegration. At the national level, each member state has also instituted its own policies and initiatives.

ASEAN Consensus on the Protection and Promotion of the Rights of Migrant Workers

As one of the initiatives of ASEAN in ensuring the rights of migrant workers in the region, ASEAN reached a Consensus on the Protection and Promotion of the Rights of Migrant Workers (ASEAN Consensus) and it was signed by the ASEAN leaders during the 31st ASEAN Summit in November 2017. The ASEAN Consensus reaffirms its commitments enshrined in the ASEAN Charter, particularly in relation to the respect for the promotion and protection of human rights and fundamental freedoms, and it also aims to implement the purposes and commitments contained in the ASEAN Declaration on the Protection and Promotion of the Rights of Migrant Workers adopted at the 12th ASEAN Summit in 2007 in Cebu, the Philippines.[14] The ASEAN Consensus stipulates "the general principles, fundamental rights of migrant workers and members of their families, specific rights of migrant workers, obligations and commitments of ASEAN Member States. It also aims to establish a framework for closer cooperation among member states on addressing migrant workers' issues in the region."[15]

Although the ASEAN Consensus is a compromise between labor-sending and -receiving countries on divisive issues relating to their respective interests after nearly eight years of negotiations, it does not carry any legal weight and thus ASEAN members are not required to ratify the document nationally for implementation. Rather, the Consensus only serves as a moral standard for national governments to implement measures that address the commitments expressed in the document. In addition, the consensus emphasizes that the implementation of the commitments of the ASEAN member states shall be "in accordance with national laws, regulations, and policies."[16] The ASEAN Consensus is a significant milestone in strengthening the efforts of ASEAN countries to revisit their labor migration policies and aim for them to reflect the fundamental human rights of migrants, the need for promoting the welfare, and to uphold the human dignity of migrant workers.[17]

There is an action plan (2018–2025) for the ASEAN member states to implement the ASEAN Consensus through the ASEAN Committee on the Implementation of the ASEAN Declaration on the Protection and Promotion of the Rights of Migrant Workers (ACMW). Every member Ssate is sought to identify and insert projects into the proposed action plan 2018–2025 where each member state commits to lead at least one project in the action plan. There are 48 projects under the action plan and Myanmar is co-leading the "Tripartite Workshop to share good practices and experiences in: strengthening Labor Market Information System (LMIS) to facilitate responsiveness of Technical Vocational Education and Training (TVET) to labor market demands and skills needed for unemployed youth, women, and other vulnerable groups in AMS" along with the Philippines and it is also a coordinator for the project on "Protection Programme for Marginalised and Vulnerable Women (e.g. victims of trafficking, migrant workers, victims of disasters)."[18]

ASEAN Forum on Migrant Labor (AFML)

Another relevant initiative by ASEAN is an annual Forum on Migrant Labor (AFML), which is an open platform for review, discussion, and exchange of good practices and ideas between governments, workers' and employers' organizations, and civil society stakeholders on key issues facing women and men migrant workers in Southeast Asia, and develop recommendations to advance the implementation of the principles of the ASEAN Declaration on Protection and Promotion of the Rights of Migrant Workers. The Forum provides an opportunity to share stakeholder activities to implement the various recommendations from AFML meetings as well as the experience of developing the draft ASEAN instrument on the Protection and Promotion of the Rights of Migrant Workers.[19]

In addition, the ASEAN Secretariat also initiated the ASEAN Migration Outlook to provide "an analysis of recent migration movements and the prospects for rehabilitating labor migration, and enhance our preparedness and resilience for future shocks and crises." It was launched in July 2022, providing recommendations to establish a common procedure or protocol on the return and reintegration of migrant workers and improve migrant workers' access to social security benefits.[20]

INTERNATIONAL LABOR MIGRATION GOVERNANCE IN MYANMAR: AN OVERVIEW

At the international level, Myanmar has affirmed, to some extent, its strong commitment in ensuring the rights of laborers by ratifying the relevant ILO conventions. Myanmar joined ILO in 1948 and has ratified 25 ILO Conventions. Among them are four fundamental Conventions: Forced Labor Convention 1930 (No. 29); Freedom of Association and Protection of the Right to Organise Convention 1948 (No. 87); Minimum Age Convention, 1973 (No. 138), and Worst Forms of Child Labor Convention 1999 (No. 182).[21] The Myanmar government has also ratified a number of other technical Conventions of the ILO.[22] By ratifying these Conventions, the Myanmar government is required to implement these standards in its domestic laws and regulations as well as policy relating to the rights of the laborers as they reflect fundamental principles and rights at work.[23] However, Myanmar is not a party to any of the ILO's Governance Conventions which are of priority in nature for ratification.[24] In addition, despite being one of the major sending countries of migrant workers, Myanmar has not ratified the UN Convention on the Protection of All Migrant Workers and Members of Their Families (1990).

At the domestic level, there are several labor laws relating to employment under the purview of the Ministry of Labor, Immigration and Population such as the Workmen's Compensation Act, 1923; Employment Restriction Act, 1959; Labor Organization Law, 2011; Minimum Wage Law, 2013; and the Law Relating to Overseas Employment, 1999; etc. As far as international migration for employment is concerned, Myanmar controls the entry of foreign workers or non-citizens under the Myanmar Immigration (Emergency Provisions) Act 1947. In addition, entry and stay measures of foreign workers in Myanmar are also concerned with the Myanmar Investment Law by implication. However, the foreign workers in Myanmar are very limited in number compared to the number of Myanmar workers employed in foreign countries.

The receiving countries of Myanmar migrant workers include Thailand, Malaysia, Singapore, Korea, UAE, and Japan.[25] International migration has long been a livelihood strategy for the people of Myanmar in search of better social, educational, and economic opportunities. Despite this reality, the existing system of international migration governance in Myanmar is not comprehensive enough to guarantee that migrants following legal procedures are fully protected, not that migration can fully contribute to the development of the country. The situation is even worse for those who entered a foreign country without documentation. For example, statistics of Myanmar migrant workers in Thailand released by the Department of Employment in Thailand reflect this situation clearly. Of the 1,903,014 Myanmar migrants registered to work in Thailand in September 2019, 71.8 percent had entered Thailand without documents and at some later point entered into a process of regularization (nationality verification).[26]

Domestic Legal and Policy Framework

There are two central international migration governance instruments in Myanmar: the Law Relating to Overseas Employment (LROE), enacted in 1999, and the National Plan of Action (NPA) for the Management of International Labor Migration. According to the Objective Statement of the 2nd National Plan of Action on the Management of International Labor migration (2018–2022), Myanmar's long-term vision is "to provide Myanmar migrant workers with increased opportunities to migrate with dignity by accessing decent work opportunities abroad, within Southeast Asia and beyond."[27]

The Law Relating to Overseas Employment (LROE) 1999 is the most relevant legislation to be discussed. According to Section 2(a) of this law, "Overseas Employment" means "employment in any foreign country for a limited period of time including the employment of seafarers and employment in a foreign country of any Government servants or experts assigned by any Government department or organization."[28] "Service Agent" means "a person or organization, who/which for a prescribed service fee, acts an agent in securing employment for those who seek overseas employment."[29] Currently, there are 174 authorized overseas employment agencies in Myanmar.[30]

The LROE is currently under the process of review and revision. This legislation sets out the basic architecture for managing international labor migration. It provides registration procedures for workers, licensing processes for employment agencies, and a range of rights and responsibilities for both workers and employment agencies. The LROE also provides for the establishment of the Overseas Employment Supervisory Committee (OESC), which oversees the coordination and cooperation necessary to achieve the law's objectives. A much more recent instrument is a national policy document that includes four strategic areas of focus: "the governance of migration, the protection and empowerment of migrant workers, the inclusion of migration in the national development agenda, and data collection and management." The plan also designates the main actors and institutions to be responsible for operationalizing the policy.

The Overseas Employment Supervisory Committee (OESC): Recent Initiatives

In January 2021, the OESC held its coordination meeting where the discussions involved the establishment of a committee to ensure the safe sending of Myanmar migrant workers to foreign countries and the protection of the rights of those working in foreign countries. The committee grants licenses to overseas employment agencies under the LROE and the agencies mainly send Myanmar workers to Thailand, Malaysia, Korea, Japan, Singapore, the UAE, Qatar, Macau, and Jordan. A total number of 1,320,914 Myanmar migrant workers were sent to foreign countries from 1990 to March 2021.[31]

Although the process of sending migrant workers to foreign countries was suspended in March 2020 due to the outbreak of COVID-19, 4,169 migrant workers were sent to Japan and Korea based on their demands. In addition, overseas employment training courses have been conducted at Skills Training Centers in Yangon and Mandalay since 2017 for those who want to work in foreign countries, particularly on labor law and occupational safety. The licensing fees for overseas employment agencies were also increased from K5 million to K25 million along with full sets of responsibilities starting from February 4, 2020, and eliminated the substandard agencies.[32] In the January 2022 coordination meeting, it is reported that only Myanmar workers who hold the passport for Job-PJ and Overseas Employment Identification Card-OWIC, issued with the permission of the Ministry of Labor, Immigration and Population, shall be able to depart the country.[33]

Bilateral Agreements (MoUs) Relating to Myanmar Migrant Workers

Myanmar signed an MoU with Thailand on cooperation in the employment of workers in 2003, which was replaced by the 2016 MoU on labor cooperation between Myanmar and Thailand.[34] In 2018, an agreement was reached on the recruitment of fishing workers between the two countries, as part of the MoU follow-up process, but this has not been made available by Thailand (and Myanmar).[35] In addition, Myanmar has also signed an MoU with South Korea on a government-to-government recruitment and memoranda/agreements with Japan and Malaysia. However, these documents are not publicly available as they are treated as confidential.[36]

MoU between Myanmar and Thailand

Experts argued that the MoU negotiations between Thailand and Myanmar were not transparent and consultations with relevant stakeholders such as the engagements with workers' groups or unions were very limited. Therefore, national security concerns and associated actors led the negotiations, and human rights concerns are therefore unlikely to have featured prominently in the negotiations leading up to the 2016 MoU, which is valid for five years and renewable upon mutual consent. As an implementation of the 2016 MoU, Myanmar and Thailand agreed to conclude the "Agreement on the Employment of Workers," which sets out the implementing details of the sending and receiving process.[37]

In addition, the 2016 MoU sheds light on some of the human rights references and promotes technical cooperation, including the exchange of information for the prevention of illegal recruiting of manpower and human trafficking for employment. As the main concern of Thailand is to prevent irregular migration, the focus of the MoU remains on admissions procedures, prevention of irregular migration and employment, and repatriation of migrant workers, with less focus on meeting labor market needs and the protection of migrants. Coordination between both state parties is well-covered and regularly takes place (with a varied group of government agencies represented). Nevertheless, some argue that the secrecy of the negotiation, particularly the lack of consultation with relevant stakeholders, resulted in a side-lining of workers' rights. This raises concern that the MoUs are little more than bureaucratic frameworks to enable better state regulation of migration, supported by private commercial interests.[38]

CHALLENGES FACED BY MYANMAR MIGRANT WORKERS IN SELECTED RECEIVING COUNTRIES

As discussed earlier, Myanmar migrant workers are mainly sent to Thailand, Malaysia, Singapore, South Korea, Japan, and GCC countries. Although a growing number of migrant workers from Myanmar are attempting to use official channels either through licensed overseas employment agencies or through a government-to-government arrangement as in the case of South Korea, the vast majority of Myanmar migrant workers are also migrating through irregular means such as smuggling due to the costly, time-consuming, and complex procedures via legal means.[39] It is estimated that around half a million migrants mainly from Myanmar (but also from Cambodia and Lao PDR) are smuggled to Thailand each year. Fees for smuggling services are low, ranging from a few dollars to a few hundred dollars, meaning it is often cheaper to use smuggling services than regular labor migration systems.[40] Within Southeast Asia, irregular migration is found to be mainly driven by economic disparities. Despite porous borders, United Nations Office on Drugs and Crime (UNODC) estimates that over 80 percent of irregular migrants rely on smugglers. In this section, the challenges of Myanmar migrant workers particularly in Thailand and Malaysia are discussed, as they are the receiving countries of the majority of Myanmar migrant workers.

Thailand

Cross-border migration between Myanmar and Thailand has existed for centuries since the time when Thailand opened up its borders to allow unskilled migrants from neighboring countries. In Thailand, major labor market sectors for Myanmar migrant workers include fisheries and seafood processing, agriculture, construction, manufacturing, and services which absorb large numbers of workers.[41] It is estimated that around 3.7 million migrants are living in Thailand while most of them are from Myanmar, which accounts for 79.28 percent of migrant workers employed in Thailand,up to 6.6 percent of the country's total gross domestic product (GDP).[42]

The main cause of the migration of Myanmar workers is a direct result of the grave political and economic disparities in their home country. In addition, following the military coup on 1 February 2021, fierce fighting between the military and units of ethnic armed groups forced thousands of

Burmese people to cross the border to Thailand.[43] According to the chairman of the Migrant Workers Rights Network, the number of people crossing into Thailand has increased from 100 per day in 2020 to 2,000 per day in 2022.[44] The majority of migrants from Myanmar who flee their country end up in neighboring Thailand, where an estimated two million people have taken up squalid residences working "3-D jobs" (dangerous, dirty, and degrading), for pay well below minimum wage. Fearing persecution, and often without recognition of their rights to receive refugee status and international protection, the vast majority of those migrating from Myanmar find themselves desperate to survive, obtaining work in underground and, often, illegal labor markets.[45]

A study shows that workers working on fishing boats in general encounter extremely poor conditions compared to the other sectors such as the seafood processing, factory, and farming sectors. It is also noted that migrant workers, especially those who are being forced by their employers to work, are more likely to end up working aboard fishing boats. In addition, physical and verbal abuse by employers is common in the fishing sector and alarmingly such treatment is faced by child workers who are under age 15.[46] A testimony given by a migrant worker stated: "I have observed that especially most child laborers they can't leave because if they leave, they won't get paid, and if they want to leave it is possible only if the employers allow them. In addition, if the young child leaves without getting their money and (pink) card, they have to obtain their permission."[47] It is significant that most migrants work under very poor conditions and they cannot leave due to the fear of police arrest. Most migrants work an average of 12 hours a day as they start work even before 5 a.m. on days when there is a heavy workload, and a few get an hour or less break time per day. In general, they can take days off at an average of 4 days per month and only a few workers get paid for those days. Migrant workers who are employed on board the fishing boats are working in extremely dangerous conditions because of the nature of work, which is tough and lonely being away from family. Therefore, migrants working in this sector are mainly those with fewer job opportunities, such as unregistered migrants or child workers.[48]

Undocumented Myanmar migrant workers in Thailand who crossed the border illegally are struggling in many ways since they are living in hiding and are far from any employment opportunities because they lack legitimate work permits and are concerned about being detained by Thai police and immigration officials. The illegal border crossing of Myanmar migrant workers increased after the military coup in February 2021. According to the representative of the Migrant Workers' Rights Network (MWRN), "Since illegal immigrants lack legal residency, they are unable to roam freely. They can be arrested at any time and deported by the authorities." Although there are many career opportunities, Thai employers only hire immigrants with legal documentation, leaving many undocumented migrants jobless or having little chance of getting a job, and many of them eventually end up committing suicide while struggling to make ends meet.[49]

It is also noted that only about half of all migrant workers in Thailand are documented workers who have permission to work under the relevant laws of Thailand, accounting for 44.7 percent of the workers in Thailand.[50] Currently, despite having an MoU between Myanmar and Thailand on labor cooperation, there are various challenges faced by Myanmar migrant workers in Thailand. Some have concerns over salary or wage inequality. Studies show that "even though nearly all the workers were poor, those who had stable employment and earned an adequate income were more satisfied with their jobs as having a stable income enabled them to meet their basic needs and send money to their families in Myanmar." On the other hand, workers who were paid less than the standard wage felt unhappy and dissatisfied with their jobs.[51] Moreover, there are also concerns relating to several aspects of their living circumstances since many people have to share a small room without privacy where they need to take turns to carry out personal activities like dressing and undressing. Concerning their hygiene condition, "most residents lacked proper cooking facilities; food was prepared and cooked on the ground. As a result of these poor environmental conditions, many were at risk to get sick. Most of their children frequently developed respiratory and digestive illnesses, such as common colds, coughs, and diarrhea."[52]

Malaysia

It is estimated that Malaysia hosts approximately 1.4 to 2 million documented migrants, and unofficial estimates of 1.2 to 3.5 million additional migrants (as reported by the World Bank), making Malaysia one of the largest migrant-receiving countries in Southeast Asia.[53] In addition, there are around 2 to 4 million more undocumented workers. Migrant workers in Malaysia mainly come from Indonesia, Bangladesh, Nepal, Myanmar, and a smaller number of workers from other Asian countries. They engage in industries such as manufacturing, plantation, agriculture, hospitality and security services, and domestic work, representing an estimated 20 percent of the Malaysian workforce (ILO) and dominating low-skilled and semi-skilled jobs. As with most destination countries in the region, labor migration in Malaysia is managed through temporary programs, and primarily for "low-skilled" work, sometimes characterized as "3D"—dirty, dangerous, and degrading. There have been many cases of abuse faced by migrant workers in Malaysia, committed by recruitment agencies and employers, "ranging from excessive recruitment fees to serious violations of the terms and conditions of employment, among others."[54]

Malaysia has MoUs with Bangladesh, China, Sri Lanka, Thailand, Pakistan, Vietnam, and Indonesia for migrant workers recruitment processes and procedures,[55] however, currently, there is no such bilateral arrangement between Myanmar and Malaysia. Although there were discussions on issuing an MoU to formalize the intention of Malaysia to "safeguard the rights and interests of Myanmar workers in Malaysia," there is yet to have further information on its development.[56] In Malaysia, there are more than 550,000 Burmese migrant workers and an estimated 250,000 are undocumented workers.[57]

In Malaysia, undocumented foreign workers are often jailed for 3 to 6 months according to its immigration laws. After serving their prison terms, they are held at immigration detention centers until their identities and citizenship are confirmed by their respective embassies. The detainees whose citizenship has been confirmed are deported back to their home countries. During COVID-19, thousands of undocumented Myanmar migrant workers lost their jobs due to lockdowns imposed, and their hardship was exacerbated by a crackdown against illegal foreign workers. There were reported cases of Myanmar workers committing suicide during the lockdown suffering from financial hardships, losing job opportunities, and fearing arrest amid an immigration crackdown.[58] It is reported that more than 3,000 people who identify themselves as Myanmar nationals are being detained in 13 immigration centers across the country.[59]

INTERNATIONAL LABOR MIGRATION GOVERNANCE IN MYANMAR: WAY FORWARD

It is fundamental for every country to have a sound governance framework relating to migrant workers from the moment they plan to head off to the receiving country until their safe return to their respective home country. Generally, a number of initiatives are necessary in order to increase the benefits of migration for everyone including: "more effective governance of migration at the national, regional and global levels; greater policy coherence; increased cooperation among stakeholders; and increased operational capacity alongside increased service provision."[60]

Despite international migration being a livelihood strategy for the people of Myanmar, providing employment opportunities and skills for millions of young people and financial resources for their families and communities, Myanmar is nowhere near having a systematic international migration governance framework to ensure the rights of Myanmar migrant workers abroad. It is evidenced by the significant numbers of migrants who have suffered and have been suffering exploitation, dangerous living and working conditions, and discrimination. In addressing the existing challenges relating to labor migration in Myanmar, it is important not only to ensure the specific laws and policies are in place but also rigorous and consistent implementation of such laws and policies by relevant authorities and stakeholders.

Apart from the international and regional instruments and initiatives which Myanmar has ratified and implemented, the most relevant national legislation is the Law Relating to Overseas Employment (LROE), 1999, which provides the overall legal basis for all the external-migration system in Myanmar. Since the labor migration trends have changed over the years, it is necessary to review the legislation to remedy gaps in legal coverage and application which have become apparent as Myanmar adjusts to new migration situations. In addition, it is also of paramount importance to ensure the "harmonization of Myanmar's national labor migration legislation with international standards; and to strengthen protection mechanisms for the recruitment and placement of Myanmar workers abroad."[61] Moreover, critical to the successful implementation is the development of Rules and Regulations (by-laws) to ensure the government officials tasked with the implementation of the LROE are fully empowered in their functions and responsibilities. As of now, only basic rules and regulations regarding the licensing and roles of overseas employment agencies have been issued.

In addition, the effective implementation of the National Plan of Action on Management of International Labor Migration (NPA) should also be a priority for the relevant stakeholders. As advocated by the ILO, the inclusion of relevant key issues in the NPA in line with the ILO Multilateral Framework on Migration and relevant international labor standard is necessary. For instance, the ratification of the Private Employment Agencies Convention, 1997 (No. 181) and the Domestic Workers Convention, 2011 (No. 189), the recognition of the Code of Conduct for the members of Myanmar Overseas Employment Agencies Federation (MOEAF)[62] and monitoring mechanism to promote more ethical recruitment practices, and a specific time frame to revise the Overseas Employment Law and to develop its accompanying rules and regulations, which are reflected in the second NPA adopted by Ministry of Labor, Immigration, and Population in May 2019.[63]

It is important to enhance bilateral and multilateral cooperation. In terms of bilateral agreements, Myanmar should review the current mechanisms in place for implementations of existing MoUs relating to the labor cooperation to come out with effective remedies to address the challenges faced by Myanmar migrant workers despite having MoUs. In addition, Myanmar should also make the best effort in entering more bilateral agreements with receiving countries such as MoUs or government–government arrangements along with comprehensive policies and guidelines for effective implementations.

Moreover, Myanmar being a member of the ASEAN is encouraged to make every effort in its implementation of relevant rules and policies on international labor migration governance to be in line with the first general principle of the 2007 ASEAN Declaration on the Protection and Promotion of the Rights of Migrant Workers:

> Both the receiving states and sending states shall strengthen the political, economic, and social pillars of the ASEAN Community by promoting the full potential and dignity of migrant workers in a climate of freedom, equity, and stability in accordance with the laws, regulations, and policies of respective ASEAN Member Countries.[64]

In order to ensure the safe and secure migration process of migrant workers, there are several general principles that should be respected in designing and implementing relevant laws and policies at the international, regional, and national levels. The protection of migrant workers' rights should be fully inclusive, covering all migrant workers irrespective of sex, age, skills, and migratory or return status (e.g., irregular status or deported). All the mechanisms in place are necessary to protect migrants from recruitment abuses, from carrying high debt burdens, and/or from being provided with misleading information not only prior to departure but also after their arrival in the receiving countries.

Planning for return and reintegration should start before migration and continue during employment as well as upon arrival back to the home countries. Similarly, it is necessary to ensure that migrant workers are protected from abuse and exploitation in the workplaces and discrimination in the destination country since it will undermine the capacity of migrant workers to safely return to their home countries with conditions of dignity. Lastly, all policies and programs should respect the human and labor rights of migrant workers in line with relevant international and ASEAN instruments.[65] In doing so, adopting the ILO Multilateral Framework on Labor Migration is recommended since it provides not only a comprehensive set of principles and guidelines for a rights-based approach to labor migration but also good practices on labor migration developed by governments and social partners.[66]

CONCLUSION

It is reported that the Myanmar government has now opened legal channels for migration to 18 different countries and is working to provide documents to the large numbers of semi-documented[67] workers in Thailand and Malaysia.[68] Nevertheless, the current governance of regular migration in Myanmar is still not comprehensive enough to guarantee that migrants following legal procedures are fully protected from exploitation, abuse, and discrimination in receiving countries. Undoubtedly, there is even more work to be done in ensuring undocumented or irregular migrant workers are protected. It would be a great move for Myanmar to ratify the International Convention on the Protection of the Rights of All Migrant Workers and Members of Their Families to show its strong commitments in ensuring the rights of migrant workers and their families. In order to make migration safer and to increase the long-term benefits of international labor migration in Myanmar, its government is also encouraged to work with all the relevant stakeholders in the industry including ILO's project on Developing International and Internal Labor Migration Governance (DIILM), the Myanmar Overseas Employment Agencies Federation, anti-trafficking police recruitment agencies, labor organizations, and civil society organizations to strengthen the legislative and policy framework governing international labor migration in Myanmar.

REFERENCES

Action plan (2018–2025) to implement the ASEAN consensus on the protection and promotion of the rights of migrant workers. https://asean.org/wp-content/uploads/Action-Plan-of-ASEAN-Consensus_EXTRACT-FOR-ASEAN-WEBSITE_25-NOV-2020.pdf, accessed on 12 April 2023.

ASEAN Declaration on the Protection and Promotion of the Rights of Migrant Workers, 2007.

ASEAN Leaders commit to safeguard the rights of migrant workers, November 14, 2017. https://asean.org/asean-leaders-commit-to-safeguard-the-rights-of-migrant-workers/, accessed on 11 April 2023.

Chantavanich, S., and Vungsiriphisal, P., 2012 "Myanmar Migrants to Thailand: Economic Analysis and Implications to Myanmar Development." In *Economic Reforms in Myanmar: Pathways and Prospects*, edited by Hank Lim and Yasuhiro Yamada, BRC Research Report No. 10, Bangkok Research Center, IDE-JETRO, Bangkok, Thailand.

Committee Meeting: Overseas Employment Supervisory Comm. Meeting Held, MITV, 22 January 2022. https://www.myanmaritv.com/news/committee-meeting-overseas-employment-supervisory-comm-meeting-held.

Duncan, K. In Thailand, Myanmar Migrants' Illicit Unions Fight to be Heard, *Aljazeera*, 30 May 2022. https://www.aljazeera.com/economy/2022/5/30/in-thailand-burmese-migrant-workers-fight-to-organise.

Five Corridors Project, Myanmar-Thailand: Bilateral Agreements. https://fivecorridorsproject.org/myanmar-thailand/myanmar-thailand-bilateral

-arrangements#:~:text=Myanmar%20has%20additionally%20signed%20a,they%20are%20treated%20as%20confidential.

ILO Governance Conventions include: Labor Inspection Convention 1947; Employment Policy Convention 1964; Labor Inspection (Agriculture) Convention 1969; and Tripartite Consultation (International Labor Standards) Convention 1976.

ILO, TRIANGLE in ASEAN Quarterly Briefing Note, Myanmar (July–September 2022).

ILO's 2006 Multilateral Framework on Labor Migration. https://www.ilo.org/africa/areas-of-work/labor-migration/policy-frameworks/WCMS_671744/lang--en/index.htm#:~:text=The%20framework%20is%20a%20comprehensive,and%20practices%20of%20ILO%20constituents. Accessed on 11 April 2023.

International Labor Organisation, 88 Generation dismisses Malaysia Migrants MOU (Myanmar Times—17 March 2015—The 88 Generation has called on Malaysia to introduce legislation to protect Myanmar workers and dismissed a plan to sign a bilateral memorandum of understanding as just for show). https://apmigration.ilo.org/news/88-generation-dismisses-malaysia-migrants-mou accessed on 15 April 2023.

International Labor Organisation, Developing International and Internal Labor Migration Governance (DIILM) Feb 2016–2021, DIILM Update No. 3, International Labor Migration Governance, November 2020. https://www.ilo.org/wcmsp5/groups/public/---asia/---ro-bangkok/---ilo-yangon/documents/briefingnote/wcms_760744.pdf, accessed on 15 April 2023.

International Labor Organisation, Labor Migration in Myanmar. https://www.ilo.org/yangon/areas/labor-migration/lang- en/index.htm#:~:text=According%20to%20the%20latest%20Myanmar,Japan%2C%20and%20the%20GCC%20countries, accessed on 10 April 2023.

International Labor Organisation, Migrant Workers' Rights and Welfare, Combating the Worst Forms of Child Labor in Shrimp and Seafood Processing Areas of Thailand THA/10/50/USA. At https://www.ilo.org/wcmsp5/groups/public/---asia/---ro-bangkok/documents/publication/wcms_230053.pdf, accessed on 10 April 2023.

International Labor Organisation, Myanmar Guide to ILO Fundamental and Governance Conventions, 2019. ISBN 9789220315194 (Print), ISBN 9789220315200 (web pdf). https://www.ilo.org/wcmsp5/groups/public/---asia/---ro-bangkok/---ilo-yangon/documents/publication/wcms_738360.pdf, accessed on 12 April 2023.

International Labor Organisation, Ratifications for Myanmar. https://www.ilo.org/dyn/normlex/en/f?p=NORMLEXPUB:11200:0::NO::P11200_COUNTRY_ID:103159, accessed on 12 April 2023.

International Labor Organisation, The Multilateral Framework on Labor Migration: Non-binding principles and guidelines for a rights-based approach to labor migration, ISBN: 92-2-119118-4 and 978-92-2-119118-6, Geneva, International Labor Office, 2006. P-55. https://www.ilo.org/wcmsp5/groups/public/---ed_protect/---protrav/---migrant/documents/publication/wcms_178672.pdf, accessed on 15 April 2023.

International Organisation for Migration, World Migration Report 2020, p. 10. https://publications.iom.int/system/files/pdf/wmr_2020.pdf, accessed on 10 April 2023.

Irena M., and O. Daquio CR., ASEAN Advances Migrant Workers' Rights in the Changing World of Work, *The SEAN*, 7 December 2022. https://theaseanmagazine.asean.org/article/asean-advances-migrant-workers-rights-in-the-changing-world-of-work/#:~:text=As%20of%202020%2C%20ASEAN%20is,cent%20since%20three%20decades%20ago. Accessed on 11 April 2023.

Labor Migration Trends and Policies in Myanmar. https://events.development.asia/system/files/materials/2019/01/201901-labor-migration-trends-and-policies-myanmar.pdf, accessed on 12 April 2023.

Memorandum of Understanding between the Government of the Kingdom of Thailand and the Government of the Union of Myanmar on Cooperation in the Employment of Workers. https://www.ilo.org/asia/info/WCMS_160932/lang--en/index.htm, accessed on 12 April 2023.

MoUs, BLAs and declarations related to migration. https://www.ilo.org/asia/areas/labor-migration/WCMS_161105/lang--en/index.htm, accessed on 11 April 2023.

MoUs, BLAs and declarations related to migration. https://www.ilo.org/asia/areas/labor-migration/WCMS_161105/lang--en/index.htm, accessed on 11 April 2023.

Myanmar Coup: Thousands of Burmese flee to Thailand after intense fighting, *BBC News*, 7 April 2023. https://www.bbc.com/news/world-asia-65210336, accessed on 13 April 2023.

Myanmar migrant workers face waves of challenges in Thailand, December 17, 2022. https://www.bnionline.net/en/news/myanmar-migrant-workers-face-waves-challenges-thailand, accessed on 13 April 2023.

Myanmar Migrants Face Being Exploited under Thai Deportation System, *Radio Free Asia*, 5 February 2023. https://www.rfa.org/english/news/myanmar/myanmar-migrants-thailand-02052023090414.html#:~:text=Chairman%20of%20the%20Migrant%20Workers,to%2045%2C000%20that%20fled%20Myanmar, accessed on 13 April 2023.

Ruhs Martin, The Human Rights of Migrant Workers: Why Do So Few Countries Care, *American Behavioral Scientists* 56 (9) 1277–93 (2012).

S. Srakaew. (2006) Assessing the Situation of the Worst Forms of Child Labor in Samuth Sakhon, Bangkok: Asian Research Centre for Migration Chulalongkorn University.

Sarapirom K., Muensakda. P, and Sriwanna T. (2020) Lifestyles of Myanmar migrant workers under Thai socio-cultural context: A challenge of state management in the future, *Interdisciplinary Research Review* 15, no. 5, 8–15.

The ASEAN Consensus on the Protection and Promotion of the Rights of Migrant Workers. https://www.ilo.org/wcmsp5/groups/public/---asia/---ro-bangkok/documents/publication/wcms_230053.pdf.

United Nations Department of Economic and Social Affairs, Population Division (2020). International Migration 2020 Highlights (ST/ESA/SER.A/452). https://www.un.org/en/globalissues/migration#:~:text=Some%20people%20move%20in%20search,disasters%2C%20or%20other%20environmental%20factors.

United Nations, Smuggling of Migrants, UNODC Regional Office for Southeast Asia and the Pacific. https://www.unodc.org/roseap/en/what-we-do/toc/smuggling-of-migrants.html.

US Department of Labor, Bureau of International Labor Affairs, Protecting the Rights of Migrant Workers through Empowerment and Advocacy in Malaysia. https://www.dol.gov/agencies/ilab/protecting-rights-migrant-workers-through-empowerment-and-advocacy-malaysia, accessed on 16 April 2023.

W. H. Mobley, Intermediate linkages in the relationship between job satisfaction and employee turnover, *Journal of Applied Psychology* 62, no. 2 (1997) 237–40.

Wickramasekara P., Effective Return and Reintegration of Migrant Workers with Special Focus on ASEAN Member States,," International Labor Organization 2019. ISBN: 978-92-2-134062-1. https://www.ilo.org/wcmsp5/groups/public/---asia/---ro-bangkok/---sro-bangkok/documents/publication/wcms_733917.pdf, accessed on 14 April 2023.

Wiki Impact, Life As a Burmese Migrant Worker in Malaysia: A Collection of Stories, November 30, 2021, https://www.wikiimpact.com/life-as-a-burmese-migrant-worker-in-malaysia-a-collection-of-stories/#:~:text=As%20migrant%20workers%20play%20such,%2C%20agriculture%2C%20forestry%20and%20fishing,accessedon15April2023.

Zaw Zaw Htwe, Malaysia Begins Deporting Nearly 1,000 Detained Myanmar Migrants, *The Irrawaddy*, 3 November 2020. https://www.irrawaddy.com/news/burma/malaysia-begins-deporting-nearly-1000-detained-myanmar-migrants.html, accessed on 15 April 2023.

NOTES

1. "Much of this increase was due to labor or family migration. Humanitarian crises in many parts of the world also contributed, with an increase of 17 million in the number of refugees and asylum seekers between 2000 and 2020. In 2020, the number of persons forcibly displaced across national borders worldwide stood at 34 million, double the number in 2000." United Nations Department of Economic and Social Affairs, Population Division (2020). International Migration 2020 Highlights (ST/ESA/SER.A/452).

2. https://www.un.org/en/globalissues/migration#:~:text=Some%20people%20move%20in%20search,disasters%2C%20or%20other%20environmental%20factors.

3. Ibid.

4. https://www.iom.int/about-migration, accessed on 10 April 2023.

5. International Organisation for Migration, World Migration Report 2020, p. 10. https://publications.iom.int/system/files/pdf/wmr_2020.pdf, accessed on 10 April 2023.

6. Article 11, Migration for Employment Convention (Revised), 1949 (o. 97).

7. Article 2(1), United Nations Convention on the Protection of the Rights of all Migrant Workers and Members of their Families, 1990.

8. International Labor Organisation, Migrant Workers' Rights and Welfare, Combating the Worst Forms of Child Labor in Shrimp and Seafood Processing Areas of Thailand THA/10/50/USA.

https://www.ilo.org/wcmsp5/groups/public/---asia/---ro-bangkok/documents/publication/wcms_230053.pdf accessed on 10 April 2023.

9. International Labor Organisation, Labor Migration in Myanmar.

https://www.ilo.org/yangon/areas/labor-migration/lang- en/index.htm#:~:text=According%20to%20the%20latest%20Myanmar,Japan%2C%20and%20the%20GCC%20countries, accessed on 10 April 2023.

10. ILO, TRIANGLE in ASEAN Quarterly Briefing Note, Myanmar (July–September 2022).

11. Ruhs Martin, The Human Rights of Migrant Workers: Why Do So Few Countries Care, *American Behavioral Scientists* 56, no. 9, 1277–93 (2012).

12. ILO's 2006 Multilateral Framework on Labor Migration.

https://www.ilo.org/africa/areas-of-work/labor-migration/policy-frameworks/WCMS_671744/lang--en/index.htm#:~:text=The%20framework%20is%20a%20comprehensive,and%20practices%20of%20ILO%20constituents, accessed on 11 April 2023.

13. Irena M., and O. Daquio CR., ASEAN Advances Migrant Workers' Rights in the Changing World of Work, *The SEAN*, 7 December 2022,

https://theaseanmagazine.asean.org/article/asean-advances-migrant-workers-rights-in-the-changing-world-of-work/#:~:text=As%20of%202020%2C%20ASEAN%20is,cent%20since%20three%20decades%20ago, accessed on 11 April 2023.

14. ASEAN Leaders commit to safeguard the rights of migrant workers, November 14, 2017.

https://asean.org/asean-leaders-commit-to-safeguard-the-rights-of-migrant-workers/, accessed on 11 April 2023.

15. Ibid.

16. Chapter 7, The ASEAN Consensus on the Protection and Promotion of the Rights of Migrant Workers.

17. https://www.ilo.org/wcmsp5/groups/public/---asia/---ro-bangkok/documents/publication/wcms_230053.pdf.

18. ACTION PLAN (2018–2025) TO IMPLEMENT THE ASEAN CONSENSUS ON THE PROTECTION AND PROMOTION OF THE RIGHTS OF MIGRANT WORKERS.

https://asean.org/wp-content/uploads/Action-Plan-of-ASEAN-Consensus_EXTRACT-FOR-ASEAN-WEBSITE_25-NOV-2020.pdf, accessed on 12 April 2023.

19. MoUs, BLAs and declarations related to migration,

https://www.ilo.org/asia/areas/labor-migration/WCMS_161105/lang--en/index.htm, accessed on 11 April 2023.

20. Irena M., and O. Daquio CR., ASEAN Advances Migrant Workers' Rights in the Changing World of Work, *The SEAN*, 7 December 2022.

https://theaseanmagazine.asean.org/article/asean-advances-migrant-workers-rights-in-the-changing-world-of-work/#:~:text=As%20of%202020%2C%20ASEAN%20is,cent%20since%20three%20decades%20ago, accessed on 11 April 2023.

21. International Labor Organisation, Ratifications for Myanmar,

https://www.ilo.org/dyn/normlex/en/f?p=NORMLEXPUB:11200:0::NO::P11200_COUNTRY_ID:103159, accessed on 12 April 2023.

22. Ibid.

23. International Labor Organisation, Myanmar Guide to ILO Fundamental and Governance Conventions, 2019. ISBN 9789220315194 (Print), ISBN 9789220315200 (web pdf). https://www.ilo.org/wcmsp5/groups/public/---asia/---ro-bangkok/---ilo-yangon/documents/publication/wcms_738360.pdf, accessed on 12 April 2023.

24. ILO Governance Conventions include: Labor Inspection Convention 1947; Employment Policy Convention 1964; Labor Inspection (Agriculture) Convention 1969; and Tripartite Consultation (International Labor Standards) Convention 1976.

25. Labor Migration Trends and Policies in Myanmar, https://events.development.asia/system/files/materials/2019/01/201901-labor-migration-trends-and-policies-myanmar.pdf, accessed on 12 April 2023.

26. International Labor Organisation, Developing International and Internal Labor Migration Governance (DIILM) Feb. 2016–2021, DIILM Update No. 3, International Labor Migration Governance, November 2020, https://www.ilo.org/wcmsp5/groups/public/---asia/---ro-bangkok/---ilo-yangon/documents/briefingnote/wcms_760744.pdf, accessed on 15th April 2023.

27. Ibid.

28. Section 2 (a), The Law Relating to Overseas Employment 1999, The State Peace and Development Council Law No. 3/99, The 12 Waning Day of First Waso. 1361 ME (9 July 1999).

29. Section 2(c), ibid.

30. Updated List of Sending Organisations for Specified Skilled Worker, 30 March 2023. https://www.moj.go.jp/isa/content/930004987.pdf, accessed on 12 April 2023.

31. COMMITTEE MEETING: OVERSEAS EMPLOYMENT SUPERVISORY COMM. MEETING HELD, MITV, 22 JANUARY 2022.

https://www.myanmaritv.com/news/committee-meeting-overseas-employment-supervisory-comm-meeting-held.

32. Ibid.

33. Ibid.

34. Memorandum of Understanding between the Government of the Kingdom of Thailand and the Government of the Union of Myanmar on Cooperation in the Employment of Workers,

https://www.ilo.org/asia/info/WCMS_160932/lang--en/index.htm, accessed on 12 April 2023.

35. Five Corridors Project, Myanmar-Thailand: Bilateral Agreements,

https://fivecorridorsproject.org/myanmar-thailand/myanmar-thailand-bilateral-arrangements#:~:text=Myanmar%20has%20additionally%20signed%20a,they%20are%20treated%20as%20confidential.

36. Ibid.

37. Article 5, Memorandum of Understanding between the Government of the Kingdom of Thailand and the Government of the Union of Myanmar on Cooperation in the Employment of Workers, 2016.

38. Five Corridors Project, Myanmar-Thailand: Bilateral Agreements,

https://fivecorridorsproject.org/myanmar-thailand/myanmar-thailand-bilateral-arrangements#:~:text=Myanmar%20has%20additionally%20signed%20a,they%20are%20treated%20as%20confidential.

39. International Labor Organisation, Labor Migration in Myanmar, https://www.ilo.org/yangon/areas/labor-migration/lang--en/index.htm.

40. United Nations, Smuggling of Migrants, UNODC Regional Office for Southeast Asia and the Pacific, https://www.unodc.org/roseap/en/what-we-do/toc/smuggling-of-migrants.html.

41. Chantavanich, S., and Vungsiriphisal, P., 2012, "Myanmar Migrants to Thailand: Economic Analysis and Implications to Myanmar Development," in *Economic Reforms in Myanmar: Pathways and Prospects*, edited by Hank Lim and Yasuhiro Yamada, BRC Research Report No. 10, Bangkok Research Center, IDE-JETRO, Bangkok, Thailand.

42. Duncan, K. In Thailand, Myanmar Migrants' Illicit Unions Fight to be Heard, *Aljazeera*, 30 May 2022, https://www.aljazeera.com/economy/2022/5/30/in-thailand-burmese-migrant-workers-fight-to-organise.

43. Myanmar Coup: Thousands of Burmese flee to Thailand after intense fighting, *BBC News*, 7 April 2023, https://www.bbc.com/news/world-asia-65210336, accessed on 13 April 2023.

44. Myanmar Migrants Face Being Exploited under Thai Deportation System, *Radio Free Asia*, 5 February 2023, https://www.rfa.org/english/news/myanmar/myanmar-migrants-thailand-02052023090414.html#:~:text=Chairman%20of%20the%20Migrant%20Workers,to%2045%2C000%20that%20fled%20Myanmar, accessed on 13 April 2023.

45. Sarapirom, K., Muensakda, P., Sriwanna, T. (2020) Lifestyles of Myanmar migrant workers under Thai socio-cultural context: A challenge of state management in the future, *Interdisciplinary Research Review* 15, no. 5, 8–15.

46. S. Srakaew (2006) Assessing the Situation of the Worst Forms of Child Labor in Samuth Sakhon, Bangkok: Asian Research Centre for Migration Chulalongkorn University.

47. Sarapirom, K., Muensakda, P., Sriwanna, T. (2020) Lifestyles of Myanmar migrant workers under Thai socio-cultural context: A challenge of state management in the future, *Interdisciplinary Research Review* 15, no. 5, 8–15.

48. Ibid.

49. Myanmar migrant workers face waves of challenges in Thailand, December 17, 2022. https://www.bnionline.net/en/news/myanmar-migrant-workers-face-waves-challenges-thailand, accessed on 13 April 2023.

50. Ibid.

51. W. H. Mobley, Intermediate linkages in the relationship between job satisfaction and employee turnover, *Journal of Applied Psychology* 62, no. 2 (1997), 237–40.

52. Ibid.

53. https://www.iom.int/countries/malaysia, accessed on 14 April 2023.

54. US Department of Labor, Bureau of International Labor Affairs, Protecting the Rights of Migrant Workers through Empowerment and Advocacy in Malaysia.

https://www.dol.gov/agencies/ilab/protecting-rights-migrant-workers-through-empowerment-and-advocacy-malaysia, accessed on 16 April 2023.

55. MoUs, BLAs and declarations related to migration, https://www.ilo.org/asia/areas/labor-migration/WCMS_161105/lang--en/index.htm, accessed on 11 April 2023.

56. International Labor Organisation, 88 Generation dismisses Malaysia Migrants MOU (Myanmar Times—17 March 2015—The 88 Generation has called on Malaysia to introduce legislation to protect Myanmar workers and dismissed a plan to sign of a bilateral memorandum of understanding as just for show), https://apmigration.ilo.org/news/88-generation-dismisses-malaysia-migrants-mou, accessed on 15 April 2023.

57. Wiki Impact, Life as a Burmese Migrant Worker in Malaysia: A Collection of Stories, November 30, 2021, https://www.wikiimpact.com/life-as-a-burmese-migrant-worker-in-malaysia-a-collection-of-stories/#:~:text=As%20migrant%20workers%20play%20such,%2C%20agriculture%2C%20forestry%20and%20fishing, accessed on 15 April 2023.

58. Zaw Zaw Htwe, Without Work and Fearing Arrest, Undocumented Myanmar Migrants in Malaysia Take Their Own Lives, *The Irrawaddy*, 17 June 2020, https://www.irrawaddy.com/news/burma/without-work-fearing-arrest-undocumented-myanmar-migrants-malaysia-take-lives.html, accessed on 15 April 2023.

59. Zaw Zaw Htwe, Malaysia Begins Deporting Nearly 1,000 Detained Myanmar Migrants, *The Irrawaddy*, 3 November 2020, https://www.irrawaddy.com/news/burma/malaysia-begins-deporting-nearly-1000-detained-myanmar-migrants.html, accessed on 15 April 2023.

60. International Labor Organisation, Developing International and Internal Labor Migration Governance (DIILM) Feb. 2016–2021, DIILM Update No. 3, International Labor Migration Governance, November 2020, https://www.ilo.org/wcmsp5/groups/public/---asia/---ro-bangkok/---ilo-yangon/documents/briefingnote/wcms_760744.pdf, accessed on 15th April 2023.

61. Ibid.

62. MOEAF Code of Conduct was developed by the Myanmar Overseas Employment Agencies Federation (MOEAF), in collaboration with the Ministry of Labor, Immigration and Population (MOLIP) and with technical input from the ILO TRIANGLE in the ASEAN project. It was signed by over 100 recruitment agencies in August 2016 to encourage more ethical recruitment practices and more fair and respectful procedures. According to the code, migrant workers are briefed about details of contracts, labor rights, complaint mechanisms, social security, access to health care, information on local currency, wages, cost of living, remittances, and banking. It also instructs the establishment of a database of all workers, and supporting agencies that can respond quickly to workers' needs.

63. International Labor Organisation, Developing International and Internal Labor Migration Governance (DIILM) Feb. 2016–2021, DIILM Update No. 3, International Labor Migration Governance, November 2020, https://www.ilo.org/wcmsp5/groups

/public/---asia/---ro-bangkok/---ilo-yangon/documents/briefingnote/wcms_760744.pdf, accessed on 15 April 2023.

64. ASEAN Declaration on the Protection and Promotion of the Rights of Migrant Workers, 2007.

65. Wickramasekara, P., Effective Return and Reintegration of Migrant Workers with Special Focus on ASEAN Member States," International Labor Organization 2019. ISBN: 978-92-2-134062-1.

https://www.ilo.org/wcmsp5/groups/public/---asia/---ro-bangkok/---sro-bangkok/documents/publication/wcms_733917.pdf, accessed on 14 April 2023.

66. International Labor Organisation, The Multilateral Framework on Labor Migration: Non-Binding principles and guidelines for a rights-based approach to labor migration, ISBN: 92-2-119118-4 & 978-92-2-119118-6, Geneva, International Labor Office, 2006, p. 55, https://www.ilo.org/wcmsp5/groups/public/---ed_protect/---protrav/---migrant/documents/publication/wcms_178672.pdf, accessed on 15 April 2023.

67. The term "semi-documented migrants" refers to migrants who have registered in the countries of destination under amnesties and registration processes but who do not yet have all the documents required by Myanmar.

68. International Labor Organisation, Developing International and Internal Labor Migration Governance (DIILM) Feb. 2016–2021, DIILM Update No. 3, International Labor Migration Governance, November 2020, https://www.ilo.org/wcmsp5/groups/public/---asia/---ro-bangkok/---ilo-yangon/documents/briefingnote/wcms_760744.pdf, accessed on 15 April 2023.

Chapter 8

Nepali Laws on Ensuring the Rights of Migrant Workers

Geeta Pathak Sangroula and
Amritha Viswanath Shenoy

Workers have migrated from Nepal for a long time. One famous example is Arniko, an architect who travelled to East Asia (China, Japan, South Korea) in the thirteenth century and introduced the Pagoda style of construction.[1] He was accompanied by many artisans. To date, most Nepali men who travel abroad for work join the construction industry whereas women join the workforce as domestic workers. Depending upon the work they undertake, they face different problems. The Convention of Migrant Workers (CMW), 1990, recognizes and ensures some of their rights. Similarly, some instruments formulated under the aegis of the International Labor Organization (ILO) refer to migrant workers. However, Nepal is not a party to them thereby exposing the migrant workers to various vulnerabilities. Nepal is a signatory to a soft law instrument, the Global Compact on Migration.

The Global Compact refers to many of the commitments toward helping migrant workers. National laws, especially the Foreign Employment Act of 2007, are a significant national endeavour to establish a mechanism for recruitment and grievance redressal for the migrant workers. The bilateral agreements are important steps in protecting the migrant workers. SAARC (South Asian Association for Regional Cooperation) has formed a plan of action for migrant workers that need to be implemented properly. The Non-governmental organizations (NGOs) working in Nepal try to fill the other gaps. This chapter elucidates these aspects one by one and reaches a conclusion along with some suggestions.

TERMINOLOGIES RELATED TO MIGRANT WORKERS

The authors would like to use the terminologies as per the Convention on Migrant Workers in the context of Nepal. Therefore, instead of legal migrant workers and illegal migrant workers, the article mentions regular or documented migrant workers and irregular or undocumented migrant workers, respectively. Article 5 of the Convention on the Protection of the Rights of All Migrant Workers and Members of their Families, 1990, states as follows:

For the purposes of the present Convention, migrant workers and members of their families:

> Are considered as documented or in a regular situation if they are authorized to enter, to stay and to engage in a remunerated activity in the State of employment pursuant to the law of that State and to international agreements to which that State is a party;
>
> Are considered as non-documented or in an irregular situation if they do not comply with the conditions provided for in subparagraph (a) of the present article.

As discussed in the succeeding section, migration of women workers from Nepal is mostly to do domestic work. Therefore, the issue of domestic workers is also discussed in the present article. The terminologies of domestic work and domestic workers is defined in Article 1 of the Domestic Workers Convention, 2011 (ILO Convention, No. 189):

For the purpose of this Convention:

> The term domestic work means work performed in or for a household or households;
>
> The term domestic worker means any person engaged in domestic work within an employment relationship;
>
> A person who performs domestic work only occasionally or sporadically and not on an occupational basis is not a domestic worker.

Since, migrant workers from Nepal contribute to the Gulf countries, we would like to use the term "West Asia" instead of "Middle East." The nomenclature related to geographical areas was imposed by the colonizers. With decolonization and self-determination, the nomenclature has changed.[2] West Asia represents a decolonized term today.

ISSUES OF MIGRANT WORKERS OF NEPAL

Migrant workers from Nepal travel to many countries for work. They contribute toward the receiving economies as well as to the Nepali economy. Remittances are a major source of income for Nepal's economy.[3] Despite the economic contribution, the labor from Nepal faces various threats like abuses, sexual exploitation, forced labor, forced marriage, among many. In many instances, they also die in unfortunate circumstances in the country of destination. Individual agents and recruitment agencies help the workers migrate to host countries. However, individual agents escape the legal obligations, putting the migrant workers at a risk of fraud.

Depending upon the destination countries of work, the problems also differ accordingly. A majority of workers migrate to Malaysia, West Asia, and India. Apart from these regions, South Korea welcomes many migrant workers from Nepal. The Department of Foreign Employment has approved 111 destination countries to work in. However, Nepalis work in unrecognized countries also. This is quite risky because minimum protection from the government would be lacking in the unrecognized countries. In such cases, they cannot access the legal remedies of approaching the embassy or law enforcement agencies.[4]

Migration to India is largest in number. Many of the migrant workers are without documentation because of open borders.[5] Undocumented migrant workers do not have many of the rights provided under the Convention on Migrant Workers. For instance, Article 40 provides the right to form associations and trade unions.[6] Article 41 ensures the right to participate in public affairs and elections of their state of origin.[7] Significantly, Article 44 protects the unity of the families of the migrant workers.[8] In any event, the undocumented or irregular migrant workers add to remittances through indirect channels.[9] They are deprived of many rights, and, specifically, the Nepali irregular migrant workers cannot avail of soft loans, or a reintegration plan in the domestic workforce[10] (reintegration is indispensable for workers who returned due to the pandemic), etc.

A problematic system underlying the migration to West Asia is the *Kafala* system—the system of sponsorship to migrant workers in the West Asian countries.[11] The employers sponsor the workers to travel and accommodate in the new country. Thereafter, they exercise a lot of control over them. They cannot change their employer. The employers seize the passports and visas of the workers.[12] Thus, an uneven power is exercised by the employer over the migrants. At times, the worker is subjected to forced and unpaid labor.

Many workers employed in Qatar to prepare for the FIFA World Cup 2022 succumbed to death.[13] A number of deaths occurred due to unanswerable situations. The exploitation of labor caught the eyes of the media and

Qatar was criticized. Those who suffered preparing for the World Cup are still demanding compensation.[14] Thereafter, with the negotiations of ILO and Qatar, the efforts to improve working conditions of workers is going on.[15]

Most male workers from Nepal join the construction sector and most women migrate as domestic helpers.[16] Some of the concerns are specific to women domestic workers. In the case of women who migrate as domestic workers, non-documentation leads to further risks of trafficking. Women workers often travel to India for work without documentation.[17] Women workers migrating abroad face various risks. Therefore, the government of Nepal restricts partially or totally (depending upon the policies) migration of women workers. The government policy of restricting women from migrating is discriminatory (Ghimire 2017). The International Labor Organization in its 2015 report titled "No Easy Exit: Migration Bans Affecting Women From Nepal" (ILO 2015) points out the restrictions/partial/total ban on women migrating to work. Because of such restrictions, women migrate without proper documents. This endangers their working conditions and life abroad. Therefore, many scholars as well as the ILO consider the restrictive policies as discriminatory.

The pandemic that hit the world in 2020, exacerbated the problems of the migrant workers. Laura Foley and Nicola Piper bring to light an important issue of "wage theft" faced by the migrant workers during the pandemic. They define wage theft as "the unlawful intentional under- or non-payment of an employee's wages or entitlements by their employer (or recruitment agency) for work carried out" (Laura Foley; Nicola Piper 2021). Migrant workers take loans to pay the recruitment fees and due to wage theft, they are unable to repay their loans (Laura Foley; Nicola Piper 2021). This worsens their financial loss leading to a bondage kind of situation. Wage theft constitutes a violation of labor rights under ILO Convention 95 on Protection of Wages.[18] During emergency situations, the migrant workers have the right to be paid the outstanding remuneration. Article 22(6) of the CMW also states the right of the migrant workers to claim the unpaid wages.[19] In addition, Article 34(1) of the ILO Migrant Workers Recommendation, 1975 (No. 151), states:

> a migrant worker who leaves the country of employment should be entitled, irrespective of the legality of his stay therein – (a) to any outstanding remuneration for work performed, including severance payments normally due.

The pandemic put a halt on migration for work affecting those who waited to migrate for work. The issuance of labor permits by the Department of Foreign Employment of Nepal decreased in number.[20] Workers were stranded abroad in difficult circumstances with financial as well as health issues. Based on interviews conducted of about 3,000 migrant workers, the International Organization for Migration published a report in 2020.[21] According to the report, the well-educated migrant workers were retained by their employees whereas the ones with less or no education were laid off.[22] The jobs of Nepali migrant workers in the UAE and Malaysia decreased by 30 percent.[23] Thus, the unskilled laborers are always at risk of losing their jobs.

RIGHTS OF FAMILY OF MIGRANT WORKERS

The Convention on Migrant Workers on the Protection of the Rights of All Migrant Workers and Members of their Families, as the name suggests, provides various rights to the family members of the migrant workers. The preambular paragraph of the convention gives the rationale behind considering the family of migrant workers, "*Taking into account* the fact that migration is often the cause of serious problems for the members of the families of migrant workers as well as for the workers themselves, in particular because of the scattering of the family." The data shows that the institution of the family in Nepal is drastically affected by migration. The divorce rate has increased since the migrant workers stay abroad for a long period of time.[24] Elderly are left alone in the villages with lack of care because the migrant workers go abroad, and joint families get converted to nuclear families.[25]

INTERNATIONAL AGREEMENTS AND NEPAL'S COMMITMENT

Convention on Migrant Workers is one of the nine core international human rights instruments. It provides vast rights to the migrant workers and their families. To date, only 58 states are parties to the Convention. Malaysia, India, UAE, Saudi Arabia, Qatar, South Korea, etc. where Nepalis usually migrate, are not parties to the convention. Nepal itself is not a party to CMW or to many of the international agreements concerning migrant workers.

The report of the Special Rapporteur on Migrant Workers on a visit to Nepal suggests various solutions to ensure human rights to the migrant workers.[26] He raises the importance of ratification of the CMW and other agreements viz. "ILO Conventions No. 87 concerning Freedom of Association and Protection of the Right to Organise Convention, No. 97 Concerning Migration for Employment (1949), No. 143 concerning Migrations in Abusive Conditions and the Promotion of Equality of Opportunity and Treatment of Migrant Workers (1975), No. 181 concerning Private Employment Agencies (1997), and No. 189 concerning Decent Work for Domestic Workers (2011)."[27] The report advises implementation of the UN Guiding Principles on Business and Human Rights, 2011. The Guiding Principles is in the form of a soft law. However, to date it remains a significant instrument of reminding business entities and other stakeholders in the field of their obligations, interlinking business and human rights. He drew attention to the lack of mechanisms for migrant workers of Nepal in India to redress human rights violations. He suggested the setting up of consulates in major cities where Nepali workers migrate in large numbers. In the detailed report, the Rapporteur draws attention to the centralized development in Nepal. If a worker wishes to migrate abroad, the procedure of application, interview, etc., take place in Kathmandu. People from remotest places have to travel and stay in the capital city, which adds to further expenses. A decentralized approach to migration policies and laws is proposed in the report. To prevent unscrupulous practices, the report opines for a standardized labor contract that provides proper details. Thus, it tries to combat the problem of misinformation. One of his innovative ideas is to introduce a rating system for the recruitment agencies, so that the migrant workers can recognize fraudulent or inefficient agencies. His emphasis is on an efficient system for access to justice so that legal remedies are easily available, especially against the recruitment agencies. He recognizes the importance of minimum wages and other good working conditions for the labor in the country of origin. The Rapporteur also makes recommendations to the private sector for better compliance.

The International Labor Organization since its inception in 1919 has played an important role in protecting the rights of migrant workers. There are also the South Asia Labor Migration Governance Project and the Work in Freedom Project: Preventing Trafficking of Women and Girls in South Asia and the Middle East.[28] Nepal has yet to ratify many of the conventions entered under the aegis of the ILO beneficial to the migrant workers.

Nepal is a signatory to the Global Compact on Migration that was envisaged as a part of the 2030 Sustainable Development Agenda.[29] The Compact is in the form of a soft law instrument. Nepal's signature to the document is the acceptance of rights of migrant workers mentioned in Objective 6 that ensures facilitation of "fair and ethical recruitment and safeguard conditions that ensure decent work." The Compact in Objective 20 recognizes the importance of remittances, stating that "We further commit to optimize the transformative impact of remittances on the well-being of migrant workers and their families, as well as on the sustainable development of countries, while respecting that remittances constitute an important source of private capital and cannot be equated to other international financial flows, such as foreign direct investment, official development assistance or other public sources of financing for development." It is incumbent on the state to fulfill its commitments made under this objective, especially reducing the transaction costs.

At present, the transaction cost in Nepal is 4.54 percent[30] on average and the commitment envisages reduction of the costs to less than 3 percent. The judicious use of technology and ease of transfer are some of the promises made in the Compact. This aspect is significant in the case of Nepal due to the immense contribution of remittances to the economy of Nepal. Objective 22 ensures adoption of social security measures for the migrant workers in the country of origin as well as in the country of work. In this regard, the Social Security Fund of Nepal has extended the benefits for migrant workers recently.[31] This is a positive move for the social security of migrant workers.

BILATERAL AND REGIONAL AGREEMENTS

Nepal has entered into bilateral labor agreements with Israel and South Korea only (Bajracharya 2022). Bilateral agreements with a standardized labor contract are imperative with the number of Nepali migrants leaving the country in unprecedented manner for work. Their contribution to the Nepali economy should be reciprocated with protection of their basic to special human rights. The weak diplomacy of Nepal risks the rights and lives of migrant workers at times.[32] Therefore, to strengthen its diplomatic power, regional cooperation would help in negotiations with the destination countries.

With regard to regional agreement, SAARC negotiated a Plan of Action on Labor Migration. The plan applauds the contribution of migrant workers to South Asian economies. It recalls the commitment of SAARC member states to international treaties on human rights. It reminds the members of the promises under the SAARC Convention on Preventing and Combating Trafficking on Women and Children for Prostitution, 2002, and the SAARC Convention on Mutual Assistance in Criminal Matters. This aspect hints that migration can lead to trafficking, and hence, the members need to be vigilant. The primary objective of the Plan is to build an institutional mechanism for labor migration. Apart from the fairness in the recruitment process, the Plan looks forward to improving access to the justice system for migrant workers.

NATIONAL LAWS

Article 51(i)(5) of the Constitution of Nepal, 2015, guides the state to formulate policies "to regulate and manage the sector in order to make foreign employment free from exploitation, safe and systematic and to guarantee employment and rights of the labours." The principal law related to migrant workers of Nepal is the Foreign Employment Act that is Act No. 18 of 2007. The Act establishes a Department of Foreign Employment that grants licenses to the recruitment agencies. As per Section 10 of the Act, an agency cannot do business related to foreign employment without a license. Section 30 provides for skill-oriented training to the workers. Section 25 mentions that before departure for work, a labor contract shall be entered into, explaining the remuneration and other working conditions in Nepali. According to Section 26, insurance of Rs. 500,000 shall be procured to the worker. Section 32 establishes a Foreign Employment Welfare Fund that credits the amount deposited by workers before going abroad, the amount received as license fees, etc. The use of the funds under Section 33 can be for repatriation, providing skills, etc. A Foreign Employment Promotion Board under Article 38 is established for the welfare of migrant workers. The Board studies labor markets and suggests steps to improve their situations. A Foreign Employment Tribunal is another institutional mechanism for access to justice under the Act.

In furtherance of the objectives of the Act, the Foreign Employment Rules were formulated in 2008. The rules further clarify the institutions established under the above Act. Detailed rules are laid down about the Foreign Employment Tribunal and its functioning. The Tribunal has solved about 3,000 cases since its establishment in 2010.

The Supreme Court of Nepal has played a significant role in pointing out the lack of implementation of the laws and directing the government to take action. Based on a Public Interest Litigation filed by the Law and Policy Forum for Social Justice for ensuring the right to vote of migrant workers, the Supreme Court ordered the government to take steps for facilitating voting in foreign countries.[33] On 9 January 2020, the Supreme Court of Nepal questioned the inexplicable death of around 1,000 migrant workers in a year. Requesting a Writ of Mandamus, the Law and Policy Forum for Social Justice and Paurakhi Nepal, drew the attention of the apex court on the death of migrant workers especially in West Asia. The Court ordered the government to take measures, with compulsory post-mortem examinations for the deaths occurring of migrant workers abroad.[34] Thereafter, the pandemic brought the world economy to a standstill in 2020. During the pandemic, the Supreme Court of Nepal played a significant role in giving timely decisions. In June 2020, the apex Court ordered the government either to provide facilities in the stranded countries or use the Foreign Employment Welfare Fund to repatriate them back to Nepal.

The Pravasi Nepali Coordination Committee, Pourakhi Nepal, and Equidem Research are a few of the NGOs working for the rights of the migrant workers. NGOs can act as "bridge-builders" in fulfilling the obligations of the state.[35] The gaps that are left by the state in implementing the laws, data collection, research, and related aspects can very well be filled by the NGOs.

MIGRANT WORKERS IN NEPAL

Migration from Nepal takes place because of a weak economy and unemployment. However, due to the temperate climatic conditions, some workers migrate to Nepal. The data regarding this is not clear and requires more empirical research and in-depth study. Most of the literature studies the migrant workers going abroad. Nevertheless, as aforementioned in the section on international agreements, Nepal is not a party to the Convention on Migrant Workers. However, it does not absolve the state from its other obligations incumbent in human rights rteaties. The state has obligations to fulfill its commitment under the treaties it has ratified viz. the International Covenant on Economic, Social and Cultural Rights, the International Covenant on Civil and Political Rights, the Convention on Elimination of Discrimination Against Women, and the Convention on Rights of the Child.

SUGGESTIONS AND CONCLUSION

There are many limitations of the state, especially in a Least Developed Country like Nepal. The inaccessible terrains of Nepal confine facilities and infrastructure largely to the capital city of Kathmandu. The migrant workers from other parts of Nepal lack information and facilities. This subjects them to problems related to migration and extra expenses. NGOs can help fill the gaps where the state cannot reach people. Furthermore, Nepal is surrounded by developing states like India. A better regional mechanism can help in strengthening the negotiating power. The diplomatic power of India is quite developed in terms of embassies and consulates. The plight of migrant workers can be speedily addressed by using better diplomatic channels and adopting a regional approach. A model bilateral agreement with strong provisions for protection can be drafted for a better protection. Moreover, bilateral agreements with West Asian countries seems to be the need of the hour. The issues of migrant workers mentioned in the present chapter is a pressing concern that needs timely solutions.

REFERENCES

Amritha V. Shenoy, Ravi Prakash Vyas, and Rachit Murarka. 2018. "State Practice of Asian Countries in International Law." Vol. 24, in *Asian Yearbook of International Law*, 398–410. Brill.

Arval, Ramesh. 2022. The Rising Nepal. July 7. Accessed March 28, 2023. https://risingnepaldaily.com/news/13586.

Bajracharya, Sugam Nanda. 2022. Nepal Economic Forum. March 28. Accessed March 15, 2023. https://nepaleconomicforum.org/6767-2/.

Bhattarai, Sewa. 2018. Nepali Times. May 15. Accessed April 24, 2023. https://nepalitimes.com/here-now/the-life-and-times-of-arniko.

Business—Human Rights. January 2020. Accessed March 29, 2023. https://www.business-humanrights.org/en/latest-news/nepal-supreme-court-orders-action-on-unexplained-high-numbers-of-migrant-worker-deaths/.

David Seddon, Jagannath Adhikari, and Ganesh Gurung. 2010. "Foreign Labor Migration and the Remittance Economy of Nepal." *Critical Asian Studies*, 19–40.

General Assembly, UN. 2019. January 11. Accessed March 28, 2023. https://documents-dds-ny.un.org/doc/UNDOC/GEN/N18/451/99/PDF/N1845199.pdf?OpenElement.

Ghimire, Barun. 2017. Law and Policy Forum for Social Justice. August 16. Accessed March 2, 2023. https://lapsoj.org/ensuring-the-rights-of-women-migrant-workers-of-nepal-need-of-integrated-approach-beyond-the-protectionist-ban/.

Human Rights Watch. November 2022. Accessed March 15, 2023. https://www.hrw.org/news/2022/11/17/fifa/qatar-migrant-workers-call-compensation-abuses#:~:text=(Beirut)%20%E2%80%93%20Migrant%20workers%20and,Human%20Rights%20Watch%20said%20today.

ILO. 2015. No Easy Exit: Migration Bans Affecting Women from Nepal. Geneva: Labor Migration Branch.

ILO. 2022. ILO. November. What has changed for migrant workers in Qatar? Accessed March 22, 2023. https://www.ilo.org/infostories/en-GB/Stories/Country-Focus/world-cup-qatar#landing.

ILO. n.d. ILO. Labour migration in Nepal. Accessed March 28, 2023. https://www.ilo.org/kathmandu/areasofwork/labor-migration/lang--en/index.htm.

IOM. 2020. Status of Nepali Migrant Workers in Relation to COVID-19. Kathmandu: International Organization for Migration.

Laura Foley and Nicola Piper. 2021. "Returning Home Empty Handed: Examining How COVID-19 Exacerbates the Non-Payment of Temporary Migrant Workers' Wages." *Global Social Policy*, 468–89.

Magnus Marsden and Till Mostowlansky. 2019. "Whither West Asia? Exploring North–South Perspectives on Eurasia." *Journal of Eurasian Studies*, 3–10.

Nandita Baruah and Shareen Tuladhar. 2013. The Diplomat. Accessed March 25, 2023. https://thediplomat.com/2013/10/the-challenge-for-nepals-migrant-workers/.

Nicola Banks, David Hulme, and Michael Edwards. 2015. "NGOs, States, and Donors Revisited: Still Too Close for Comfort?" *World Development*, 707–18.

Pandey, Pawan. 2022. The Kadmandu Post. September 24. Accessed April 25, 2023. https://kathmandupost.com/money/2022/09/24/migrant-workers-biggest-moneymakers-but-the-country-doesn-t-care-enough.

Rai, Diwakar. 2022. DW. January 11. Accessed March 22, 2023. https://www.dw.com/en/why-nepal-sends-so-many-migrant-workers-to-the-middle-east/a-63616875.

Rapporteur, UN Special. 2018. "End-of-mission statement of the UN Special Rapporteur on the human rights of migrants on his visit to Nepal."

Republica. 2023. My Republica. March 22. Accessed March 29, 2023. https://myrepublica.nagariknetwork.com/news/social-security-scheme-to-cover-nepali-migrant-workers-self-employed-in-foreign-lands/.

Rimal, Suswopna. 2021. The Asia Foundation. May 21. Accessed February 28, 2023. https://asiafoundation.org/2021/05/12/pandemic-dramatically-alters-path-of-migrant-workers/.

Shivakoti, Richa. 2020. "Protection or Discrimination? The Case of Nepal's Policy Banning Female Migrant Workers." *Urban Spaces and Gender in Asia*, 17–34.

Susan Thieme, Raju Bhattrai, Ganesh Gurung, Michael Kollmair, Siddhi Manandhar, and Ulrike Müller-Böker. 2005. "Addressing the Needs of Nepalese Migrant Workers in Nepal and in Delhi, India." *Mountain Research and Development*, 109–14.

NOTES

1. Bhattarai, Sewa. 2018. *Nepali Times.* May 15. Accessed April 24, 2023. https://nepalitimes.com/here-now/the-life-and-times-of-arniko.

2. Magnus Marsden and Till Mostowlansky. 2019. "Whither West Asia? Exploring North-South Perspectives on Eurasia." *Journal of Eurasian Studies*, 3–10.

3. Pandey, Pawan. 2022. *The Kadmandu Post.* September 24. Accessed April 25, 2023. https://kathmandupost.com/money/2022/09/24/migrant-workers-biggest-moneymakers-but-the-country-doesn-t-care-enough.

4. Nandita Baruah and Shareen Tuladhar. 2013. *The Diplomat.* Accessed March 25, 2023. https://thediplomat.com/2013/10/the-challenge-for-nepals-migrant-workers/.

5. Susan Thieme, Raju Bhattrai, Ganesh Gurung, Michael Kollmair, Siddhi Manandhar, and Ulrike Müller-Böker. 2005. "Addressing the Needs of Nepalese Migrant Workers in Nepal and in Delhi, India." *Mountain Research and Development*, 109–14.

6. Article 40 states, "1. Migrant workers and members of their families shall have the right to form associations and trade unions in the State of employment for the promotion and protection of their economic, social, cultural and other interests.

7. Article 41 states, "1. Migrant workers and members of their families shall have the right to participate in public affairs of their State of origin and to vote and to be elected at elections of that State, in accordance with its legislation. 2. The States concerned shall, as appropriate and in accordance with their legislation, facilitate the exercise of these rights."

8. Article 44 provides, "1. States Parties, recognizing that the family is the natural and fundamental group unit of society and is entitled to protection by society and the State, shall take appropriate measures to ensure the protection of the unity of the families of migrant workers. 2. States parties shall take measures that they deem appropriate and that fall within their competence to facilitate the reunification of migrant workers with their spouses or persons who have with the migrant worker a relationship that, according to applicable law, produces effects equivalent to marriage, as well as with their minor dependent unmarried children. 3. States of employment, on

humanitarian grounds, shall favourably consider granting equal treatment, as set forth in paragraph 2 of the present article, to other family members of migrant workers."

9. David Seddon, Jagannath Adhikari, and Ganesh Gurung. 2010. "Foreign Labor Migration and the Remittance Economy of Nepal." *Critical Asian Studies*, 19–40.

10. Rimal, Suswopna. 2021. *The Asia Foundation.* May 21. Accessed February 28, 2023. https://asiafoundation.org/2021/05/12/pandemic-dramatically-alters-path-of-migrant-workers/.

11. Laura Foley and Nicola Piper. 2021. "Returning Home Empty Handed: Examining How COVID-19 Exacerbates the Non-Payment of Temporary Migrant Workers' Wages." *Global Social Policy*, 468–89.

12. Rai, Diwakar. 2022. *DW.* January 11. Accessed March 22, 2023. https://www.dw.com/en/why-nepal-sends-so-many-migrant-workers-to-the-middle-east/a-63616875.

13. Rai, Diwakar. 2022. *DW.* January 11. Accessed March 22, 2023. https://www.dw.com/en/why-nepal-sends-so-many-migrant-workers-to-the-middle-east/a-63616875.

14. 2022. *Human Rights Watch.* November 17. Accessed March 15, 2023. https://www.hrw.org/news/2022/11/17/fifa/qatar-migrant-workers-call-compensation-abuses#:~:text=(Beirut)%20%E2%80%93%20Migrant%20workers%20and,Human%20Rights%20Watch%20said%20today.

15. ILO. 2022. *ILO.* November. Accessed March 22, 2023. https://www.ilo.org/infostories/en-GB/Stories/Country-Focus/world-cup-qatar#landing.

16. Nandita Baruah and Shareen Tuladhar. 2013. *The Diplomat.* Accessed March 25, 2023. https://thediplomat.com/2013/10/the-challenge-for-nepals-migrant-workers/.

17. Nandita Baruah and Shareen Tuladhar. 2013. *The Diplomat.* Accessed March 25, 2023. https://thediplomat.com/2013/10/the-challenge-for-nepals-migrant-workers/.

18. Article 12 states, "1. Wages shall be paid regularly. Except where other appropriate arrangements exist which ensure the payment of wages at regular intervals, the intervals of payment of wages shall be prescribed by national laws or regulations or fixed by collective agreement or arbitration award. 2. Upon the termination of a contract of employment, a final settlement of all wages due shall be effected in accordance with national laws or regulations, collective agreement or arbitration award or, in the absence of any applicable law, regulation, agreement or award, within a reasonable period of time having regard to the terms of the contract."

19. Article 22(6) states "In case of expulsion, the person concerned shall have a reasonable opportunity before or after departure to settle any claims for wages and other entitlements due to him or her and any pending liabilities."

20. Bajracharya, Sugam Nanda. 2022. *Nepal Economic Forum.* March 28. Accessed March 15, 2023. https://nepaleconomicforum.org/6767-2/.

21. IOM. 2020. *Status of Nepali Migrant Workers in Relation to COVID-19.* Kathmandu: International Organization for Migration.

22. IOM. 2020. *Status of Nepali Migrant Workers in Relation to COVID-19.* Kathmandu: International Organization for Migration.

23. Rimal, Suswopna. 2021. *The Asia Foundation.* May 21. Accessed February 28, 2023. https://asiafoundation.org/2021/05/12/pandemic-dramatically-alters-path-of-migrant-workers/.

24. Rai, Diwakar. 2022. *DW.* January 11. Accessed March 22, 2023. https://www.dw.com/en/why-nepal-sends-so-many-migrant-workers-to-the-middle-east/a-63616875.

25. Rai, Diwakar. 2022. *DW.* January 11. Accessed March 22, 2023. https://www.dw.com/en/why-nepal-sends-so-many-migrant-workers-to-the-middle-east/a-63616875.

26. Rapporteur, UN Special. 2018. "End-of-mission statement of the UN Special Rapporteur on the human rights of migrants on his visit to Nepal."

27. Rapporteur, UN Special. 2018. "End-of-mission statement of the UN Special Rapporteur on the human rights of migrants on his visit to Nepal."

28. ILO. n.d. *ILO.* Accessed March 28, 2023. https://www.ilo.org/kathmandu/areasofwork/labor-migration/lang--en/index.htm.

29. General Assembly, UN. 2019. January 11. Accessed March 28, 2023. https://documents-dds-ny.un.org/doc/UNDOC/GEN/N18/451/99/PDF/N1845199.pdf?OpenElement.

30. Arval, Ramesh. 2022. *The Rising Nepal.* July 7. Accessed March 28, 2023. https://risingnepaldaily.com/news/13586.

31. Republica. 2023. *My Republica.* March 22. Accessed March 29, 2023. https://myrepublica.nagariknetwork.com/news/social-security-scheme-to-cover-nepali-migrant-workers-self-employed-in-foreign-lands/.

32. Pandey, Pawan. 2022. *The Kadmandu Post.* September 24. Accessed April 25, 2023. https://kathmandupost.com/money/2022/09/24/migrant-workers-biggest-moneymakers-but-the-country-doesn-t-care-enough.

33. Amritha V. Shenoy, Ravi Prakash Vyas, Rachit Murarka. 2018. "State Practice of Asian Countries in International Law." Vol. 24, in *Asian Yearbook of International Law*, 398–410. Brill.

34. 2020. *Business—Human Rights.* January 10. Accessed March 29, 2023. https://www.business-humanrights.org/en/latest-news/nepal-supreme-court-orders-action-on-unexplained-high-numbers-of-migrant-worker-deaths/.

35. Nicola Banks, David Hulme, and Michael Edwards. 2015. "NGOs, States, and Donors Revisited: Still Too Close for Comfort?" *World Development*, 707–18.

Chapter 9

The Law Relating to Migrant Laborers

A Study of Indian Law and ILO Instruments

S. Anandha Krishna Raj and Aathira Raju

Human migration has a long history of time immemorial. Without migration, humanity would have been stuck on the African continent forever. Humanity flourished because of migration. Migration happens in search of better living standards and the quest for survival. Labor migration in general is understood as the *movement of persons from one state to another, or within their own country of residence, for the purpose of employment.*[1] The factors that are responsible for migration can be demographic, political, economic, ecological, etc. However, the significant reason for migration is regional disparity in economic development, which is linked to inequality of opportunity and is true regarding international as well as internal migration. People from underdeveloped regions prefer developed and prosperous regions to upgrade their standard of living.[2] Migration for work and education has been a historical phenomenon. A structural transformation of the economy happens due to the migration of labor from low-productive agricultural activities to high-productive sectors. The movement of this surplus labor increases the household spending of the host regions and facilitates the economic development of underdeveloped regions.[3]

In India, internal migration has been common and people migrate from rural to urban areas as well as seasonal or circular migration within rural areas. Historically no restrictions were imposed on the movement of people within the country. During the colonial period, the labor market was built on migrant laborers and they were employed in tea, cotton, and jute industries, which facilitated industrialization and urbanization in the colonial era.[4] After the ban on the slave trade by the colonial countries, they had to look for other sources. This led to the creation of contracts between the laborers and the owners. The uneducated Indians were simply taken away for plantation work. Internal migrants are those who migrate from one state to another or within the same state in search of an occupation, the former ones are known as inter-state migrant workers and the latter are tagged as intra-state migrant workers. The migrant workers occupy a major portion of the unorganized sector. Out of the 50 core workers in the organized and unorganized sector, 90 percent belongs to the unorganized sector.[5]

In India, the migrant workers were dealt with under the Contract Labor (Regulation and Abolition) Act, 1970, until the adoption of the Inter-State Migrant Workmen (Regulation of Employment and Conditions of Service) Act, 1979. The Contract Labor Abolition Act was inadequate in combating the vicious acts of contractors who recruited migrant workers for establishments. The migrant workers were treated badly without being provided even basic amenities. The contractors flouted the then-existing labor laws in the case of migrant workers and were subjected to various malpractices and consequently, their condition became miserable. The Union government took notice of the situation and appointed a committee for recommendations. On the basis of the proposal submitted by this committee, the parliament adopted the Interstate Migrant Workmen Act, 1979. The Act was in existence for almost three decades and was merged into the New Labor Code of 2020. Some of the provisions in the Act with modifications are included in the New Labor Code. The Occupational Safety, Health, and Working Conditions Code and Social Security Code cover provisions relating to inter-state migrant workers.

At the international level, the International Labor Organization (ILO) has been addressing the issue of migrant workers since its inception. Reference to the protection of interests of migrant workers can spotted in the preamble to the Constitution of the ILO. To address the issues related to migrant workers, it adopted two Conventions, namely the Migration for Employment (Revised) Convention, 1949 (No. 97), the Migrant Workers (Supplementary Provisions) Convention, 1975 (No. 143), and their accompanying non-binding Recommendations.

The chapter aims to examine the existing law relating to migrant workers in India as well as the initiatives of ILO in this regard. Section 2 of the chapter will examine national legal documents that deal with migrant workers. In this section, the constitutional provisions that cover the welfare of workers will be dealt with. It is followed by an analysis of the Interstate Migrant Workers Act 1979 along with a critical perception. The following subsection sketches the new Labor Codes 2020 that address inter-state migrant workers. Section 3 touches upon the case of overseas migrants from India from colonial times to the post-independence period. In this section, the existing Emigration Act 1983 will be analyzed followed by an examination and critical evaluation of the Draft Emigration Bill 2021. Section 4 examines the initiatives of ILO in this regard. This section limits its discussion by examining the two main conventions adopted by the ILO in the years 1949 and 1975. Section 5 delivers concluding remarks.

LEGAL DOCUMENTS THAT DEAL WITH MIGRANT WORKERS IN INDIA

Constitutional Law of India

The Constitution of India (hereinafter referred to as the Constitution) envisages social, economical, and political justice. To accomplish justice, the Constitution guarantees fundamental rights under Part III. The Constitution also lays down Directive Principles of State Policy (DPSP) under Part IV which are fundamental for the governance of the country. With respect to the welfare of workers in general, DPSP outlines guiding principles for the state. It provides that the state shall direct its policy toward securing the rights of all, irrespective of gender, to adequate means of livelihood, and to equal pay for equal work. The state shall also make provisions for securing the right to work, education, and public assistance in the case of unemployment. It shall also secure workers humane conditions of work, decent standards of life, and a living wage.[6]

Inter-state migration and inter-state quarantine are covered under Union List/List I as Item 81, which indicates that only the Union government can legislate on this matter. Matters such as trade unions; industrial and labor disputes (Item 22); social security and social insurance; employment and unemployment (Item 23); welfare of labor including conditions of work, provident funds, employers' liability, workmen's compensation, invalidity and old age pensions, and maternity benefits (Item 24); fall under the concurrent list[7] upon which both state and center can enact laws.

The Inter-State Migrant Workmen (Regulation of Employment and Conditions of Service) Act 1979

This Act was enacted to effectively address the miserable conditions of inter-state migrant laborers (known as Dadan in Orissa) in Orissa and in some other states. The contractors who recruited these workers exploited them with prolonged working hours and terrible working conditions. The contractors flouted the then-existing labor laws that were applicable to these workers. The seriousness of the issue led the representatives in the 28th session of Labor Ministers Conference 1976 to recommend the setting up of a Compact Committee. The Committee was entrusted with the obligation to propose measures that could eliminate the mishaps faced by the migrant workers. The Committee found that the Contract Labor (Regulation and Abolition) Act 1970 is limited in addressing the issues faced by migrant workers. The Committee recommended the enactment of Union government legislation that regulates the employment of inter-state migrant workers as well as curbs the vicious acts indulged by the employers. The recommendations of the Committee were taken into account at the drafting of the legislation.

The Act was adopted in 1979 and its objective is to regulate the employment of inter-state migrant workmen and to provide their conditions of service. The Act defines an inter-state migrant workman as a person recruited by a contractor for employment in another state. The recruitment can be done by the contractor with or without the knowledge of the principal employer of the establishment for which the workman is recruited.[8] The terms "contractor" and "principal employer" are defined under Section 2(b) and (g) respectively.[9] The Act applies to establishments[10] as well as contractors employing five or more inter-state workmen on any day within the preceding year.[11] It is the responsibility of the establishment that employs migrant workers to register with the respective government. If the establishment fails to obtain a certificate of registration within the stipulated time, it shall not employ inter-state migrant workers in that establishment.[12] If the contractor recruits or employs the inter-state migrant worker, he has to obtain a license from the specified authority as provided under Section 8 of the Act. The appropriate authority can fix the terms and conditions under which the inter-state workmen will be recruited, his remuneration, hours of work, fixation of wages, and other essential amenities.[13]

It is obligatory for the contractor to furnish all the details of the migrant worker to the specified authority of the home and host state.[14] The contractor is also required to issue to migrant workmen a passbook containing all details of his employment including (i) the name and place of the establishment wherein the workman is employed; (ii) the period of employment; (iii) the proposed rates and modes of payment of wages; (iv) the displacement allowance payable; (v) the return fare payable to the workman on the expiry of the period of his employment and in such contingencies as may be prescribed and in such other contingencies as may be specified in the contract of employment; (vi) deductions made; and (vii) such other particulars as may be prescribed.[15] It is the duty of the contractor to maintain the passbook up-to-date. In the case of a migrant worker who ceases to be employed, the contractor shall furnish a return including a declaration that all the wages and other dues including the fare for the return journey have been paid to the specified authority in the home and host state.[16]

Section 13 states that the establishment as well as the contractor has to adhere to the special guidelines with respect to the payment of wages[17] and in no case shall shall be paid less than the minimum wages fixed under the Minimum Wages Act, 1948. This Section also deals with the wage rates, holidays, hours of work, and other conditions of service of inter-state migrant workmen.[18] Every inter-state migrant workman is entitled to a displacement allowance at the time of recruitment.

The contractor employing migrant workers shall have the duty (a) to ensure regular payment of wages to such workmen; (b) to ensure equal pay for equal work irrespective of sex; (c) to ensure suitable conditions of work to such workmen having regard to the fact that they are required to work in a state different from their own state; (d) to provide and maintain suitable residential accommodation to such workmen during the period of their employment; (e) to provide the prescribed medical facilities to the workmen, free of charge; (f) to provide such protective clothing to the workmen as may be prescribed; and (g) in case of fatal accident or serious bodily injury to any such workman, to report to the specified authorities of both the states and also the next of kin of the workman.[19] The contractor shall pay wages to the migrant workers before the expiry of the prescribed period. He can disburse such payment only in the presence of the representative of the principal employer.[20] If the contractor fails to pay wages or provide any facility, then the duty to make such payment or provide the facility shifts to the principal employer and the latter can recover the same from the contractor.[21] It is the duty of the contractors and the principal employer to maintain registers and records containing particulars of migrant workers. It shall include the nature of the work the migrant worker performs, the rates of wages paid to him, and other particulars. The principal employer and contractor are also required to exhibit notices containing particulars about hours of work, nature of duty, and other information on the premises where the migrant worker is employed.[22]

To ensure compliance of the Act, the appropriate government shall appoint inspectors. His responsibilities include entering any premises where the inter-state workmen are employed, examining whether payment of wages, conditions of service, or provision for facilities are complied with; and going through any register or record or notices or seizing or taking copies of such register, the record of wages, or notices or portions thereof as he may consider relevant in respect to an offense under this Act which he has reason to believe has been committed by a principal employer or contractor. The home state can also appoint inspectors to ascertain the conditions of migrant workers. However, the home state can appoint such an inspector only after consultation with the host state.[23] Whoever obstructs the inspector from performing his duties or willfully refuses to produce any document or register on the demand of the inspector shall be punished with imprisonment for a term, which may extend to two years, or with fine, which may extend to two thousand rupees or with both.[24]

The Act also prescribes punishment for those who contravene the provisions of the Act or its rules or violate the condition of a licence granted with imprisonment for a term, which may extend to one year, or with a fine, which may extend to one thousand rupees or with both.[25] If any person flouts any other provision of the Act and no penalty is provided, then the violator shall be punished with imprisonment for a term, which may extend to two years, or with fine, which may extend to two thousand rupees or with both.[26] If the offense is committed by a company, then the person responsible shall be deemed to be guilty and punished accordingly.[27] In case of an industrial dispute, the migrant worker can either complain in the host state or home state after his return to his home state and after completion of the contract of employment.[28]

The appropriate government has the power to exempt any establishment or contractor or any inter-state migrant workmen in such an establishment from the purview of the Act if the government is satisfied that it is just and proper to do so. The government can make such an exemption only after a notification in the official gazette, with such restrictions and conditions. The exemption can be done only for the period specified in the notification. The exemption can be done with all or any of the provisions of the Act or rules.[29]

The Act elaborately covers all aspects that touch the interests of the inter-state migrant workers. Nevertheless, the Act has many flaws that have the potential to undermine the very objective of the Act. The Act applies to establishments or contractors that employ five or more migrant workers, which is inadequate because a large portion of migrant workers who work in small establishments or under a contractor will be left behind, which undermines the very objective of the Act. The Act does not cover intra-state migrant workers albeit the percentage of migration within the state is much higher than the inter-state migration.[30] The data collected during the decade of 1991–2001 reveals that out of 9.8 crore persons migrated to a new place from their last place of residence, 8.1 crore were intra-state migrants, 1.7 crore inter-state migrants, and 700,000 lakh international migrants. Migration from one village to another was about 5.3 crore whereas number of migrants from villages to towns was around 2.1 crore, from towns to villages was around 62 lakhs, and from one town to another about 1.4 crore.[31] According to the available data from the census 2011, around 85 percent of migrant workers were intra-state workers. Also, studies based on the 2011 census show that migration within states is around four times more than migrant flows across states.[32]

New Labor Code and the Migrant Workers

In India, multiplicity of labor laws has been a matter of concern since 2002. The colonial influence on the provisions of Indian labor laws was not taken into account and most of these laws became obsolete and hardly have any relevance in the current world. The report of the second National Commission of Labor submitted in 2002 deliberated on the issue of the proliferation of labor laws and recommended codifying these laws into four or five Labor Codes. No steps were taken in this regard until 2014. The Ministry of Labor and Employment after extensive discussion uploaded draft labor codes on its website. The ministry from 2015 to 2019 convened nine tripartite discussions on labor reforms. Around 50 crore workers occupy organized and unorganized sectors. Out of this, 90 percent have been working in the unorganized sector. The Union government has amalgamated 29 labor laws into four labor codes. The Wage Code was passed by the Parliament in the year 2019, whereas the other three codes, which are the Occupational Safety, Health and Working Conditions Code, 2020; the Industrial Relations Code, 2020; and the Code on Social Security, 2020, got the assent of the Parliament in September 2020. These new codes ensured that the demarcating line between organized and unorganized sectors would fade since the code guarantees minimum wage and social security to workers in the unorganized sectors. The Wage Code is the result of an amalgamation of four laws, whereas the Social Security Code merged nine laws, the Occupational Safety, Health and Working Conditions Code is the combination of 13 laws, and the Industrial Code combined three laws.[33]

The informal workers in India are covered under the Occupational Safety, Health and Working Conditions Code and the Code on Social Security. The inter-state migrant worker now includes persons who move from one state to another for employment on their own or who are directly recruited by employers besides those recruited by contractors as mentioned in the 1979 Interstate Migrant Workmen Act. Under the Occupational Safety Code, the definition of contract labor includes inter-state migrant workers.[34] Section 2(zf) of the Occupational Safety Code and 2(41) of the Social Security Code deals with the definition of the inter-state migrant worker.[35]

The Occupational Safety, Health and Working Conditions Code 2020 covers provisions dealing with inter-state migrant workers under Part II of Chapter XI, though Part I of the same chapter has a reference to inter-state migrant workers. The Code is applicable to establishments that employ 10 or more migrant workers, which is a total departure from the 1979 inter-state migrant workers Act that encompassed establishments or contractors employing five or more persons. As per the 2013–2014 economic census, around 70 percent of the establishments employ less than six workers. This will restrict migrant workers who are employed in small establishments from the benefits of the Code. Like its predecessor, the Code also failed to address the intra-state migrant workers.[36]

The requirement of mandatory registration of inter-state migrant workers as provided by the 1979 Act to an extent was flawless. Nevertheless, this mandatory condition has been flouted for years or one can say no state has observed this requirement. The failure of the state to collect and record data on inter-state migrant workers as provided under the 1979 Act was unveiled at the time of lockdown when millions of migrant workers were deprived of any basic amenities like food, shelter, and transportation. The lack of data on the number of interstate migrants either with the host or the home state has worsened the situation that ended with the loss of lives of workers.[37] The Occupational Safety Code retains the registration requirement. On top of that, it directs the migrant workers to register themselves with anAadhaar card (unique identification number) and a telephone authentication. Regarding the collection of statistics, the Union and state governments shall maintain the database electronically or otherwise in such portal, for inter-state migrant workers.[38] The Code casts a duty on the contractor or employer, as the case may be, to ensure suitable conditions of work and provide medical facilities, journey allowance, and other benefits including benefits under the Employees' State Insurance Act, 1948, or the Employees' Provident Funds and Miscellaneous Provisions Act, 1952, or any other law for the time being in force to the migrant workers.[39]

The Code also prescribes the portability of the public distribution system. It directs the government to frame schemes to provide an option to migrant workers for availing the benefits of the public distribution system in their home or host state. The inter-state portability of ration cards (public delivery system) was flagged off to implement the One Nation One Ration Card plan. As an initial attempt, the inter-state portability of ration cards was implemented in two clusters: Maharashtra-Gujarat and Andhra Pradesh-Telangana. It was reported that all states have ration card portability, with Assam implementing the plan in June 2022.[40]

The punishment for offenses under the Code has been slashed when compared to the 1979 Act. The Code imposes penalties in the form of a fine in case of contravention of its certain provision, unlike the 1979 Act that prescribed one-year imprisonment or fine, or both. However, the Code imposes a fine of a minimum amount of 50,000 rupees, which may extend to one lakh rupees. Punishment for other violations prescribes imprisonment ranging from three to six months whereas in the 1979 Act, the imprisonment period was two years.

The inadequacy of the law relating to migrant workers became apparent at the time of the COVID-19 pandemic. The absence of comprehensive and systematic data on migrant workers was one of the biggest difficulties faced by the Indian government during this period. The government has been grappling with the lack of data on migrant workers for years and its lethargic approach to the cause surfaced at the time of the COVID-19 pandemic. The pandemic was in a sense an eye-opener since the whole world has witnessed the trauma the migrant laborers in India have undergone when the lockdown was declared. The exodus of migrant laborers immediately following the announcement of the lockdown drew attention to the actual plight they have been enduring for years. It also threw light on various mammoth issues including the fragility of the informal sector and the lack of documentation of data on migrant workers. Though lockdown was imminent at the time of the pandemic, the short-sightedness in declaring it, discounting the interest of subaltern working class, was criticized for class bias in framing public policy.[41]

OVERSEAS MIGRATION FROM INDIA

As we have seen in the introduction, the migration of Indian laborers started during the period of colonialism. When the slave trade was banned by the European nations and the United States at the beginning of the nineteenth century, the slave trade took a new turn. The colonial powers, particularly the United Kingdom, started transferring the laborers from its colony to other colonies. The laborers were taken by way of a contract. As most of the Indians during that time were illiterate, it was hard to know if they understood the conditions of that contract. The contract was merely a formality to show consent from the migrant laborer through a legal document. Nevertheless, it was no different from the slave trade. Indian laborers migrated to the then-British colonies all over the world. They were forced to work in the rubber, tea, coffee, and sugarcane plantations. They were taken to Burma, Ceylon (Sri Lanka), Mauritius, South Africa, Fiji, etc. According to the overseas Indian data, Indians form the second-largest migrant community after China. It is estimated that Indian migrants number over 30 million across 208 countries.

The colonial Indian migration laborers mostly settled in their respective countries, otherwise sent back to India in some exceptional cases like Sri Lanka. The Sirimavo-Shastri Pact was signed between the then Sri Lankan president Sirimavo Bandaranaike and the Indian prime minister Lal Bahadur Shastri on October 30,1964 to repatriate more than 5 lac Tamils. After Indian independence, this is one incident where migrants were sent back to their home country forcefully after staying there for centuries. The Rohingya Muslim community in Burma is also the colonial migration from India to Burma to work in rubber plantations.

In the contemporary non-resident Indian (NRI) diaspora spread across the world, the Ministry of External Affairs reports that there are 32 million NRIs and persons of Indian origin (PIO) including overseas citizenship of India (OCI) residing outside India. The regulatory framework for Indian migrant workers for contractual overseas employment is provided by the Emigration Act of 1983. It also seeks to safeguard their interests and ensure their welfare. The salient features of the Act are 1). Any Indian national can be recruited for a job abroad either through a recruiting agent registered under the Act or by an employer with a valid permit issued by the Protector General of Emigrants. 2). No Indian citizen (unless exempted) can emigrate without obtaining emigration clearance from the concerned Procter of Emigrants.[42]

The draft Emigration Bill of 2021[43] aims to replace the Emigration Act of 1983. It tried to fill the loopholes of the Emigration Act of 1983. This bill attempts to address the long-term problem of corruption, middlemen, recruitment charges, contract substitution, deception, retention of passports, non-payment, and underpayment of wages, poor living conditions, discrimination, and other forms of ill-treatment of the Indian migrant workers. The bill intends to develop a comprehensive emigration management and a regulatory mechanism governing the overseas employment of Indian nationals abroad. It further intends to protect and promote the welfare of the emigrants. Moreover, the bill proposes a three-tier institutional framework. It proposes a new emigration policy and a Bureau of Emigration policy and planning which will handle the day-to-day affairs of the overseas emigrants. The welfare and protection of the emigrants will be overseen by a chief emigration officer. There could be a provision to punish workers by way of canceling and suspending their passports and a fine, if there is any violation of the provisions. This seems to control the middlemen, unregistered brokers, and the migration through tourist visas. The authorities of the Bureau will have the power equivalent to a civil court.

But there is a lack of vision in the bill in addressing the geo-political and geo-strategic impact of global migration. Moreover, the human rights aspect is missing in the bill. The rights of migrants and their family members is not addressed properly. The heavy punishment leads the emigrants, because of their lack of awareness of law, not to report the frauds by the middlemen. The missing migrants in a foreign country is partially addressed by the bill. Unlike the International Labor Organization (ILO), which states the employers will bear the recruitment fees, the bill allows the agencies to charge fees from the workers and even set their own rules. Moreover, there is no clarity on the gender aspect, and female workers are given less preference.

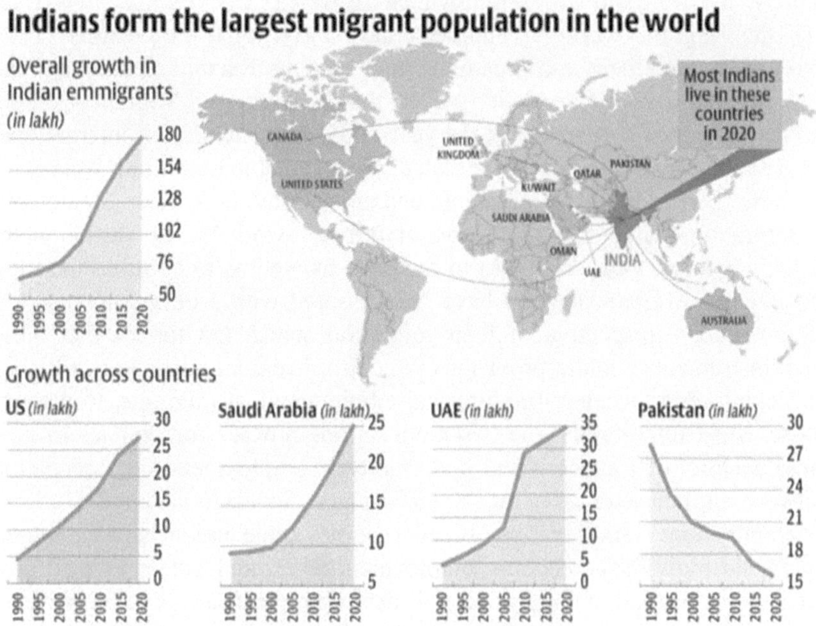

Figure 9.1 Indians form the Largest Migrant Population in the World

ILO AND MIGRANT LABORERS

In 2019, the number of international migrant workers totaled 169 million and constituted 4.9 percent of the global labor force. The increasing number of labor migrants is triggered by many factors including economic, political, and environmental crises and demographic changes. Nevertheless, the significant reason is the economic inequalities one faces in their home country, and to improve one's life they prefer to cross the border in search of employment.[44] The impact of the COVID-19 pandemic adversely affected the economy across the world, and the world of work was no exception to this. The estimate of the ILO demonstrates that 93 percent of the global working population was affected by the closure of their workplace and among them, the most vulnerable were the international migrant laborers. The pandemic has negatively impacted the international flow of migrant workers.[45]

The ILO, being the precursor of labor rights, has been addressing the issue of migrant laborers since its inception. One of the objectives of ILO as provided under the Preamble to the ILO Constitution is the "protection of interests of workers when employed in countries other than their own." This principle has been reaffirmed by the 1944 Declaration of Philadelphia. To address the issues related to migrant workers, it adopted two conventions, namely, the Migration for Employment (Revised) Convention, 1949 (No. 97), the Migrant Workers (Supplementary Provisions) Convention, 1975 (No. 143), and their accompanying non-binding Recommendations. The ILO adopted a recommendation called the Protection of Migrant Workers (Underdeveloped Countries) in the year 1955. In principle, all international labor standards, unless otherwise stated, are applicable to migrant workers.

These Conventions and Recommendations provide a basic framework of migration policy, the protection of migrant workers, the development of their potential, and measures to facilitate as well as to control migration movements. Migrant laborers have been assured with a minimum standard of protection irrespective of their migration status. On top of that these legal instruments contain provisions to control irregular migration and labor trafficking, and to detect the informal employment of migrants, to prevent abuse. Most importantly, the two Conventions provide for policies to promote equality of treatment and opportunity in employment and occupation between migrant workers in regular status and nationals in the areas of access to employment, remuneration, social security, trade union rights, cultural rights and individual freedoms, employment taxes, and access to legal proceedings.[46] The following section will deal with the features of the migrant conventions.

Migration for Employment Convention (Revised), 1949 (No. 97)

The Convention came into force on 22 January, 1952.[47] Article 11 of the Convention defines "migrant for employment" as a person who migrates from one country to another with a view to being employed other than on his own account and includes any person regularly admitted as a migrant for employment. The Convention excludes frontier workers, short-term entry of members of the liberal professions and artistes, and seamen from the definition. The Convention mandates the members to make available information on national law, policies, and regulations relating to emigration and immigration and information on special provisions concerning migration for employment and the conditions of work and livelihood of the migrants for employment. The convention directs the members to provide assistance to migrants and provide them with accurate information. Each member shall take measures to facilitate the departure, journey, and reception of migrants for employment. Members shall be responsible for maintaining appropriate medical services to ascertain the health of both migrant worker and their accompanying family. The Convention promotes equal treatment of migrants with the nationals by promoting social security measures such as remuneration, including family allowances, hours of work, overtime arrangements, holidays with pay, restrictions on homework, the minimum age for employment, apprenticeship and training, women's work and the work of young persons, membership in trade unions with benefits of collective bargaining, accommodation, and social security. However, the social security measures are subjected to the limitation prescribed under (i) and (ii) of Clause (b) of Article 6. The members shall ensure that their employment service related to migration will cooperate with the corresponding services of other members. The members should ascertain that public services rendered to the migrants by its public employment service shall be made free. If a migrant is permanently admitted in the host state, he shall not be returned to his country of origin if he is unable to follow his occupation by reason of illness or injury. This shall be applied to his family members too. However, this provision shall take effect only after a reasonable period of time and shall exceed five years from the date of admission of such migrants. If the migrants going from the territory of one member to another territory are large, then the competent authorities of the territories shall enter into agreements for regulating matters of common concern.

The convention provides for three annexes. Annex I deals with recruitment, placing, and conditions of labor of migrants for employment recruited other than under government-sponsored arrangements for a group transfer. Annex II deals with recruitment, placing, and conditions of labor of migrants for employment recruited under government-sponsored arrangements for group transfer. Annex III deals with the importation of the personal effects, tools, and equipment of migrants for employment.

The Migrant Workers (Supplementary Provisions) Convention, 1975 (No. 143)

This Convention was adopted to give effect to certain proposals with respect to migrant workers, that have the potential to supplement the Migration for Employment Convention (Revised), 1949, and the Discrimination (Employment and Occupations) Convention, 1958. At the time of the adoption of this Convention, one can witness a shift in the focus of ILO due to several external factors it was facing during that period. It was marked by the oil crisis, and the international institutions were struggling to provide a solution to this crisis. During this period there was chronic unemployment and underdevelopment and the countries were demanding the transfer of capital and technology rather than the transfer of human resources. The preamble to the Convention emphasizes the need to avoid migratory movements that are excessive and uncontrolled or unassisted since such movements have negative social and human consequences.

Put into force on 9 December 1978, the Convention is divided into three parts. The first part deals with "Migrations in abusive conditions"; Part II deals with equality of opportunity and treatment and final provisions under Part III. The first part is mainly concerned with the prevention of migration in abusive conditions and the promotion of equality of opportunity and treatment of migrant workers.[48] For promoting the human rights of migrant workers, the convention imposes a duty on the member states to determine whether the migrant workers are employed illegally on its territory. For this purpose, the member countries shall consult the representative organizations of employers and workers enabling them to furnish any information on this subject. To suppress the clandestine movement of migrants for employment and illegal employment of migrants, the members in collaboration with other members shall take appropriate measures. Manpower trafficking of migrant workers shall be prosecuted to prevent abuse of migrant workers. The Convention also directs the member countries to frame national laws for the effective detection of illegal employment of migrant workers and the application of effective sanctions including imprisonment in this regard. If a legal migrant worker loses his employment, his authorization for the residence shall not be withdrawn and in such circumstances, he is entitled to equality of treatment with nationals.

The Convention promotes equality of opportunity and treatment of migrant workers and is dealt with under Part II of the Convention. For the purpose of this part, Article 11(1) of the Convention defines the term "migrant worker" as a person who migrates or who has migrated from one country to another with a view to being employed other than on his own account and includes any person regularly admitted as a migrant worker. The following categories are excluded from the application of this part: (a) frontier workers; (b) artistes and members of the liberal professions who have entered the country on a short-term basis; (c) seamen; (d) persons coming specifically for purposes of training or education; (e) employees of organizations or undertakings operating within the territory of a country who have been admitted temporarily to that country at the request of their employer to undertake specific duties or assignments, for a limited and defined period of time, and who are required to leave that country on the completion of their duties or assignments. Comparing the definition and exclusion provision of this Convention with the 1949 Convention, one can see the definition of migrant workers or migrants for employment remains the same, but the number of categories under the exclusion list has been widened.

The convention in its Article 10 mandates its members to design national policies that guarantee equality of opportunity and social security, cultural and trade union rights, and individual and collective freedom of migrant workers who are lawfully staying in their territory. To achieve this mandate, the members have to seek the cooperation of employers and workers' organizations. The members shall promote educational programs and other activities for migrant workers to make them acquainted with the policy.[49]

CONCLUSION

The migrant workers mostly from rural parts of India have been a significant contributor to the informal labor sector. Nevertheless, their status hasn't improved even after the enactment of the Interstate Migrant Workmen Act 1979. The Act has been barely observed by governments and the issues of migrant workers were underrated until the outbreak of the COVID-19 pandemic, and the subsequent announcement of nationwide lockdown led to migrant labor exodus from the cities. The situation went out of hand and the authorities were struggling to control it. One of the reasons for such a hapless situation was the nonavailability of migrant workers' data with the authorities. Though the 1979 Act clearly directed the authorities to systematically keep the data of migrant workers up to date, the neglectful approach of the government authorities toward the migrant workers prevented them from keeping accurate data of migrant workers. But the new labor code prescribes the collection of statistics and keeping the database electronically. If the authorities under the labor code observe the directions mentioned in the Code, then it will improve the situation of downtrodden migrant workers. Since the labor code came into existence recently, the extent of its effectiveness cannot be measured in such a short span of time.

As far as the overseas Indian migrants are concerned, overseas migration was in existence in the colonial days. In this period, Indian laborers were carried to other colonies where they were forced to toil in plantations. Most of them stayed back and in a few cases, they were returned due to political exigencies. Currently, the Indian diaspora is covered under the Emigration Act of 1983 and a draft bill is in the pipeline. Further, the draft Emigration Bill of 2021 aims to clear the ambiguities posed by the 1983 Act but still needs some improvement for the welfare of Indian migrants overseas. The human rights and gender issues need to be addressed in the bill in line with the ILO rules and regulations.

From its inception, the ILO addressed the issue of migrant workers. Its Preamble declares the "protection of the interests of workers when employed in countries other than their own." It was reiterated in the 1944 Declaration of Philadelphia. The ILO adopted two conventions that specifically dealt with the issues of migrant workers. The first convention was adopted in the year 1949 and the second convention was adopted on 1975. At the time of the adoption of the second convention, i.e., the Migrant Workers (Supplementary

Provisions) Convention, 1975, one can view a shift in the focus of ILO due to external factors it was facing at that time. This period was marked by the oil crisis and the world had not recovered from the crisis yet and international institutions were struggling to provide a solution. During this period there was chronic unemployment and underdevelopment and the countries were demanding the transfer of capital and technology rather than the transfer of human resources. The preamble to the Convention emphasizes the need to avoid migratory movements that are excessive and uncontrolled or unassisted since such movements have negative social and human consequences.

REFERENCES

Akhileshwari Reddy, Lack of Updated Data led to Massive Migrant Crisis During Covid-19, VIDHI Centre for Legal Policy, 16 Jul 2020 Lack of Updated Data Led to Massive Migrant Crisis During COVID-19. Vidhi Centre for Legal Policy (vidhilegalpolicy.in).

Akhileshwari Reddy, New Labor Codes: What changes for interstate migrants? An analysis of two critical codes, VIDHI Centre for Legal Policy, 25 Nov 2020 New Labor Codes: What Changes for Interstate Migrants? Vidhi Centre for Legal Policy (vidhilegalpolicy.in).

Census of India, https://censusindia.gov.in/nada/index.php/catalog/40447/download/44081/DROP_IN_ARTICLE-08.pdf.

Chandani G. S. (2021), "Inter State Migrant Workmen (Regulation of Employment and Conditions of Service) Act, 1979: A critical Perspective," *International Journal of Law Management & Humanities* 4 (4): 1754–69; 1762–63.

Directive Principles of State Policy, https://knowindia.india.gov.in/profile/directive-principles-of-state-policy.php#: ~:text=Directive%20Principle%20of%20State%20Policy&text=These%20lay%20down%20that%20the,all%20institutions%20of%20national%20life.

ILO Global Estimated on International Migrant Workers: Results and Methodology Executive Summary, https://www.ilo.org/wcmsp5/groups/public/---ed_protect/---protrav/---migrant/documents/publication/wcms_808939.pdf.

India on the Move and Churning: New Evidence, https://www.indiabudget.gov.in/budget2017-2018/es2016-17/echap12.pdf Pg 264- 284; p. 264.

International Labor Office, Rights, Labor Migration and Development: The ILO Approach http://www.ilo.org/migrant; http://www.ilo.org/dyn/normlex/en/f?p=NORMLEXPUB:12100:0::NO::P12100_INSTRUMENT_ID:312242.

Kamala Sankaran (2021), The fundamental freedom to migrate within India, Vol. LVI, No. 23, pp. 10–12; 10.

Labor Migration, ILO, 18 Feb. 2022, https://www.migrationdataportal.org/themes/labor-migration.

Neeraj Kumar, Inter-State Migration in India, https://www.ies.gov.in/pdfs/Seminar-neerajkumar.pdf; pp. 1–16.

New Labor Code for New India Biggest Labor Reforms in Independent India, https://labor.gov.in/sites/default/files/labor_code_eng.pdf.

The 1979 Act, https://clc.gov.in/clc/acts-rules/inter-state-migrant-workmen#INTRODUCTION.

The Occupational, Safety, Health and Work Conditions Code, https://labor.gov.in/sites/default/files/osh_gazette.pdf.

Yagnya Valkya Misra (2022). The long walk home: India's migrant labor, livelihood, and lockdown amid COVID-19, *Journal of Applied Communication Research*, 50:supl., S10–S17, DOI: 10.1080/00909882.2022.2079916; pp. S12–13.

NOTES

1. https://home-affairs.ec.europa.eu/networks/european-migration-network-emn/emn-asylum-and-migration-glossary/glossary/labor-migration_en#:~:text=Definition(s),for%20the%20purpose%20of%20employment.

2. Neeraj Kumar, Inter- State Migration in India, https://www.ies.gov.in/pdfs/Seminar-neerajkumar.pdf, pp. 1–16.

3. India on the Move and Churning: New Evidence, https://www.indiabudget.gov.in/budget2017-2018/es2016-17/echap12.pdf, pp. 264–84;264.

4. Kamala Sankaran (2021), The fundamental freedom to migrate within India, Vol. LVI, No. 23, pp. 10–12; 10.

5. New Labor Code for New India Biggest Labor Reforms in Independent India, https://labor.gov.in/sites/default/files/labor_code_eng.pdf.

6. Directive Principles of State Policy, https://knowindia.india.gov.in/profile/directive-principles-of-state-policy.php#:~:text=Directive%20Principle%20of%20State%20Policy&text=These%20lay%20down%20that%20the,all%20institutions%20of%20national%20life.

7. Seventh Schedule, https://www.mea.gov.in/Images/pdf1/S7.pdf.

8. Section 2(e) of the 1979 Act, https://clc.gov.in/clc/acts-rules/inter-state-migrant-workmen#INTRODUCTION.

9. Section 2(b) "contractor," in relation to an establishment, means a person who undertakes (whether as an independent contractor, agent, employee, or otherwise) to produce a given result for the establishment, other than a mere supply of goods or articles of manufacture to such establishment, by the employment of workmen or to supply workmen to the establishment, and includes a sub-contractor, Khatadar, Sardar, agent or any other person, by whatever name called, who recruits or employs workmen; Section 2(g) "principal employer" means (i) in relation to any office or department of the government or a local authority, the head of that office, department or authority or such other officer as the government or the local authority, as the case may be, may specify in this behalf; (ii) in relation to a factory, the owner or occupier of the factory and where a person has been named as the manager of the factory under the Factories Act, 1948 (63 of 1948), the person so named; (iii) in relation to a mine, the owner or agent of the mine, and where a person has been named as the manager of

the mine, the person so named; (iv) in relation to any other establishment, any person responsible for the supervision and control of the establishment.

10. Section 2(d)(d) "establishment" means: (i) any office or department of the government or a local authority; or (ii) any place where any industry, trade, business, manufacture, or occupation is carried on;

11. Section 1 (4) of the 1979 Act.

12. Section 4, 5 and 6 of the 1979 Act.

13. Section 8(2) of the 1979 Act.

14. Section 12(a) of the 1979 Act.

15. Section 12(b) of the 1979 Act.

16. Section 12 © of the 1979 Act.

17. Section 2(i) wages shall have the meaning assigned to it in clause (vi) of section 2 of the Payment of Wages Act, 1936.

18. Comment to Section 13 of the 1979 Act.

19. Section 16 of the 1979 Act.

20. Section 17 of the 1979 Act.

21. Section 18 of the 1979 Act.

22. Section 23 of the 1979 Act.

23. Section 20 of the 1979 Act.

24. Section 24 of the 1979 Act.

25. Section 25 of the 1979 Act.

26. Section 26 of the 1979 Act.

27. Section 27 of the 1979 Act.

28. Section 22 of the 1979 Act.

29. Section 31 of the 1979 Act.

30. Chandani G S (2021), the Inter State Migrant Workmen (Regulation of Employment and Conditions of Service) Act, 1979: A critical Perspective, *International Journal of Law Management & Humanities* 4 (4): 1754–69; 1762–63.

31. Census of India, https://censusindia.gov.in/nada/index.php/catalog/40447/download/44081/DROP_IN_ARTICLE-08.pdf.

32. India on the Move and Churning: New Evidence, https://www.indiabudget.gov.in/budget2017-2018/es2016-17/echap12.pdf, pp. 264–84; 276.

33. New Labor Code for New India: Biggest Labor Reforms in Independent India https://labor.gov.in/sites/default/files/labor_code_eng.pdf.

34. Section 2(m) of the Occupational Safety, Health and Working Conditions Code 2020.

35. "Inter-State migrant worker" means a person who is employed in an establishment and who: (i) has been recruited directly by the employer or indirectly through a contractor in one state for employment in such establishment situated in another state; or (ii) has come on his own from one state and obtained employment in an establishment of another state (hereinafter called destination state) or has subsequently changed the establishment within the destination state, under an agreement or other arrangement for such employment and draws wages not exceeding the amount of rupees 18,000 per month or such higher amount as may be notified by the central government from time to time.

36. Akhileshwari Reddy, New Labor Codes: What changes for interstate migrants? An analysis of two critical codes, VIDHI Centre for Legal Policy, 25 Nov. 2020, New Labor Codes: What Changes for Interstate Migrants? Vidhi Centre for Legal Policy (vidhilegalpolicy.in).

37. Akhileshwari Reddy, Lack of Updated Data Led to Massive Migrant Crisis During Covid-19, VIDHI Centre for Legal Policy, 16 Jul. 2020, Lack of Updated Data Led to Massive Migrant Crisis During COVID-19, Vidhi Centre for Legal Policy (vidhilegalpolicy.in).

38. Section 21 of the Occupational, Safety, Health and Work Conditions Code, https://labor.gov.in/sites/default/files/osh_gazette.pdf.

39. Sections 60 and 61 of the Occupational, Safety, Health and Work Conditions Code, https://labor.gov.in/sites/default/files/osh_gazette.pdf.

40. https://www.indiaspend.com/governance/why-ration-card-portability-scheme-is-mostly-limited-to-delhi-867957#:~:text=With%20Assam%20implementing%20it%20in,to%20have%20ration%20card%20portability&text=Delhi%2C%20which%20had%20only%20started,financial%20year%20of%202021%2D22.

41. Yagnya Valkya Misra (2022), The long walk home: India's migrant labor, livelihood, and lockdown amid COVID-19, *Journal of Applied Communication Research*, 50:sup1, S10–S17, DOI: 10.1080/00909882.2022.2079916; pp. S12–13.

42. https://www.mea.gov.in/Images/attach/20_Emigration_and_You.pdf.

43. https://mea.gov.in/Images/amb1/Emigration-Bill-2021.pdf.

44. Labor Migration, ILO 18 Feb. 2022, https://www.migrationdataportal.org/themes/labor-migration.

45. ILO Global Estimated on International Migrant Workers: Results and Methodology Executive Summary, https://www.ilo.org/wcmsp5/groups/public/---ed_protect/---protrav/---migrant/documents/publication/wcms_808939.pdf.

46. International Labor Office, Rights, Labor Migration and Development: The ILO Approach, http://www.ilo.org/migrant.

47. http://www.ilo.org/dyn/normlex/en/f?p=NORMLEXPUB:12100:0::NO::P12100_INSTRUMENT_ID:312242.

48. http://www.ilo.org/dyn/normlex/en/f?p=NORMLEXPUB:12100:0::NO::P12100_ILO_CODE:C143.

49. https://www.ilo.org/dyn/normlex/en/f?p=NORMLEXPUB:12100:0::NO::p12100_instrument_id:312288.

Chapter 10

Indonesian Laws on Ensuring the Rights of Migrant Workers

Dodik Setiawan Nur Heriyanto

Indonesia is an alternative location for migrant workers from abroad to work. The opening of investment in strategic sectors in natural resource management is one of the factors for foreign workers to come[1] and work in Indonesia. It is not surprising that the presence of multinational companies in Indonesia sometimes requires them to recruit foreign workers with specific skills to fill human resources. This is because it is not easy to employ them considering that the regulations in Indonesia are still very strict for foreign workers to work in Indonesia.

A series of laws and regulations have been established in Indonesia to ensure that foreign workers working in Indonesia meet their needs. The tightening carried out by the government is aimed at strengthening national security. What's more, the number of unemployed people in Indonesia is still an important concern so that the existence of the labor market can be put to good use by them.[2]

Workers from Indonesia who work abroad receive excessive attention from the Indonesian government. They mostly work at the countries whose majority of the population are Moslem and who offer high income such as Malaysia and Saudi Arabia.[3] Apart from being foreign exchange heroes for Indonesia, Indonesian migrant workers also contribute to promoting Indonesia, which is superior in terms of its cultural diversity. Various regulations have been formed to provide protection to Indonesians who will work abroad. In general, Indonesian migrant workers work at the household level and are very vulnerable to legal problems such as being victims of violence.[4] The regulations formed are intended to ensure that workers from Indonesia get legal protection.

This chapter provides an explanation related to the legal framework for ensuring the rights of legal migrant workers in Indonesia. It also discusses the implementation of international agreements and Indonesian laws on ensuring the rights of migrant workers. This chapter also analyzes challenges in ensuring the rights of migrant workers from Indonesia to other countries.

THE NATIONAL LEGAL FRAMEWORK FOR ENSURING THE RIGHTS OF LEGAL MIGRANT WORKERS

The Indonesian constitution guarantees the right of work and a decent living for its citizens. This guarantee of rights is also part of Indonesia's participation in the Covenant on Economic, Social and Cultural Rights (1976). In addition, the existence of this guarantee of rights also shows Indonesia's commitment to fulfilling Article 27 of the Universal Declaration of Human Rights even though legally the Declaration does not provide legal binding power. Indonesia's commitment is very important in order to guarantee welfare for its people by providing job opportunities without discrimination and in as wide a scope as possible.[5]

A series of government programs and policies were implemented in order to provide employment opportunities and create jobs not only for their own citizens but also opportunities for migrant workers from abroad. With a large population and limited job opportunities, the government is always looking for ways to ensure that the unemployment rate can be reduced. Joko Widodo's government program, for example, created the Indonesia Pre-Employment Card policy,[6] which is a work competency development program aimed at job seekers, workers affected by layoffs, and/or workers who need competency improvement.

Migrants in the context of this research can be categorized into two types, namely, domestic migrants and international migrants. Those who move from one region to another within the same country in search of a decent living and job can be classified as domestic migrants. In Indonesia, domestic migrants often occur, especially those who have the ability and competence to work in big cities in Java. Other areas with high natural resource potential are also targeted by domestic migrant workers for work.

Kutai Kartanegara is the area targeted by domestic migrant workers, especially those from Java, to support the management of natural resources in Kutai Kartanegara, such as the processing of petroleum, natural gas, and coal. Kutai Kartanegara Regency produces the most coal in East Kalimantan Province, reaching 65.11 million tons of the total production of companies holding Mining Business Permits (IUP) in East Kalimantan Province 5, which reaches 82.87 million tons.[7] Coal production from Kutai Kartanegara, which totaled 65.11 million tons, came from 60 companies holding IUP in the district. It is not surprising that the workforce needed in this Regency is quite high when compared to other regions.[8]

Apart from East Kalimantan Province, several other regions have also become targets of domestic migrants in Indonesia, such as: DKI Jakarta Province, Surabaya City, Bandung City, and Papua Province. DKI Jakarta Province also has the largest number of domestic migrants because apart from being the center of the central government, this province is also the center of the economy and business at the national level. Many large and multinational companies have been established and located in the Province of Jakarta, making them a destination for domestic migrants seeking high wages and decent work.

Protection for Domestic/Internal Migrant Workers

Indonesia has Law No. 13 of 2003 concerning manpower as the main and first legal framework that provides protection for workers. Labor here includes domestic migrant workers. However, in its development, in 2021, the government stipulates an omnibus law in the form of Law No. 11 of 2020 concerning job creation to accommodate the latest developments to create a conducive investment climate that will absorb more jobs and increase economic growth. Some of the provision of Law No. 13 of 2003 was declared null and void and replaced with the substance regulated in Law No. 11 of 2020.

In general, the principles underlying the protection of employment under the two recent statutory laws include:

a. Every worker has the right to get protection for workers in realizing welfare both for themselves and for their families[9];
b. Every worker has the same opportunity without discrimination to get a job;[10]
c. Every worker/laborer has the right to receive equal treatment without discrimination from employers;[11]
d. Each develops work competencies in accordance with their talents, interests, and abilities through job training;[12]
e. Every worker/laborer has the same opportunity to attend job training in accordance with his/her field of work;[13]
f. Every worker has the same rights and opportunities to choose, get, or change jobs and earn a decent income inside or outside the country;[14]
g. Every worker/laborer has the right to receive protection for occupational safety and health, morals and decency, and treatment that is in accordance with human dignity and values and religious values;[15]

h. Every worker/laborer has the right to a decent living for humanity;[16]
i. Every worker/laborer and their family have the right to obtain social security for workers;[17]
j. Every worker/laborer has the right to form and become a member of a worker/labor union.[18]

The manpower law of Indonesia regulates the employment relationship between workers/laborers and employers or companies, which also regulates the interests of every individual in the company. The employment relationship that regulates between workers and employers basically contains the rights and obligations of the parties. Law No. 13 of 2003 regulates employment relationships between workers/laborers and entrepreneurs/companies, which requires them to be realized in the form of a Work Agreement, Work Agreement for Indefinite Time (PKWT), Work Agreement. Specific Time (PKWTT), Company Regulations, Collective Work Agreements, and Contracting Agreements.

Regarding work agreements for a certain period of time (PKWT) and work agreements for a certain time, conceptually there are fundamental changes in the Job Creation Law. PKWT can only be carried out for limited types of work and only for work that is not permanent in nature with a period of no more than five years. In PKWT, the employment relationship ends by law when the term of certain work is completed, and compensation is still given even if the termination of employment is carried out by one of the parties unilaterally.

Occupational health is one of the rights of workers or laborers, for which employers are obliged to implement it systematically and in an integrated manner with the company's management system.[19] Occupational health aims to protect workers or laborers in order to achieve optimal work productivity, by preventing work-related accidents and diseases, controlling workplace hazards, health promotion, treatment, and rehabilitation. The Indonesian government has made a series of regulations on occupational safety and health, including the following:

a. Law No. 1 of 1970 on Job Safety. This law is the main law related to the job safety and health security in Indonesia. This law has become the main reference to all job safety frameworks even at small unit levels such as corporations.
b. Regulation of the Ministry of Manpower No. 4 of 1987 on Occupational Safety and Health Advisory Committee (P2K3).
c. Law No. 17 of 2023 on Health. In this regulation, employers are obliged to guarantee the health of workers through promotive, preventive,

curative, rehabilitative, and palliative efforts and are obliged to bear all the costs of maintaining the health of their workers.[20]

d. Law No. 40 of 2004 on the National Social Security System, which was then technically elaborated under Government Regulation No. 84 of 2013 on Social Security for Worker's Program.
e. Government Regulation No. 50 of 2012 on Implementation of the Occupational Safety and Health Management System (SMK3).
f. Presidential Regulation No. 7 of 2019 on Occupational Illness.
g. Regulation of Ministry of Manpower No. 5 of 2018 on Occupational Health and Safety Work Environment.

A form of labor protection is also provided by ensuring that workers receive adequate wages. The government's role in this case is to determine the regional minimum wage determined by each regional government. The minimum wage is the lowest monthly wage set annually as a safety net in a region. The decision is always awaited because regulations prohibit employers from paying their workers' wages lower than the minimum wage.

According to Article 23, paragraphs (1) and (2), of Government Regulation No. 36 of 2021 concerning wages, the minimum wage as intended is the lowest monthly wage, consisting of: wages without allowances or basic wages and fixed allowances; or in the case where the wage component in the company consists of a basic wage and non-fixed allowances, the basic wage is at least the minimum wage.[21] Article 24 paragraph (1) of Government Regulation No. 36 of 2021 confirms that the minimum wage only applies to workers with a working period of less than one year.[22] Meanwhile, wages for workers with a service period of one year or more must be guided by the wage structure and scale that must be prepared and implemented by the company.

Apart from playing a role in determining minimum wages, the Indonesian government has an obligation to provide socio-economic protection to the community, including workers, in the form of implementing social security programs. Social security for workers, which is currently managed by the Social Security Administering Agency (BPJS), will play a role in understanding the need for job security guarantees, which will certainly influence the business world, further develop work discipline, and increase work efficiency. Bosses who include people, business actors, legal elements, or other elements who utilize labor as intended in Article 15 of Law No. 24 of 2011 concerning the Social Security Administering Agency are expected to include themselves and their workers as BPJS participants in accordance with the pension program borne by the government.

BPJS Employment provides certainty protection from work accidents, death, or old age to employee retirement. Despite the importance of BPJS benefits for employment, there are still many employers, legal entities, or other bodies who do not register workers for reasons of efficiency, even though the company's participation in BPJS can be categorized as part of the implementation of Good Corporate Governance. Even though the regulations stipulate sanctions for companies that do not include their workers in the BPJS, in practice law enforcement is still very weak. The forms of sanctions given are in the form of written warnings, fines, and/or not receiving services provided by the government.[23] Such forms of sanctions do not provide a deterrent effect for companies.

Protection for Indonesian Migrant Workers Abroad

Some Indonesians also migrate abroad to find a decent living. Law No. 18 of 2017 defines "Indonesian migrant worker" as every Indonesian citizen who will work, is working, or has done work for receiving wages outside the territory of the Republic of Indonesia. This definition is only applied to Indonesians who plan to or currently do work in another country. The flow of Indonesian working abroad has resulted in at least two advantages: reducing unemployment in Indonesia and increasing the country's foreign exchange.[24]

The existence of Law No. 18 of 2017 is motivated by the important factor of ensuring that there is legal protection for Indonesian migrant workers who will work abroad. This is because Indonesian migrant workers often receive discrimination and become objects of violence when they work.[25] The problem is increasingly complex because most of them are not equipped with sufficient skills to be able to target much more worthy and respected fields of work. Moreover, workers in Indonesia who work abroad do not have a high level of education. Their average level of education is senior high school graduate or below.

So far, Indonesian workers abroad have often become victims of violence. Nirmala Bonat, an Indonesian worker who worked in Malaysia in 2004, was rescued because she experienced torture from her employer in the form of hot water being poured on her body, iron marks on her body, beating her head with a clothes hanger, and hitting her with a cup. Rasi, who worked in Singapore, experienced violence which resulted in a broken nose. Rasi's employer was later sentenced to 15 years in prison by the Singapore Court.[26] In Saudi Arabia, it is also common to find Indonesian workers receiving violence or being victims of torture from their employers.[27]

The existence of Law No. 18 of 2017 basically replaces Law No. 39 of 2004 on Placement and Protection of Indonesian Workers Abroad, which is substantially less than optimal in providing legal protection for Indonesian migrant workers. Moreover, the existence of Law No. 18 of 2017 also adopts provisions regarding aspects of protection that have been adopted from the International Convention Concerning the Protection of the Rights of All Migrant Workers and Members of Their Families, which has also been ratified.

The protection of prospective Indonesian migrant workers aims to: guarantee the fulfillment and upholding of human rights for citizens and Indonesian migrant workers; and guarantee legal, economic, and social protection for Indonesian migrant workers and their families.[28] Law No. 18 of 2017 regulates two differences in the responsibilities of central and regional governments. The Central Government's responsibilities include:

a. Guarantee the protection of prospective Indonesian migrant workers and/or Indonesian migrant workers and their families;
b. Organize, develop, implement, and supervise the placement of Indonesian migrant workers;
c. Ensure the fulfillment of the rights of prospective Indonesian migrant workers and their families;
d. Establish and develop an integrated information system in organizing the placement and protection of Indonesian migrant workers;
e. Coordinating cooperation between relevant agencies in responding to complaints and handling cases of prospective Indonesian migrant workers and/or Indonesian migrant workers;
f. Managing the return of Indonesian migrant workers in the event of war, natural disasters, disease outbreaks, deportation, and problematic Indonesian migrant workers;
g. Make efforts to ensure optimal fulfillment of the rights and protection of Indonesian migrant workers in the destination country of placement;
h. Develop policies regarding the protection of Indonesian migrant workers and their families;
i. Stop or prohibit the placement of Indonesian migrant workers in certain countries or in certain positions abroad;
j. Open certain countries or positions that are closed to the placement of Indonesian migrant workers;
k. Issue and revoke Company Permits for Placement of Indonesian migrant workers;
l. Issue and revoke Indonesian Migrant Worker Recruitment Permits;
m. Coordinate between relevant agencies regarding policies for the protection of Indonesian migrant workers;
n. Appoint officials as labor attachés who are placed at the Representative Office of the Republic of Indonesia on the recommendation of the minister; and
o. Providing and facilitating training for prospective Indonesian migrant workers through vocational training whose budget comes from the education function.[29]

Meanwhile, Law No. 18 of 2017 also gives responsibility to the Provincial Government for:

a. Organizing education and job training by accredited government and/or private educational institutions and job training institutions;
b. Managing the return of Indonesian migrant workers in the event of war, natural disasters, disease outbreaks, deportation, and problems with Indonesian migrant workers in accordance with their authority;
c. Issue permits for branch offices of companies placing Indonesian migrant workers;
d. Report the results of evaluations of companies placing Indonesian migrant workers in stages and periodically to the minister;
e. Providing protection for Indonesian migrant workers before work and after work;
f. Providing assistance posts and services at the departure and return points for Indonesian migrant workers that meet health requirements and standards;
g. Providing and facilitating training for prospective Indonesian migrant workers through vocational training whose budget comes from the education function;
h. Organize, develop, implement, and supervise the placement of Indonesian migrant workers; and
i. Form an integrated service for the placement and protection of Indonesian migrant workers at the provincial level.[30]

Meanwhile, the forms of responsibility given to Regency/City Regional Governments include:

a. Disseminate information and requests for Indonesian migrant workers to the public;
b. Create a database of Indonesian migrant workers;
c. Report the results of the evaluation of the Indonesian migrant workers placement company periodically to the provincial regional government;
d. Managing the return of Indonesian migrant workers in the event of war, natural disasters, disease outbreaks, deportation, and problematic migrant workers in accordance with their authority;
e. Provide protection for Indonesian migrant workers before working and after working in the district/city areas under their duties and authority;
f. Provide education and job training to prospective Indonesian migrant workers who can collaborate with accredited government and/or private educational institutions and job training institutions;

g. Provide guidance and supervision of educational institutions and job training institutions in districts/cities;
h. Carry out social and economic reintegration for Indonesian migrant workers and their families;
i. Provide and facilitate training for prospective Indonesian migrant workers through vocational training whose budget comes from the education function;
j. Organize, develop, implement, and supervise the placement of Indonesian migrant workers; and
k. Form a one-stop integrated service for the placement and protection of Indonesian migrant workers at the district/city level.[31]

Meanwhile, the Village Government (sub-region government)[32] is also given duties and responsibilities (although only limited to certain roles due to budget limitations), namely, among others:

a. Receive and provide information and job requests from agencies that carry out government affairs in the field of employment;
b. Verifying data and the recording of prospective Indonesian migrant workers;
c. Facilitate the fulfillment of residency administration requirements for prospective Indonesian migrant workers;
d. Monitoring the departure and return of Indonesian migrant workers; and empower prospective Indonesian migrant workers and Indonesian migrant workers and their families.

With the division of tasks and responsibilities between the Central Government, Provincial Government, District/City Governments, and Village Governments, it is hoped that this will strengthen the readiness of prospective Indonesian migrant workers to work abroad, particularly related to improving their skills through effective education and training activities. Some of the materials in education and training include catering, caretaker/babysitter, housekeeping, foreign languages, and introduction to foreign cultures. In general, Indonesian migrant workers are very enthusiastic about participating in the training to make them confident about being able to work abroad.[33] The training equips them with work skills which are demonstrated through work certification. Short training like this is preferred because it is more practical, faster, and at a lower cost than formal education.[34] This is the reason why most Indonesian migrant workers work in the household sector.

Even though a statutory law has been established that provides protection for Indonesian migrant workers, there are still many cases that cause them to become victims of violence and discrimination abroad. Law No. 18 of 2017, although it has regulated many things so that before being placed, migrant workers can have adequate skills, is unable to enforce the problems experienced by migrant workers abroad. This law does not have extraterritorial reach because each country has its own sovereignty.

Law No. 18 of 2017 states that Indonesian migrant workers must be protected from human trafficking, slavery and forced labor, violence, abuse, crimes against human dignity, as well as other treatment that violates human rights.[35] This law does not reflect in reality where there are many cases experienced by migrant workers both during the placement process and while working. The reach of this article is only limited to protecting them while they are in the country (Indonesia). However, when they enter the border immigration gate in another country, they must comply with the laws of that country with all existing protection schemes that have been established by the other country.

Article 21 Law No. 18 of 2017 regulates the existence of a protection scheme for Indonesian migrant workers abroad, namely, among others:

- data collection and registration by the labor attaché or appointed foreign service official;
- monitoring and evaluation of employers, jobs and working conditions;
- facilitating the fulfillment of the rights of Indonesian migrant workers;
- facilitating the resolution of employment cases;
- provision of consular services;
- assistance, mediation, advocacy, and provision of legal assistance in the form of facilitating advocate services by the Central Government and/or representatives of the Republic of Indonesia as well as guardianship in accordance with local state law;
- coaching Indonesian migrant workers; and
- repatriation facility.[36]

The form of technical facilitation regulated in Article 21 is of course not carried out by the foreign country but can be carried out through cooperation and diplomacy mechanisms between Indonesian representatives in the foreign country and the local government. For this reason, the Indonesian government is trying to strengthen the existence of diplomatic and consular functions in recipient countries such as Malaysia, Singapore, and Taiwan,[37] and Saudi Arabia because these countries receive many migrant workers from Indonesia. Law No. 18 of 2017 also provides structural support for the Indonesian embassies by positioning labor attachés.[38] However, technically their activities are only limited to collecting information on problematic migrant workers from Indonesia, including collecting data on business partners who channel Indonesian workers abroad.

Numbers of labor attachés stationed at Indonesian embassies abroad[39] are not enough.[40] Apart from that, the affairs of Indonesian migrant workers should also receive sufficient attention from the embassy to ensure they receive adequate legal protection.[41] For this reason, the affairs of Indonesian migrant workers must actually be a shared responsibility for all structures in the embassy. In addition, increasing the capacity of diplomatic and consular personnel is very necessary[42] and equipping them with knowledge and skills in dealing with the problems experienced by Indonesian migrant workers abroad. Creating an information system or employment database, especially to collect data on Indonesian migrant workers abroad, is also very necessary. This is to ensure the whereabouts of migrant workers and the extent of their progress working abroad.

Apart from that, bilateral and multilateral cooperation is very necessary to become the basis for cooperation in providing protection for migrant workers abroad. However, what is generally done is the preparation of a Memorandum of Understanding (MoU) between the Indonesian government and the other country.[43] In fact, legally, the existence of an MoU according to custom is a pre-contractual text and does not give rise to binding legal force. In 2022, for example, Indonesia will carry out cooperation with Malaysia in the form of signing an MoU on the Placement and Protection of Indonesian Migrant Workers in the Domestic Sector in Malaysia.[44] Although in reality, at the time of implementation of this MoU, there were still problems with migrant workers that had not been resolved properly. Based on data released by the Malaysian embassy to Indonesia, from January to June 2022, as many as 48 Indonesian citizens died in immigration detention centers in Malaysia. Still in the same year, namely 2022, there were 746 Indonesian migrant workers who were arrested in raids on the border between Indonesia and Malaysia.

Based on the 2022 data from the Indonesian Migrant Worker Protection Agency (BP2MI) processed by the Central Statistics Agency (BPS), there are 200,000 migrant workers recorded as working in Asia, Africa, Europe, the Middle East, America, and the Pacific in 2022.[45] That number is from data on legal and documented migrant workers. Meanwhile, there is also data on migrant workers who enter illegally. In 2021, based on BP2MI data, Nunukan, North Kalimantan, received deportation of 1,386 Indonesian illegal migrant workers. In a situation like this, coordination and alertness are needed from government units to tighten supervision and carry out law enforcement effectively. The coordination function between ministries, including enabling them to carry out direct coordination with Indonesian diplomatic representatives abroad, must be given space and facilities in order to encourage them to not tend to ignore each other and pass on responsibilities.[46]

Apart from that, Indonesia's diplomatic efforts also need to be strengthened, especially for countries that still need the role of Indonesian migrant workers.

There needs to be a binding bilateral cooperation forum so that there is legal certainty to provide protection for Indonesian migrant workers abroad.[47] The initiation and negotiations for the establishment of bilateral cooperation must be supervised by Indonesian diplomatic representatives abroad. Binding treaties must be the goal of these negotiation activities. Indonesian diplomatic representatives abroad need to prepare a strategy to create Indonesia's bargaining power to be able to have this bilateral cooperation. For example, if Taiwan still needs free market cooperation with Indonesia, then as a form of agreement Taiwan must agree to Indonesia's proposal to on norms for protecting migrant workers in Indonesia.

PROTECTION FOR FOREIGN MIGRANT WORKERS

The presence of foreign investors also influences the economy in Indonesia, especially in terms of managing natural resources and utilizing them for the welfare of society. Primarily in the case of a free market, foreign investors not only provide benefits in the form of capital, money, and technology to enter Indonesian territory but also foreign workers. The presence of foreign workers is of course not only used for their energy to work but also for the transfer of knowledge. Their very specific skills and expertise are very important to teach to the rest of the workforce who work with them.

Whether or not you can employ foreign workers is regulated in the regulation of Foreign Workers (TKA) as stated in Article 42, paragraph (1), of Law Number 13 of 2003 concerning manpower that "Every employer who employs foreign workers is obliged to obtain written permission from the Minister or appointed official." The Law of Job Creation also regulates employment relationships for certain positions and certain times and having competencies in accordance with the position to be occupied.[48]

Those who can provide work to foreign workers are called foreign migrant worker employers, which include:

a. government agencies, foreign country representatives and international bodies;
b. foreign trade representative offices, foreign company representative offices, and foreign news agencies carrying out activities in Indonesia;
c. foreign private companies doing business in Indonesia;
d. legal entities in the form of limited liability companies or foundations established under Indonesian law or foreign business entities registered with the competent authorities, except for limited liability companies in the form of individual legal entities;
e. social, religious, educational, and cultural institutions;

f. impresario service businesses; and
g. business entities to the extent permitted by law to use foreign migrant workers.[49]

Every institution, both government and private, in Indonesia that will employ foreign workers is required to have an Plan for the Use of Foreign Workers (RPTKA) document. This document is issued by the Ministry of Manpower of the Republic of Indonesia to regulate and provide approval for the use of foreign workers by companies in Indonesia. Its function is as a basis for obtaining a Permit to Employ Foreign Workers (IMTA). The RPTKA is a document that contains plans for the use of foreign workers by the company and contains information related to work, the number of foreign workers needed, and the term or duration of the contract for the use of foreign workers. The RPTKA contains complete information regarding the company identity, including company name, address, business license number, and company contact. There are also job details which contain information about the job description that will be carried out by foreign workers and information about the position and qualifications of the worker. Apart from that, the RPTKA must also show the contract that has been agreed on between the foreign worker and the company/institution that uses them. The contract must state when they start working and when they finish working so that it is known that their existence is not permanent, and they must carry out a transfer of knowledge so that there is no element of dependency on their existence. All RPTKA processing is carried out online through the digital service system[50] owned by the Indonesian Ministry of Manpower.

Furthermore, RPTKA must be ratified RPTKA or approval for the use of TKA which is authorized by the minister who handles government affairs in the field of employment or an appointed official.[51] Ratification of the RPTKA consists of:

a. RPTKA for temporary work, namely, a maximum of 6 months, cannot be extended;
b. RPTKA for work of more than 6 months is given for a maximum period of two) years and can be extended;
c. Non-DKPTKA RPTKA (Working Permit without government incentives) given for a maximum period of two years and can be extended;
d. RPTKA KEK (Working Permit in the Specific Region), given for a maximum period of five years and can be extended. Meanwhile, RPTKA KEK approval for the position of director or commissioner is given once and is valid as long as the TKA concerned is a director or commissioner.[52]

After the RPTKA has received approval from the Ministry, the next document that must be processed is the IMTA (or Permit to Employ Foreign Workers). Only with an IMTA can foreign workers work in Indonesia. The IMTA validity period is one year and can then be extended if the requirements are met. Requirements for documents for making an IMTA include a copy of the RPTKA ratification decision letter, curriculum vitae, copy of passport, one 4 x 6–size color photograph, a copy of a diploma or work experience letter, and a copy of the letter of appointment of accompanying foreign workers employed. In the draft IMTA application petitioners must also attach a copy of the work agreement document, proof of payment of compensation money for the use of foreign workers through a bank appointed by the government, a copy of the insurance policy, a copy of the notification letter approving the granting of a visa, and a recent passport photo.

Apart from RPTKA and IMTA documents, foreign workers must also obtain KITAS documents to ensure they can stay in Indonesia. Every foreigner residing in Indonesian territory, based on Article 48, paragraph (1), of Law No. 6 of 2011, is required to have a stay permit. The immigration stay permits that foreigners can have consist of visit stay permits, limited stay permits, and permanent stay permits. Foreign workers generally get limited stay permits. Under certain conditions, they can apply for a change of status to obtain a permanent residence permit that is valid for five years.

Furthermore, Regulation of the Ministry of Law and Human Rights No. 29 of 2021 regulates that the request for the transfer of ITAS (temporary) status to ITAP (permanent) is submitted by foreign migrant workers by filling in a data application and attaching documents:

a. valid and legal national passport;
b. residence certificate;
c. statement of integration except for children under 18 years of age and unmarried;
d. ITAS of the foreigner concerned;
e. letter of guarantee from the guarantor or proof of immigration deposit;
f. identity card and family card of the guarantor or person in charge; and
g. ITAP in the event that the guarantor or person in charge is a foreign citizen.

Apart from these documents, foreign migrant workers must also attach additional evidence: a Temporary Residence Permit, which shows that the person concerned has lived for more than three consecutive years in Indonesian territory; and recommendations from government agencies that carry out government affairs in the field of employment. Hence, it can be concluded that in fact foreign workers can have a permanent residence permit with a maximum of five years to live and work in Indonesia provided that they integrate with their families in Indonesia and have at least obtained a temporary residence permit of at least three years.

THE NEED TO RATIFY RELEVANT TREATIES TO ENSURE THE PROTECTION OF THE RIGHTS OF MIGRANT WORKERS

Indonesia is actively involved in carrying out international cooperation with the aim of providing direct benefits to society. Apart from being aimed at adapting to international standards, especially in the field of employment, Indonesia also really hopes that this collaboration can support improving the country's economy. Furthermore, Indonesia's participation in both bilateral and multilateral agreements regarding employment is also aimed at showing Indonesia's reputation as a country that guarantees protection for workers' rights. It is also hoped that Indonesia's involvement can encourage other countries to also provide equal protection to our migrant workers in countries participating in other international agreements.

Currently, Indonesia has ratified the International Convention on the Protection of the Rights of All Migrant Workers and Members of their Families. This Convention was created by taking into account the principles contained in the basic instruments of the United Nations regarding human rights, in particular the Universal Declaration of Human Rights; the International Covenant on Economic, Social and Cultural Rights; the International Covenant on Civil and Political Rights; the International Convention on the Elimination of All Forms of Racial Discrimination; the International Convention on the Elimination of All Forms of Discrimination Against Women; and the Convention on the Rights of the Child.

This Convention applies to all migrant workers and members of their families without any distinction such as gender, race, color, language, religion or belief, political or other opinion, nationality, ethnic or social origin, nationality, age, economic position, wealth, marital status, and birth status, or others. This convention also covers all migrant workers during the process as well as all migration statuses, whether documented or not.[53]

This convention protects the rights of migrant workers and their families comprehensively, starting from the protection of human rights, the right not to be tortured, economic rights, as well as rights and decent working conditions. However, in reality there have been several cases of abuse and torture against Indonesian migrant workers, especially female migrant workers who work as household helpers, which often lead to death. Likewise, rights related to decent working conditions[54] state that migrants have the right to decent working hours, overtime pay, weekly rest, occupational safety and health, guarantees during layoffs, minimum wage, and other working conditions in accordance with legal practices.

The existence of this Convention is of course still insufficient in providing protection to migrant workers because it does not specifically regulate domestic workers, protection of workers during emigration and immigration, as well as protection of the rights of migrant workers from acts of violence and discrimination. For this reason, in this study it is recommended for Indonesia to consider the ratification process for other relevant multilateral agreements, namely, as follows:

ILO Convention No. 97 on Migration on Employment[55]

The migration for work convention is very important to ratify considering the situation in Indonesia which makes it possible for everyone to move from one place to another for work reasons, especially those who target industrial cities in other countries. This Convention provides guarantees to migrant workers so that they do not become victims of regulations either because they immigrate or when they emigrate. Emigration is also defined as leaving a country for the purpose of living or staying permanently in another country. Meanwhile, immigration is the movement of people from abroad to another country.

This Convention will be very beneficial for Indonesia because it will reduce or prevent illegal immigration. This Convention stipulates that anyone who immigrates illegally will be given legal sanctions.[56] To prevent such actions, the Convention encourages each country participating in ratification to simplify administrative bureaucracy during movement, guarantee protection while the migrant worker's family lives with them, guarantee protection for the transfer of their property, and provide security during their journey to another country.[57]

ILO Convention No. 143 on Migrant Workers (Supplementary Provisions)

This convention provides guarantees to prevent acts of violence/mistreatment and discrimination against migrant workers because differences in age, gender, ethnicity, race, and class are often the basis for acts of violence or abuse against migrant workers. Migrant workers are then exploited and treated discriminatorily, especially because their position is not equal to that of their employers. This clearly violates the basic provisions of human rights, and it is very important to provide protection to ensure respect for their dignity.

This Convention specifically asks countries participating in the Convention to suppress clandestine movements of migrants for employment and illegal employment of migrants, and against the organizers of illicit or clandestine movements of migrants for employment departing from, passing through, or arriving in its territory, and against those who employ workers who have immigrated in illegal conditions, in order to prevent and to eliminate the abuses.[58] Apart from that, other norms in this Convention also request that each country participating in the ratification of the Convention regulates its national law to promote and to guarantee, by methods appropriate to national conditions and practice, equality of opportunity and treatment in respect to employment and occupation, social security, trade union and cultural rights, and individual and collective freedoms for persons who as migrant workers or as members of their families are legally within its territory.[59]

ILO Convention No. 189 on Domestic Workers[60]

According to the International Labor Organization (ILO), the definition of a domestic worker is someone who is employed in domestic work within an employment relationship. Domestic workers usually work in private homes, doing household work such as cleaning the house, cooking, gardening, looking after children, and so on. In Indonesia, the majority of domestic workers work in an informal and private manner, so that domestic workers do not receive the same rights and protections as other workers in other sectors.[61] Especially for female workers, their honor and dignity must also be respected while working.[62]

This Convention carries the main mission of placing the position of domestic workers at the level they should be, namely, as workers who are equal to other workers in general. Thus, in principle, this Convention functions as an instrument that aims to improve the working conditions and dignity of domestic workers throughout the world, which is done through providing a basis for ensuring that domestic workers can access and enjoy the rights that workers have long enjoyed in the formal economic sector and provides minimum standards that must be met in order to protect the rights of domestic workers.

The Philippines is the only Asian country that has ratified ILO Convention No. 189 and has a national policy regarding the protection of domestic workers and has similar social characteristics to Indonesia. Indonesia can learn from the good practices, challenges, and opportunities related to the policies to protect domestic workers that the Philippines already has. ILO Convention No. 189 as a meta norm, provides minimum standard measures and a basic framework regarding the protection of domestic workers.

Indonesia is also preparing a Draft Law on Domestic Workers. The bill on domestic workers has been discussed several times in the House of Representatives, although it has not yet been approved for ratification. However, this bill still has several weaknesses because it does not provide regulations regarding procedures for determining minimum wages and wage systems, working time limits, rights to freedom, and minimum limits for domestic workers in working. By ratifying ILO Convention No. 189, it is expected to be the main basis for drafting the bill on domestic workers. At least international standards related to the protection of domestic workers can be adopted and regulated more technically in the bill of domestic workers.

Basically, there are still other ILO Conventions that are still very relevant and need to be ratified by Indonesia. For example, ILO Convention 181 concerning Private Employment Agencies, ILO Convention 118 concerning Equal Treatment (Social Security), and ILO Convention No. 157 concerning Safeguarding Social Security Rights. It's just that based on existing empirical conditions, the three Conventions above need to receive priority considering the many problems that often occur in society. Apart from that, ratification/ratification of international agreements also requires time and mutual consent from both the legislature and the executive.

CHALLENGES IN ENSURING THE RIGHTS OF MIGRANT WORKERS FROM INDONESIA TO OTHER COUNTRIES

The presence of Indonesian migrant workers who go abroad is part of their right to get work and a decent living. To be able to work abroad, migrant workers in Indonesia must meet the following qualifications: at least 18 (eighteen) years of age; have competence; physically and mentally healthy; registered and having a social security participation number; and have complete documents required.[63] Generally Indonesian migrant workers abroad work as domestic workers.[64] Apart from that, they work as caregivers/caretakers, plantation workers, operators, deck hands, and others.[65] There are also some who work abroad as professionals, but those who have the skills are easily tempted to change citizenship.[66]

In fact, many violations often occur, especially for migrant workers abroad, ranging from their document status to the violence they experience. Some of the challenges that are often faced are as follows:

Strengthening Improvements in the Quality of Education and Specialization of Skills

To reduce the number of migrant workers in Indonesia, who are generally in the household sector, it is very necessary to improve the quality of education. For example, it is very necessary to organize a skills program for them in cooking so that they are ready to become chefs in restaurants abroad. Indonesia, which is rich in culinary delights, can be the basic capital for learning to cook. Moreover, many Asian or Indonesian restaurants have started to open abroad, such as in the Netherlands. Apart from that, prospective migrant workers need to be equipped with high education and good literacy awareness.[67] Currently, there are many undergraduate degrees with specializations, for example, in the use of leather technology, drug/pharmaceutical processing, and etc. It is time for Indonesian migrant workers to target industrial areas abroad.

Mastery of Technology

The challenge of the industrial era 4.0 is that Indonesian migrant workers will compete with artificial intelligence and/or robots. For this reason, it is necessary to prepare an Indonesian workforce that is professional, productive, able to compete, and ready to face global challenges and the industrial revolution 4.0. Mastery of technology is mandatory for Indonesian migrant workers so that their skills are not easily replaced by robots. In developed countries, robots already have a role in helping households. Their homes are also equipped with technology that adopts artificial intelligence so that the entire system is run autonomously.

Supervision of the Border Area

In order to prevent the presence of illegal and undocumented migrant workers, the immigration authorities[68] need to prepare an information system that is integrated and easy to monitor in real time. This system must be single and integrated, namely, combining documents held by the immigration unit and units in the Ministry of Manpower. This unification is important so that detection of document forgery can be carried out directly, especially at immigration offices, particularly those located at the border. Companies or agents who commit acts of counterfeiting and smuggling illegal and undocumented migrant workers need to be given punishments that have a deterrent effect.[69]

Cooperation with other Countries and Strengthening Diplomacy

One of the weaknesses of the Indonesian government in dealing with cases of migrant workers is weak cooperation with law enforcement units in other countries. State sovereignty is an obstacle for law enforcement officials in Indonesia to obtain sufficient evidence or information to resolve the problems of migrant workers abroad. By establishing more detailed cooperation, it will be easier to get assistance or assist law enforcement officials in other countries in resolving cases faced by migrant workers. Even if binding cooperation is difficult to realize, Indonesia can strengthen its diplomatic role with other countries. Strengthening this diplomacy can take the form of encouraging additional attachés to deal with employment issues or become part of the priority agenda of Indonesian diplomats abroad.

The Indonesian government must always make the issue of migrant workers a priority discussion scale in both the legislative and executive branches. At the legislative level, apart from encouraging the ratification of other relevant ILO Conventions, it is also necessary to monitor whether the existence of Law No. 18 of 2017 and all relevant statutory laws have been implemented properly or are still causing problems. Apart from that, at the executive level, it is necessary to think about how Indonesian migrant workers can "move up" to not only work at the household level but can target large industrial sectors in developed countries. With an optimistic spirit, encouragement for them to be able to move up in class at work can be realized because many Indonesians are starting to have bachelor's/master's/doctoral degrees from universities abroad. Several conveniences need to be arranged so that they can work comfortably, and their rights are protected.

What should not be forgotten is that efforts to increase the existence of Indonesian migrant workers can also be done through the Association of Southeast Asian Nations (ASEAN) mechanism. As a regional institution, ASEAN has a very strategic role in providing guarantees for migrant workers to feel safe and comfortable at work, especially in Southeast Asia. To date, there has been a Consensus on the Protection and Promotion of Migrant Workers' Rights which was formed in 2018. However, this consensus only provides moral force and does not have legally binding force. For this reason, a multilateral agreement that is binding and technical and detailed is needed by adopting the standard norms set out by the ILO Convention to be implemented in Southeast Asian countries.

REFERENCES

Antlöv, Hans. "Village Government and Rural Development in Indonesia: The New Democratic Framework." *Bulletin of Indonesian Economic Studies* 39, no. 2 (August 2010): 193–214.

Audrey, Josephine, Fakhri Sabiq Muawal, and Eva Firsha. "The Influence of Globalization on Migration Flows of Indonesian Female Migrant Workers to Saudi Arabia." *Publica: Jurnal Pemikiran Administrasi Negara* 15, no. 2 (July 29, 2023): 414–25.

Constant, A. F., Nottmeyer, O., and K. F. Zimmermann. "The Economics of Circular Migration." In *International Handbook on the Economics of Migration*, 55–74. Edward Elgar Publishing, 2013.

Dzulviqor, Ahmad, and Dita Angga Rusiana. "Jumlah PMI Di Malaysia Yang Berangkat Dan Pulang Secara Ilegal Meningkat, Pengaruh Calo Masih Kuat." Last modified 2023. Accessed September 16, 2023. https://regional.kompas.com/read/2023/01/11/140859178/jumlah-pmi-di-malaysia-yang-berangkat-dan-pulang-secara-ilegal-meningkat.

Elvianti, Witri, and Jihan Djafar Sidik. "The Consignment of Indonesian Migrant Workers in Saudi Arabia and Its Resilience: Examining the Impacts of Indonesia's Moratorium Policy (2011–2015)." *Andalas Journal of International Studies (AJIS)* 7, no. 1 (June 22, 2018): 14–32.

Febriari. "Quality Education and Skills of Indonesian Labor, Towards Equality Wages in Foreign Countries." *Jurnal Ekonomi Pembangunan* 14, no. 2 (2013): 203–13.

Firlana, Habbi, and Cahyoko Edi Tando. "Peran Imigrasi Dalam Pengawasan Pekerja Migran Indonesia." *Jurnal Ilmiah Kajian Keimigrasian* 5, no. 1 (October 28, 2022): 69–77.

Ghofar, M. "Kukar Produksi 65,11 Juta Ton Batu Bara, Terbanyak Di Kaltim Pada 2017." Last modified 2018. Accessed September 14, 2023. https://www.antaranews.com/berita/687168/kukar-produksi-6511-juta-ton-batu-bara-terbanyak-di-kaltim-pada-2017.

Hamalik, Oemar. *Manajemen Pelatihan Ketenagakerjaan Pendekatan Terpadu*. Jakarta: Bumi Aksara, 2007.

H.R., Syaukani. "Karakteristik Dan Stuktur Kesempatan Kerja Di Kabupaten Kutai Kartanegara." *Jurnal Ekonomi Pembangunan* 8, no. 1 (2003): 63–71.

Hussin, Mutia Hariati. "Factors Influencing Indonesian Women Becomes Migrant Workers." *Jurnal Hubungan Internasional* 2, no. 1 (2013): 65–74.

Indonesian Ministry of Foreign Affairs. "Indonesia Malaysia Sepakati Mou Perlindungan Pekerja Migran Indonesia Di Malaysia." Last modified 2022. Accessed September 12, 2023. https://kemlu.go.id/portal/id/read/3475/berita/indonesia-malaysia-sepakati-mou-perlindungan-pekerja-migran-indonesia-di-malaysia.

Jain, Prakash C., and Ginu Zacharia OOmmen. *South Asian Migration to Gulf Countries: History, Policies, Development*. London: Routledge, 2016.

Koser, Khalid. *International Migration: A Very Short Introduction*. Oxford: Oxford University Press, 2007.

Kusdarini, Eny, Chandra Dewi Puspitasari, Sri Wahyu Krida Sakti, and Purwaningdyah Murti Wahyuni. "The Urgency of Legal Literacy for Indonesian Migrant Workers through Distance Education." *Fiat Justisia Jurnal Ilmu Hukum* 15, no. 4 (2021): 399–416.

Kusuma, Ardli Johan, Michael Ryan York, and Rizki Hari Wibowo. "Violence against Indonesian Migrant Workers: A Causal Analysis." *Jurnal Hubungan Internasional* 4, no. 1 (August 22, 2015): 47–57.

Laraspati, Angga. "Menaker Ingatkan Atase Ketenagakerjaan Tak Hanya Urusi Persoalan PMI." Accessed September 12, 2023. https://news.detik.com/berita/d-5704437/menaker-ingatkan-atase-ketenagakerjaan-tak-hanya-urusi-persoalan-pmi.

Maksum, Ali, Ching Lung Tsay, and Ali Muhammad. "Indonesian Migrant Workers in Taiwan: The State Dilemma and People's Realities." *Jurnal Ilmu Sosial dan Ilmu Politik* 24, no. 1 (January 12, 2021): 80–96.

MAMPU. "Improving Conditions for Women's Overseas Labour Migration." Last modified 2017. Accessed September 11, 2023. http://mampu.bappenas.go.id/en/theme/migrant-workers-protection/.

National Commission of Human Rights of Indonesia. "Urgensi Ratifikasi Konvensi ILO 189 Untuk Pemenuhan Dan Perlindungan Hak PRT: Komnas HAM." Last modified 2022. Accessed September 12, 2023. https://www.komnasham.go.id/index.php/news/2022/9/23/2237/urgensi-ratifikasi-konvensi-ilo-189-untuk-pemenuhan-dan-perlindungan-hak-prt.html.

Nuraeni, Yeni, and Suryadi. "Strategy for the Development of the Indonesian Migrant Worker (PMI) Placement Program in the Formal Sector." *Italienisch* 12, no. 1 (2021): 12–22.

Office of Assistant to Deputy Cabinet Secretary for State. "President Jokowi Tells Pre-Employment Card Recipients to Never Stop Learning." Last modified 2021. Accessed September 14, 2023. https://setkab.go.id/en/president-jokowi-advises-tells-pre-employment-card-recipients-to-never-stop-learning/.

Rahmawati, Anggun, Arief Budiono, Syaifuddin Zuhdi, and Nuria Siswi Enggarani. "Legal Issues Behind Village Autonomy and Village Head Role in Village Governments." *Audito Comparative Law Journal* 4, no. 2 (May 15, 2023): 68–75.

Santika, Erlina F. "Pekerja Migran Indonesia Di Asia Meningkat Pada 2022, Penempatan Hong Kong Terbanyak." Last modified 2023. Accessed September 16, 2023. https://databoks.katadata.co.id/datapublish/2023/03/07/pekerja-migran-indonesia-di-asia-meningkat-pada-2022-penempatan-hong-kong-terbanyak#.

Sentinel Villages Report. *Indonesian Village Governance under the New Village Law (2015–2018)*. Washington DC, 2020. Accessed September 15, 2023. https://documents1.worldbank.org/curated/en/220661590726265687/pdf/Indonesian-Village-Governance-Under-the-New-Village-Law-2015-2018-Sentinel-Villages-Report.pdf.

Setijaningrum, Erna, Asiyah Kassim, Rochyati Triana, and Reza Dzulfikri. "Going Back with Glee: A Case Study of Indonesian Migrant Workers Engaging in Circular Migration." *Journal of ASEAN Studies* 11, no. 1 (June 20, 2023): 219–43.

Wahyono, Sri. "The Problems of Indonesian Migrant Worker's Rights Protection in Malaysia." *Jurnal Kependudukan Indonesia* II, no. 1 (2007): 27–44.
Wahyudi, Deny Tri. "Perlindungan Hukum Terhadap Tenaga Kerja Indonesia Di Luar Negeri." *Mimbar Hukum* (2015): 170–84.
Yuniar, Resty Woro. "Young Indonesians Secure Singapore Citizenship as Many Lament 'Skills Mismatch' Back Home." *This Week in Asia*. Last modified 2023. Accessed September 11, 2023. https://www.scmp.com/week-asia/people/article/3229314/young-indonesians-secure-singapore-citizenship-many-lament-skills-mismatch-back-home.
Zulfikar, Achmad. "Peluang Dan Tantangan Pekerja Migran Indonesia Dalam Masyarakat Ekonomi ASEAN." In *National Convention Association of International Relations VII Year 2016, University of Hasanuddin*. Makasar, 2016.
"Alasan Depresi, Wanita Singapura Siksa TKI Hingga Babak Belur." Last modified 2019. Accessed September 14, 2023. https://www.cnnindonesia.com/internasional/20191121140013-106-450348/alasan-depresi-wanita-singapura-siksa-tki-hingga-babak-belur.
"Convention on the Protection of the Rights of All Migrant Workers and Their Families." Last modified 2003. Accessed October 2, 2020. https://www.culturalsurvival.org/publications/cultural-survival-quarterly/convention-protection-rights-all-migrant-workers-and-their.
Government Regulation No. 34 of 2021 on the Use of Foreign Migrant Worker, n.d.
Government Regulation No. 36 of 2021 on Wages, n.d.
"Jumlah Atase Ketenagakerjaan Tidak Memadai, Banyak Kasus TKI Tidak Tertangani." Last modified 2018. Accessed September 12, 2023. https://www.merdeka.com/uang/jumlah-atase-ketenagakerjaan-tidak-memadai-banyak-kasus-tki-tidak-tertangani.html.
"Kemnaker Perkuat Peran Dan Tugas Atase Ketenagakerjaan." Last modified 2019. Accessed September 16, 2023. https://kemnaker.go.id/news/detail/kemnaker-perkuat-peran-dan-tugas-atase-ketenagakerjaan.
Law No. 11 of 2020 on Job Creation, n.d.
Law No. 13 of 2013 on Manpower, n.d.
Law No. 18 of 2017 on the Protection of Indonesian Migrant Workers, n.d.
Law No.17 of 2023 on Health, n.d.
Regulation of Minister of Manpower and Transmigration No. PER.12/MEN/X/2011 on Manpower Attaché and Technical Staffs on Manpower in the Indonesian Representative Abroad, n.d.
"TKA-Online: Sistem Informasi Pelayanan Penggunaan Tenaga Kerja Asing Online." Last modified 2023. Accessed September 16, 2023. https://tka-online.kemnaker.go.id/alur.asp.

NOTES

1. Khalid Koser, *International Migration: A Very Short Introduction* (Oxford: Oxford University Press, 2007).

2. A. F. Constant, Nottmeyer, O., and K. F. Zimmermann, "The Economics of Circular Migration," in *International Handbook on the Economics of Migration* (Edward Elgar Publishing, 2013), 55–74.

3. Prakash C. Jain and Ginu Zacharia OOmmen, *South Asian Migration to Gulf Countries: History, Policies, Development* (London: Routledge, 2016).

4. Josephine Audrey, Fakhri Sabiq Muawal, and Eva Firsha, "The Influence of Globalization on Migration Flows of Indonesian Female Migrant Workers to Saudi Arabia," *Publica: Jurnal Pemikiran Administrasi Negara* 15, no. 2 (July 29, 2023): 414–25.

5. Erna Setijaningrum et al., "Going Back with Glee: A Case Study of Indonesian Migrant Workers Engaging in Circular Migration," *Journal of ASEAN Studies* 11, no. 1 (June 20, 2023): 219–43.

6. Office of Assistant to Deputy Cabinet Secretary for State, "President Jokowi Tells Pre-Employment Card Recipients to Never Stop Learning," last modified 2021, accessed September 14, 2023, https://setkab.go.id/en/president-jokowi-advises-tells-pre-employment-card-recipients-to-never-stop-learning/.

7. M. Ghofar, "Kukar Produksi 65,11 Juta Ton Batu Bara, Terbanyak Di Kaltim Pada 2017," last modified 2018, accessed September 14, 2023, https://www.antaranews.com/berita/687168/kukar-produksi-6511-juta-ton-batu-bara-terbanyak-di-kaltim-pada-2017.

8. Syaukani, H.R., "Karakteristik Dan Stuktur Kesempatan Kerja Di Kabupaten Kutai Kartanegara," *Jurnal Ekonomi Pembangunan* 8, no. 1 (2003): 63–71.

9. *Law No. 13 of 2013 on Manpower*, n.d. Art. 4 (c).

10. Ibid. Art. 5.

11. Ibid. Art. 6.

12. Ibid. Art. 11.

13. Ibid. Art. 12(3).

14. Ibid. Art. 31.

15. Ibid. Art. 86(1).

16. *Law No. 11 of 2020 on Job Creation*, n.d., Art. 21, point 4.

17. Ibid. Art. 99(1).

18. Ibid. Art. 104(1).

19. *Law No. 13 of 2013 on Manpower* Art. 86(1)(a).

20. *Law No.17 of 2023 on Health*, n.d., Art.100.

21. *Government Regulation No. 36 of 2021 on Wages*, n.d. Art. 23 (1) and (2).

22. Ibid. Art. 24 (1).

23. Ibid. Art. 79.

24. MAMPU, "Improving Conditions for Women's Overseas Labour Migration," last modified 2017, accessed September 11, 2023, http://mampu.bappenas.go.id/en/theme/migrant-workers-protection/.

25. Ardli Johan Kusuma, Michael Ryan York, and Rizki Hari Wibowo, "Violence against Indonesian Migrant Workers: A Causal Analysis," *Jurnal Hubungan Internasional* 4, no. 1 (August 22, 2015): 47–57.

26. "Alasan Depresi, Wanita Singapura Siksa TKI Hingga Babak Belur," last modified 2019, accessed September 14, 2023, https://www.cnnindonesia.com/

internasional/20191121140013-106-450348/alasan-depresi-wanita-singapura-siksa-tki-hingga-babak-belur.

27. Witri Elvianti and Jihan Djafar Sidik, "The Consignment of Indonesian Migrant Workers in Saudi Arabia and Its Resilience: Examining the Impacts of Indonesia's Moratorium Policy (2011–2015)," *Andalas Journal of International Studies (AJIS)* 7, no. 1 (June 22, 2018): 14–32.

28. *Law No. 18 of 2017 on the Protection of Indonesian Migrant Workers*, n.d., Art. 3.

29. Ibid. Art. 39.

30. Ibid. Art. 40.

31. Ibid. Art. 41.

32. Village government is a government institution tasked with managing village-level areas and has autonomy to manage and allocate their owned fund. Anggun Rahmawati et al., "Legal Issues Behind Village Autonomy and Village Head Role in Village Governments," *Audito Comparative Law Journal* 4, no. 2 (May 15, 2023): 68–75; Sentinel Villages Report, *Indonesian Village Governance under the New Village Law (2015–2018)* (Washington DC, 2020), accessed September 15, 2023, https://documents1.worldbank.org/curated/en/220661590726265687/pdf/Indonesian-Village-Governance-Under-the-New-Village-Law-2015-2018-Sentinel-Villages-Report.pdf; Hans Antlöv, "Village Government and Rural Development in Indonesia: The New Democratic Framework," *Bulletin of Indonesian Economic Studies* 39, no. 2 (August 2010): 193–214.

33. Oemar Hamalik, *Manajemen Pelatihan Ketenagakerjaan Pendekatan Terpadu* (Jakarta: Bumi Aksara, 2007).

34. Febriari, "Quality Education and Skills of Indonesian Labor, Towards Equality Wages in Foreign Countries," *Jurnal Ekonomi Pembangunan* 14, no. 2 (2013): 203–13.

35. *Law No. 18 of 2017 on the Protection of Indonesian Migrant Workers*, Considerant point c.

36. Ibid. Art. 21.

37. Ali Maksum, Ching Lung Tsay, and Ali Muhammad, "Indonesian Migrant Workers in Taiwan: The State Dilemma and People's Realities," *Jurnal Ilmu Sosial dan Ilmu Politik* 24, no. 1 (January 12, 2021): 80–96.

38. *Law No. 18 of 2017 on the Protection of Indonesian Migrant Workers*, Art. 9 and 10.

39. *Regulation of Minister of Manpower and Transmigration No. PER.12/MEN/X/2011 on Manpower Attaché and Technical Staffs on Manpower in the Indonesian Representative Abroad*, n.d.

40. Angga Laraspati, "Menaker Ingatkan Atase Ketenagakerjaan Tak Hanya Urusi Persoalan PMI," accessed September 12, 2023, https://news.detik.com/berita/d-5704437/menaker-ingatkan-atase-ketenagakerjaan-tak-hanya-urusi-persoalan-pmi.

41. Yeni Nuraeni and Suryadi, "Strategy for the Development of the Indonesian Migrant Worker (PMI) Placement Program in the Formal Sector," *Italienisch* 12, no. 1 (2021): 12–22, esp. 20.

42. "Jumlah Atase Ketenagakerjaan Tidak Memadai, Banyak Kasus TKI Tidak Tertangani," last modified 2018, accessed September 12, 2023, https://www.merdeka.com/uang/jumlah-atase-ketenagakerjaan-tidak-memadai-banyak-kasus-tki-tidak-tertangani.html.

43. Deny Tri Wahyudi, "Perlindungan Hukum Terhadap Tenaga Kerja Indonesia Di Luar Negeri," *Mimbar Hukum* (2015): 170–184, 181–182.

44. Indonesian Ministry of Foreign Affairs, "Indonesia Malaysia Sepakati Mou Perlindungan Pekerja Migran Indonesia Di Malaysia," last modified 2022, accessed September 12, 2023, https://kemlu.go.id/portal/id/read/3475/berita/indonesia-malaysia-sepakati-mou-perlindungan-pekerja-migran-indonesia-di-malaysia.

45. Erlina F. Santika, "Pekerja Migran Indonesia Di Asia Meningkat Pada 2022, Penempatan Hong Kong Terbanyak," last modified 2023, accessed September 16, 2023, https://databoks.katadata.co.id/datapublish/2023/03/07/pekerja-migran-indonesia-di-asia-meningkat-pada-2022-penempatan-hong-kong-terbanyak#.

46. Ahmad Dzulviqor and Dita Angga Rusiana, "Jumlah PMI Di Malaysia Yang Berangkat Dan Pulang Secara Ilegal Meningkat, Pengaruh Calo Masih Kuat," last modified 2023, accessed September 16, 2023, https://regional.kompas.com/read/2023/01/11/140859178/jumlah-pmi-di-malaysia-yang-berangkat-dan-pulang-secara-ilegal-meningkat.

47. "Kemnaker Perkuat Peran Dan Tugas Atase Ketenagakerjaan," last modified 2019, accessed September 16, 2023, https://kemnaker.go.id/news/detail/kemnaker-perkuat-peran-dan-tugas-atase-ketenagakerjaan.

48. *Law No. 11 of 2020 on Job Creation*, Art. 81 par. (1).

49. *Government Regulation No. 34 of 2021 on the Use of Foreign Migrant Worker*, n.d., Art. 34 par. (1) and (2).

50. "TKA-Online: Sistem Informasi Pelayanan Penggunaan Tenaga Kerja Asing Online," last modified 2023, accessed September 16, 2023, https://tka-online.kemnaker.go.id/alur.asp.

51. *Government Regulation No. 34 of 2021 on the Use of Foreign Migrant Worker*, Art. 1, point 5.

52. Ibid. Arts. 16 and 17.

53. "Convention on the Protection of the Rights of All Migrant Workers and Their Families," last modified 2003, accessed October 2, 2020, https://www.culturalsurvival.org/publications/cultural-survival-quarterly/convention-protection-rights-all-migrant-workers-and-their Art. 7.

54. Ibid. Art. 25.

55. *ILO Convention No.97 on Migration on Employment*, 1949.

56. Ibid. Annex II, art. 13.

57. Ibid. Annex II, art.7.

58. *ILO Convention No. 143 on Migrant Workers (Supplementary Provisions)*, 1975, art. 3.

59. Ibid. Art. 10.

60. *ILO Convention No. 189 on Domestic Workers*, 2011.

61. National Commission of Human Rights of Indonesia, "Urgensi Ratifikasi Konvensi ILO 189 Untuk Pemenuhan Dan Perlindungan Hak PRT: Komnas HAM," last

modified 2022, accessed September 12, 2023, https://www.komnasham.go.id/index.php/news/2022/9/23/2237/urgensi-ratifikasi-konvensi-ilo-189-untuk-pemenuhan-dan-perlindungan-hak-prt.html.

62. Mutia Hariati Hussin, "Factors Influencing Indonesian Women Becomes Migrant Workers," *Jurnal Hubungan Internasional* 2, no. 1 (2013): 65–74.

63. *Law No. 18 of 2017 on the Protection of Indonesian Migrant Workers*, Art. 5.

64. Achmad Zulfikar, "Peluang Dan Tantangan Pekerja Migran Indonesia Dalam Masyarakat Ekonomi ASEAN," in *National Convention Association of International Relations VII Year 2016, University of Hasanuddin* (Makasar, 2016), 16–17.

65. Ibid.

66. Resty Woro Yuniar, "Young Indonesians Secure Singapore Citizenship as Many Lament 'Skills Mismatch' Back Home," *This Week in Asia*, last modified 2023, accessed September 11, 2023, https://www.scmp.com/week-asia/people/article/3229314/young-indonesians-secure-singapore-citizenship-many-lament-skills-mismatch-back-home.

67. Eny Kusdarini et al., "The Urgency of Legal Literacy for Indonesian Migrant Workers through Distance Education," *Fiat Justisia Jurnal Ilmu Hukum* 15, no. 4 (2021): 399–416.

68. Habbi Firlana and Cahyoko Edi Tando, "Peran Imigrasi Dalam Pengawasan Pekerja Migran Indonesia," *Jurnal Ilmiah Kajian Keimigrasian* 5, no. 1 (October 28, 2022): 69–77.

69. Sri Wahyono, "The Problems of Indonesian Migrant Worker's Rights Protection in Malaysia," *Jurnal Kependudukan Indonesia* II, no. 1 (2007): 27–44.

PART III

Identifying the Challenges of Asia Origin Countries in Ensuring the Rights of Migrant Workers

In the fast-changing global context, deeper international integration, the legitimate needs, and aspirations of each individual have contributed to promoting the migration flow, making it more diverse in morphology and scale. Unlike developed countries that mainly receive immigrant workers, developing countries in Asia have a high proportion of migrant workers. In addition to the benefits of migration, this issue also poses many challenges for the origin country. The cognition of the challenges produces important implications, helping to identify the problems facing Asian countries, especially the destination countries. On that basis, the search for and identification of measures on migrant workers will ensure objectivity, comprehensiveness, and practical integration. With the above objectives, Part 3 will focus on the following: i) The challenges posed to the governments of the origin countries; ii) The challenges facing migrant workers; and iii) Assessment of migration trends and recommendations for solutions.

Chapter 11

Challenges for Ensuring the Rights of Migrant Workers

from Developing Countries in Asia

Nguyen Toan Thang and Mac Thi Hoai Thuong

In the era of globalization and deep international economic integration, migrant workers have become an integral part of economies. The reality demonstrates that migrant workers have made positive contributions to the economic development of both labor-importing and labor-exporting countries. However, with the increasing magnitude of international migration, especially in Asia, labor-exporting countries face significant challenges in protecting the rights of their workers. Migrant workers often confront daunting issues such as working in hazardous and unsafe environments, experiencing physical abuse or exploitation without adequate protection, receiving insufficient wages, and facing wage discrimination compared to native workers. Additionally, language barriers and cultural differences act as further obstacles, exacerbating the disadvantages faced by migrant workers.[1]

CHALLENGES IN ENSURING EMPLOYMENT AND SOCIAL SECURITY

As Mr. Mohammed Azman of the Malaysian Social Security Organisation states, when migrant workers go to another country for employment, they frequently don't give much thought to insurance regime participation—rather, they are primarily concerned with pay and working conditions. Notably, a sizable fraction of female migrant workers are employed in low-paying, precarious occupations like domestic assistance, health care, and agriculture. In

Asia, finding jobs for migrant laborers is becoming a more pressing concern. The labor market in Malaysia has historically relied on migrant laborers, whose numbers have steadily increased over time (from 1.8 million licenced individuals in 2014 to over 2.2 million in 2017).[2]

Due to the fact that their covered period is typically fewer than 10 years, migrant workers frequently face difficulties when it comes to receiving retirement benefits. Furthermore, the allowance may be withheld or decreased if a person returns to their home country after being eligible for a pension in another nation. There are roughly 500,000 Vietnamese employed overseas, and the figure rises yearly. However, only 6,000 members of this category take advantage of social security, therefore social security needs to be managed well.[3] It requires countries to quickly develop solutions to change perceptions and ensure the rights of migrant workers. This is a significant challenge to Asia countries, particularly the developing ones. There are several distinct social security systems and models throughout Asia, and the Association of Southeast Asian Nations (ASEAN) in particular. Furthermore, the social security systems of many nations are underdeveloped and have poor coverage rates, which means that there are insufficient resources or a lack of experience when it comes to enforcing social security laws and defending the rights of migrant workers.

Equality and non-discrimination are fundamental principles in ensuring human rights. This principle is recognized in multilateral international treaties on human rights and international treaties in the field of labor, including those related to providing social security policies for migrant workers.[4] To implement international law in social life, nations must incorporate its provisions into their own legal systems. However, only approximately 70 out of 120 countries mandate equality between citizens and foreign workers when putting social security laws into practice, according to Internation Labor Organization (ILO) figures.[5]

A comprehensive, rights-based approach and social discourse are crucial for creating and executing policies and mechanisms to support social protection for migrant workers and their families. An approach like this should consider the various factors that impact migrant workers' access to social security rights, such as the labor mobility and migration context; the availability, extent, and scope of social security guarantees in immigration and host countries; and the diversity and uniqueness of migrant workers and their families, including their demographics, employment status, length of stay and work, skills, income, and industry or field of work.[6] In addition to understanding the global trend of social security development, it is important to consider how the Internet of Things and free labor movement will affect the economy, labor, and employment in each nation, and how this will affect the requirements for the social security system in the future.

Promoting and ensuring the rights of migrant workers requires not only each country to perfect its policies and regulations, but also the signing of bilateral and multilateral agreements between nations on social security and migrant worker protection. These accords serve as the foundation for international cooperation among nations to support migrant workers' rights, end discriminatory laws, adhere to international migrant worker principles, and assist migrant workers in progressively gaining access to the social security programs of the receiving nation.

With social security agreements, workers can handle many disadvantages in this field. The Social Security Agreement helps eliminate dual insurance, paid in both countries, reducing the financial burden on workers abroad. Workers who have enough qualify for pension benefits through the total period of coverage and ensure that foreign workers are treated equally with nationals of the contracting country. However, signing social security agreements still faces many barriers and challenges. Agreements often take a lot of time to complete and sign, especially when some countries need help finding common understanding.

International labor standards form the basis and provide helpful guidance for developing such agreements. In 2020, there were 660 social security agreements worldwide, steadily increasing from around 100 agreements in 1980. This trend is common in all regions, although the largest number of bilateral agreements have been signed in Europe, followed by the Americas, Asia, the Pacific, and Africa. Nearly 90 percent of the agreements provide benefits for the elderly and disabled, while less than 50 percent cover other social security issues. These agreements do not cover migrant workers in the informal economy or irregular migration.[7]

To further ensure that migrant workers are not treated unfairly in comparison to domestic workers under international labor standards, social protection clauses should be included in bilateral agreements on labor cooperation and temporary labor migration programs. The Annex to the Migration for Employment Recommendation (Revised), 1949 (No. 86), provides a model agreement for signing and concluding a bilateral agreement. Although ILO standards and other international instruments encourage countries to sign bilateral labor agreements to manage and facilitate labor migration and ensure migrant workers enjoy their rights, these agreements have almost no provisions for social security. The scope of social security protection available to migrant workers under bilateral labor agreements depends on national laws and other relevant agreements to which countries are parties. Practice shows that countries should simultaneously sign bilateral labor agreements and social security agreements to ensure the benefits of migrant workers. In 2022, the UN will publish Guidance on Bilateral accords on Migrant Labour, which will assist nations in developing accords based on human rights.[8]

The ratification and implementation of relevant international labor standards is also an important measure to ensure the universal enjoyment of social security rights by migrant workers. These standards guide the development of national policy, legislation, and social security arrangements. The main principles relating to migrant workers in these standards are equality and non-discrimination, maintaining existing rights and exercising interests abroad, maintaining rights during labor, determining applicable laws, and providing administrative support.[9]

The process of deepening economic integration has made it easier for workers to move between nations. While this is good news for the job market, it also presents a number of difficulties for enforcing foreign workers' rights and putting social security laws into practice.

HUMAN TRAFFICKING CRIME AND ITS IMPLICATIONS FOR ENSURING THE RIGHTS OF MIGRANT WORKERS

Along with the increase in demand for migration, there has been a parallel rise in transnational crimes related to human trafficking. The profits generated by this illegal activity in Asia alone amount to tens of billions of dollars annually. The significant financial gains have led to the strong development of human trafficking and related transnational organized crime, employing increasingly sophisticated, complex, and brutal methods and tactics. Combating and preventing this type of crime is extremely dangerous and challenging. According to the United Nations Protocol against Trafficking in Persons (Palermo Protocol, 2000), which supplements the Convention on Transnational Organized Crime (UNTOC), the crime of human trafficking is composed of three key elements: (1). Action (activity): Carrying out one of the following actions: recruitment, transportation, transfer, harboring, receipt; (2). Means (methods): Utilizing threats, violence, coercion, abduction, deception, abuse of power, or taking advantage of a person's vulnerability. This includes giving or receiving money or benefits to gain control over another person. (3). Purpose: Exploiting victims, which may include: prostitution or other forms of sexual exploitation, orced labor or services, slavery or practices similar to servitude, and organ trafficking, which ranks as the third most prevalent global crime, following drug trafficking and arms trafficking.[10] Globalization has facilitated the rise of human trafficking by making cross-border transportation of victims less complicated and more cost-effective, thereby increasing the profitability of trafficking operations.[11]

The number of migrant workers falling victim to human trafficking crimes in developing countries in Asia is increasing and becoming more complex, with perpetrators employing increasingly sophisticated and diverse methods and tactics. There is a disturbing level of collusion between buyers, sellers, brokers, and guides, leading to the formation of inter-provincial and cross-border criminal networks. The victims of these crimes are not only women and children but also include men. Furthermore, there are alarming instances of the trafficking of babies and fetuses, organ trading, and exploitation through surrogacy, which exacerbate the gravity of the situation.

Developing countries in Asia are both source and destination countries for migrant workers who are vulnerable to becoming victims of human trafficking. Recent reports from regional media in Cambodia, Thailand, Vietnam, Indonesia, Malaysia, and Myanmar have highlighted alarming increases in the incidence of forced labor and human trafficking within these nations.[12] Across Southeast Asia, a region plagued by "modern slavery," an estimated 40 million men, women, and children are trapped in a complex network of forced labor, sexual exploitation, and other forms of exploitation.[13] According to the Global Slavery Index, around 1,220,000 Indonesians are currently enslaved. Many of these individuals, including men, women, and children, are trafficked domestically and internationally for labor or subjected to exploitation in the sex trade. Shockingly, 43 percent of Indonesian human trafficking victims fall between the ages of 14 and 17.[14]

All such countries are developing countries in Asia, but the purposes, nature, methods, and tactics of human trafficking in these countries are different due to many reasons. Some countries are primarily considered places of origin, transit, or destination for victims of human trafficking. For example, Singapore is primarily considered a destination country for men, women, and girls trafficked for the sex tradeand forced labor. Migrant workers from countries like the Philippines, Indonesia, Cambodia, and Vietnam are often coerced into working on fishing boats that pass through Singapore or its territorial waters.[15] On the other hand, Thailand has a significant issue with sex trafficking due to its well-developed commercial sex industry. Migrant workers trafficked to Thailand are predominantly women from neighboring countries such as Myanmar, Cambodia, Laos, and Myanmar. In addition to sexual exploitation, victims of human trafficking in Thailand, including migrant workers, may also be subjected to forced labor in industries such as fishing, poultry, agriculture, domestic work, and even forced begging.[16] It's important to note that Thai citizens can also become victims of human trafficking and may be trafficked to various countries worldwide, including Australia, Bahrain, China, Germany, Israel, Japan, South Africa, and the United States.

Vietnam is another country where a significant number of its citizens fall victim to human trafficking and migrate overseas for work. Certain provinces along the Vietnam–China border, such as Lao Cai, Lai Chau, and Ha Giang, have experienced cases of abduction and trafficking of women and children.

Typically, these victims are sold for purposes such as prostitution, forced marriage, or labor exploitation. In some distressing instances, Vietnamese children are illegally transported to Thailand and coerced into selling goods on the streets to tourists. Cases involving organ trafficking or surrogacy have also been discovered, where victims are taken abroad for these purposes. In terms of air travel, victims are often routed through international airports such as Noi Bai and Tan Son Nhat, connecting to various countries and territories including Malaysia, Hong Kong, Macau, European countries, the United States, and others. These trafficking operations are carried out through different means, such as disguising the purpose as tourism, marriage, labor migration, or foreign adoption. Human trafficking crimes continue to persist in many regions, employing highly sophisticated and complex methods.[17]

During the five-year period from 2018–2023, in Indonesia, each of Indonesia's 38 provinces was a source and destination of human trafficking. Traffickers use direct and secondary recruitment agents to withhold identification documents and threaten violence to keep migrants in forced labor.

The situation of migrant workers becoming victims of human trafficking in developing countries in Asia is increasingly complicated due to the following main reasons:

First, due to economic reasons: The slow economic development in these countries, influenced by their colonial history, has resulted in a significant number of nations with low or below-average income levels. The uneven economic growth and the demand for low-skilled, low-cost labor in Asia are key drivers of human trafficking within the region and to other parts of the world. Many victims of human trafficking in developing Asian countries initially migrate across borders in search of better job opportunities that offer higher wages. However, they are often deceived or coerced into working in industries such as fishing, agriculture, construction, or services. Consequently, a majority of trafficking victims originate from less-developed countries in the region, including Cambodia, Laos, Myanmar, and Vietnam. These victims are then transported to more developed countries such as Thailand, Malaysia, Singapore, as well as destinations outside the region, including China, Japan, South Korea, Europe, North America, the Middle East, and Australia. Thailand is a primary destination for human trafficking victims from Cambodia, Laos, and Myanmar, while Malaysia serves as a major destination for victims from Indonesia, the Philippines, and Vietnam.[18] According to data provided by the Japanese government, individuals from 12 countries were convicted of human trafficking crimes in Japan between 2014 and 2016. Approximately 16 percent of these cases (74 individuals) involved nationals from Southeast Asian countries, mainly Thailand and the Philippines, with others originating from China, Brazil, and Taiwan. In recent years, Japan has identified a total of 129 trafficking victims, including 50 from Japan (39%), 48 from the Philippines (37%), 20 from Thailand (15.5%), and 7 from Cambodia (5%).[19]

Victims of human trafficking are often concentrated in rural areas, particularly in remote and border provinces. These areas are characterized by challenging living conditions, low levels of education, and many families facing extreme difficulties. As a result, individuals, including women and children, aspire for a better life and actively seek job opportunities, often resorting to migration as a means to improve their circumstances.[20] Unfortunately, their desperation and desire for a better life make them susceptible to exploitation by human traffickers. In many cases, victims of human trafficking willingly accept the risks involved and agree to cross borders illegally in search of employment. According to the Vietnamese Consulate General in Cambodia, only 50 out of 270 human trafficking victims rescued in April 2022 had valid documents. This highlights how a significant number of victims engage in illegal border crossings as they seek work opportunities.[21]

Uneven economic development and the demand for cheap, low-skilled labor are indeed factors that contribute to migrant workers becoming victims of human trafficking, not only within Asian countries but also globally. Many migrant workers who fall prey to human trafficking originate from less-developed countries such as Cambodia, Laos, Myanmar, and Vietnam, and are trafficked to more developed countries like Thailand, Malaysia, Singapore, and other destinations worldwide, including China, Europe, North America, the Middle East, and Australia. Among these destinations, Thailand is a prominent hub for human trafficking victims from Cambodia, Laos, and Myanmar. Malaysia serves as the primary destination for victims from Indonesia, the Philippines, and Vietnam.[22] In Indonesia, human traffickers often target Indonesian fishermen from Java, as well as poor agricultural workers. They lure them with false promises of high wages and good working conditions, provide them with illegal travel documents, and make them sign exploitative contracts that are incredibly difficult to break, earning them the term "slave contracts."

Trafficked victims from Laos are often low-income, underemployed people, who migrate in search of jobs with better income from abroad. These people are exploited for labor or sex in Thailand, Vietnam, Malaysia, China, Taiwan, and Japan. A large number of victims are women and girls, exploited in Thailand's commercial sex industry and forced domestic, factory, and agricultural labor. Laotian men and boys are victims of forced labor in Thailand's fishing, construction, and agricultural industries.[23]

Second, due to the limited qualifications and awareness of migrant workers in developing countries in Asia: the majority of human trafficking victims in these countries have low levels of education and limited understanding. The challenges they face in life, combined with their limited awareness, make them vulnerable to exploitation and increase their likelihood of becoming victims of human trafficking. Traffickers often exploit this vulnerability by offering false promises of stable, high-income jobs and providing support in order to deceive and manipulate them.[24]

In Vietnam, traffickers often target women who are experiencing difficult economic circumstances, conflicts in family relationships, have limited understanding, and are susceptible to manipulation and trust. Teenage girls are also at risk, particularly those with limited understanding, playful behavior, and a lack of family supervision. In most cases, the areas where crimes occur are often in border areas or areas where ethnic minorities live. Statistics reveal that over 90 percent of trafficking victims in Vietnam are women and children, with a concentration in rural, mountainous, remote, and border areas. The main reasons victims fall into the trap of human trafficking are linked to poor economic conditions, low educational levels, and a lack of awareness. Approximately 37.2 percent of victims are trafficked due to challenging family relationships and low education levels. Moreover, 6.8 percent of young girls and students lack life skills, social understanding, and vigilance, often seeking enjoyment and engaging in risky behaviors.[25]

Third, globalization, along with the advancements in science and technology, including the Fourth Industrial Revolution, has also created conditions that make migrant workers susceptible to human trafficking crimes. Human traffickers take advantage of sophisticated recruitment scams, making it difficult to distinguish between legal and illegal recruitment processes. They exploit technology as a tool to deceive and facilitate the sale of individuals, making it faster, more cost-effective, and harder to detect. By exploiting the digital divide between children and adults, traffickers utilize social media as a primary tool to lure vulnerable individuals with false promises of job opportunities and non-existent employment. They then coerce them into forced labor and sexual slavery. Many victims are trafficked from countries such as Indonesia, Vietnam, Thailand, Malaysia, Taiwan, and China to Cambodia. They may be enticed through online advertisements or even by acquaintances who advertise high-paying and peaceful jobs.[26] Furthermore, in the context of globalization, human trafficking criminals often exploit open immigration policies to organize rings that send people abroad under the pretense of tourism, visiting relatives, or seeking illegal employment. Once the victims arrive, their documents and passports are confiscated, residence procedures are left incomplete, and they are subjected to forced labor and sexual abuse.

And finally, climate change and natural disasters in Asia widen the gap between the rich and the poor, making it difficult for vulnerable populations to access essential services. Climate change, including rising sea levels and extreme weather events, contributes to food and water insecurity due to crop failures, the loss of arable land, overpopulation, poor health and hygiene, and increased competition for limited employment opportunities. These factors create favorable conditions for human trafficking criminals to deceive and exploit migrant workers in the region. For instance, in Bangladesh, which is one of the countries most vulnerable to climate change,[27] extreme weather events have been associated with child marriages as families seek to minimize costs and protect girls from the heightened risks of sexual violence during times of crisis.[28]

Migrant workers who are victims of human trafficking face many risks, such as forced labor, forced sex, forced marriage, and begging.[29] The risk of forced labor and sexual exploitation is particularly prevalent in these cases.

It can be seen that migrant workers from Asia are often burdened with debts, which both Indonesian and foreign recruitment agents exploit to coerce and retain their workers. Labor traffickers exploit many Asian migrant workers through forced coercion and debt bondage in various regions, including Asia (such as China, Korea, and Singapore) and the Middle East (especially Saudi Arabia). They are subjected to exploitative conditions in domestic work, factories, construction, manufacturing, Malaysian oil palm plantations, and fishing vessels.[30] In addition, sex traffickers target Indonesian women and girls, recruiting them for legal work abroad and then exploiting them in sex trafficking. This particularly occurs in countries such as Malaysia, Taiwan, the Middle East, and Timor-Leste.[31]

According to the ILO, there are currently at least more than 12 million victims of forced labor. Of these, about 2.4 million were sold into forced labor.[32] The majority of victims of forced labor are found in Asia (9.5 million).[33] Human trafficking for labor exploitation can be found in many economic sectors, including agriculture, construction, hospitality, and home services. About 4 out of 10 victims discovered between 2012 and 2014 were trafficked for forced labor, and of these victims, 63 percent were men.

Human trafficking for forced labor in the fishing industry is widespread in some developing Asian countries. A significant number of Cambodian men are believed to be recruited in Thailand to work on fishing boats, where they are subjected to forced labor on Thai-owned vessels in international waters.[34] According to the International Labour Organization (ILO), fishing workers are among the most exploited groups compared to other sectors of migration. The victims often find themselves trapped with no means of escape as they are isolated at sea. The Indonesian National Fisheries Center has recorded at least 90 reports involving 280 victims between 2019 and 2022, with "failure to pay wages" being the most commonly reported issue among the cases.[35]

Human trafficking for sexual exploitation and forced labor are the most commonly reported forms, although victims of human trafficking can also be exploited in various other ways. Some examples include trafficking for the purpose of begging, forced or sham marriages, benefit fraud, pornography production, and organ harvesting, among others. In the past, human trafficking for different forms of marriage was frequently reported, but it is now becoming more prevalent. In Southeast Asia, forced marriages or marriages without the woman's or girl's consent are often involved. Trafficking for fake marriages primarily occurs in wealthier countries. This can occur, for instance, on large fishing vessels at sea, often facilitated by major international fishing companies, or in onshore processing facilities.

In Indonesia, traffickers exploit adults and children for fishing, fish processing, construction, mining and manufacturing, and work on palm oil and other plantations. Traffickers subject children to criminal charges in the illegal drug trade. Government regulations exempt employers in certain sectors—including Small and Medium Enterprises (SMEs) and textile manufacturing—from minimum wage requirements, increasing risks for workers to debt-based coercion. More than 100,000 Thais work in South Korea, where traffickers subject Thai men and women to forced labor and sex trafficking. Victims are forced into debt bondage, owing money to business owners, entertainment establishments, or loan sharks as a means of control. Thai citizens are also subjected to forced labor and sex trafficking in various countries across North America, Europe, Africa, Asia, and the Middle East. In Switzerland, Thai women and LGBTQI+ individuals are particularly vulnerable to exploitation in the sex trade. Thai citizens traveling to Norway for family reunions are at risk of falling victim to labor and sex trafficking. Additionally, traffickers subject Thai men and women to forced labor in Israel's agricultural sector, imposing grueling working conditions such as long hours, no days off, confiscating their passports, and making it difficult to change employers due to restrictive work permit regulations.

The challenges for governments of developing countries in Asia to protect the rights of migrant workers who are victims of human trafficking are as follows:

First, the challenge in identifying migrant workers as victims of human trafficking crimes in developing countries in Asia. Due to factors such as poverty, natural disasters, climate change, and lack of job opportunities, it becomes difficult to determine whether a migrant worker is a victim of human trafficking. Some victims may not perceive themselves as slaves or trafficking victims because they willingly enter into employment arrangements, fully aware of the working conditions that await them. They may believe that their situation abroad is still preferable to the conditions they face back home in impoverished areas. This raises the question of whether such migrants should be considered modern slaves and victims of human trafficking. When a victim is identified, it refers to someone recognized by a competent authority as a victim of human trafficking, entitling them to various forms of assistance for their protection. However, the majority of victims of human trafficking worldwide remain unidentified. These victims may have recently escaped an exploitative environment or are currently in one but have not been officially recognized as victims of human trafficking. Consequently, they often face vulnerabilities, particularly if they are trafficked to another country, as they may be viewed as illegal migrant workers or as engaging voluntarily in prostitution, which can lead to their treatment as criminals rather than victims. As a result, the support needs of these unidentified victims are often not recognized or adequately addressed.

Second, challenges in allocating resources to implement measures that ensure the rights of migrant workers who are victims of human trafficking are indeed significant. Asia is a region characterized by substantial disparities in economic development across countries. Many developing countries in Asia share common features such as high levels of poverty, low GDP per capita, significant foreign debts, and low Human Development Index (HDI) scores. Consequently, there is a lack of material resources to effectively support and protect migrant workers who are victims of human trafficking. Essential measures like establishing temporary shelters, crisis support centers, community-based security, and specialized support services for children are often inadequately provided.

The challenge comes from the limitations of the legal systems of developing countries in Asia. In many countries there is no legal provision against slavery, which means that a person cannot be prosecuted and punished in criminal court for enslaving another person. Most Asian countries have labor and anti-trafficking laws, but such laws do not necessarily address the issue of slavery.

RETURNING AND THE DOWNSIDES OF THE COMMUNITY REINTEGRATION RETURN

According to the definition offered by the United Nations Statistics Division for collecting data on international migration (UNSD, 1998), returning migrants are "persons returning to their country of citizenship after having been international migrants (whether short-term or long-term) in another country and who are intending to stay in their own country for at least a year." This definition embraces four dimensions: i) country of origin, ii) place of residence abroad, iii) length of stay in the host country, and iv) length of stay in the home country after return.[36] The 2018 ILO guidelines on migration statistics state: "return international migrant workers are defined as all current residents of the country who were previously international migrant workers in another country or countries. . . . The minimum duration of labor attachment abroad for a person to be considered as a return international migrant worker [is] relatively short, such as 6 months."[37]

Return period: The return can be permanent or temporary. For example, for highly skilled migrants who wish to contribute to the development of their country of origin by imparting the knowledge and experience they acquired abroad, temporary assistance may be the preferred choice.

Returns with or without assistance: Spontaneous returns occur when individuals decide and carry out returns on their own. Repatriation assistance occurs when the state or a third party provides financial and logistical support to returnees for repatriation, and sometimes reintegration measures.

Voluntary or forced return: Forced return is the act of returning an individual, against their will, to their country of origin, to a place of transit, or to a third country that has agreed to receive that person, usually made on the basis of an administrative or judicial act or decision. Voluntary repatriation is an assisted or independent return to the country of origin, transit country, or other country based on the returnee's voluntary decision. However, a migrant's decision to return does not necessarily mean that return is the migrant's explicit desire. It is possible that other options are limited, for example, if economic opportunities are scarce or if a migrant has no legal right to remain on the territory of a state. There is no uniform definition of voluntary reimbursement.

In developing countries in Asia, returning migrant workers can make an important contribution to the country's economic and social development due to the fact that:

- Returning migrant workers are a labor force that easily and willingly gets used to the local working environment. This is because the bond between migrant workers in these countries often has a close relationship with the country of origin as shown by the amount of remittances sent back home.[38]
- Returning migrant workers can facilitate the transfer of labor skills acquired abroad for the benefit of the domestic economy.
- Returning migrants can stimulate investment in new businesses. Returning workers tend to be self-employed, even though they may have been employed before migrating.[39]

Migrant workers return for many different reasons such as: achieving the goals set when migrating; reaching retirement age; unsuccessful and difficult attempts to integrate in the destination country; expiration of short-term work contract; family reasons; conditions at home have improved compared to the time of migration; and many other reasons, including deportation. In the fixed-term migration cycle, mainly in Asian and Middle Eastern countries, migrant workers must return to the original country at the end of their contract. Some migrant workers are better prepared for reintegration with minimal support from the state, while some may return in difficult situations, requiring attention and special support. Therefore, there is a need for flexible reintegration programs to meet the different needs of returning migrant workers.

Developing countries in Asia, represent a labor market where the majority of them are low-skilled migrant workers working temporarily on short-term contracts. Therefore, there is always a significant number of migrant workers returning home. For example, most migrants from Cambodia, Laos, and Myanmar to Thailand intend to return home after a certain period of time, unless they are refugees. In the absence of comprehensive support services, returning migrant workers may encounter many difficulties that affect their ability to reintegrate into their home community, resolve psychosocial issues, find sustainable livelihood opportunities, or re-enter the country and integrate into the labor market. The lack of adequate reintegration policies and options is a loss for migrant workers, communities, and society as a whole.

Reintegration

Reintegration is the return of a returnee to the society of the country of origin, a process that includes many psychological, social, health, and economic aspects. Reintegration is an essential part of the return migration process because it generally contributes to the sustainability of migration benefits after the return of migrants. Along with the term "reintegration," there is also the term "sustainable reintegration." "Sustainable reintegration" is understood to mean that returning migrant workers have achieved a level of economic self-sufficiency, social stability in their communities, and psychosocial well-being that allows them to cope with the agents of (re)migration. Once sustainable reintegration is achieved, returnees can make subsequent migration decisions a matter of choice, rather than necessity.[40] United Nations High Commissioner for Refugees' (UNHCR) 2004 Handbook on Repatriation and Reintegration Operations states that "the 'end state' of the reintegration process is the full enjoyment of all political, civil, economic, and social rights."[41] According to this definition, reintegration is a necessary precondition for a meaningful sustainable return, and it also emphasizes that returnees must perceive that they are in safe and secure conditions upon return.

Challenges of Return and Reintegration: Causes Leading to Negative Aspects of Reintegration of Migrant Workers in Developing Countries in Asia

As analyzed, returning migrant workers is an inevitable trend in the context of globalization and labor mobility. Returning migrant workers can be a human resource that actively contributes to the economic and social development of developing countries in Asia if these countries have timely management and support policies. However, in developing countries in Asia, in addition to a number of objective reasons combined with a lack of attention to management measures and policies to support migrant workers, this leads to negative impacts. Difficulties for developing Asian countries in managing and supporting returning migrant workers include:

First, lack of data on returning migrant workers. Practice shows that the majority of migrants return to their homeland. Although data on international migration is more complete, data on return migration is lacking and incomplete. On average, it is estimated that two out of every five migrants will leave the host country within five years of arrival.[42] The lack of information makes it difficult to provide services or measures to support the reintegration of returning migrant workers. For example, the Philippines has no systematic data collection and analysis process on repatriated Filipinos. There is no agency to process and analyze information about repatriated Filipinos.[43] Many migrant workers who are victims of human trafficking are never identified as victims of human trafficking in either the country of origin or the receiving country. This results in trafficked migrant workers being detained and deported, forced to pay their own way home (sometimes going into debt to do so), and/or at risk of further trafficking or exploitation during the refund process. At the same time, these individuals will not be supported upon their return.

Second, there are inadequacies in policies and laws in developing countries in Asia related to migrant workers' return and reintegration. Indonesia and the Philippines are large-scale migrant exporting countries compared to developing countries in Asia; however, reintegration of migrant workers in this country mainly refers to skilled labor or semi-skilled, such as nurses from the Philippines. For returning workers in Indonesia, reintegration aspects mainly refer to social aspects, economic aspects, and skill development of unskilled or low-skilled workers, which are not pay due attention.[44] There are no regulations on skills certification and skills recognition. Most returning workers, including low-skilled workers, gain new social and vocational skills while working abroad. However, there is no streamlined system for certifying skills by employers in destination or origin countries upon return.

Third, slow economic development, lack of jobs, and the risk of unemployment. The economic and social situation greatly influences repatriation decisions. If the structural economic problems, unemployment, poverty, and conflict that cause migration in the first place do not change significantly, there will be little incentive for migrant workers to return. Reintegration policies and an individual's reintegration process depend greatly on the general economic, political, and social circumstances of the country of origin. Research conducted by IOM on the repatriation intentions of migrant workers from Cambodia, Lao People's Democratic Republic, and Myanmar in Thailand has demonstrated this. IOM found that Myanmar migrant workers are more likely to return to Myanmar, which is experiencing higher economic growth, while most Cambodian workers and about half of Laotian workers do not want to return to their country, due to lower employment prospects and wages. The unwillingness of migrant workers to return and reintegrate leads to migrant workers finding ways to continue working in the destination country by overstaying their contracts or by revolving migration. Overstaying or staying illegally creates the risk of labor exploitation and human trafficking by migrant workers, etc. Poor and underdeveloped economy can also be the cause of the lack of interest in training, skills development, and finding jobs among returning migrants.

Fourth, limited access to information. Many migrant workers do not know what they are entitled to or supported with. Where to go for support? Lack of information about available support acts as a barrier for returning migrant workers to receive the support they need to reintegrate into their communities.

Finally, there are resource limitations. Resources are needed to carry out repatriation and reintegration activities, as well as to arrange travel and support at the final destination. Reintegration requires longer-term support and significantly more resources, and many countries of origin or destination are unable or unwilling to provide this level of support.[45] In Indonesia, for example, the support currently available to returning migrant workers is mainly short-term and designed to meet only immediate and urgent needs. Short-term support was assessed as not nearly enough to assist individuals in reintegration.

The above difficulties and challenges lead to the negative side of returning and the reintegration of migrant workers. Not only do they miss out on development opportunities, but ineffective management of the return process of migrant workers can expose them to health and safety risks, and they can be forced to pay high brokerage and service fees, or suffer a failure to reclaim deposits/escrows and unpaid wages, especially for groups of migrants who work freely or without documents, or groups who migrate legally but must return before the contract expires. Upon return, migrants face unemployment, debt, social alienation, family conflicts, and migration-related poor health, including psychological and physical problems.

Unemployment rates were very high among the returnees surveyed. Eighty percent of Lao people are unemployed after returning, 46 percent of Cambodians are unemployed. Twenty-six percent of Cambodian returnees are doing unpaid work for their families, with women (32%) more likely than men (19%) to say this is their current job. Seventy-seven percent of women and 89 percent of men are looking for work but don't know how to find it or are skeptical about any available jobs.[46] The Philippines is one of the developing countries in Asia with a large source of migrant workers in the world. Migrant workers from the Philippines include not only low-skilled workers but also highly qualified workers. However, returning migrant workers in many regions of the Philippines also face high unemployment rates (about 65%) and have difficulty reintegrating into the labor market. Additionally, three-quarters of repatriated migrant workers surveyed said they received no financial or reintegration support upon returning to the Philippines.

The majority of returning Vietnamese migrants return to unskilled labor jobs, jobs they held before migrating and unrelated to the skills and knowledge they acquired while working abroad. The reason is that returning workers cannot apply the skills and working style of working abroad to working conditions in Vietnam or to start a business.[47]

When repatriated, migrant workers face many difficulties in re-engaging in the domestic labor market, with the common situation being low income and not being able to take advantage of the skills accumulated during their work abroad, or no job. Migrant workers upon returning face many difficulties in finding jobs. Employers do not prioritize returning migrants when there are similar workers with the same skill set and educational background. Because: first, employers consider return migration as a negative signal, indicating negative choices when migrating or failure abroad; second, employers believe that returning migrants demand a high salary; third, employers think that returning migrants are overrated; and fourth, employers believe that returning migrants have high job turnover rates.[48]

Returning migrant workers often face difficulties when faced with lower wages and living standards, and difficulty establishing businesses. In the Philippines, the majority of migrant workers face a significant reduction in their monthly income after returning from abroad and find it very difficult to earn the same level of income as in the immigration country.[49]

Returnees may face stigma and discrimination within their own communities and families because of their failed migration experiences, losing family assets upon return due to debt and forced repatriation or departure from destination countries. Migrant women may experience additional stigma when their migration may involve sex work and abuse. These migrant workers may need counseling and psychosocial support to address and cope with their experiences.

Children of returning migrant workers often encounter problems related to education due to differences between the languages, teaching content, and educational methods implemented in the two countries. The experience of return migration has a significant negative impact on children's mental health as measured by risk of depression, self-esteem, and resilience.[50]

COMMENT ON FACTORS AFFECTING CHALLENGES IN ENSURING THE RIGHTS OF MIGRANT WORKERS

The question is how to promote the protection of the rights of migrant workers in Asia, ensuring both free labor movement and decent job opportunities for all workers. In the context that Asia does not have a common legal framework, ASEAN plays an important role in promoting the rights of migrant workers within the sub-region. Besides, many ASEAN countries are both developing and emigration countries. In that context, the following factors can be noted:[51]

First, ASEAN has not yet established binding regulations and clear mechanisms for promoting decent working conditions and basic labor standards at the regional level. Although the bloc countries adopted the ASEAN Declaration on the Protection and Promotion of the Rights of Migrant Workers in January 2007, which acknowledged the responsibilities of receiving and origin countries, as well as the ASEAN Association in protecting and promoting the rights of migrant workers, this Declaration is not a legally binding document. Therefore, the impact of the Declaration is very limited.

Second, although there are no effective common mechanisms and documents to protect migrant workers, the majority of ASEAN member countries currently lack widely applied social protection systems that effectively safeguard all workers across various fields. Moreover, many ASEAN countries still lack mechanisms to promote improved living conditions and reduce poverty for their growing populations. These factors have a negative impact on workforce protection. Practical experience has shown that without effective protection for domestic workers, progress in safeguarding the rights of migrant workers remains limited.

Third, the majority of ASEAN countries still lack effective mechanisms established by trade unions and civil society organizations to provide consultation and support services to workers in general, including migrant workers. These mechanisms are crucial to strengthening relations and resolving conflicts between employers and employees, thereby protecting workers' rights and implementing basic international labor standards. The absence of such mechanisms poses a significant obstacle to the protection of migrant workers, as trade unions and civil society organizations are typically at the forefront of these efforts.

Fourth, there is still a significant gap in the technical and professional qualifications of workers in general, including migrant workers, among ASEAN countries. This disparity, combined with various other factors, contributes to the unequal treatment of workers from less-developed countries. Migrant workers from these countries often have to accept lower wages compared to workers in the receiving country, resulting in lower remittances sent back home than the expected income they should be entitled to. To address this issue, it is not sufficient to solely rely on complaints about the rights of migrant workers. It is necessary to implement a comprehensive approach that includes raising awareness and enhancing the capacity of key stakeholders responsible for addressing this issue in the region. Additionally, fostering strong connections between trade unions, civil society organizations, and relevant international and regional organizations is crucial in tackling this matter effectively.[52]

In summary, regional economic integration can exacerbate the situation of migrant workers, particularly those who are poor or working in the informal sector, if the implementation and protection of basic international labor standards are not prioritized. It is crucial to address standards related to various issues, including the creation of decent jobs, ensuring minimum wages, protecting and promoting the rights of migrant workers, establishing universal social security, providing access to health care, housing, education, and training, as well as promoting improved living conditions and poverty reduction. These standards should be given high priority to mitigate the negative impact of regional economic integration on migrant workers.

REFERENCES

Abarcar, Paolo. 2016. Do Employers Value Return Migrants? An Experiment on the Returns to Foreign Work Experience. Working Paper 48, Mathematica Policy Research.

Abul Muamar, Modern Sea Slavery in Indonesia and Beyond, at: https://greennetwork.asia/brief/modern-sea-slavery-in-indonesia-and-beyond/.

Alkida Ndreka, Return migration and re-integration of returnees' challenges in the origin country, https://sciendo.com/article/10.2478/rsc-2019-0012?tab=article#j_rsc-2019-0012_ref_057_w2aab3b7b1b1b6b1ab2ac58Aa. Accessed on June 15 2023.

Assarino, J. P. 2014a. "Bridging the policy gap between reintegration and development," in J. P. Cassarino (ed.): Reintegration and development, *CRIS Analytical Study* (Florence, European University Institute), 1–18.

Bachtiar, P. P. and Prasetyo, D. D. 2017. Return migration and various reintegration programs for low-skilled migrant workers in Indonesia, Research Report (Jakarta, SMERU Research Institute).

Bali Process Regional Support Office (BPRSO). 2019. A policy guide on returns and reintegration for Bali Process Members (Bangkok). Available at: https://www.baliprocess.net/UserFiles/baliprocess/File/BP%20Policy%20Guide%20on%20Returns%20 and%20Reintegration.pdf. 2 July 2019.

Clara Van Panhuys, Samia Kazi-Aoul, and Geneviève Binette, "Migrant Access to Social Protection under Bilateral Labour Agreements: A Review of 120 Countries and Nine Bilateral Arrangements," Extension of Social Security Working Paper No. 57, 2017.

Coelho, S., Martens, J., Cole, A., and Lee, S. 2016. *The Climate Change-Human Trafficking Nexus*, International Organization for Migration, p. 3. Available from: https://publications.iom.int/books/climate-change-human-trafficking-nexus. 9 November 2022.

Connell, John. 2009. " 'I Never Wanted to Come Home': Skilled Health Workers in the South Pacific." *Migration and Transnationalism, Pacific Perspectives*, ANU Press.

Cook, T. L., Shannon, P. J., Vinson, G. A., Letts, J. P., and Dwee, E. 2015. War trauma and torture experiences reported during public health screening of newly resettled Karen refugees: A qualitative study. *BMC International Health and Human Rights*, 15(1), 8. https://doi.org/10.1186/s12914-015-0046-y.

Consular Department, Ministry of Foreign Affairs of Vietnam, general report on the migration situation of Vietnamese citizens abroad, https://phapluatdansu.edu.vn/wp-content/uploads/2020/06/ bao_cao_tong_quan_ve_di_dan_VN-2.pdf. Accessed on June 23, 2023.

DANH, T. (2022) Difficulties in rescuing Vietnamese people in Cambodia. VnExpress. Available from: https://vnexpress.net/tong-lanh-su-neu-khokhan-khi-giai-cuu-nguoi-viet-o-campuchia4509632.htm. Accessed on June 23, 2023.

Deanna Davy, Regional Overview: Sexual Exploitaton of Children in Southeast Asia, https://www.ecpat.org/wp-content/uploads/2021/05/Regional-Overview_Southeast-Asia.pdf. Accessed on June 23, 2023.

Eckstein, D., Künzel, V., and Schäfer, L. 2021. Global Climate Risk Index 2021: Who Suffers Most from Extreme Weather Events? Weather-Related Loss Events in 2019 and 2000–2019, GermanWatch, pp. 13–15. Available from: https://reliefweb.int/sites/reliefweb.int/files/resources/Global%20Climate%20Risk%20Index%202021_1_0.pdf. 2 February 2022.

Environmental Justice Foundation, "Sold to the Sea: Human Trafficking in Thailand's Fishing Industry." 2013; IOM, "Trafficking of fishermen in Thailand" (2011), http://www.iom.int/jahia/webdav/shared/shared/mainsite/activities/countries/docs/thailand/Trafficking-of-FishermenThailand.pdf.

Farahdilah Ghazali and Siti Fazilah Abdul Shukor, Human Trafficking and Forced Labour in Southeast Asia: Legal Framework and a Way Forward,

DOI: 10.4018/978-1-6684-6334-5.ch003; https://www.ilo.org/hanoi/Whatwedo/Publications/WCMS_316803/lang--vi/index.htm. Accessed on June 23, 2023.

ILO, Securing social protection for migrant workers and their families: Challenges and options for building a better future, GB.344/POL/1, 16 February 2022, https://www.ilo.org/wcmsp5/groups/public/---ed_norm/---relconf/documents/meetingdocument/wcms_837401.pdf. Accessed on 3 October 2023.

ILO, Universal Social Protection for Human Dignity, Social Justice and Sustainable Development: General Survey Concerning the Social Protection Floors Recommendation, 2012 (No. 202), ILC.108/III/B, 2019, para. 418; and Promoting Fair Migration: General Survey Concerning the Migrant Workers Instruments, ILC.105/III/1B, 2016, para. 313.

ILO, Extending Social Protection to Migrant Workers, Refugees and their Families: A Guide for Policymakers and Practitioners, 2021.

ILO, WALK FREE FOUNDATION. 2017. Global Estimates of Modern Slavery. Report. International Labour Organizationand Walk Free Foundation. Available from: https://www.ilo.org/global/publications/book s/WCMS_575479/lang—en/index.htm

Jesperson, S., Alffram, H., Denney, L., and Domingo, P. 2022. Labour migration in Cambodia, Laos, Thailand and Vietnam: Migrants' vulnerabilities and capacities across the labour migration cycle. ODI Thematic brief. London: ODI. https://cdn.odi.org/media/documents/Thematic_b rief_4_FINAL_MR.pdf.

Khanh Vu. Protecting the rights of migrant workers/Protecting the rights of migrant workers, https://hanoimoi.vn/bao-ve-quyen-loi-nguoi-lao-dong-di-cu-561841. html. Accessed on 3 October 2023.

Konrad Adenauer. EU-Asia Dialogue, "Trafficking in Human Beings: Learning from Asian and European Experiences" (2014) 86; US TIP 2017 Report 357.

Koser, K., and Kuschminder, K. 2015. Comparative research on assisted voluntary return (Geneva, IOM). Kuschminder, K. 2017. "Interrogating the relationship between remigration and sustainable return," in *International Migration*, Vol. 55, No. 6, pp. 107–21.

Li, Xu, Zhisheng Zhu, and Hong Zuo. 2019. "The impact of return migration on the mental health of children." *Applied Economics Letters* 26(3): 217–21.

LO, IOM, and UN Women. Policy Discussion Summary: Let returning migrant workers contribute positively to Vietnam. https://www.ilo.org/hanoi/Whatwedo/Publications/WCMS_316803/lang--vi/index.htm. Accessed on June 15, 2023.

Nam Khanh. Migrant workers and social security challenges/Migrant workers and social security challenges, https://www.tinnhanhchungkhoan.vn/lao-dong-di-cu-va-nhung-thach- food-vehicle-an-sinh-xa-hoi-post197280.html. Acceessed on 3 October 2023.

Nguyen Dang Dung and Pham Hong Thai (eds.). Protecting and promoting human rights in the ASEAN region, Publishing House. Social Labor, Hanoi, 2012, p. 95.

OSCE, Human Trafficking for Labour Exploitation/Forced and Bonded Labour: Identification—Prevention—Prosecution Human Trafficking for Labour Exploitation/Forced and Bonded Labour: Prosecution of Offenders, Justice for Victims, tại. https://www.osce.org/files/f/documents/9/0/31923.pdf. Accessed on June 15, 2023.

Renshaw, C. 2016. Human trafficking in Southeast Asia: Uncovering the Dynamics of State Commitment and Compliance. *Michigan Journal of International Law*, 37(4). https://repository.law.umich.edu/cgi/viewcon tent.cgi?article=1341&context=mjil.

Return and Reintegration to the Philippines: An Information Guide for Migrant Filipino Health Workers, https://www.ilo.org/dyn/migpractice/docs/294/Return .pdf. Accessed on June 18, 2023.

SMERU. 2015. Return Migration and the Importance of Reintegration Policies. *SMERU Policy Brief*, No.3. http://www.smeru.or.id/sites/default/files/publication/03_pb _rm.pdf.

Susan Kneebone and Julie Debeljak, Transnational Crime and Human Rights: Responses to Human Trafficking in the Greater Mekong Subregion (Routledge, 2012).

UN-ACT, "Human Trafficking Vulnerabilities in Asia: A Study on Forced Marriage between Cambodia and China" (UNDP, 2016).

UN, Report of the Special Rapporteur on trafficking in persons, especially women and children, Joy Ngozi Ezeilo: Mission to Thailand (2 May 2012) A/HRC/20/18 /Add.2.

United Nations High Commissioner for Refugees (UNHCR). 2004. Handbook for repatriation and reintegration activities (Geneva). Available at: https:// refugeesmigrants.un.org/sites/default/files/180713_agreed_outcome_global_ compact_for_migration.pdf. Accessed on June 15, 2023.

United Nations High Commissioner for Refugees. 2021. *Displaced on the frontlines of the climate emergency*. Available from: https://storymaps.arcgis.com/stories /065d18218b654c798ae9f360a626d903. 13 January 2022.

Van Panhuys et al., "Migrant Access to Social Protection under Bilateral Labour Agreements," 2017.

Wu, J. 2022. Human Trafficking widespread in Southeast Asia. Online scammers send victims to Cambodia and Myanmar. WORLD. Available from: https://wng.org /roundups/widespread-humantrafficking-in-southeast-asia-1661544586.

NOTES

1. ILO, International labour migration. A rights-based approach, Geneva, 2010, p. 13.

2. Khanh Vu, *Bảo vệ quyền lợi người lao động di cư/Protecting the rights of migrant workers* [Protecting the rights of migrant workers/Protecting the rights of migrant workers], https://hanoimoi.vn/bao-ve-quyen-loi-nguoi-lao-dong-di-cu -561841.html, accessed on 3 October 2023.

3. Nam Khanh, *Lao động di cư và những thách thức về an sinh xã hội* [Migrant workers and social security challenges], https://www.tinnhanhchungkhoan.vn/lao -dong-di-cu-va-nhung-thach-thuc-ve-an-sinh-xa-hoi-post197280.html, accessed on 3 October 2023.

4. The principle of equality and non-discrimination is recognized in fundamental international legal documents such as: Universal Declaration of Human Rights; the International Covenant on Civil and Political Rights; the International Covenant on

Economic, Social and Cultural Rights, Social Security (Minimum Standards) Convention, 1952 (No. 102); Migrant Workers (Supplementary Provisions) Convention, 1975 (No. 143). See also: ILO, Universal Social Protection for Human Dignity, Social Justice and Sustainable Development: General Survey Concerning the Social Protection Floors Recommendation, 2012 (No. 202), ILC.108/III/B, 2019, para. 418; and Promoting Fair Migration: General Survey Concerning the Migrant Workers Instruments, ILC.105/III/1B, 2016, para. 313.

5. Clara Van Panhuys, Samia Kazi-Aoul, and Geneviève Binette, "Migrant Access to Social Protection under Bilateral Labour Agreements: A Review of 120 Countries and Nine Bilateral Arrangements," Extension of Social Security Working Paper No. 57, 2017.

6. ILO, Securing social protection for migrant workers and their families: Challenges and options for building a better future, GB.344/POL/1, 16 February 2022, https://www.ilo.org/wcmsp5/groups/public/---ed_norm/---relconf/documents/meetingdocument/wcms_837401.pdf, accessed on 3 October 2023.

7. ILO, Extending Social Protection to Migrant Workers, Refugees and their Families: A Guide for Policymakers and Practitioners, 2021.

8. Van Panhuys et al., "Migrant Access to Social Protection under Bilateral Labour Agreements," 2017.

9. Refer to some international standards in the field of labor: Social Security (Minimum Standards) Convention, 1952 (No. 102); Social Protection Floors Recommendation, 2012 (No. 202); Equality of Treatment (Social Security) Convention, 1962 (No. 118); Maintenance of Social Security Rights Convention, 1982 (No. 157); Equality of Treatment (Accident Compensation) Convention, 1925 (No. 19); Migration for Employment Convention (Revised), 1949 (No. 97).

10. Farahdilah Ghazali and Siti Fazilah Abdul Shukor, Human Trafficking and Forced Labour in Southeast Asia: Legal Framework and a Way Forward, DOI: 10.4018/978-1-6684-6334-5.ch003; see also The Reality of Human Trafficking in Indonesia, https://www.darkbali.org/. Accessed on June 23, 2023.

11. Ibid.

12. Jesperson, S., Alffram, H., Denney, L., and Domingo, P. (2022). Labour migration in Cambodia, Laos, Thailand and Vietnam: Migrants' vulnerabilities and capacities across the labour migration cycle. ODI Thematic brief. London: ODI. https://cdn.odi.org/media/documents/Thematic_b rief_4_FINAL_MR.pdf.

13. ILO, Walk Free Foundation (2017). Global Estimates of Modern Slavery. Report. International Labour Organizationand Walk Free Foundation. Available from: https://www.ilo.org/global/publications/book s/WCMS_575479/lang—en/index.htm.

14. Deanna Davy, Regional Overview: Sexual Exploitaton of Children in Southeast Asia, https://www.ecpat.org/wp-content/uploads/2021/05/Regional-Overview_Southeast-Asia.pdf. Accessed on June 23, 2023.

15. Konrad Adenauer EU-Asia Dialogue, "Trafficking in Human Beings: Learning from Asian and European Experiences" (2014) 86; US TIP 2017 Report 357.

16. UN, Report of the Special Rapporteur on trafficking in persons, especially women and children, Joy Ngozi Ezeilo: Mission to Thailand (2 May 2012)

A/HRC/20/18/Add.2; Environmental Justice Foundation, "Sold to the Sea: Human Trafficking in Thailand's Fishing Industry" (2013); IOM, "Trafficking of fishermen in Thailand" (2011), http://www.iom.int/jahia/webdav/shared/shared/mainsite/activities/countries/docs/thailand/Trafficking-of-FishermenThailand.pdf. See also Susan Kneebone and Julie Debeljak, Transnational Crime and Human Rights: Responses to Human Trafficking in the Greater Mekong Subregion (Routledge, 2012).

17. Consular Department, Ministry of Foreign Affairs of Vietnam, general report on the migration situation of Vietnamese citizens going abroad, https://phapluatdansu.edu.vn/wp-content/uploads/2020/06/bao_cao_tong_quan_ve_di_dan_VN- 2.pdf. Accessed on June 23, 2023.

18. Walk Free Foundation Global Slavery Index (2022) at https://www.walkfree.org/global-slavery-index/findings/regional-findings/asia-and-the-pacific/. Accessed on June 25, 2023.

19. UNODC, Questionnaire for the Global Report on Trafficking in Persons 2018, Japan Ministry of Foreign Affairs, 2017.

20. Although many people who are economically well-off and highly educated also wish to migrate to find suitable jobs and better income. However, because they have economic conditions and knowledge, they often find out enough information and migrate by legal means.

21. Danh, T. (2022) Difficulties in rescuing Vietnamese people in Cambodia. VnExpress. Available from: https://vnexpress.net/tong-lanh-su-neu-khokhan-khi-giai-cuu-nguoi-viet-o-campuchia4509632.htm. Accessed on June 25, 2023.

22. Renshaw, C. (2016) Human trafficking in Southeast Asia: Uncovering the Dynamics of State Commitment and Compliance. *Michigan Journal of International Law*, 37(4). https://repository.law.umich.edu/cgi/viewcon tent.cgi?article=1341&context=mjil.

23. IOM, Report on Human Trafficking, Forced Labour and Fisheries Crime in the Indonesian Fishing Industry (2016).

24. Education and especially literacy can also make migrants more vulnerable. Children's literacy significantly increases awareness of the risk of human trafficking. See more at: World Vision (n.d.) "Human trafficking in Lao PDR." Vientiane: World Vision Lao PDR.

25. Preventing and repelling human trafficking crimes, Communist Party of Vietnam Magazine, at https://dangcongsan.vn/xa-hoi/ngan-chan-day-lui-toi-pham-mua-ban-nguoi- 506789.html. Accessed on June 23, 2023.

26. Wu, J. (2022) Human Trafficking widespread in Southeast Asia. Online scammers send victims to Cambodia and Myanmar. WORLD. Available from: https://wng.org/roundups/widespread-humantrafficking-in-southeast-asia-1661544586.

27. Eckstein, D., Künzel, V., and Schäfer, L. (2021) Global Climate Risk Index 2021: Who Suffers Most from Extreme Weather Events? Weather-Related Loss Events in 2019 and 2000–2019, GermanWatch, pp. 13–15. Available from: https://reliefweb.int/sites/reliefweb.int/files/resources/Global%20Climate%20Risk%20Index%202021_1_0.pdf. 2 February 2022.

28. Coelho, S., Martens, J., Cole, A., and Lee, S. (2016). *The Climate Change-Human Trafficking Nexus*, International Organization for Migration, p. 3. Available from: https://publications.iom.int/books/climate-change-human-trafficking-nexus. 9 November

2022; United Nations High Commissioner for Refugees 2021, *Displaced on the front-lines of the climate emergency*. Available from: https://storymaps.arcgis.com/stories/065d18218b654c798ae9f360a626d903. 13 January 2022.

29. Cook, T. L., Shannon, P. J., Vinson, G. A., Letts, J. P., and Dwee, E. (2015). War trauma and torture experiences reported during public health screening of newly resettled Karen refugees: A qualitative study. *BMC International Health and Human Rights*, 15(1), 8. https://doi.org/10.1186/s12914-015-0046-y.

30. 2023 Trafficking in Persons Report, https://www.state.gov/reports/2023-trafficking-in-persons-report/indonesia/.

31. 2023 Trafficking in Persons Report, https://www.state.gov/reports/2023-trafficking-in-persons-report/indonesia/.

32. 2002. ILO, A Global Alliance Against Forced Labour. 2005 (https://www.ilo.org/declaration/lang--en/index.htm). Accessed on May 16, 2023.

33. OSCE, Human Trafficking for Labour Exploitation/Forced and Bonded Labour: Identification—Prevention—Prosecution Human Trafficking for Labour Exploitation/Forced and Bonded Labour: Prosecution of Offenders, Justice for Victims, at: https://www.osce.org/files/f/documents/9/0/31923.pdf. Accessed on May 16, 2023.

34. UN-ACT, "Human Trafficking Vulnerabilities in Asia: A Study on Forced Marriage between Cambodia and China" (UNDP, 2016).

35. Abul Muamar, Modern Sea Slavery in Indonesia and Beyond, at: https://greennetwork.asia/brief/modern-sea-slavery-in-indonesia-and-beyond/.

36. Jean-Christophe Dumont and Gilles Spielvogel (OECD), Return Migration: A New Perspective, in International Migrant Outlook 2008, OECD, p. 164.

37. ILO, 2018. Guidelines concerning statistics of international labour migration, ICLS/20/2018/Guidelines, 20th International Conference of Labour Statisticians, Geneva, 10–19 October.

38. Bachtiar, P. P. and Prasetyo, D.D. (2017). Return migration and various reintegration programs for low-skilled migrant workers in Indonesia, Research Report (Jakarta, SMERU Research Institute).

39. Assarino, J. P. (2014a). "Bridging the policy gap between reintegration and development," in J.P. Cassarino (ed.), Reintegration and development, *CRIS Analytical Study* (Florence, European University Institute), pp. 1–18.

40. Koser, K. and Kuschminder, K. 2015. Comparative research on assisted voluntary return (Geneva, IOM). Kuschminder, K. 2017. "Interrogating the relationship between remigration and sustainable return," in *International Migration*, Vol. 55, No. 6, pp. 107–21.

41. United Nations High Commissioner for Refugees (UNHCR). 2004. Handbook for repatriation and reintegration activities (Geneva). Available at: https://refugeesmigrants.un.org/sites/default/files/180713_agreed_outcome_global_compact_for_migration.pdf. Accessed June 15, 2023.

42. Alkida Ndreka, Return migration and re-integration of returnees challenges in the origin country, https://sciendo.com/article/10.2478/rsc-2019-0012?tab=article#j_rsc-2019-0012_ref_057_w2aab3b7b1b1b6b1ab2ac58Aa. Accessed June 15, 2023.

43. Return and Reintegration to the Philippines: An Information Guide for Migrant Filipino Health Workers, https://www.ilo.org/dyn/migpractice/docs/294/Return.pdf. Accessed June 18, 2023.

44. S. Meru (2015), Return Migration and the Importance of Reintegration Policies. *SMERU Policy Brief*, No.3. http://www.smeru.or.id/sites/default/files/publication/03_pb_rm.pdf.

45. Bali Process Regional Support Office (BPRSO). 2019. A policy guide on returns and reintegration for Bali Process Members (Bangkok). Available at: https://www.baliprocess.net/UserFiles/baliprocess/File/BP%20Policy%20Guide%20on%20Returns%20 and%20Reintegration.pdf.

46. Greater Mekong, Mekong Dialouge on Labour Mobility, https://www.greatermekong.org/sites/default/files/Background%20slides%20for%20Mekong%20Dialogue.pdf.

47. LO, IOM, and UN Women, Summary of policy discussion: Let returning migrant workers contribute positively to Vietnam, https://www.ilo.org/hanoi/Whatwedo/Publications/WCMS_316803/lang--vi/index.htm. Accessed June 15, 2023.

48. Abarcar, Paolo. 2016. Do Employers Value Return Migrants? An Experiment on the Returns to Foreign Work Experience. Working Paper 48, Mathematica Policy Research.

49. Connell, John. 2009. " 'I Never Wanted to Come Home': Skilled Health Workers in the South Pacific." *Migration and Transnationalism, Pacific Perspectives*, ANU Press.

50. Li, Xu, Zhisheng Zhu, and Hong Zuo. 2019. "The impact of return migration on the mental health of children." *Applied Economics Letters* 26(3): 217–21.

51. Nguyen Dang Dung and Pham Hong Thai (eds.), Protecting and promoting human rights in the ASEAN region, Publishing House. Social Labor, Hanoi, 2012, p. 95.

52. See more at: IOM, International Organization for Migration (IOM), 2023. Labour Migration in Asia: What Does the Future Hold? IOM, Geneva.

Chapter 12

Recommendations to Effectively Ensure the Rights of Migrant Workers

from Developing Countries in Asia

Nguyen Thi Kim Ngan, Nguyen Toan Thang, and Nguyen Thi Hong Yen

Undoubtedly, Asia is steadily taking the lead globally in providing migrant workers for the international labor market. The temporary migration trends with primary and medium-skilled occupations account for the majority of the labor movement in the region. It does not mean that this area does not have skilled migrant workers, but compared to the huge population in this region, skilled migrant workers seem relatively modest. In 2021, it is anticipated that more than 25 percent of migration flows into OECD (Organisation for Economic Co-operation and Development) countries will come from Asia and the Pacific.[1]

However, there are still significant loopholes in the legal systems of the Asian exporting countries that protect migrant workers' rights, and the regional cooperation mechanism is not strong enough. As a result, migrant workers from these nations still face challenges in exercising their rights. Based on that practice, the authors suggest the following fixes to guarantee the proper application of migrant workers' rights from Asian countries:

ENHANCEMENT OF POLICIES AND LAWS ON MIGRANT WORKERS

Governments need to continue to improve policies and laws and promote the signing of international treaties to protect the rights of migrant workers abroad, including legal and illegal migrant workers.

The reality is that legal migrant workers and contract employees continue to be the primary protected persons under both national and international law. Undocumented or illegal migrant workers, on the other hand, appear to be growing increasingly vulnerable and "forgotten" even though their presence in the global labor market is clear and undeniable.

As mentioned in previous chapters, migrant workers, whether legal or illegal, documented or undocumented, are still human beings, and, in principle, they will still enjoy fundamental human rights. Therefore, protecting their legitimate rights is especially urgent for governments because their rights can be violated at any time. Therefore, one of the critical measures that governments can take immediately is to actively develop laws and regulations toward fairness and transparency to protect the rights of migrant workers, including legal and illegal, documented and undocumented migrant workers and to facilitate their access to justice as much as possible. It is significant for female migrant workers who are subject to gender-based abuses. Countries should simplify the procedures for women to obtain legal assistance in cases of abuse and provide routine legal aid. This support aims to help them get the fairest, most transparent and timely help possible when abused.

To provide the best circumstances and assistance for migrant workers before, during, and following their overseas employment, policies and regulations on migrant workers must be settled. In particular, a post-migration social reintegration policy is essential because unfavorable repatriation conditions affect migrant workers' decisions to overstay or turn around.[2] According to International Labor Organization (ILO) research, legalizing labor migration will help reduce the flow of illegal migrants and related rights violations. At the same time, sending countries should reduce their excessive dependence on work abroad by reducing internal migration pressures. ILO Employment Policy (para. 39 [X]. Additional Provisions), Recommendation, 1984 (No. 169)[3] calls on member states to improve working conditions and employment prospects in the origin countries to reduce the need to migrate in search of work.[4]

In addition, sending countries also need to focus on developing specific social security policies for migrant workers, focusing on employment and reintegration support policies. The purpose is to create favorable conditions for them to return. To do this, governments should provide vocational and skill-training programs to assist individuals in stabilizing their lives and promoting the occupations and skills they have acquired when working abroad.[5] For low-skilled or undocumented migrant workers, governments should pay particular attention and take effective social protection measures for them. Low-skilled and illegal migrant workers are more vulnerable to abuse and exploitation because of their illegality or the low-skilled nature of the work they are required to do. Therefore, the more specific and transparent legal regulations will be a tool to prevent them from being left behind, regardless of their migration path. Mainly, the social security system does not provide insurance for housemaids abroad. Low-skilled migrants are often denied the same rights as high-skilled immigrant workers due to discriminatory policies in destination countries. This includes denying mobile work permits, the possibility of permanent settlement, and family reunification. These refusals violate their right to social protection.[6]

The report also claimed that formal short-term benefits including primary health care and injuries sustained at work are frequently offered in destination countries; however, access to these benefits may be restricted or denied in reality.[7] However, long-term benefits—particularly retirement benefits including old age, disability, survivor, and aftercare—are a significant issue for low-skilled or illegal workers. While some sending countries have expressed interest in setting up migrant welfare funds and related migration support services to ensure that their workers are adequately protected overseas, the main functions of these funds are to offer emergency and repatriation services, work-related benefits and legal assistance, and welfare provisions for the remaining families. They can offer restricted reintegration support, like loans for starting small enterprises. But usually, they also don't include long-term advantages.[8]

One issue that is "necessary to consider" for countries to encourage legal migration and decrease illegal migrant flows was also mentioned by the International Organisation for Migration (IOM) in its 2016 document called "Promoting Safe Migrant." The answer lies in integrating migration policies with other comprehensive development objectives, including but not limited to food security, equitable access to health care, education, water and electricity, decent housing, decent jobs, and justice. This will help ensure migration is an option, not a necessity.[9]

Equally important is that countries need to develop official programs, communication campaigns, and dialogues on migrant workers, thereby helping people, especially workers, have the most general understanding of the rights and obligations of workers when going to work abroad; issues to remember when working abroad: a system of agencies and organizations they can contact when they need help; the risks and dangers of illegal migration; and issues of human trafficking must be made available to all parties in sending and receiving countries.[10]

Consideration to Promote and Facilitate Migration by Ratifying the International Convention for the Protection of Migrant Workers (ICMW) and Related Treaties, Including Signing the Bilateral and Multilateral Cooperation Agreements

To establish a legal foundation for improved and more direct protection of migrant workers' rights, countries, especially sending countries, ought to think about ratifying the International Convention for the Protection of Migrant Workers (ICMW) as well as other bilateral and multilateral agreements. As mentioned above, the ICMW is an international convention that stipulates the rights and obligations of migrant workers. However, governments are approaching the Convention with "caution" because, similar to earlier ILO agreements, it only establishes "one-way responsibility" for receiving countries, ignoring the role of sending countries.[11]

Furthermore, expanding the commitment to protect relatives of migrant workers when they are present in the receiving country is also a challenge for them when considering applying this Convention.[12] Although there are different views on the "hesitancy" of countries with the ICMW, it cannot be denied that ratifying this Convention will contribute to providing an essential legal foundation for the protection of migrant workers and their family members because the implementation of the provisions of this Convention will then become a State's obligation under the principle of Pacta Sunt Servanda.

In addition to ICMW, non-members should also consider ratifying relevant ILO instruments such as the ILO Migration for Work Convention (Amendment), 1949 (No. 97); ILO Migrant Workers (Additional Provisions) Convention, 1975 (No. 143); ILO Conventions No. 181 and No. 189; and Forced Labor Protocol P029 should also be promoted to implement in countries of origin and destination.

In addition, the governments need to continue to promote the signing of bilateral and multilateral cooperation agreements on migrant workers. Even so, the governments may aim to establish a regional protection mechanism to share information and create a support system when related problems arise. According to the IOM, a significant proportion of low-skilled and skilled migrants, especially women migrants, find themselves unable to access professional employment and apply their education level due to the different regulations in qualifications of the countries. Because of this, many female migrant workers are frequently restricted to low-skilled positions in housekeeping, hotel, and food services—jobs that do not align with their skills.[13] It is also mentioned in the document of *Safeguarding the rights of*

Asian migrant workers from home to the workplace. Accordingly, some Asian countries have strict regulations on licensing and implementing overseas recruitment, but achieving fair employment is elusive. The problem stems from a combination of scarce jobs, poor governance, and complex cross-border regulations. Because labor supply in countries of origin with low wages far exceeds demand in wealthier destination countries, migrant workers are vulnerable to abuses in the recruitment process.[14] In light of this, the objective of international cooperation initiatives should include agreements on the establishment of a system for the recognition of foreign degrees as well as the application of beneficial labor market policies that enable migrant workers, regardless of gender, to contribute most effectively with their professional and skillful abilities to the advancement of social progress.[15] In addition, signed Memoranda of Understanding (MOUs) should aim to simplify immigration and recruitment regulations.

It is important to note that to ensure comprehensive protection for workers in the sending and destination countries, the design of any international treaty between governments should involve the participation of social partners and associations and apply a periodic review system, especially concerning the protection of migrant workers. Such arrangements can help low-skilled migrant workers file labor complaints and access remedial proceedings easier, the ILO says. They can also avoid hiring errors by informing employees of their legal rights, including the maximum amount they can be required to pay.[16]

CONSTRUCTION AND IMPROVEMENT OF INSTITUTIONS AND MANAGEMENT FOR MIGRANT WORKERS

To protect migrant workers' rights, managing migrant employees must be developed and refined in a contemporary, professional, and rights-based manner.

According to the author's research in the World Bank publication, many ASEAN (Association of Southeast Asian Nations) nations have set up specialized bodies to handle and address migrant worker–related concerns more efficiently (Indonesia has two agencies, the Ministry of Manpower and the National Authority for the Placement and Protection of Indonesian Overseas Workers [BNP2TKI]; the Philippines has got the Overseas Workers Welfare Administration [OWWA] and Philippine Overseas Labor Offices [POLOs]; Vietnam has got the Department of Overseas Labor within the Ministry of Labor, Invalids, and Social Affairs).[17] In South Asia, three countries,

Bangladesh, India, and Sri Lanka, have established independent ministries on labor migration. There, Bangladesh established the Ministry of Expatriates' Welfare and Overseas Employment (2001), India created the Ministry of Overseas Indian Affairs (2004), and Sri Lanka created the Ministry of Foreign Employment Promotion and Welfare (2007) and renamed the Ministry of Foreign Employment in 2015.[18] Some other countries have delegated the authority on labor migration management to ministries, agencies with general labor and social competence, etc. However, this study also shows that these agencies face challenges, such as overlapping authority functions and a lack of migration data and financial resources.[19] Some other countries have delegated the authority on labor migration management to ministries, agencies with general labor, and social competence, etc.

Therefore, to specialize and improve the capacity of agencies in migration management, it is thought that countries of origin need to focus on building organizational structures and delineating functional authority for these agencies clearly; besides that, it empowers them to protect the rights of migrant workers fully. To modernize the management of migrant workers, governments should simultaneously encourage digital transformation. They should also establish a data platform for information exchange, support, and international collaboration among agencies of countries to enhance their capacity to address migrant workers' issues.

In addition to perfecting the institutions in the state system, strengthening the capacity and responsibility of labor recruitment enterprises is also extremely important because managing migrant labor recruitment is incredibly complicated. It requires surveillance of hundreds of thousands of private subjects operating formally and informally across national and international borders. Apart from giving millions of prospective low-wage workers access to unattainable job chances overseas, they also provide prospective workers with employment-related information, aid in acquiring requisite documentation, and manage intricate government inquiries once employed overseas.[20] Therefore, building a rights-based governance framework for these agencies and organizations is necessary because it will contribute to sharing the burden of migration management for the state. On the other hand, businesses that operate with transparency, fairness, and employee-centeredness will help migrant workers receive the rights and benefits they have been defined by law more fully. Of course, like Farbenblum Bassina said in his study, a rights-based hiring governance framework is not a panacea that can end all ills overnight. Nor does it simply involve the creation of rights and obligations under the law—although this is an essential component. More specifically, it offers a prism through which the effects of governance frameworks on marginalized migrant worker groups can be more fully recognized and effectively dealt with.[21]

Build a database to digitize and share information about immigrant workers in countries

The lack of information is one reason that makes the migration and work process of workers and employers' recruitment and management process become more complex. In actuality, to plan logistics, contact target data receivers, as well as provide them updates and coordinate relief or repatriation efforts, authorities in both the nation of origin and the workplace must have comprehensive and full information on the migrant worker.[22]

Moreover, countries should establish a migrant worker data system as soon as possible to gather, manage, analyze, and assess data on trends, difficulties, and the present state of migrant workers overseas. According to IOM, collecting accurate data on migrants' enjoyment of their rights and contributions to development can also promote a more precise understanding of migration and the circumstances of migrants. Furthermore, meticulous data gathering on migrants is necessary to lay the groundwork for safeguarding their human rights and promoting access to basic services.[23]

The governments can consider being more proactive in empowering professional-social organizations such as trade unions, migrant associations, and other social organizations in providing support services for immigrant workers by using grievance mechanisms, promoting media campaigns, and policy advocacy toward fair recruitment in their countries. Twenty-six migrant worker resource centers have been established throughout Southeast Asia by unions, society organizations, and government employment centers with ILO support. These facilities offer protective services to migrant workers, prospective migrants, and their families. These facilities also offer legal counsel and assistance to migrants who wish to file complaints over mistreatment related to hiring or employment. However, in addition to providing services, migrant workers need to be empowered to represent their interests and protect their rights through migrant associations and unions.[24]

Effective labor migration governance requires coordination between relevant government agencies to develop and achieve common goals.[25]

For migration activities to comply with the provisions of international law and national law, organizations and agencies responsible in this field need to cooperate and support each other to share common goals. They have to fulfill their human rights responsibilities toward all workers, including migrant workers, in a long-lasting manner that produces consistent results. According to P. Maximilian, and others, businesses should build their migration management systems on four pillars: (i) a commitment to policy, (ii) protection of human rights, (iii) corrective actions, and (iv) interaction with immigrant workers. This system should control and operate the entire process of labor migration.[26] Maximilian and the authors specifically suggest that businesses need to develop policies that demonstrate respect for human rights generally and the labor rights of migrant workers specifically. They also suggest integrating these approaches into internal management systems to guarantee consistent and efficient enforcement of these policies.[27] In order to proactively manage actual and prospective negative human rights consequences resulting from or connected to their commercial activities, relationships, products, or services, organizations should next undertake human rights due diligence.[28] Regarding remedies, companies must set up or participate in migrant worker-accessible grievance procedures; provide effective and timely remedies when harm occurs; monitor corrective action; and capture lessons for continuous improvement. Lastly, companies should foster a relationship with migrant workers by involving them in the development, implementation, and monitoring of corporate policies and related management systems to human rights and labor migration and provide effective support services to address the specific vulnerabilities of migrant workers; collaborating with reputable organizations can aid in overcoming challenges.[29]

APPLICATION OF EFFECTIVE MEASURES FOR THE MANAGEMENT OF AND ASSURANCE FOR ENSURING THE RIGHTS OF MIGRANT WORKERS

The ILO's report in 2017 states that "States have the sovereign right to develop their own to manage labour migration and that opportunities and risks may vary nationally and within migration corridors, it is necessary to develop tailored and effective policy responses"[30]; and "Effective labour migration governance must also respond to the changing needs of business and workers, including addressing skills, education and training gaps, with particular attention to women and youth, and persons with disabilities and other vulnerable groups."[31] Developing policies and laws to manage migrant labor is indeed the sovereignty of each country, based on the country's economic, social, human, and cultural development. Based on the current situation of migrant labor management in sending countries in Asia, to strengthen effective migrant labor governance and ensure better their rights and benefits, the authors suggest the application of the following measures:

Continue to effectively enforce the fundamental human rights of migrant workers in the workplace and without discrimination based on their migration status.

Protect the rights of migrant workers at work as set out in relevant ILO Conventions, such as the Migration for Employment (Revised) Convention, 1949 (No. 97), on Migrant Workers (Supplementary Provisions), 1975 (No. 143), and other standards, including the Private Employment Agencies Convention, 1997 (No. 181), and the Domestic Workers Convention Family, 2011 (No. 189).[32] In addition, countries also need to develop appropriate social protection policies to create favorable conditions for migrant workers and their families to access social protection bylaws and regulations of national and international obligations, ensuring the implementation of their rights to social security, creating an equal labor environment between domestic and migrant workers, and supporting the labor migration process in attempts to be fair and transparent.[33]

Implement fair recruitment policies and develop sustainable employment programs to ensure basic working rights for workers.

Fair recruitment, as the ILO states in its study, is crucial to enhancing skills and finding suitable jobs for migrant workers in both the countries of origin and destination while reducing the likelihood that migrant workers would be the victims of gender-based violence, child and forced labor, exploitation and abuse, and human trafficking. It is more necessary when the number of temporary migrants rises and supply chains get more complex.[34] Besides, the government needs to limit recruitment fees and implement measures to combat illegal recruitment and migration. At the same time, it is also essential to implement specific protection measures for workers who belong to vulnerable groups, such as young women and kids, to prevent, combat, and restrict the human trafficking.[35]

Strengthen the inspection and examination mechanism, and at the same time, improve the accountability of stakeholders in ensuring and promoting the rights and interests of migrant workers.

Labor inspection is globally recognized as an essential tool in labor market management. In countries that receive large numbers of migrant workers, specific procedures are needed to allow labor inspectors to monitor their working conditions.[36] As noted above, migrant workers often work in sectors or geographies that are difficult for the government to access, including domestic work, the fishing industry, and agriculture. Furthermore, it is becoming more challenging to share duties regarding employment and working conditions due to outsourcing and tripartite connections involving migrant employees (i.e., individuals hired by one firm to work for another).[37] Therefore, strengthening a team of professional, courageous, and well-qualified labor inspectors is necessary for building and perfecting institutions, helping to make migrant labor management activities more scientific and responsible.

In addition, governments should stipulate accountability, transparency, and integrity in the information of relevant agencies and organizations to bind the responsibilities and awareness of agencies in ensuring and supporting migrant activities. The accountability should be carried out regularly, according to procedures and authority, with the participation of all parties involved in the migration process, such as state agencies (including domestic agencies from central to local and foreign agencies, civil servants), businesses with the function of sending workers to work abroad, associations, and workers. The reports from the various parties will provide the governments with a precise and all-encompassing image of migrant workers, enabling them to recognize the obstacles, difficulties, and current issues in this domain. This provides more of a foundation for the timely and appropriate development of laws and policies that will better safeguard the rights and interests of migrant workers, whether they are employed legally or not. Furthermore, the government must fulfill its obligation to keep an eye on and assess how policies and their execution affect migrant workers. Concurrently, government should monitor the actions of the agencies providing social security services to ensure that low-skilled immigrant laborers are not being exploited here.[38]

Last but not least, the government needs to develop policies and support for institutions/organizations to provide some support services for migrant workers like pre-departure consulting services, on-site labor attaché services, and social insurance services; training services for returnees and employment support; emergency evacuation and repatriation arrangements; and the establishment of facilities and community centers for workers abroad.[39]

PROMOTION OF INTERNATIONAL COOPERATION IN ADDRESSING ISSUES RELATED TO MIGRANT WORKERS

International cooperation is essential for the protection and promotion of migrant workers' rights as well as for expanding organized labor migration and curbing irregular movement. Moreover, successful governance of international migration is an inherently multilateral concern requiring cooperation between various stakeholders. Cooperation on migration issues takes place at the global, regional, subregional, bilateral, and national levels. The ILO Multilateral Framework on Labour Migration 2006 recognized that "issues related to the movement of workers across national borders cannot be effectively addressed when countries act in isolation; hence, international cooperation in managing labour migration can be valuable in addressing national interests."[40] Principle 2 of ILO Multilateral Framework states: "Governments, in consultation with employers' and workers' organizations, should engage in international cooperation to promote managed migration for employment purposes."[41] There are several types of international cooperation. These can be either formal or informal, such as bilateral labor agreements and memoranda of understanding (MoUs); and cooperation among non-state actors.

Bilateral labor migration agreements (BLMAs*)* and Memoranda of Understanding (MoUs*)* between *origin and destination country governments* in Asia

The ILO has long recognized the potential of BLMAs and MoUs in promoting well-regulated labor migration and protection of migrant workers. BLMAs and MoUs formalize each side's commitment to ensure that migration takes place in accordance with agreed principles and procedures. In addition BLMAs and MoUs provide a means to address labor shortages for destination countries and labor market access for countries of origin. Apart from national laws and multilateral treaties, BLMAs and MoUs have provided a useful mechanism to regulate cross-border labor migration. However, their effectiveness in the region (and globally) has varied. Some good practices found in the agreements are:

- Exchange of relevant information between the country of origin and destination on labor migration
- Provisions relating to employment contracts and applicable labor laws
- Implementation, monitoring, and evaluation procedures
- Defining clear responsibilities between parties
- Mechanisms for complaints and dispute resolution procedures
- Provision for free transfer of savings and remittances

BLMAs and MoUs will continue to be important, and can indeed focus on labor market access and shortages as well as migrant protection. To increase their efficiency, a number of measures are needed:

Safeguard human rights and international labour standards for the protection of migrant workers. All BLMAs should respect, promote, and realize all human rights, including those expressed in international labor standards, and in particular fundamental principles and rights at work. BLMAs should include explicit provisions on addressing exploitation and rights abuse of migrant workers, and on providing assistance to trafficked and/or smuggled migrants. The BLMA should also respect and facilitate the enforcement of national laws and regulations governing human and labor rights and collective agreements.

Guarantee equality of treatment and non-discrimination. Equality of treatment and non-discrimination should be extended to all migrant workers and members of their families regardless of sex, sexual orientation, gender expression, and gender identity; race; color; disability; language; religion; political or other opinion; national, ethnic, or social origin; nationality; age; economic position; property; marital status; migration status; or birth or other status. BLMAs should also preserve the cultural identity of migrant workers.

Provide access to justice and effective, independent, and accessible rights protection mechanisms, free of charge, in case of labor disputes and violation of human, labor, and civil rights. The provisions should also include clarity on complaints procedures or mechanisms for follow-up on complaints, including those pending after a migrant has returned to their country of origin.

Ensure prevention and elimination of violence and harassment, exploitation, or abuse, including gender-based, against migrant workers. Migrant workers should have meaningful access to appropriate and effective remedies and safe, fair, and effective, gender-responsive reporting and complaint mechanisms and support in cases of abuse, violence, and harassment, with protection from retaliation and negative repercussions regarding their status. Legal assistance and legal aid should be available and free of charge and migrant workers should not have to pay fees at a rate which impedes access to justice. This may include allowing migrant workers who are subject to violations at work to change their workplace, and providing continued residence and work authorization in the country, at least until a decision on their case is made. BLMAs should include provisions for the involvement of social partners and other stakeholders in countering violence and harassment at work.

Allow freedom of movement of migrant workers. Migrant workers should be able to freely move and choose their place of residency within the destination country, in accordance with human rights standards. This implies the facilitation of the entry in the destination country and the right to leave it, integration measures, geographical mobility, and the right to return to the origin country. The withholding or confiscation of a migrant worker's passport, other identity documents, or work permit by an employer or a recruitment agency constitutes a violation of human and labor rights and can negatively impact the right to freedom of movement.

Facilitate admission of family members of migrant workers, and family reunification. Provisions are included for both parties to exchange updated information on the rules for admission of family members of migrant workers, and family reunification, and pathways to stay, including permanent residence and citizenship. BLMAs should consider the best interests of the dependent children of migrant workers and the preservation of the family unit in their family reunification policies. When family accompaniment is not viable or taken up by migrant workers, BLMAs should include specific provisions addressing the need to create opportunities for regular reunification between migrant workers and dependent children.

Ensure protection of migrant workers and their families in case of loss or change of employment, allowing for appropriate flexibility and time to change workplace and employer, or exit the country. Migrant workers should not fall into an irregular situation due to the mere loss of employment and should enjoy equality of treatment in respect to particular guarantees of security of employment, protection against dismissal, ability to seek alternative employment and relief work, and retraining receipt of unemployment benefits. If subsequent to the migrant worker's arrival, the job does not materialize (or the authority considers that the job for which the migrant worker has been recruited does not correspond to his or her physical capacity or occupational qualifications) or the contract prematurely ends, he/she should be entitled to alternative employment. Restricting the ability of migrant workers to leave an employment relationship of their own free will can lead to or reinforce exploitation and abuse and may therefore be explicitly prohibited in the BLMA.

Cooperation among non-state actors (trade unions, employer organizations)

Trade union cooperation for migrant protection is essential for several reasons. The widespread exploitation of migrant workers in destination countries is due to lax enforcement of labor laws and the exclusion of some workers from the coverage of labor law. Low-skilled workers, in particular, have issues lodging complaints or accessing redress. Most migrant workers lack information on their rights and obligations. Unions can also prevent recruitment malpractices by alerting workers to their legal rights and the maximum fees payable. Restrictions on the formation of trade unions or support for freedom of association principles in some destination countries constrain the role that unions can play in destination countries. The main challenges faced by trade unions in supporting and organizing migrant workers in destination countries have been summarized as follows:

- The extremely vulnerable position of migrant workers in society; segregation into a separate entity from the national labor force;
- The exclusion of trade unions from intergovernmental agreements and the migrant recruitment process; severe restrictions on trade union rights, mostly in destination countries;
- The absence of a consolidated and common strategy between trade unions; and the exclusion of migrants during policy debates and discussions.

Given the significant gaps in the protection of migrant workers in destination countries, it is important to establish partnerships among trade unions, civil society, and other non-state actors.

Partnerships among employer organizations in Asia on the issue of labor migration have yet to come up prominently so far. However, industry associations in the region (and globally) have developed codes of practice and self-regulation in the framework of corporate social responsibility. While trade unions have generally been active in labor migration issues in Asia, it is also essential that employers' organizations play a role here given its implications for migration governance, including recruitment malpractices, high migration costs, human resource development, and protection of migrant workers in workplaces abroad. The considerable abuse and exploitation of these migrant workers by employers in destination countries, and intermediaries in both origin and destination countries, is well documented. Employers' organizations should play a role in negotiations with their counterparts in destination countries based on corporate social responsibility considerations to minimize these abuses. Other recommendations include:

- Work with workers' organizations and the government to develop a code of practice of good conduct or ethical framework for recruitment. High migration costs and related debt burdens of migrant workers is a major governance issue to be addressed partly through a code of conduct.
- Given that private sector employers mostly employ migrant workers in Asia, it is important to look at the potential for collaboration between employers' organizations in origin and destination countries. Such cooperation can have high potential given that employers' organizations in destination countries may be able to address issues of contract substitution, wage protection, occupational safety and health, and other related issues in a direct manner. Origin country employers' organizations can sensitize employers in destination countries on the rights of migrant workers.
- Employers' organizations can play a helpful role in contributing to skill development programs for migrant workers and recognition of skills of migrant workers on their return. Employers' organizations can also contribute to pre-departure orientation training with information on employers in destination countries, and dos and don'ts. In addition, they can review the curricula of pre-departure orientation programs to check whether employer issues have been properly addressed.

REFERENCES

ADBI, ILO, or OECD, Labor Migration in Asia: Building Effective Institutions, 2016, https://www.oecd.org/migration/labor-migration-in-asia-building-effective-institutions.pdf, pp.18–20.

ADBI, OECD, or ILO, Safeguarding the rights of Asian migrant workers from home to the workplace, 2017, https://www.adb.org/sites/default/files/publication/230176/adbi-safeguarding-rights-asian-migrant-workers.pdf, pp. 27–30.

ASEAN Secretariat, ASEAN Migration Outlook, 2022, https://asean.org/wp-content/uploads/2022/08/ASEAN-Migration-Outlook-Final.pdf.

Farbenblum, B. (2017). Governance of Migrant Worker Recruitment: A Rights-Based Framework for Countries of Origin. *Asian Journal of International Law*, 7(1), 152–84. doi:10.1017/S2044251316000011, https://www.cambridge.org/core/journals/asian-journal-of-international-law/article/governance-of-migrant-worker-recruitment-a-rightsbased-framework-for-countries-of-origin/02C4527B323828B2BA2B55406837A8B4, accessed on 1 September 2023.

ILO Regional Office for Asia and the Pacific, Complaint mechanisms for Vietnamese migrant workers: An overview of law and practice / Tripartite Action to Protect the Rights of Migrant Workers within and from the Greater Mekong Subregion (GMS TRIANGLE project), Hanoi, 2015. Available at https://www.ilo.org/wcmsp5/groups/public/---asia/---ro-bangkok/---ilo-hanoi/documents/publication/wcms_482928.pdf, accessed on 2 July 2023.

ILO, *Labour migration in Asia and the Pacific and the Arab States*, 2014, https://www.ilo.org/wcmsp5/groups/public/---asia/---ro-bangkok/documents/publication/wcms_534954.pdf.

ILO International Migration Programme and Subregional Office for East Asia Labour Migration Policy and Management: Training materials, Bangkok, International Labour Office, 2005, pp. 20–33.

ILO, Labour migration in Asia and the Pacific, https://www.ilo.org/asia/areas/labour-migration/WCMS_634559/lang--en/index.htm.

ILO, R169—Employment Policy (Supplementary Provisions) Recommendation, 1984 (No. 169), available at https://www.ilo.org/dyn/normlex/en/f?p=NORMLEXPUB:12100:0::NO::P12100_INSTRUMENT_ID:312507.

Inter-Agency Task Force on Financing for Development, IOM, Promoting safe migration, Issue Brief Series, 2016, https://www.un.org/esa/ffd/wp-content/uploads/2016/01/Promoting-safe-migration_IOM_IATF-Issue-Brief.pdf, accessed on 28 August 2023, pp. 3–4.

IOM International Organization for Migration, International Labour Organisation, UN Women, "Making the return of migrant workers work for Vietnam: An issue in brief," available at https://www.ilo.org/hanoi/Whatwedo/Publications/WCMS_316802/lang--en/index.htm.

Maximilian, P., C. Pütz, L. Pham, and H. Plumb, 2021. Migrant Worker Guidelines for Employers. International Organization for Migration (IOM), Geneva, https://publications.iom.int/system/files/pdf/Migrant-Worker-Guidelines-for-Emloyers_1.pdf.

Migrant Forrum in Asia, Social Protection for Low-Skilled Migrant Workers and their Families, Policy Brief No. 7, at https://www.ilo.org/dyn/migpractice/docs/137/PB7.pdf, accessed on 1 September 2023.

Piyasiri Wickramasekera, Asian Labour Migration: Issues and Challenges in an Era of Globalization, 2002, https://www.ilo.org/asia/publications/WCMS_160632/lang--en/index.htm.p

Testaverde, Mauro, et al. Migrating to Opportunity: Overcoming Barriers to Labor Mobility in Southeast Asia, World Bank Publications, 2017. ProQuest, Ebook Central, http://ebookcentral.proquest.com/lib/deakin/detail.action?docID=5109742, pp. 207–10.

Nguyen, Thi Hong Yen. "Challenges in Ensuring the Rights of Vietnamese Migrant Workers in the Globalization Context – The Two Sides of the Development Process". In Asian Yearbook of International Law, (Leiden, The Netherlands: Brill | Nijhoff, 2021) doi: https://doi.org/10.1163/9789004501249_008

Nguyen, Thi Hong Yen and Tran, Thi Thu Thuy. "Ensuring the Rights of Vietnamese Migrant Workers in the Context of the Covid - 19 Pandemic." Journal of Contemporary Sociological Issues (2022): 40-58. Available at: https: // jurnal.unej .ac .id /index .php /JCSI /article /view/27916. Date accessed: June 29 2023.

NOTES

1. ILO, Labour migration in Asia and the Pacific, https://www.ilo.org/asia/areas/labour-migration/WCMS_634559/lang--en/index.htm.

2. IOM International Organization for Migration, International Labour Organisation, UN Women, "Making the return of migrant workers work for Vietnam: An issue in brief," available at https://www.ilo.org/hanoi/Whatwedo/Publications/WCMS_316802/lang--en/index.htm.

3. ILO, R169—Employment Policy (Supplementary Provisions) Recommendation, 1984 (No. 169), available at https://www.ilo.org/dyn/normlex/en/f?p=NORMLEXPUB:12100:0::NO::P12100_INSTRUMENT_ID:312507.

4. Piyasiri Wickramasekera, Asian Labour Migration: Issues and Challenges in an Era of Globalization, 2002, https://www.ilo.org/asia/publications/WCMS_160632/lang--en/index.htm.

5. Yen, Nguyen Thi Hong; Thuy, Tran Thi Thu. Ensuring the Rights of Vietnamese Migrant Workers in the Context of the Covid-19 Pandemic. Journal of Contemporary Sociological Issues, [S.l.], 2(1), pp. 40–58, February 2022. ISSN 2775–2895. Available at: https://jurnal.unej.ac.id/index.php/JCSI/article/view/27916. Date accessed: 29 June 2023.

6. Migrant Forrum in Asia, Social Protection for Low-Skilled Migrant Workers and Their Families, Policy Brief No. 7, at https://www.ilo.org/dyn/migpractice/docs/137/PB7.pdf, accessed on 1 September 2023.

7. Ibid.

8. Ibid.

9. Inter-Agency Task Force on Financing for Development, IOM, Promoting safe migration, Issue Brief Series, 2016, https://www.un.org/esa/ffd/wp-content/uploads/2016/01/Promoting-safe-migration_IOM_IATF-Issue-Brief.pdf, accessed on 28 August 2023, pp. 3–4.

10. ILO Regional Office for Asia and the Pacific, Complaint mechanisms for Vietnamese migrant workers: An overview of law and practice / Tripartite Action to Protect the Rights of Migrant Workers within and from the Greater Mekong Subregion (GMS TRIANGLE project), Hanoi, 2015. Available at https://www.ilo.org/wcmsp5/groups/public/---asia/---ro-bangkok/---ilo-hanoi/documents/publication/wcms_482928.pdf, accessed on 2 July 2023.

11. Thi Hong Yen Nguyen, "Challenges in Ensuring the Rights of Vietnamese Migrant Workers in the Globalization Context: The Two Sides of the Development Process," in *Asian Yearbook of International Law*, Vol. 25 (2019), pp.154–84, Brill NV, Leiden, The Netherlands, DOI: https://doi.org/10.1163/9789004501249_008, at https://brill.com/display/book/edcoll/9789004501249/BP000017.xml, truy cập ngày, accessed 10 June 2023.

12. Ibid.

13. Inter-Agency Task Force on Financing for Development, IOM, *Supra note 9.*

14. ADBI, OECD, or ILO, Safeguarding the rights of Asian migrant workers from home to the workplace, 2017, https://www.adb.org/sites/default/files/publication/230176/adbi-safeguarding-rights-asian-migrant-workers.pdf, pp. 27–30.

15. Inter-Agency Task Force on Financing for Development, IOM, *Supra note 9.*

16. ILO, Labour migration in Asia and the Pacific and the Arab States, 2014, https://www.ilo.org/wcmsp5/groups/public/---asia/---ro-bangkok/documents/publication/wcms_534954.pdf.

17. Testaverde, Mauro, et al. Migrating to Opportunity: Overcoming Barriers to Labor Mobility in Southeast Asia, World Bank Publications, 2017. ProQuest, Ebook Central, http://ebookcentral.proquest.com/lib/deakin/detail.action?docID=5109742, pp. 207–10.

18. ADBI, ILO, or OECD, Labor Migration in Asia: Building Efective Institutions, 2016, https://www.oecd.org/migration/labor-migration-in-asia-building-effective-institutions.pdf, pp. 18–20.

19. Ibid.

20. Farbenblum, B. (2017). Governance of Migrant Worker Recruitment: A Rights-Based Framework for Countries of Origin. *Asian Journal of International Law*, 7(1), 152–84. doi:10.1017/S2044251316000011, https://www.cambridge.org/core/journals/asian-journal-of-international-law/article/governance-of-migrant-worker-recruitment-a-rightsbased-framework-for-countries-of-origin/02C4527B323828B2BA2B55406837A8B4, accessed on 1 September 2023.

21. Ibid.

22. ASEAN Secretariat, ASEAN Migration Outlook, 2022, https://asean.org/wp-content/uploads/2022/08/ASEAN-Migration-Outlook-Final.pdf.

23. Inter-Agency Task Force on Financing for Development, IOM, *Supra note 9.*

24. ADBI, OECD, or ILO, *Supra note 14.*

25. Ibid.

26. Maximilian, P., C. Pütz, L. Pham, and H. Plumb, 2021. Migrant Worker Guidelines for Employers. International Organization for Migration (IOM), Geneva, https://publications.iom.int/system/files/pdf/Migrant-Worker-Guidelines-for-Emloyers_1.pdf.
27. Ibid.
28. Ibid.
29. Ibid.
30. Source: https://www.ilo.org/wcmsp5/groups/public/---ed_norm/---relconf/documents/meetingdocument/wcms_561871.pdf, date accessed 15 October 2023.
31. Ibid.
32. Ibid., p. 2.
33. Ibid.
34. Ibid., pp. 2–3.
35. ILO International Migration Programme and Subregional Office for East Asia Labour Migration Policy and Management: Training materials, Bangkok, International Labour Office, 2005, pp. 20–33.
36. Ibid., p. 52.
37. Ibid.
38. Migrant Forum in Asia, *Supra note 6*, p. 8.
39. ILO International Migration Programme and Subregional Office for East Asia Labour Migration Policy and Management: Training materials, Bangkok, International Labour Office, 2005, pp. 20–33.
40. ILO Multilateral Framework on Labour Migration, https://www.ilo.org/wcmsp5/groups/public/---ed_protect/---protrav/---migrant/documents/publication/wcms_178672.pdf, p. 3.
41. Ibid., p. 7.

Index

About the Contributors

Nguyen Thi Kim Ngan (Editor) is an Associate Professor of law and the Director of the Postgraduate Education Department of Hanoi Law University (HLU), Vietnam. She has 28 years of working experience and is one of the leading experts in Public International Law in Vietnam. She is a member of the Executive Council of Viet Nam Society of International Law (VSIL). Assoc. Prof. Ngan has completed numerous projects and published books and articles in renowned national and international law journals. Several of her written works, including *"The Process of Viet Nam's Preparation of the National Report under the United Nations Human Rights Council's Universal Periodic Review"*, Asia Pacific Journal on Human Rights and the Law, 17(2016); *"Human rights in International law and Vietnamese law"*, People Police Publishing House, Hanoi, 2023; *"Law and Practice of Implementing Recommendations of International Institutions on Civil and Political Rights in Vietnam"*, National Political Publishing House, Hanoi 2023. etc. She was also well-known for being an impartial expert who contributed to making the laws of the Parliament. She also actively participated in the Ministry of Justice's law evaluation process and has previous experience working on the UN human rights reporting processes and the ICCPR reporting processes. She is particularly interested in the legal and practical aspects of treaty law, international law of the sea, and international human rights law. Regarding human rights law matters, she has focused on the rights of weaker demographics like women, children, and migratory laborers. She has done some research on the subject. Her work has significantly contributed to advancing Vietnamese law and human rights legislation.

Su Wai Mon (Editor) is currently a senior lecturer at the Faculty of Law, and an associate member of the Institute of Ocean and Earth Sciences (IOES), at the University of Malaya (UM), Malaysia. She is also an adjunct professor at the Woxen University, Hyderabad, India. Dr. Su holds a Ph.D. in maritime security and law enforcement. She teaches Public

International Law, and International Trade Law and supervises masters and Ph.D. students at the Faculty of Law, University of Malaya. She is a managing editor of the *Journal of Malaysian and Comparative Law* (JMCL). She has a special research interest in artificial intelligence in maritime security, cybersecurity in the maritime domain, and IUU fishing.

Nguyen Toan Thang (Editor) is the general director of the Comparative Law Institute, Hanoi Law University. Dr. Nguyen Toan Thang received his Ph.D. in international law from Université Libre de Bruxelles (Belgium) in 2005. Dr. Nguyen Toan Thang lectures at Hanoi Law University, with over 13 years in researching, lecturing, and training in international law; experience working in legal aid and human rights; experience working with vulnerable groups (children, ethnic minorities); and in activities regarding legal education and dissemination. Dr. Nguyen Toan Thang holds teaching assignments (associate professor) at the International School (Hanoi National University) and Hanoi Open University. Dr. Nguyen Toan Thang has research interests in comparative law, human rights law, and law of the sea in Southeast Asia. Dr. Nguyen Toan Thang took part in several projects dealing with ASEAN's direction and was a speaker at various national and international conferences.

Nguyen Thi Hong Yen (Editor) has 16 years of experience in teaching and researching public international law. She is currently the Head of the Public International Law Division of Hanoi Law University (HLU), Vietnam. She has published some books and articles in this field in prestigious national and international legal journals. Her research focuses on various areas of public international law such as human rights law, sea law, environmental law, and more. Dr. Yen held visiting appointments and fellow positions at famous European universities/institutes like the Raoul Wallenberg Institute of Human Rights and Humanitarian Law (Lund University, Sweden), The Hague Academy of International Law (the Netherlands). Some of her typical research in human rights law such as Impacts of Sinosphere on Ensuring Equal Rights of Ethnic Minority Women in Southeast Asian Countries: Barriers, Challenges and Recent Developments (co-author), a chapter in the book of The Wretched of the Global South: Critical Approaches to International Human Rights Law, Springer Publisher (2024); Challenges in Ensuring the Rights of Vietnamese Migrant Workers in the Globalization Context – The Two Sides of the Development Process, a chapter of the book of Asian Yearbook of International Law, Volume 25 (2019), Brill Nijhoff Publisher; Climate Change and the Challenges for Developing Countries in the Implementation of the Human Right to a Healthy Environment: Case of Vietnam (co-author). Asia-Pacific Journal on Human Rights and the Law 22,

2 (2021): 222-254; For further information, please visit her Orcid at https://orcid.org/my-orcid?orcid=0000-0003-2703-2363.

Aathira Raju is an assistant professor in the Department of Law at the Central University of Kerala, Kerala, India. She is a graduate of law from Government Law College,Thiruvananthapuram, Kerala, and a postgraduate in human rights and environmental law from Cochin University of Science and Technology, Kerala. She has acquired an MPhil in international law from Jawaharlal Nehru University. Ms. Aathira Raju has published articles in various journals. She has participated in and presented research papers at several national and international conferences. She is currently pursuing her Ph.D. from Jawaharlal Nehru University, New Delhi, India.

Amritha V. Shenoy is assistant professor, Kathmandu School of Law, Bhaktapur, Nepal, since 2018. She was awarded a Ph.D. in 2018 from the Centre for International Legal Studies, Jawaharlal Nehru University, New Delhi. Her area of work includes history of international law from an Indian perspective, international human rights law, international environmental law, and jurisprudence. Relevant book publications: "International Crimes Tribunal, Bangladesh: Case Study on the Chief Prosecutor v. Delowar Husain Sayee," in Kumar, Ashish (ed.), Contemporary Developments in International Law: Some Random Reflections, Satyam Law International; "Freedom of the Seas, International Law and South China Sea Dispute," in South China Sea: Emerging Scenario, Pentagon Press; Thamil Venthan Ananthavinayagan and Amritha V. Shenoy (eds.), The Wretched of the Global South, Springer Publications (published on March 8, 2024)

.

Dr. Chu Manh Hungis secretary of the Party Committee—Chairman of Hanoi Law University Council. In 2012, he defended his PhD thesis on the topic: "Human security issues in international law". With 28 years of research, teaching and management at Hanoi Law University; Dr. Chu Manh Hung has many studies on different fields of international law and Vietnamese law, especially in the field of human rights. Dr. Chu Manh Hung directly guides many students in carrying out scientific research in different topics, Graduation theses, Master's theses and PhD theses on international law as well as on human rights. At the same time, he has many articles published in law journals and participates in writing books on human rights. Besides, he also participates in implementing scientific research projects at the central and local levels. In addition to research and teaching activities, Dr. Hung also actively collaborates with state agencies to provide scientific arguments for law building and implementation activities in Vietnam. He has many years of cooperation with the Government's Human Rights Steering

Committee and directly trains localities on human rights such as international law and Vietnamese law on human rights; ensuring and promoting human rights in Vietnam; rights of vulnerable groups according to international standards as well as specific characteristics in Vietnam.

Dodik Setiawan Nur Heriyanto is currently an associate professor at the Department of International Law, Faculty of Law, Universitas Islam Indonesia. He is the founder and chair of the Base for International Law and ASEAN Legal Studies (BILALS) in Indonesia. He is very active in conducting research with particular interests in international law and has received domestic and international research grants, i.e., iHiLead Erasmus Grant (2023), George Mason University (2023), and National Research Foundation of Korea (NRF; in 2023). He can be reached at dodiksetiawan@uii.ac.id.

Geeta Pathak Sangroula is a senior advocate, Nepal Supreme Court Bar Association, and professor in charge, Kathmandu School of Law, Bhaktapur, Nepal. She is the convenor and a faculty member of Asia-Pacific Masters of Human Rights and Democratisation. She pursued her LL.M. from Hong Kong University and was the top of her class. She has over two decades of experience in practicing and teaching law. Her area of expertise includes human rights, gender justice, international criminal law, and international humanitarian law, among others.

Mac Thi Hoai Thuong is a lecturer at the faculty of International Law, Hanoi Law University, Vietnam. She was awarded a doctorate in 2018 from Hanoi Law University and has done various studies on international law, international sea law, law on international treaties, law on human rights, and international business law. She is a full member of the Asian Association of Law Professors.

Nguyen Phuong Dung earned her LL.B. degree from Hanoi Law University (Class of 2009–2013) in Hanoi, Vietnam, and subsequently pursued an LL.M. in international business law at Newcastle Law School (Class of 2013–2014), Newcastle University, Newcastle upon Tyne, England, the United Kingdom. Currently, she holds the position of associate lecturer (law) at the Department of Economics and Finance, the Business School, RMIT University Vietnam. Previously, she worked as a legal practitioner specializing in international business law, corporate-related issues, and regulatory compliance. Her scholarly pursuits are anchored in the realm of public international law, specifically international human rights, international environmental law, international law of the seas, climate change, migrant workers' rights, and related areas.

She has co-authored numerous publications featured in prestigious national and international journals. Additionally, she is a qualified solicitor licensed to practice law in Vietnam. For additional information, please visit: https://orcid.org/0000-0002-1882-2956.

Nguyen Thi Thanh Hai is currently Deputy Director of the Institute for Human Rights, Ho Chi Minh National Academy of Politics, Hanoi, Vietnam. She has more than 20 years of professional experience in the field of human rights and rule of law with a particular focus in human rights, business and trade, human rights of vulnerable groups including migrant workers, children, women and persons with disability, human rights-based approaches and judicial reform in Vietnam. She has extensive experience working as human rights expert and consultant for major UN and other international and local agencies on human rights in Vietnam. She is an editor, author of many journal articles and book on human rights. Hai holds a PhD in human rights and business from the University of Sydney, Australia.

Nguyen Tien Duc received Bachelor of Laws from Hanoi Law University (Vietnam, 2012), Master of Philosophy from the University of Oslo (Norway, 2016), and Doctor of Philosophy from the University of Campania (Italy, 2022). Duc interned at the Norwegian National Human Rights Institution and UNICEF Vietnam. Since 2013, Duc has worked as a research fellow at the Institute of State and Law (Vietnam Academy of Social Sciences). Duc has participated in various research projects for building the capacity of the government of Vietnam in various aspects. His works have been published in esteemed journals such as Statute Law Review, Asian Journal of Comparative Law, Nordic Journal of Human Rights. His research interests cover international law, constitutional law, human rights, and the rule of law. He can be reached at ng.tien.duc@gmail.com.

Tran Thi Thu Thuy received her LLB and LLM from Hanoi Law University in 2012 and 2014, respectively. Since 2013, she has been a lecturer of international law at Hanoi Law University. In 2017, she was a visiting fellow at Norwegian Centre for Human Rights. Her research focus is on the recent developments of international law, international law of the sea, international human rights law, climate change law, and the use of force in cyberspace. Her research has been published in some journals such as Asian Journal of Comparative Law, Journal of Southeast Asian Human Rights. She is also a contributors of some specialize book in human rights such as *"Human rights in International law and Vietnamese law"*, People Police Publishing House, Hanoi, 2023; *"Law and Practice of Implementing Recommendations of*

International Institutions on Civil and Political Rights in Vietnam", National Political Publishing House, Hanoi 2023.etc. She can be reached at thuthuy-tran65.hlu@gmail.com

www.ingramcontent.com/pod-product-compliance
Ingram Content Group UK Ltd.
Pitfield, Milton Keynes, MK11 3LW, UK
UKHW041450071026
15587UKWH00010B/727

9 781666 940374